SPY×FAMILY

CRUISE ADVENTURE

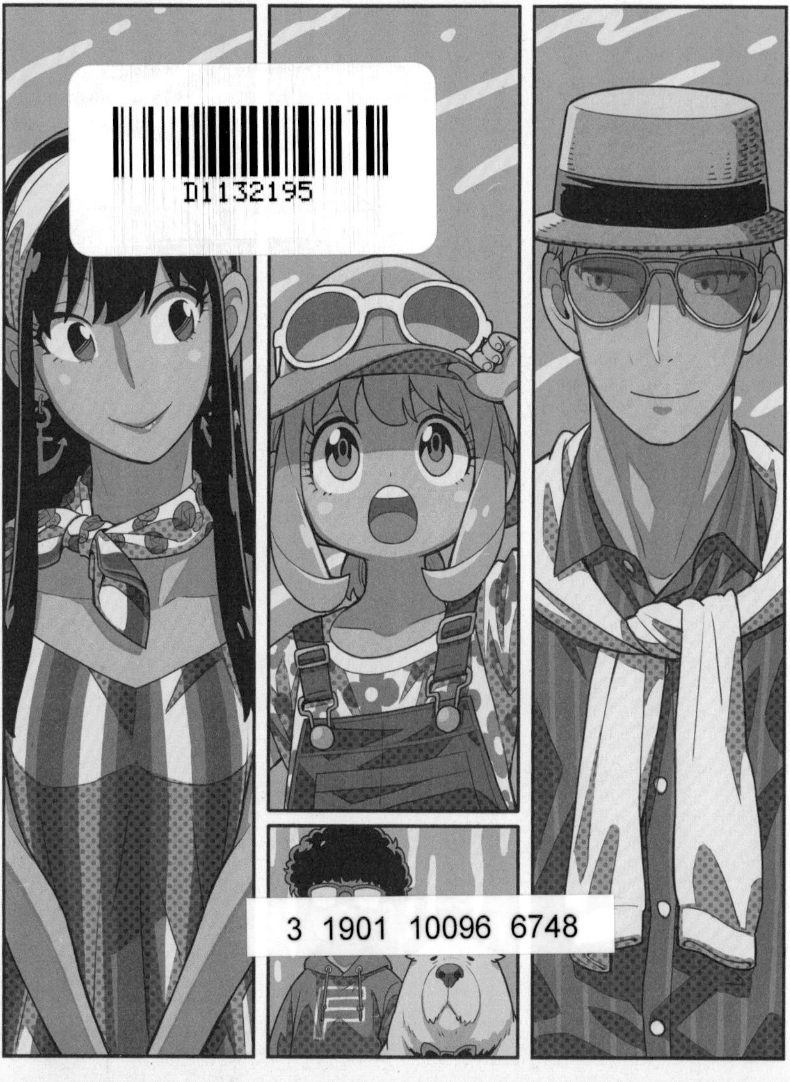

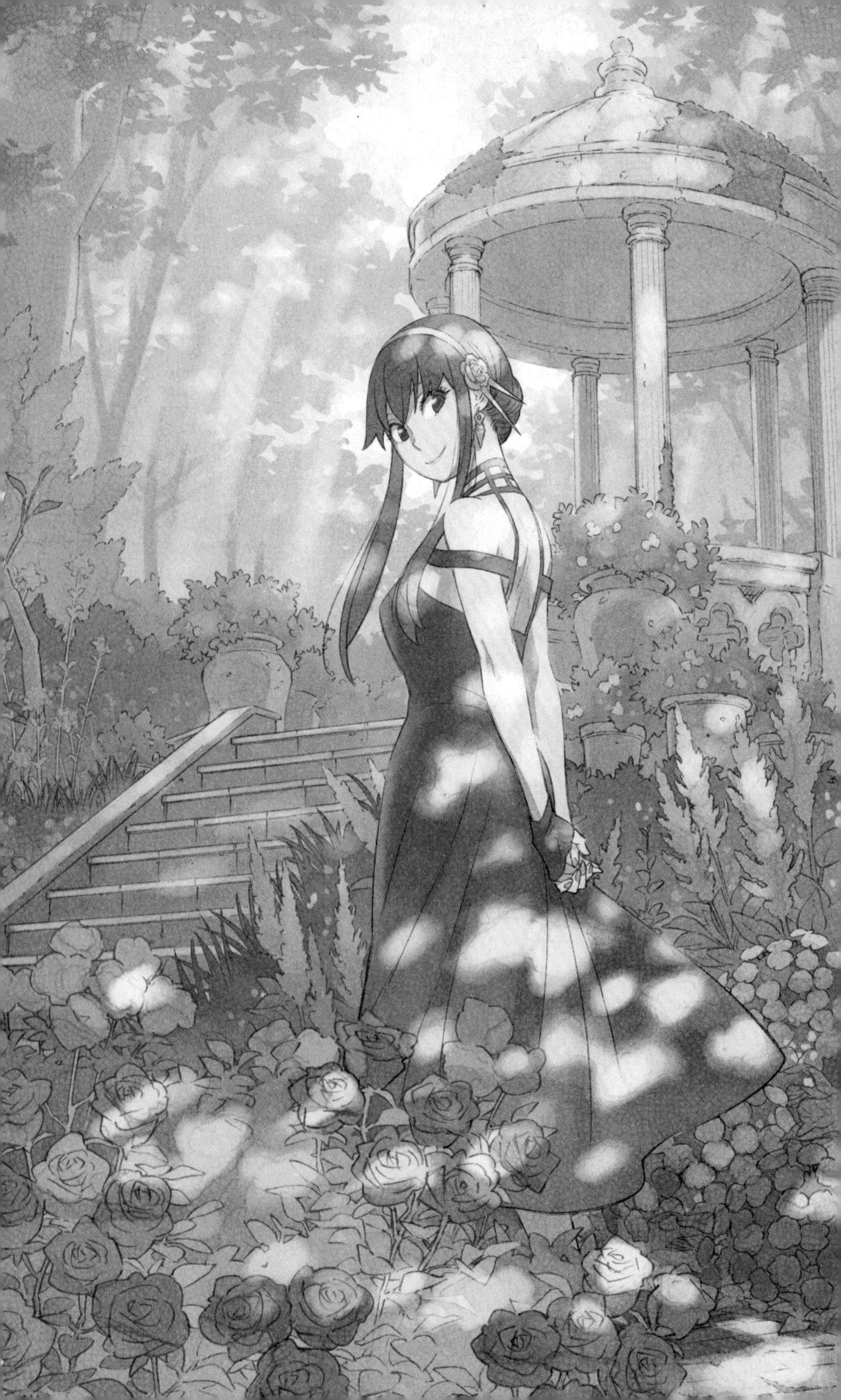

SPY×FAMILY

8

STORY AND ART BY
TATSUYA ENDO

CONTENTS

SPY×FAMILY CHARACTERS

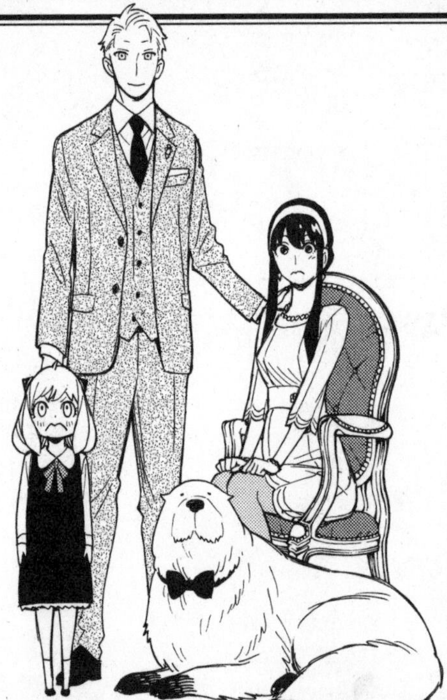

LOID FORGER

ROLE: Husband

Known as a skilled psychiatrist, Loid is actually "Twilight," a spy and master of disguise serving the nation of Westalis.

YOR FORGER

ROLE: Wife

A city hall clerk who also lives a secret life as a talented contract killer. Her code name is "Thorn Princess."

ANYA FORGER

ROLE: Daughter

Anya is a first grader at the prestigious Eden Academy. A telepath whose abilities were created in an experiment conducted by a certain organization. She can read minds.

BOND FORGER

ROLE: Dog

Anya's playmate and the family guard dog. As a former military test subject, he can see the future.

KEY PEOPLE

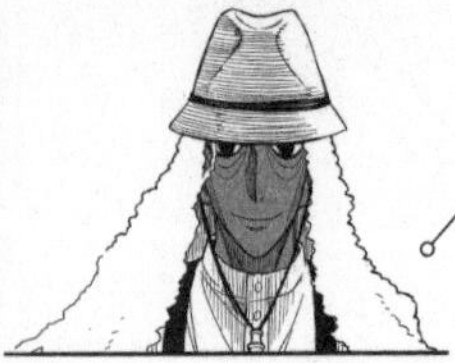

Head of the secret organization known as Garden.

MATTHEW MCMAHON

Policy director at city hall and member of Garden.

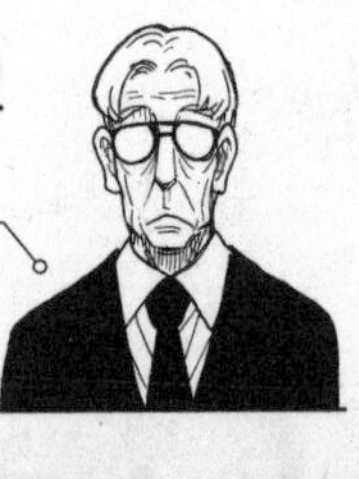

STORY

Westalis secret agent Twilight receives orders to uncover the plans of Donovan Desmond, the warmongering chairman of Ostania's National Unity Party. To do so, Twilight must pose as Loid Forger, create a fake family, and enroll his child at the prestigious Eden Academy. However, by sheer coincidence, the daughter he selects from an orphanage is secretly a telepath! Also, the woman who agrees to be in a sham marriage with him is secretly an assassin! While concealing their true identities from one another, the three now find themselves living together as a family.

Twilight has succeeded in making contact with his target. Meanwhile, the underground organization Garden has ordered Yor to protect the scion of an organized crime family during a luxury cruise. But it turns out Loid and Anya will be vacationing on the same ship!

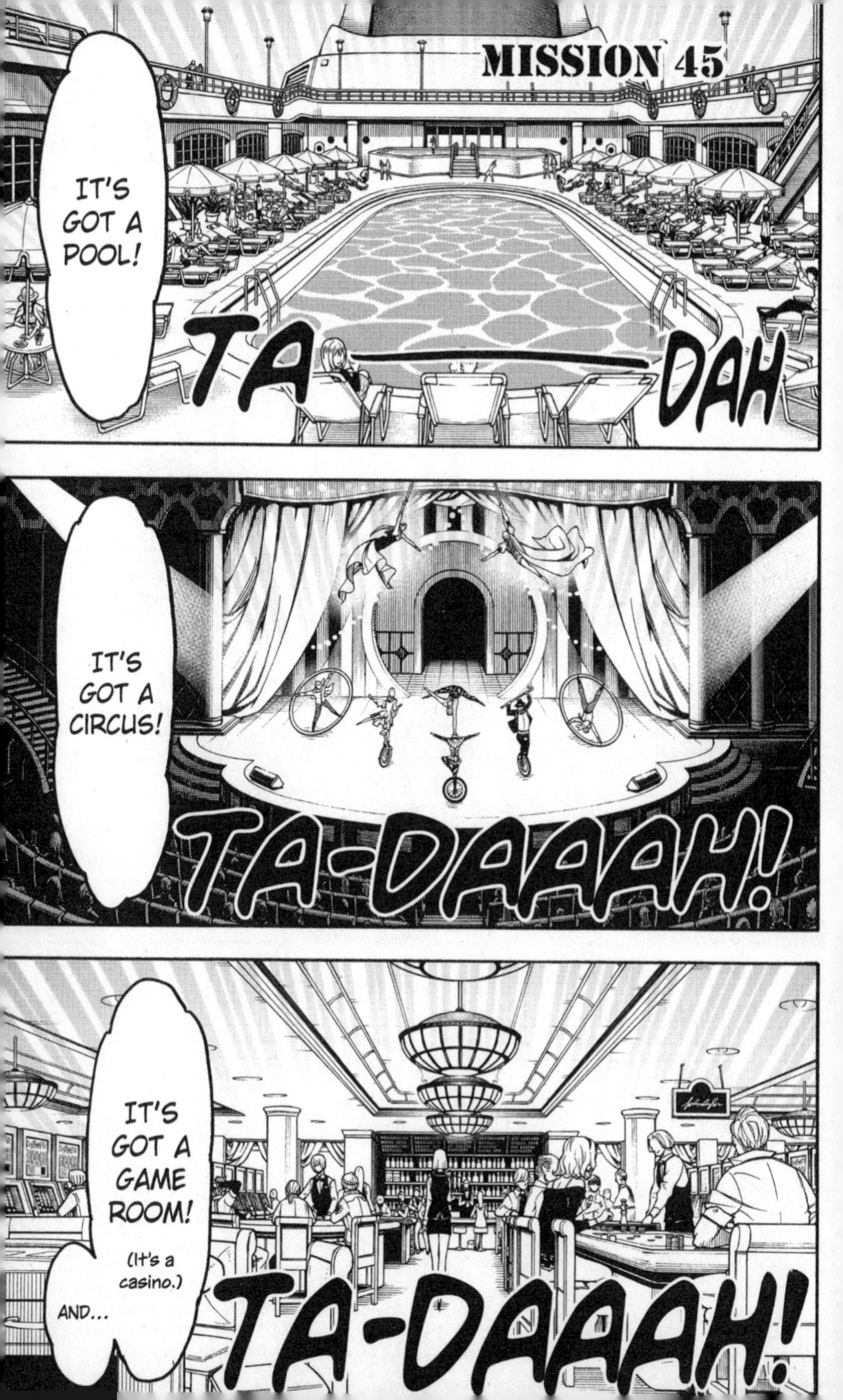
MISSION 45
IT'S GOT A POOL!
TA—DAH
IT'S GOT A CIRCUS!
TA-DAAAH!
IT'S GOT A GAME ROOM!
(It's a casino.)
AND...
TA-DAAAH!

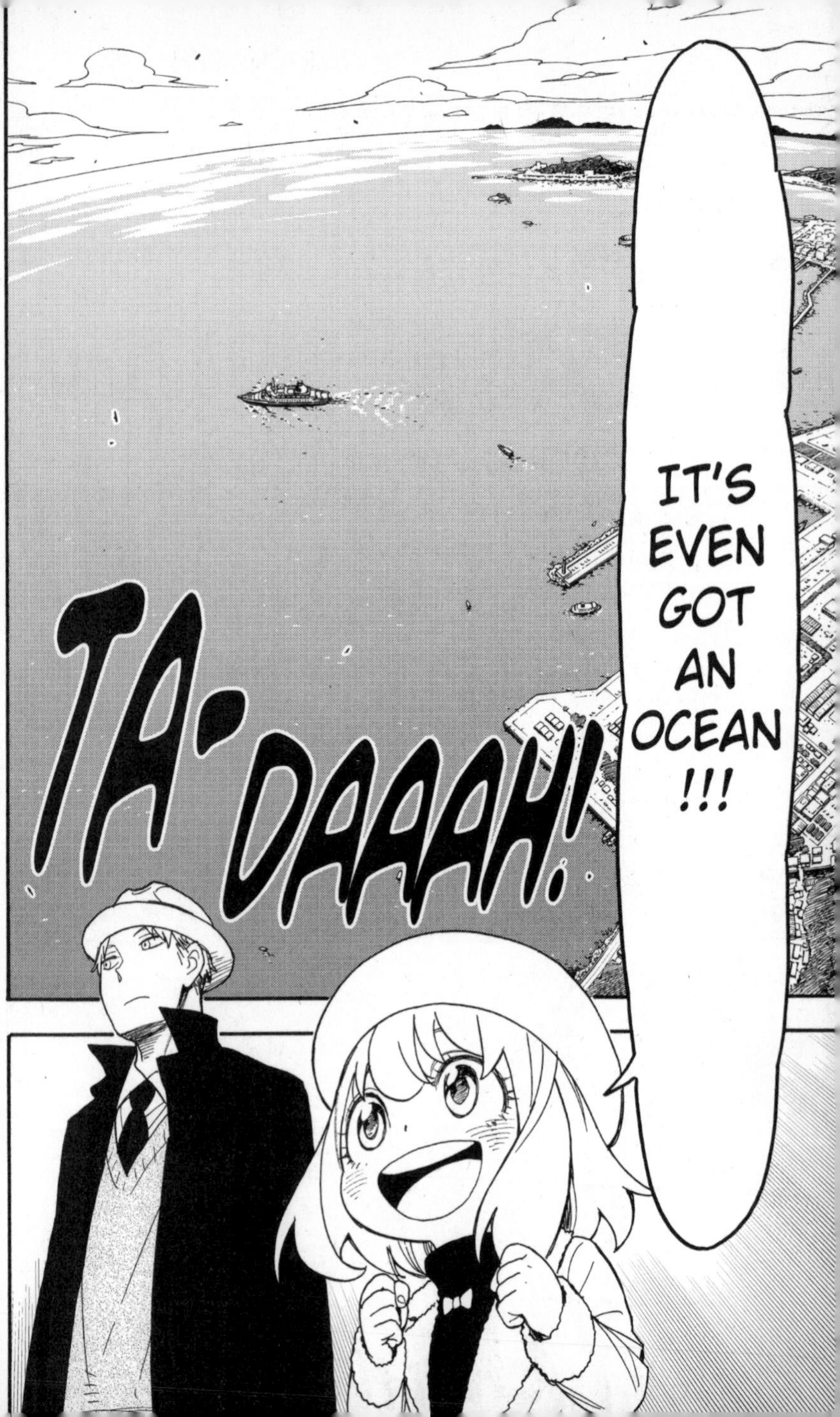
IT'S EVEN GOT AN OCEAN !!!
TA-DAAAH!

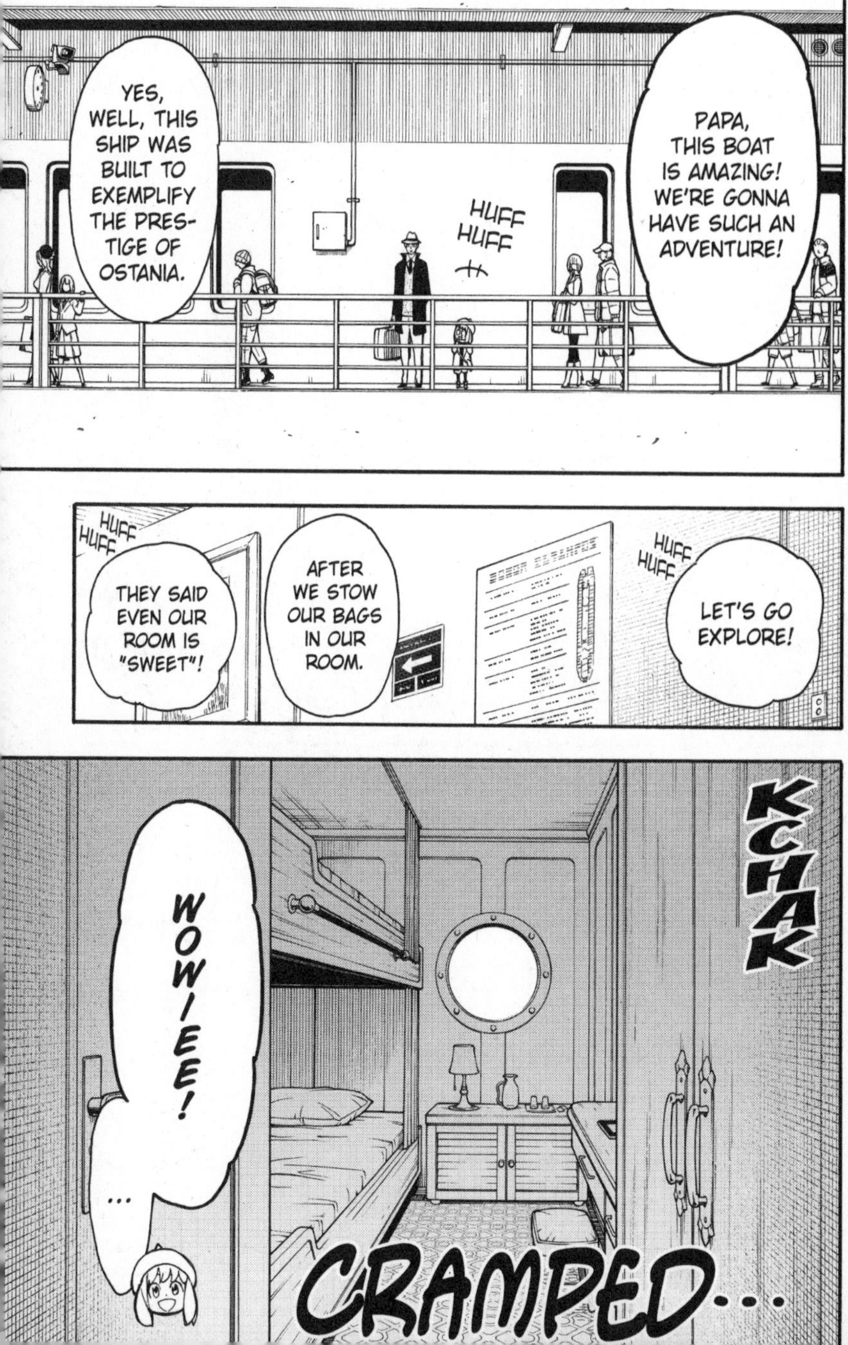
PAPA, THIS BOAT IS AMAZING! WE'RE GONNA HAVE SUCH AN ADVENTURE!
HUFF HUFF
YES, WELL, THIS SHIP WAS BUILT TO EXEMPLIFY THE PRES-TIGE OF OSTANIA.
HUFF HUFF
LET'S GO EXPLORE!
AFTER WE STOW OUR BAGS IN OUR ROOM.
HUFF HUFF
THEY SAID EVEN OUR ROOM IS "SWEET"!
KCHAK
WOWIEE!
...
CRAMPED...

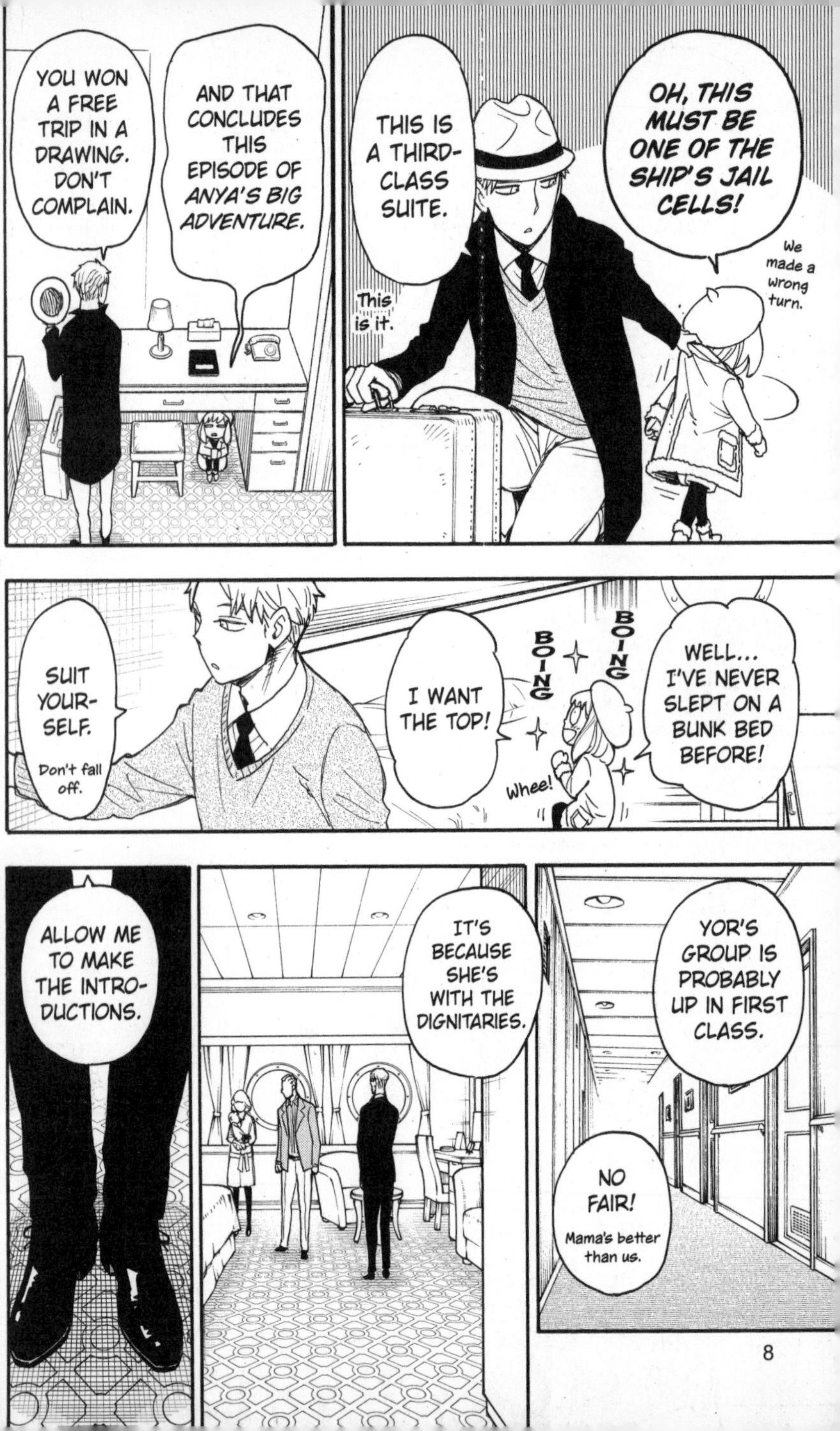
OH, THIS MUST BE ONE OF THE SHIP'S JAIL CELLS!
We made a wrong turn.
THIS IS A THIRD-CLASS SUITE.
This is it.
AND THAT CONCLUDES THIS EPISODE OF *ANYA'S BIG ADVENTURE.*
YOU WON A FREE TRIP IN A DRAWING. DON'T COMPLAIN.
BOING
BOING
WELL... I'VE NEVER SLEPT ON A BUNK BED BEFORE!
I WANT THE TOP!
Whee!
SUIT YOURSELF.
Don't fall off.
YOR'S GROUP IS PROBABLY UP IN FIRST CLASS.
NO FAIR!
Mama's better than us.
IT'S BECAUSE SHE'S WITH THE DIGNITARIES.
ALLOW ME TO MAKE THE INTRODUCTIONS.

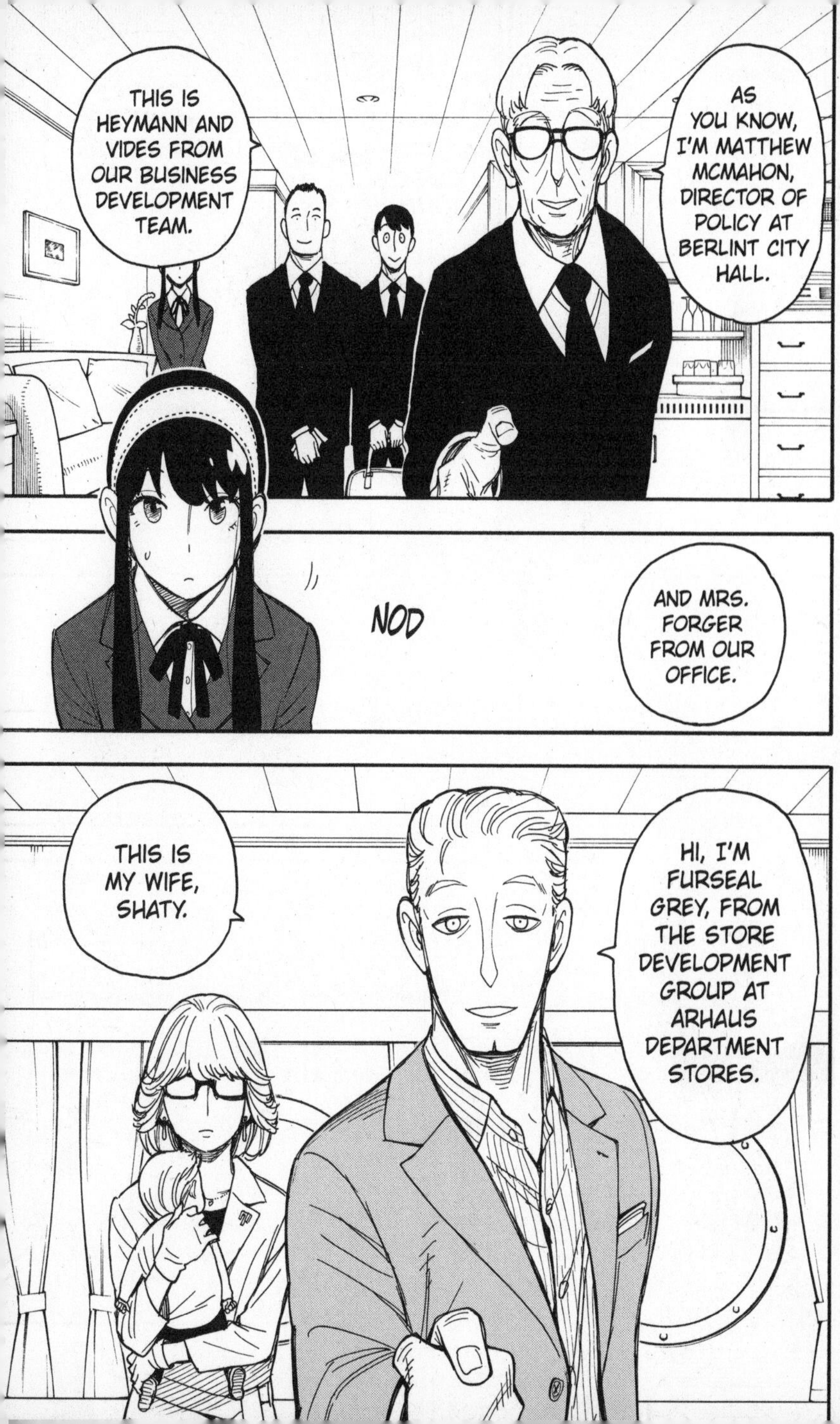
AS YOU KNOW, I'M MATTHEW MCMAHON, DIRECTOR OF POLICY AT BERLINT CITY HALL.
THIS IS HEYMANN AND VIDES FROM OUR BUSINESS DEVELOPMENT TEAM.
AND MRS. FORGER FROM OUR OFFICE.
NOD
HI, I'M FURSEAL GREY, FROM THE STORE DEVELOPMENT GROUP AT ARHAUS DEPARTMENT STORES.
THIS IS MY WIFE, SHATY.

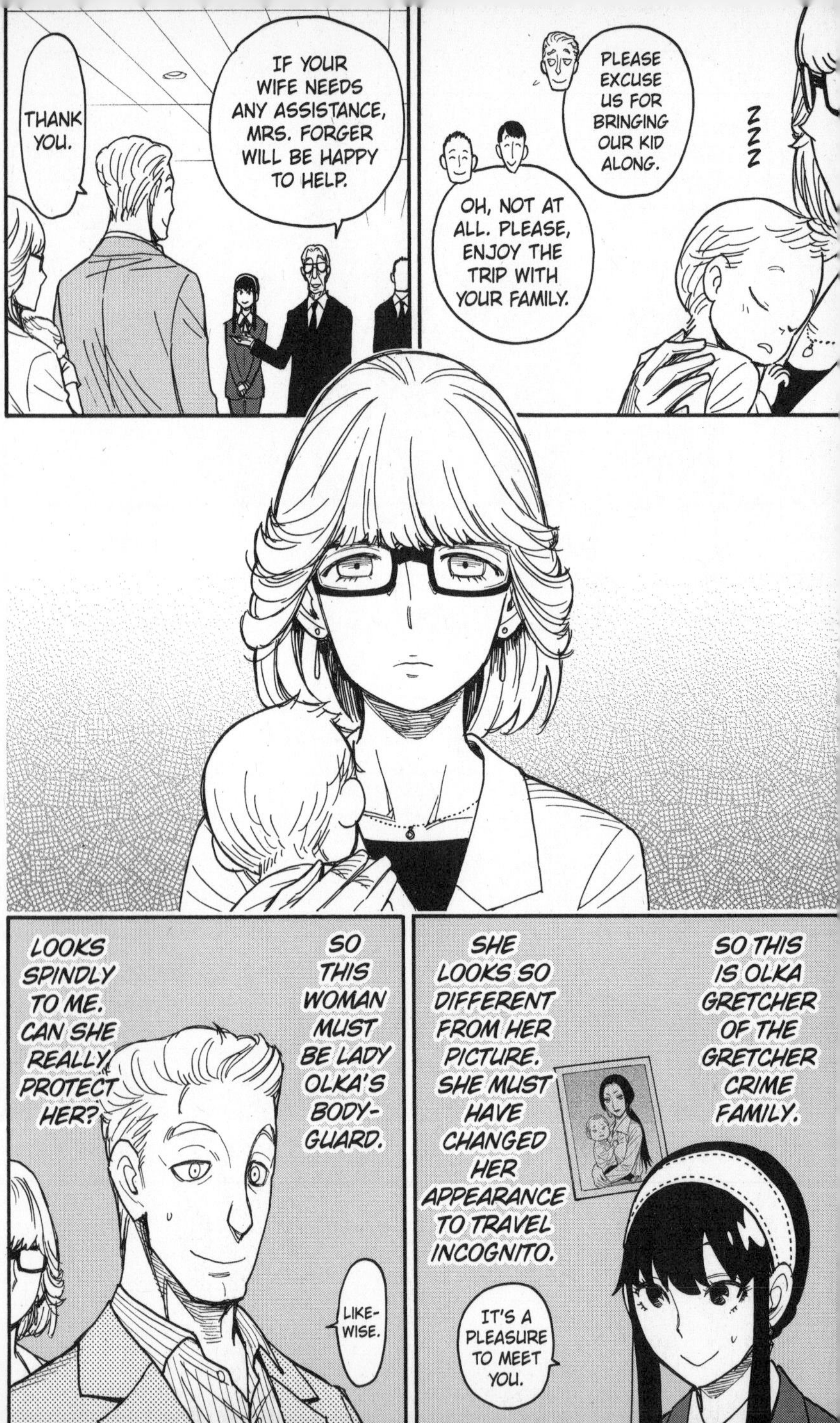
PLEASE EXCUSE US FOR BRINGING OUR KID ALONG.
ZZZ
OH, NOT AT ALL. PLEASE, ENJOY THE TRIP WITH YOUR FAMILY.
IF YOUR WIFE NEEDS ANY ASSISTANCE, MRS. FORGER WILL BE HAPPY TO HELP.
THANK YOU.
SO THIS IS OLKA GRETCHER OF THE GRETCHER CRIME FAMILY.
SHE LOOKS SO DIFFERENT FROM HER PICTURE. SHE MUST HAVE CHANGED HER APPEARANCE TO TRAVEL INCOGNITO.
IT'S A PLEASURE TO MEET YOU.
SO THIS WOMAN MUST BE LADY OLKA'S BODY-GUARD.
LOOKS SPINDLY TO ME. CAN SHE REALLY PROTECT HER?
LIKE-WISE.

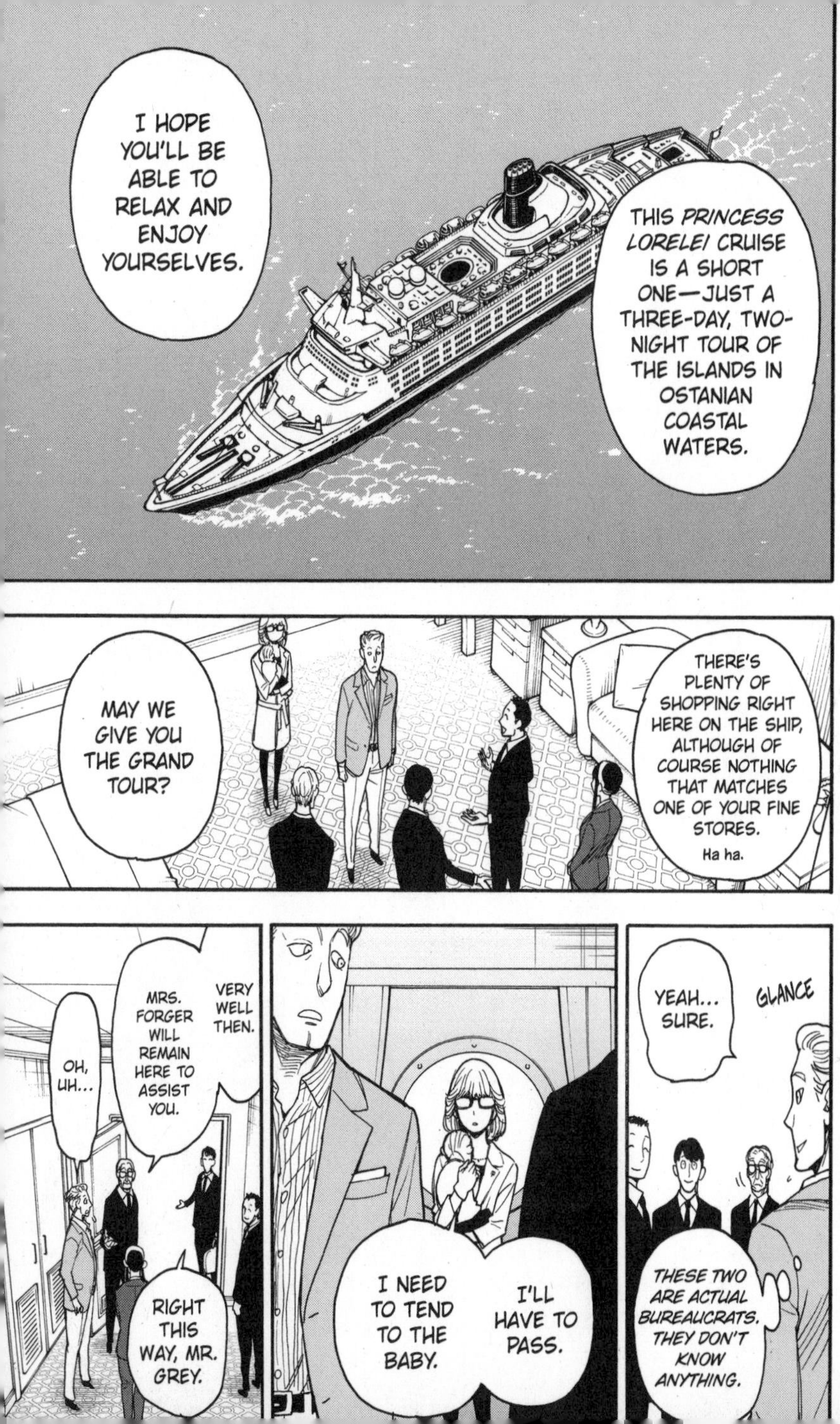
THIS *PRINCESS LORELEI* CRUISE IS A SHORT ONE—JUST A THREE-DAY, TWO-NIGHT TOUR OF THE ISLANDS IN OSTANIAN COASTAL WATERS.
I HOPE YOU'LL BE ABLE TO RELAX AND ENJOY YOURSELVES.
THERE'S PLENTY OF SHOPPING RIGHT HERE ON THE SHIP, ALTHOUGH OF COURSE NOTHING THAT MATCHES ONE OF YOUR FINE STORES.
Ha ha.
MAY WE GIVE YOU THE GRAND TOUR?
YEAH... SURE.
GLANCE
THESE TWO ARE ACTUAL BUREAUCRATS. THEY DON'T KNOW ANYTHING.
I'LL HAVE TO PASS.
I NEED TO TEND TO THE BABY.
VERY WELL THEN.
MRS. FORGER WILL REMAIN HERE TO ASSIST YOU.
OH, UH...
RIGHT THIS WAY, MR. GREY.

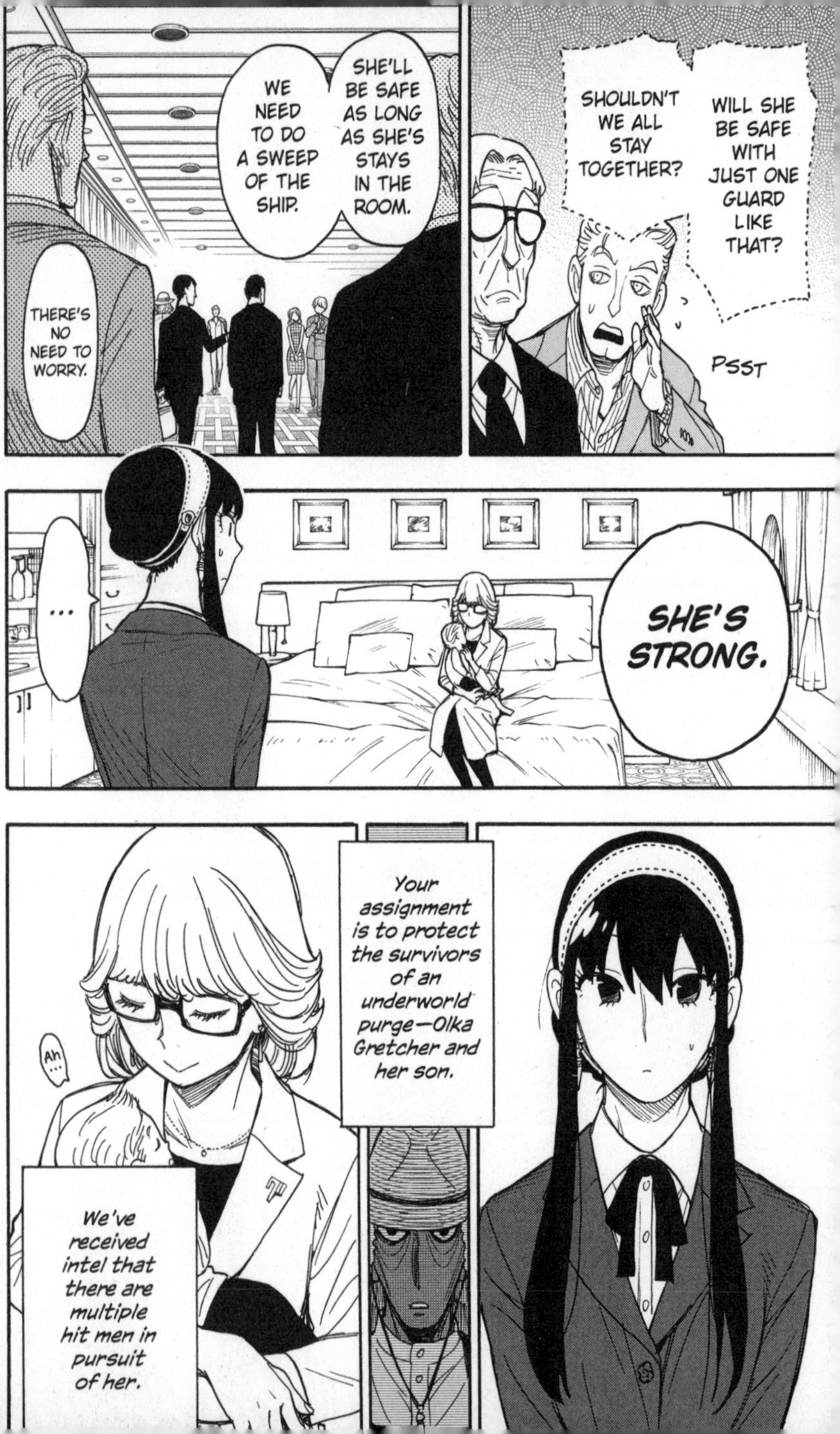
WILL SHE BE SAFE WITH JUST ONE GUARD LIKE THAT?
SHOULDN'T WE ALL STAY TOGETHER?
PSST
SHE'LL BE SAFE AS LONG AS SHE'S STAYS IN THE ROOM.
WE NEED TO DO A SWEEP OF THE SHIP.
THERE'S NO NEED TO WORRY.
SHE'S STRONG.
...
Your assignment is to protect the survivors of an underworld purge—Olka Gretcher and her son.
Ah...
We've received intel that there are multiple hit men in pursuit of her.

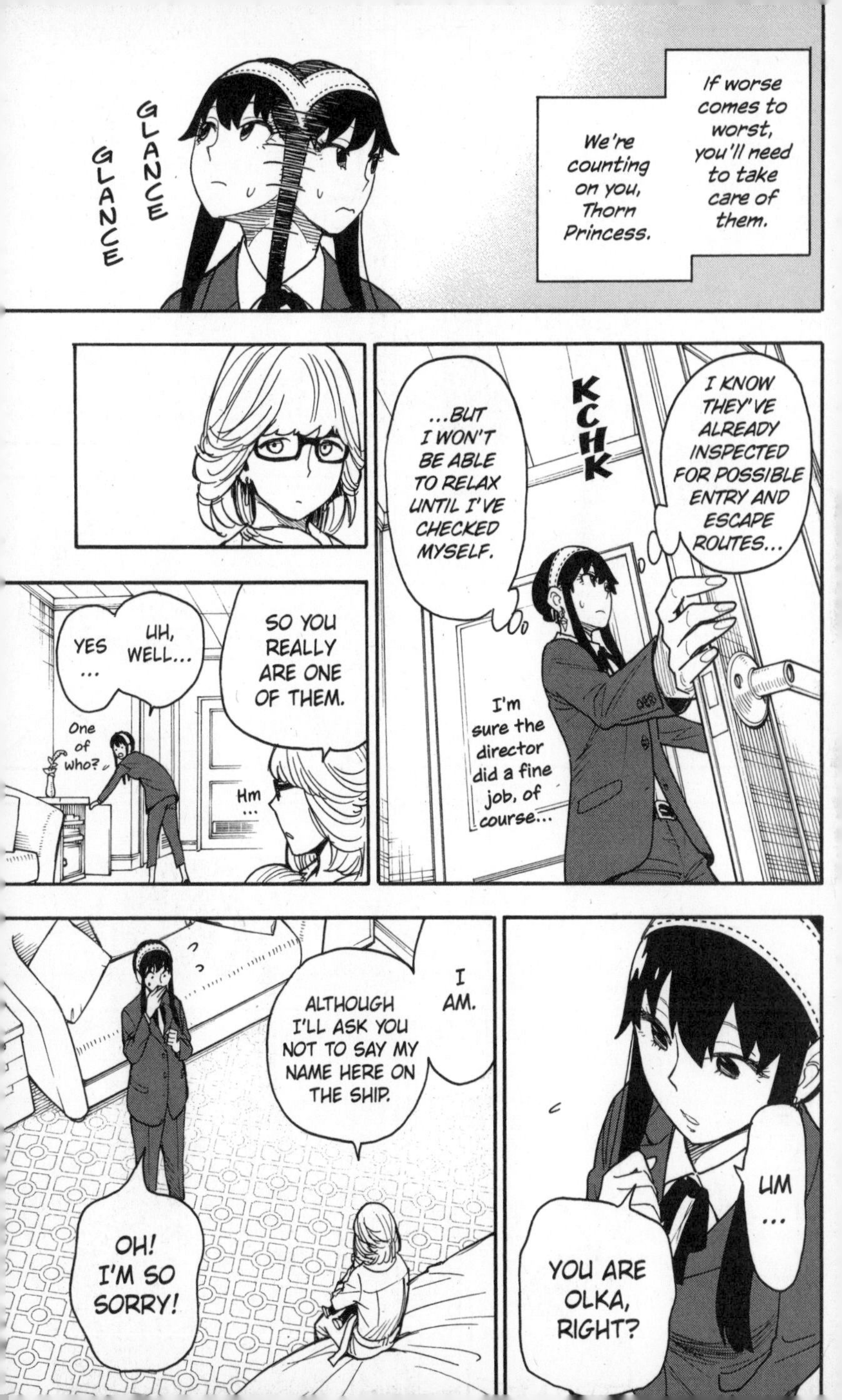
If worse comes to worst, you'll need to take care of them.
We're counting on you, Thorn Princess.
GLANCE
GLANCE
I KNOW THEY'VE ALREADY INSPECTED FOR POSSIBLE ENTRY AND ESCAPE ROUTES...
KCHK
...BUT I WON'T BE ABLE TO RELAX UNTIL I'VE CHECKED MYSELF.
I'm sure the director did a fine job, of course...
SO YOU REALLY ARE ONE OF THEM.
Hm...
UH, WELL...
YES...
One of who?
UM...
YOU ARE OLKA, RIGHT?
I AM.
ALTHOUGH I'LL ASK YOU NOT TO SAY MY NAME HERE ON THE SHIP.
OH! I'M SO SORRY!

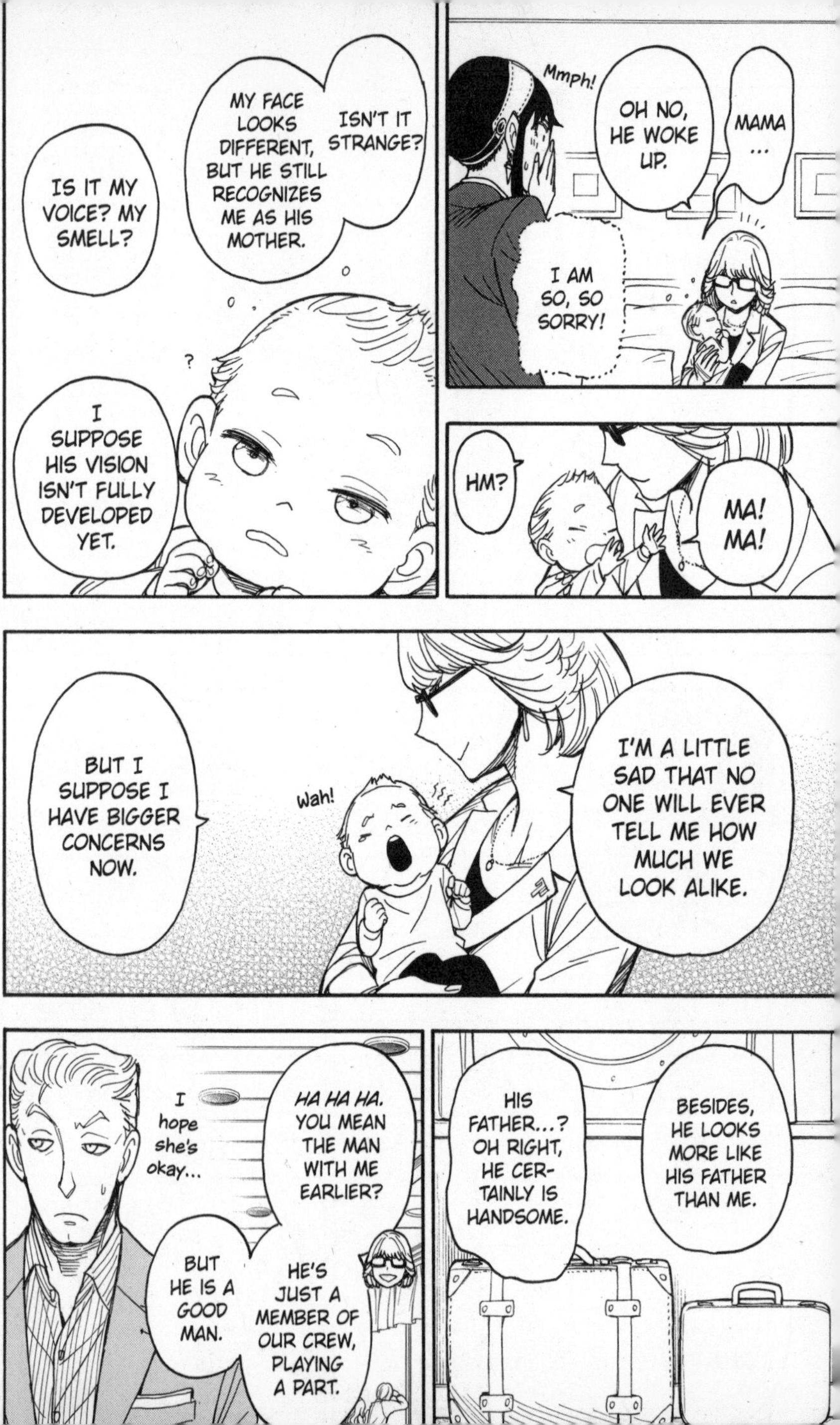
MAMA ...
OH NO, HE WOKE UP.
Mmph!
I AM SO, SO SORRY!
MA! MA!
HM?
ISN'T IT STRANGE?
MY FACE LOOKS DIFFERENT, BUT HE STILL RECOGNIZES ME AS HIS MOTHER.
IS IT MY VOICE? MY SMELL?
I SUPPOSE HIS VISION ISN'T FULLY DEVELOPED YET.
I'M A LITTLE SAD THAT NO ONE WILL EVER TELL ME HOW MUCH WE LOOK ALIKE.
Wah!
BUT I SUPPOSE I HAVE BIGGER CONCERNS NOW.
BESIDES, HE LOOKS MORE LIKE HIS FATHER THAN ME.
HIS FATHER...? OH RIGHT, HE CER-TAINLY IS HANDSOME.
HA HA HA. YOU MEAN THE MAN WITH ME EARLIER?
HE'S JUST A MEMBER OF OUR CREW, PLAYING A PART.
BUT HE IS A GOOD MAN.
I hope she's okay...

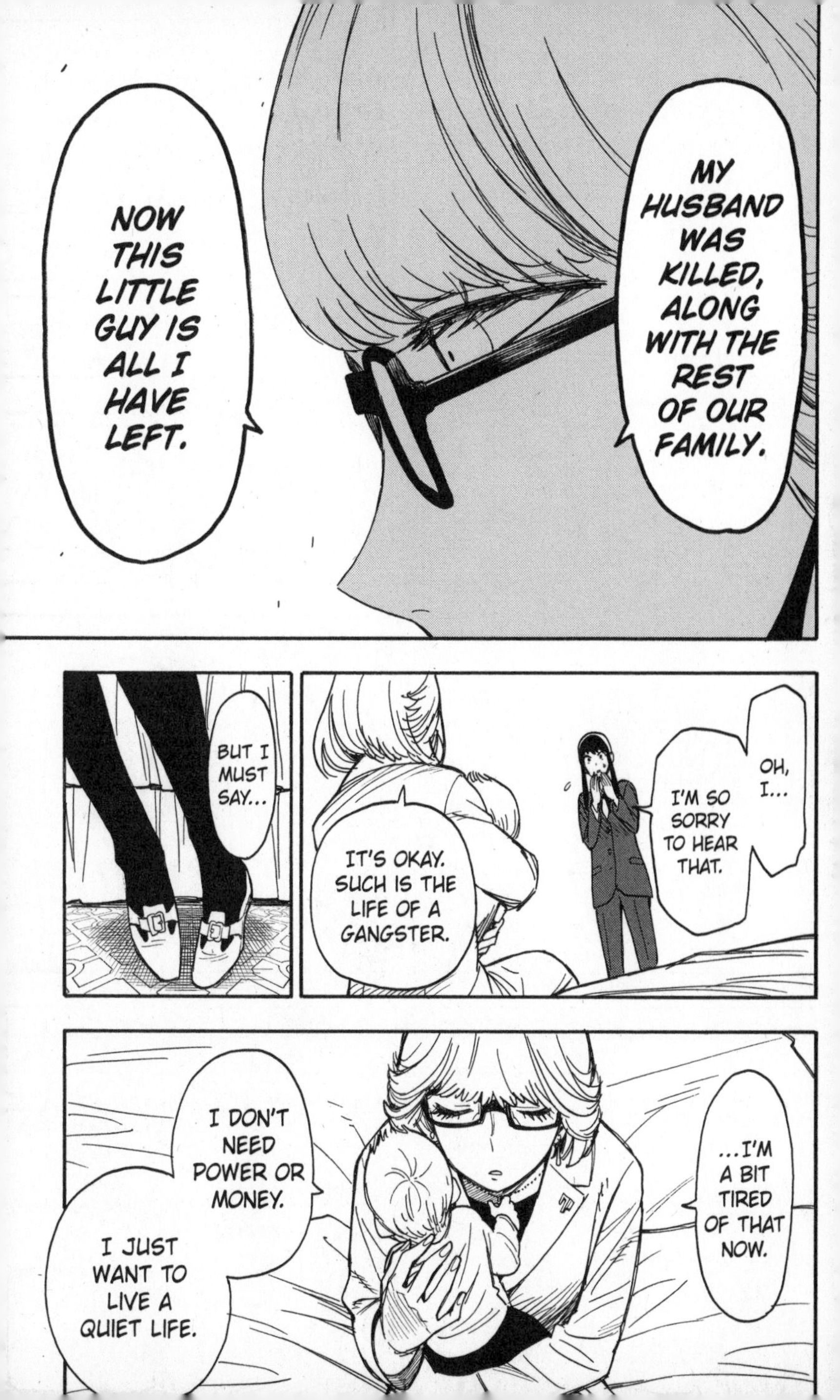
MY HUSBAND WAS KILLED, ALONG WITH THE REST OF OUR FAMILY.
NOW THIS LITTLE GUY IS ALL I HAVE LEFT.
OH, I...
I'M SO SORRY TO HEAR THAT.
IT'S OKAY. SUCH IS THE LIFE OF A GANGSTER.
BUT I MUST SAY...
...I'M A BIT TIRED OF THAT NOW.
I DON'T NEED POWER OR MONEY.
I JUST WANT TO LIVE A QUIET LIFE.

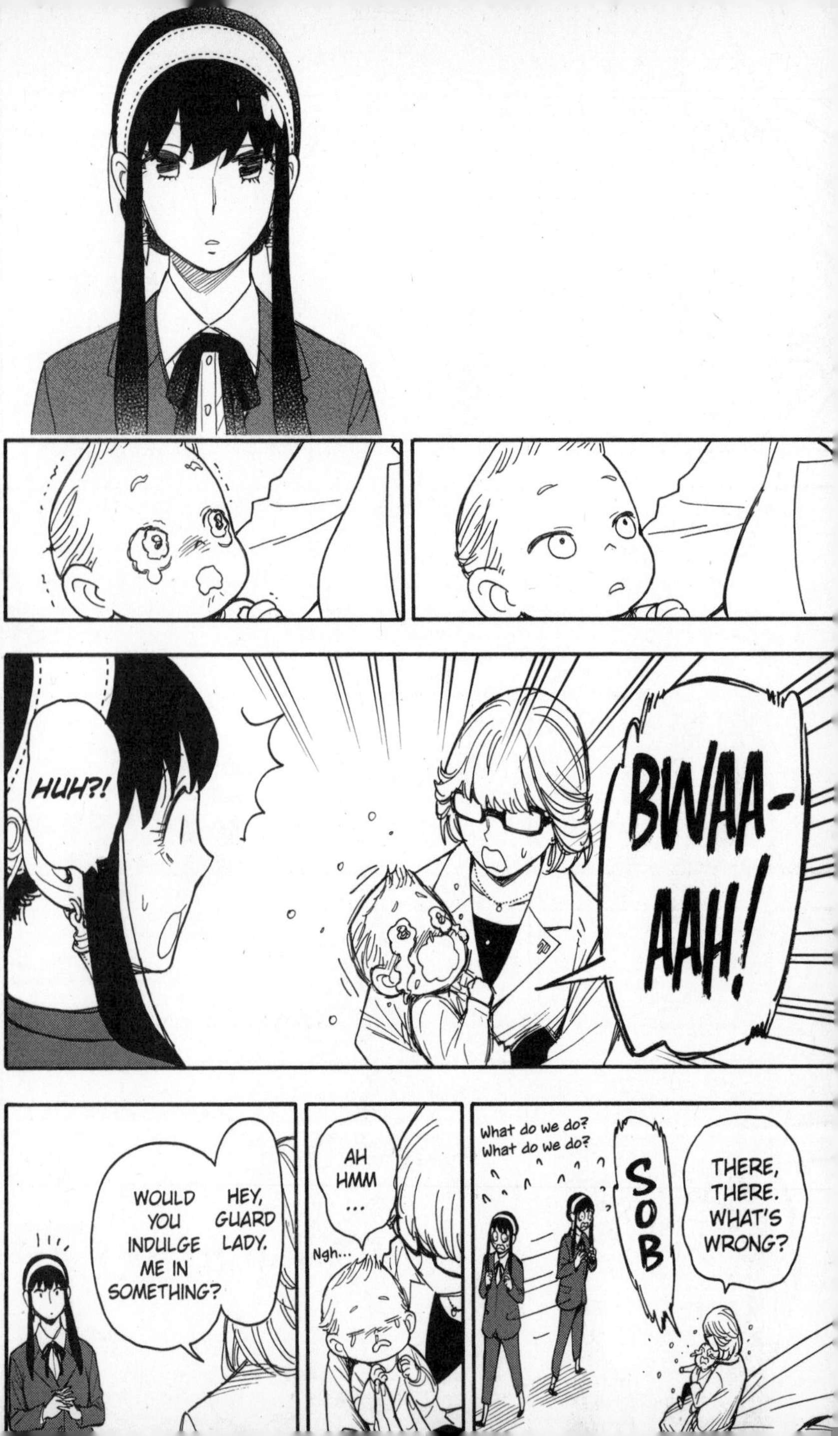
BWAA-AAH!
HUH?!
THERE, THERE. WHAT'S WRONG?
SOB
What do we do? What do we do?
AH HMM ...
Ngh...
HEY, GUARD LADY.
WOULD YOU INDULGE ME IN SOMETHING?

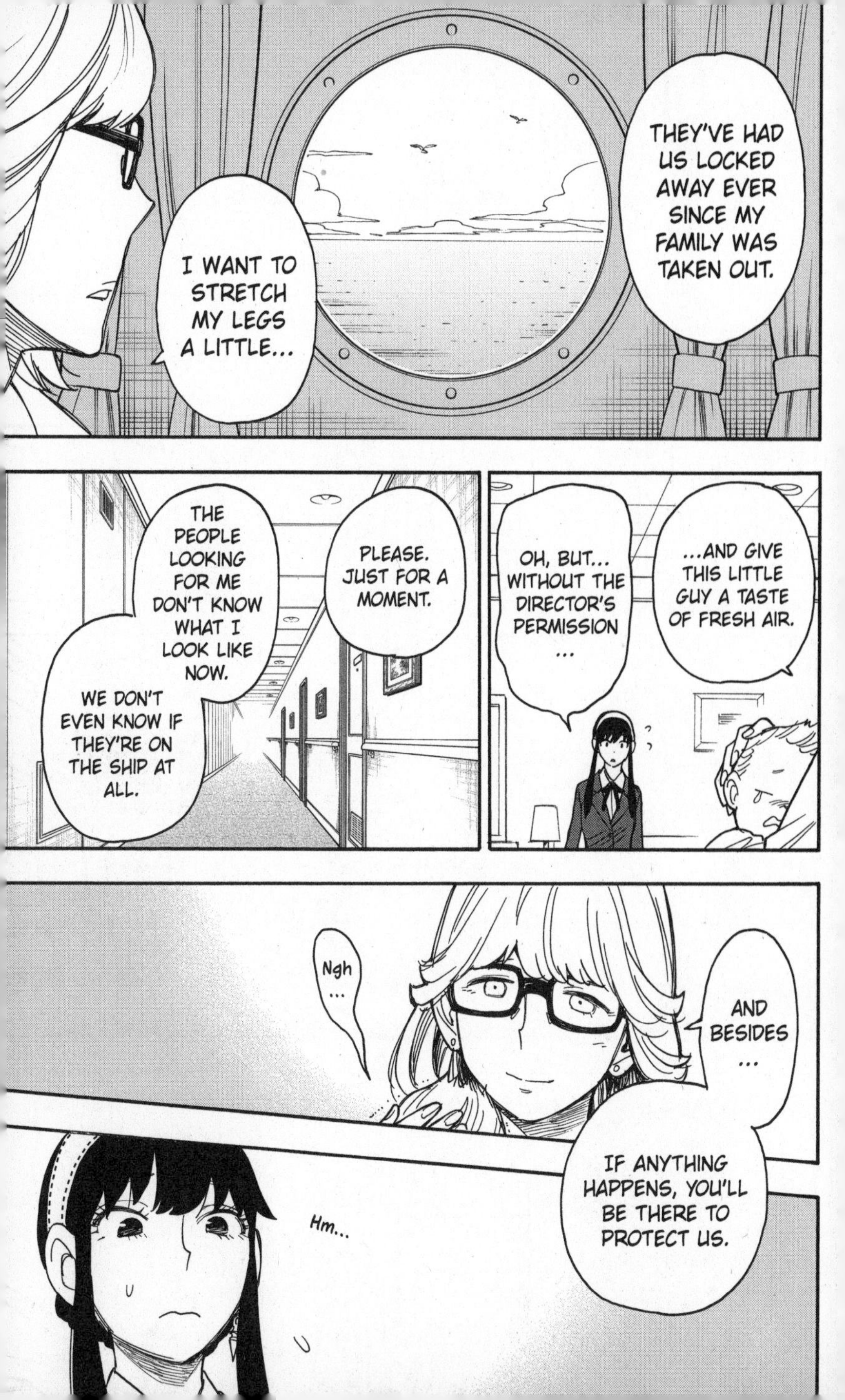
THEY'VE HAD US LOCKED AWAY EVER SINCE MY FAMILY WAS TAKEN OUT.
I WANT TO STRETCH MY LEGS A LITTLE...
...AND GIVE THIS LITTLE GUY A TASTE OF FRESH AIR.
OH, BUT... WITHOUT THE DIRECTOR'S PERMISSION ...
PLEASE. JUST FOR A MOMENT.
THE PEOPLE LOOKING FOR ME DON'T KNOW WHAT I LOOK LIKE NOW.
WE DON'T EVEN KNOW IF THEY'RE ON THE SHIP AT ALL.
AND BESIDES ...
Ngh ...
IF ANYTHING HAPPENS, YOU'LL BE THERE TO PROTECT US.
Hm...

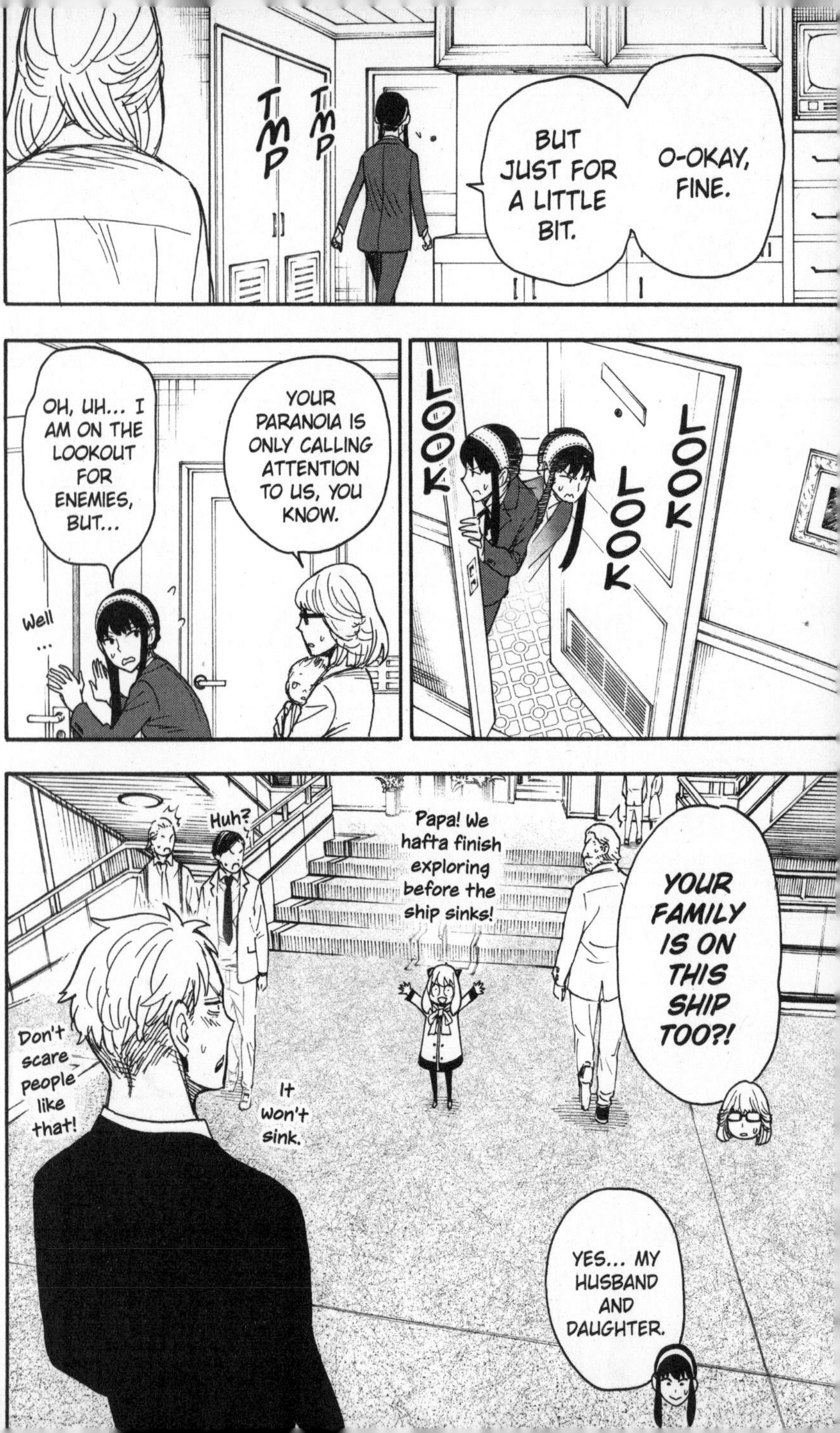
O-OKAY, FINE.
BUT JUST FOR A LITTLE BIT.
TMP TMP
LOOK LOOK LOOK
YOUR PARANOIA IS ONLY CALLING ATTENTION TO US, YOU KNOW.
OH, UH... I AM ON THE LOOKOUT FOR ENEMIES, BUT...
Well...
YOUR FAMILY IS ON THIS SHIP TOO?!
Papa! We hafta finish exploring before the ship sinks!
Huh?
It won't sink.
Don't scare people like that!
YES... MY HUSBAND AND DAUGHTER.

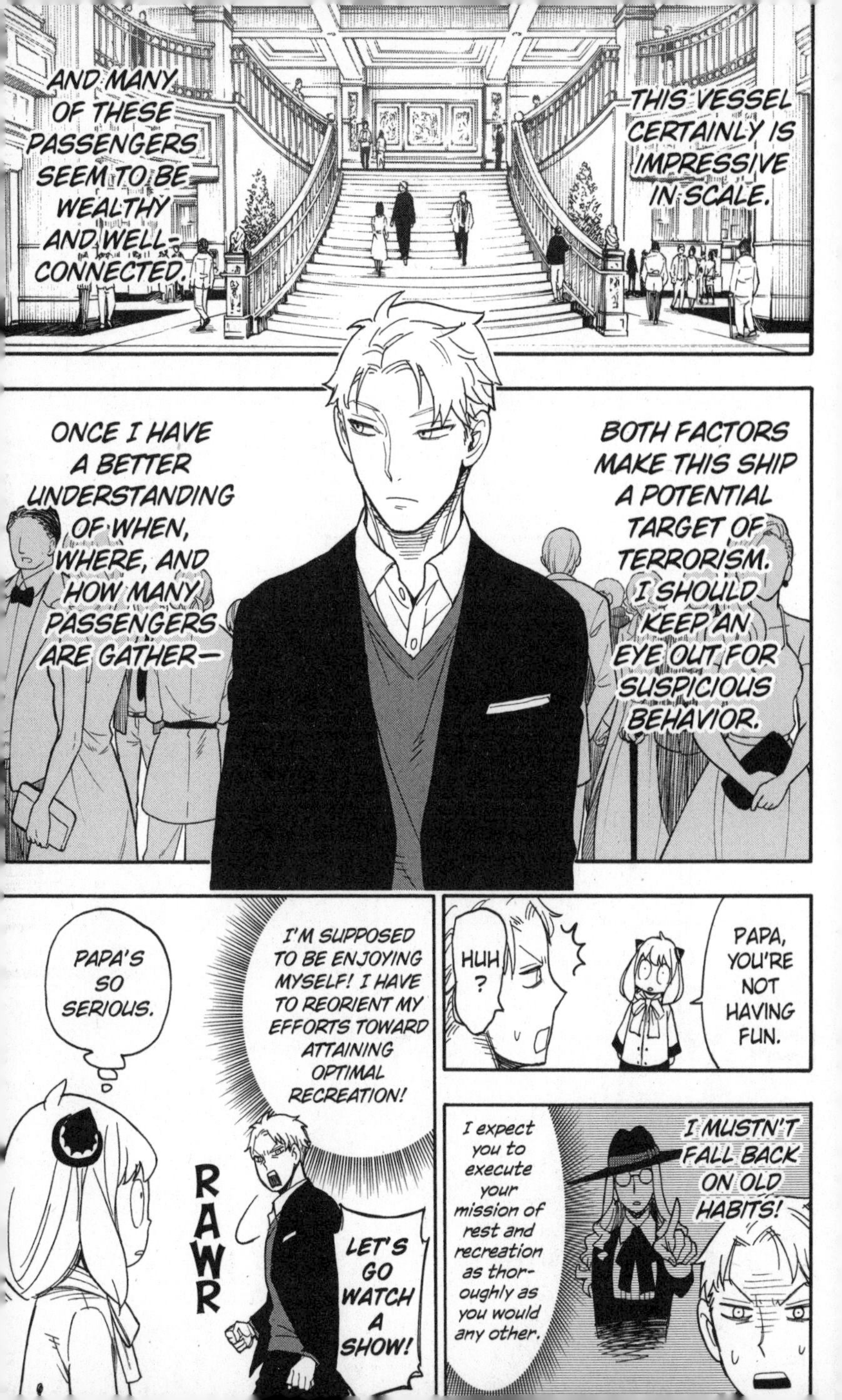
THIS VESSEL CERTAINLY IS IMPRESSIVE IN SCALE.
AND MANY OF THESE PASSENGERS SEEM TO BE WEALTHY AND WELL-CONNECTED.
BOTH FACTORS MAKE THIS SHIP A POTENTIAL TARGET OF TERRORISM. I SHOULD KEEP AN EYE OUT FOR SUSPICIOUS BEHAVIOR.
ONCE I HAVE A BETTER UNDERSTANDING OF WHEN, WHERE, AND HOW MANY PASSENGERS ARE GATHER—
PAPA, YOU'RE NOT HAVING FUN.
HUH?
I MUSTN'T FALL BACK ON OLD HABITS!
I expect you to execute your mission of rest and recreation as thoroughly as you would any other.
I'M SUPPOSED TO BE ENJOYING MYSELF! I HAVE TO REORIENT MY EFFORTS TOWARD ATTAINING OPTIMAL RECREATION!
PAPA'S SO SERIOUS.
LET'S GO WATCH A SHOW!
RAWR

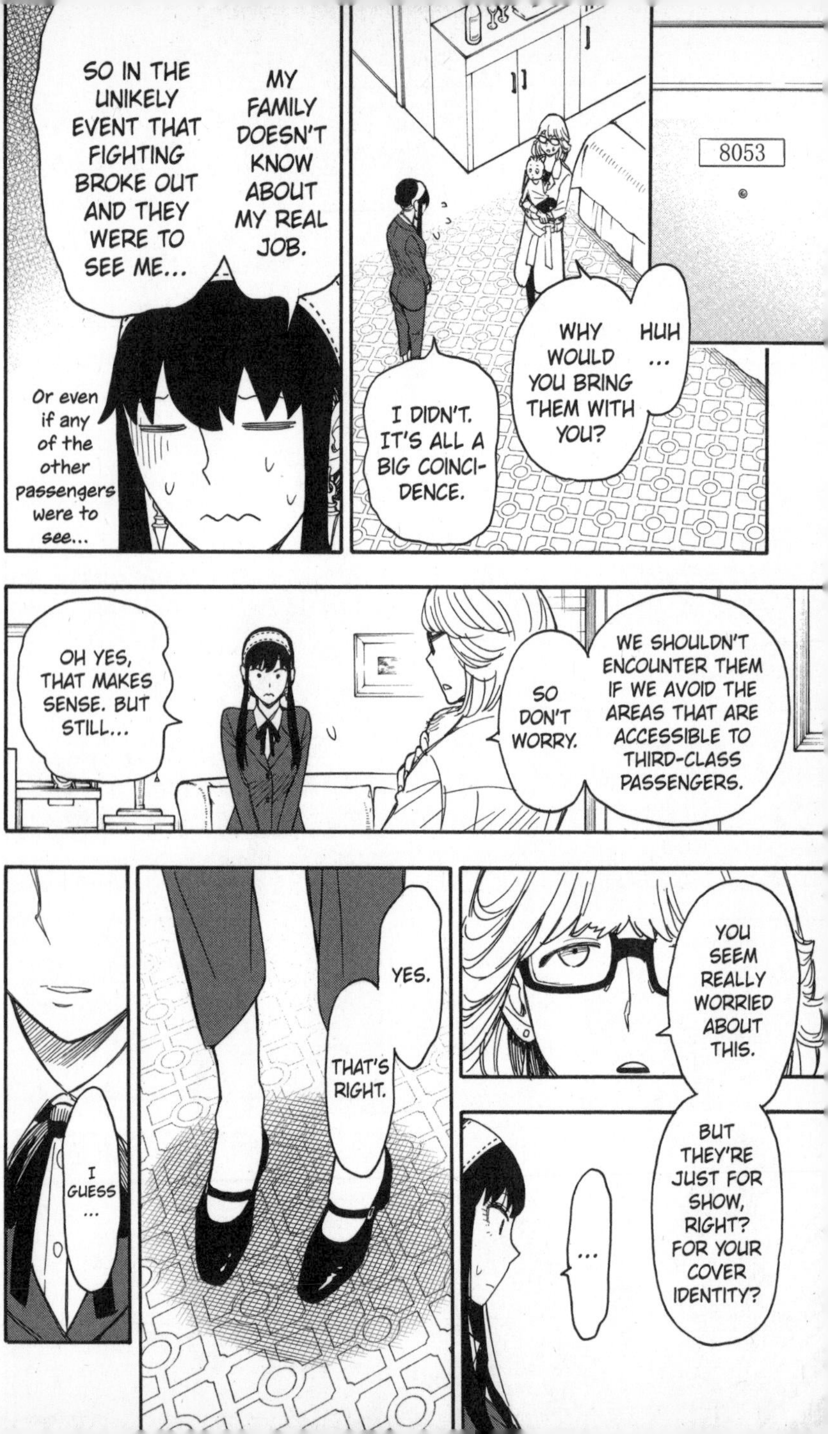
8053
HUH...
WHY WOULD YOU BRING THEM WITH YOU?
I DIDN'T. IT'S ALL A BIG COINCIDENCE.
MY FAMILY DOESN'T KNOW ABOUT MY REAL JOB.
SO IN THE UNIKELY EVENT THAT FIGHTING BROKE OUT AND THEY WERE TO SEE ME...
Or even if any of the other passengers were to see...
WE SHOULDN'T ENCOUNTER THEM IF WE AVOID THE AREAS THAT ARE ACCESSIBLE TO THIRD-CLASS PASSENGERS.
SO DON'T WORRY.
OH YES, THAT MAKES SENSE. BUT STILL...
YOU SEEM REALLY WORRIED ABOUT THIS.
BUT THEY'RE JUST FOR SHOW, RIGHT? FOR YOUR COVER IDENTITY?
...
YES.
THAT'S RIGHT.
I GUESS...

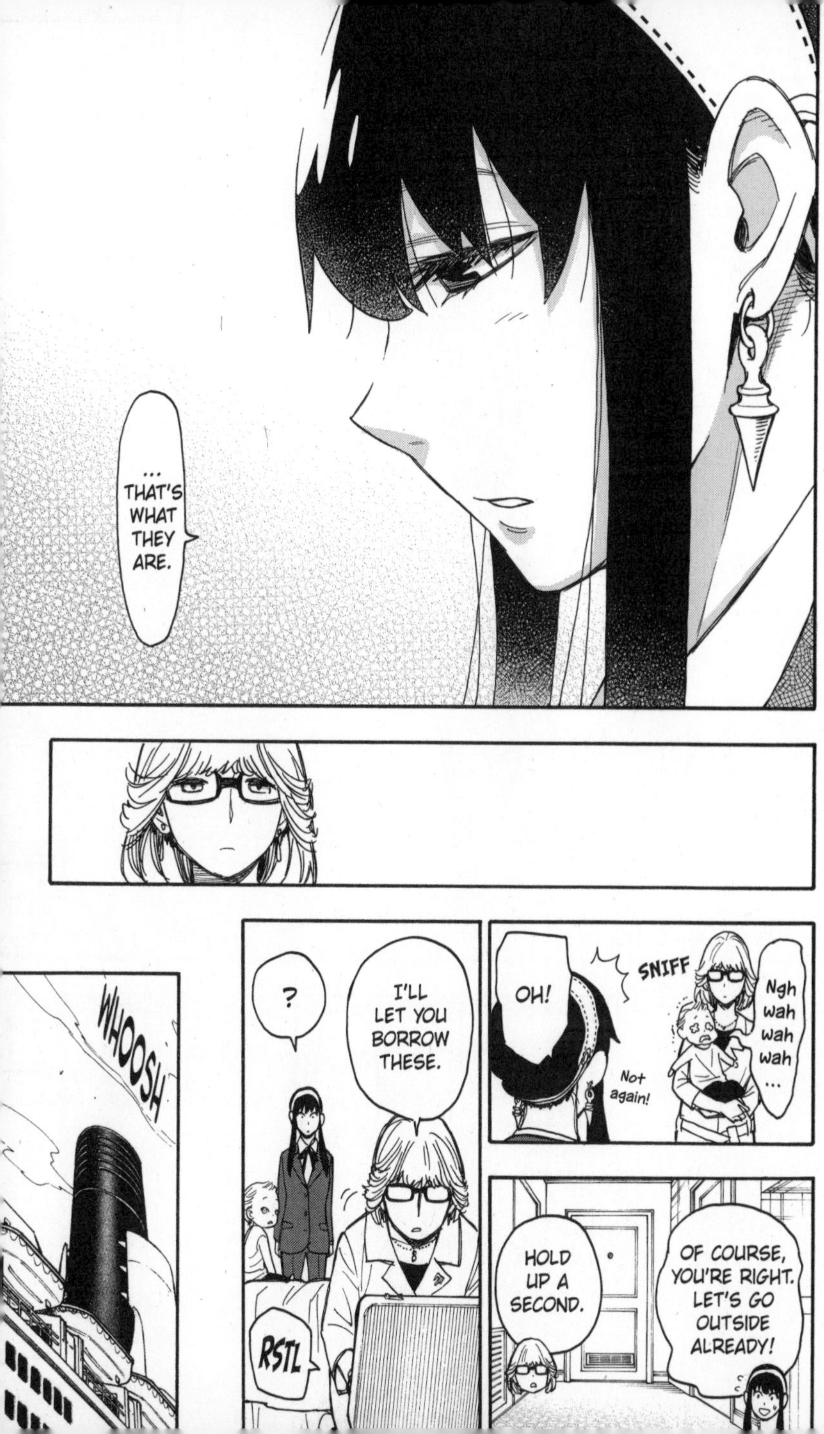
...THAT'S WHAT THEY ARE.
Ngh wah wah wah ...
SNIFF
OH!
Not again!
OF COURSE, YOU'RE RIGHT. LET'S GO OUTSIDE ALREADY!
HOLD UP A SECOND.
I'LL LET YOU BORROW THESE.
?
RSTL
WHOOSH

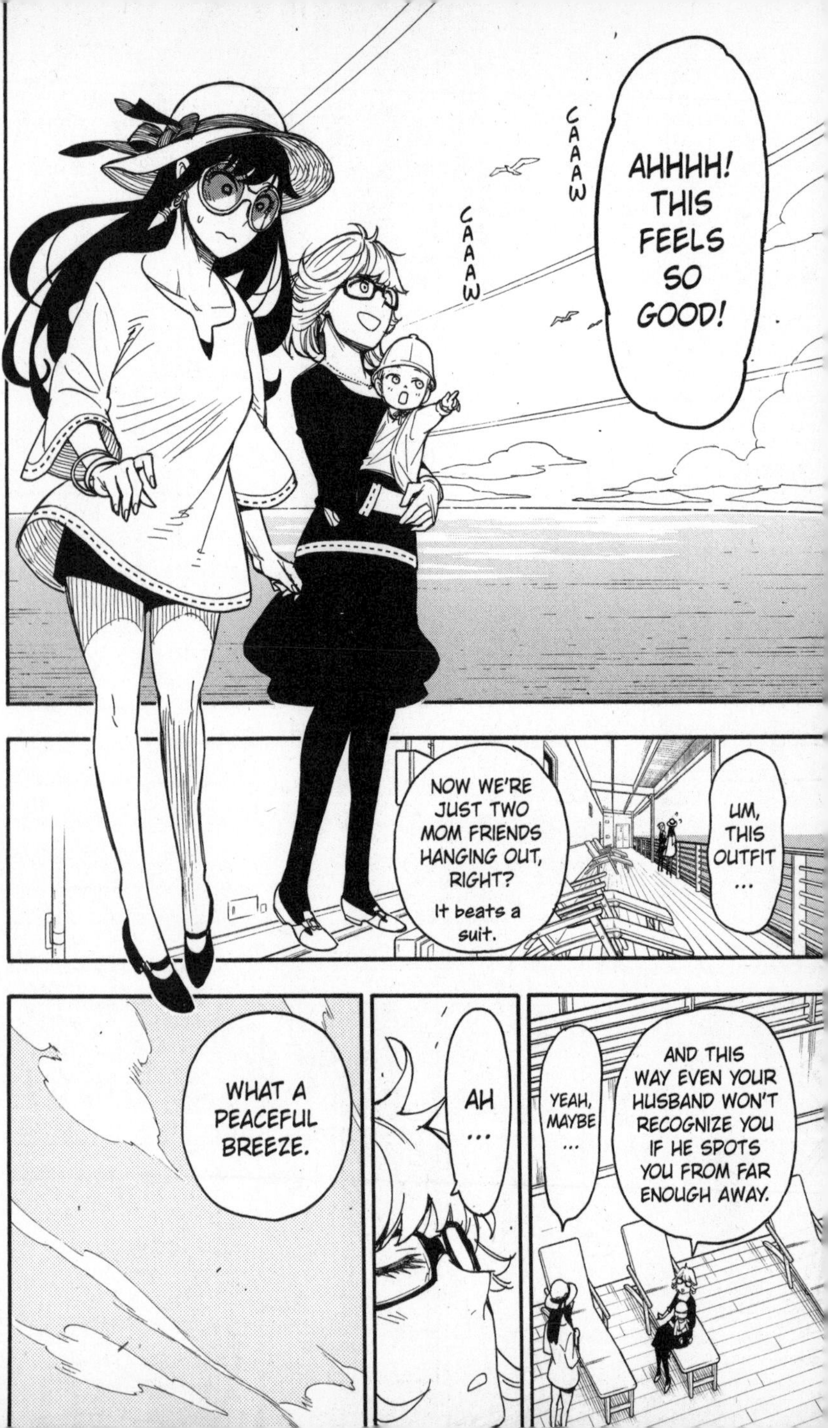
AHHHH! THIS FEELS SO GOOD!
CAAAW
CAAAW
UM, THIS OUTFIT ...
NOW WE'RE JUST TWO MOM FRIENDS HANGING OUT, RIGHT?
It beats a suit.
AND THIS WAY EVEN YOUR HUSBAND WON'T RECOGNIZE YOU IF HE SPOTS YOU FROM FAR ENOUGH AWAY.
YEAH, MAYBE ...
AH ...
WHAT A PEACEFUL BREEZE.

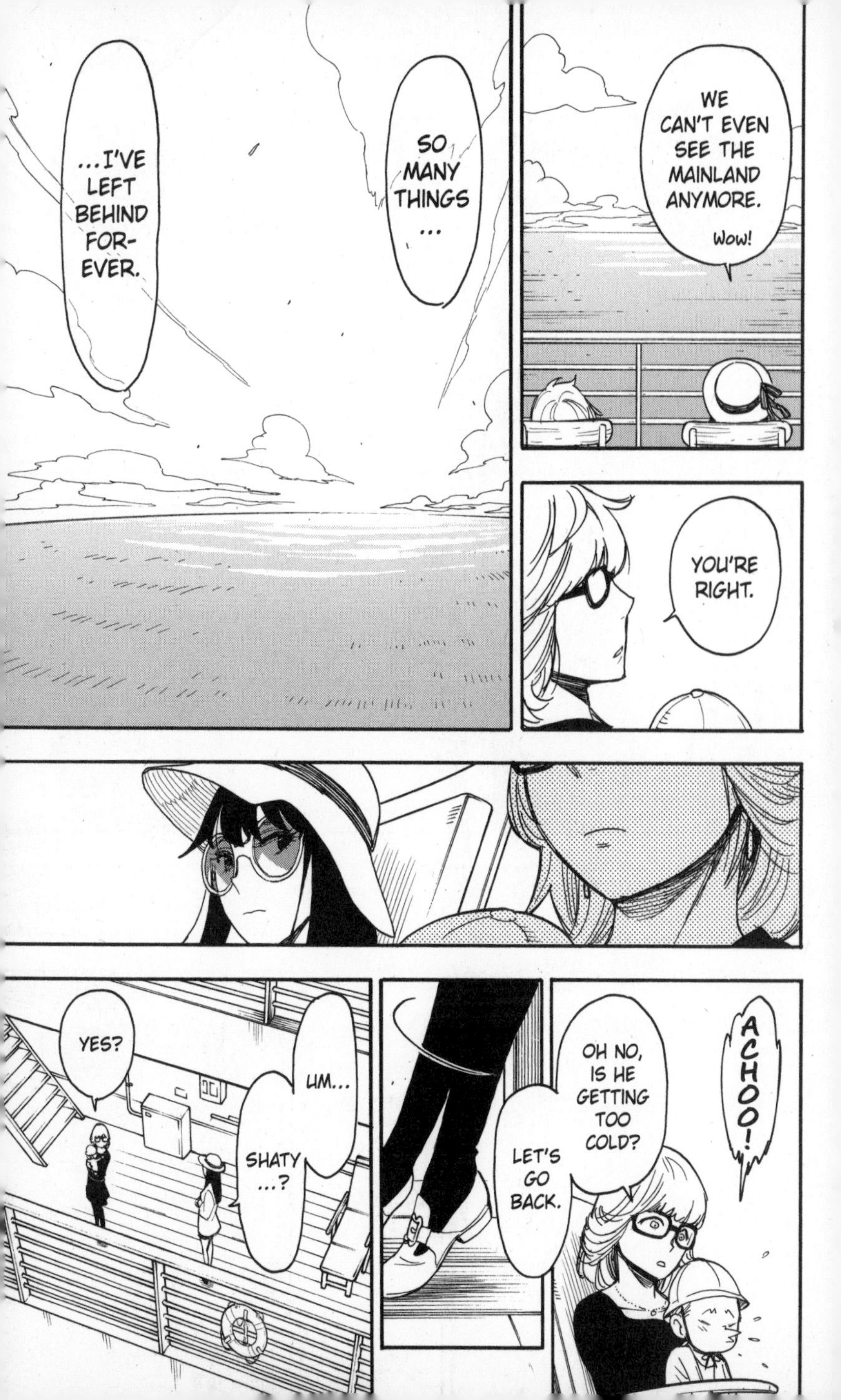
WE CAN'T EVEN SEE THE MAINLAND ANYMORE.
Wow!
YOU'RE RIGHT.
SO MANY THINGS ...
...I'VE LEFT BEHIND FOR-EVER.
ACHOO!
OH NO, IS HE GETTING TOO COLD?
LET'S GO BACK.
UM...
SHATY ...?
YES?

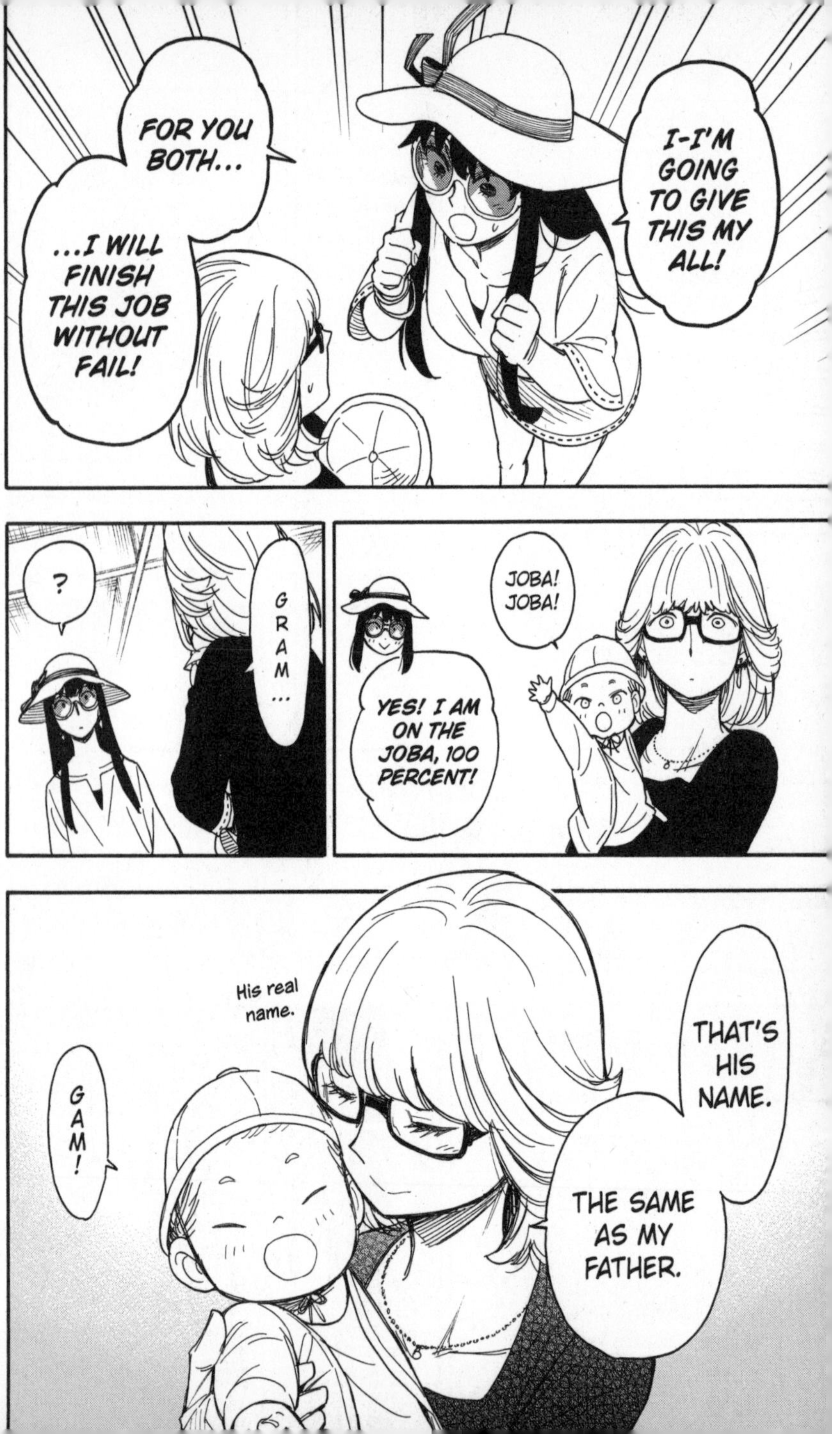
I-I'M GOING TO GIVE THIS MY ALL!
FOR YOU BOTH...
...I WILL FINISH THIS JOB WITHOUT FAIL!
JOBA! JOBA!
YES! I AM ON THE JOBA, 100 PERCENT!
GRAM...
?
THAT'S HIS NAME.
THE SAME AS MY FATHER.
His real name.
GAM!

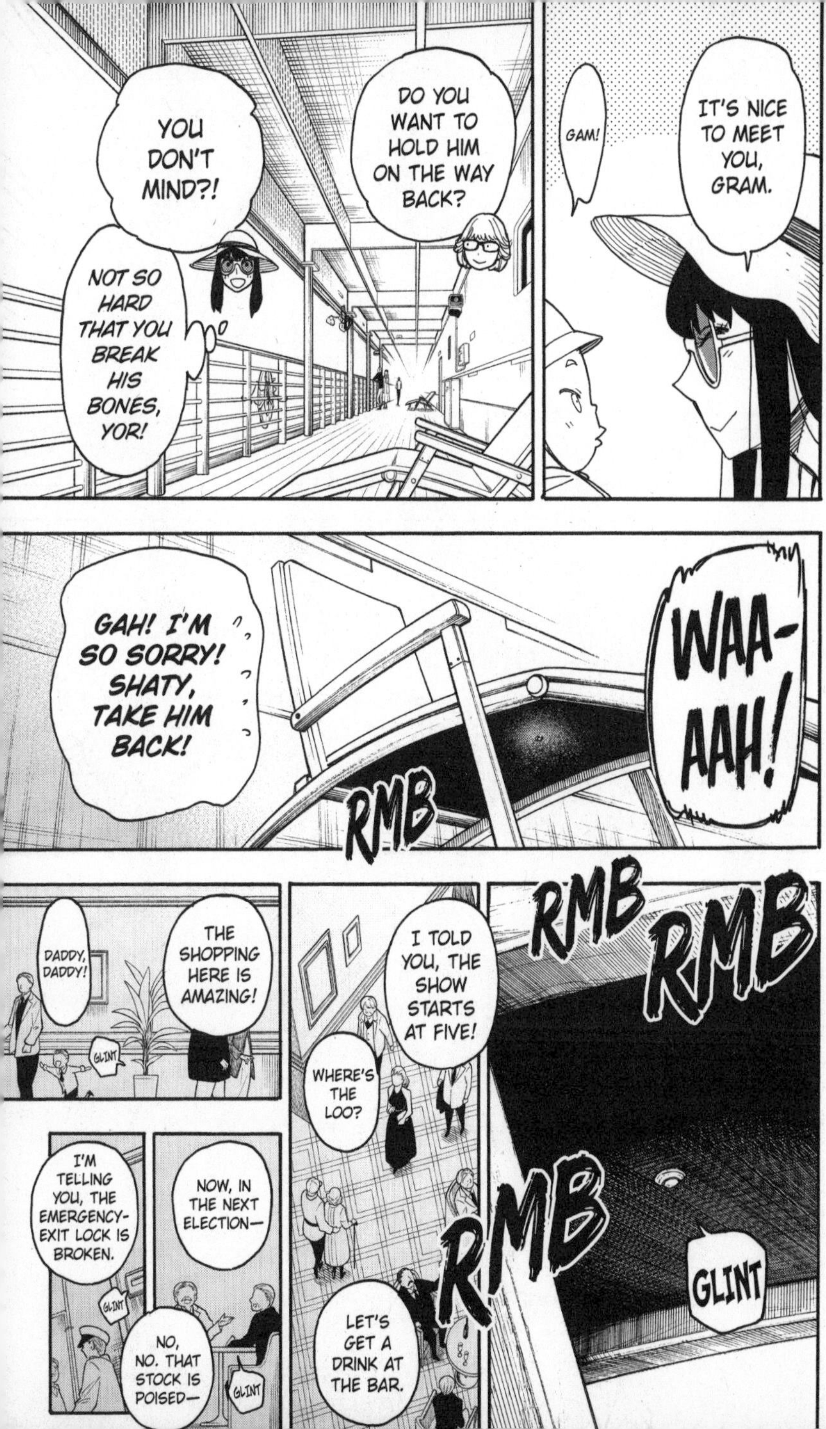
IT'S NICE TO MEET YOU, GRAM.
GAM!
DO YOU WANT TO HOLD HIM ON THE WAY BACK?
YOU DON'T MIND?!
NOT SO HARD THAT YOU BREAK HIS BONES, YOR!
WAA-AAH!
GAH! I'M SO SORRY! SHATY, TAKE HIM BACK!
RMB
RMB
RMB
RMB
GLINT
I TOLD YOU, THE SHOW STARTS AT FIVE!
WHERE'S THE LOO?
LET'S GET A DRINK AT THE BAR.
THE SHOPPING HERE IS AMAZING!
DADDY, DADDY!
GLINT
NOW, IN THE NEXT ELECTION—
NO, NO. THAT STOCK IS POISED—
GLINT
I'M TELLING YOU, THE EMERGENCY-EXIT LOCK IS BROKEN.
GLINT

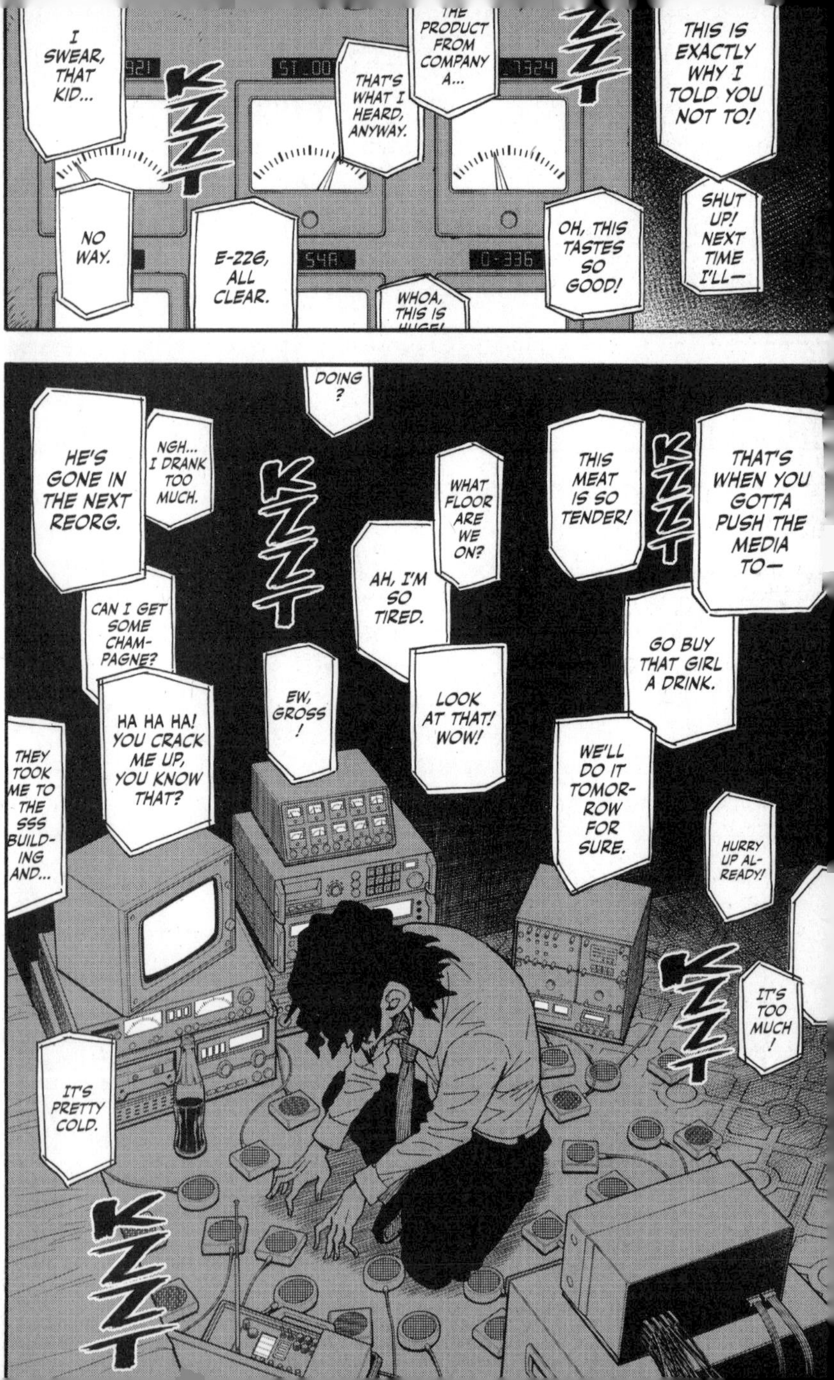
THIS IS EXACTLY WHY I TOLD YOU NOT TO!
SHUT UP! NEXT TIME I'LL—
THE PRODUCT FROM COMPANY A...
OH, THIS TASTES SO GOOD!
THAT'S WHAT I HEARD, ANYWAY.
WHOA, THIS IS
E-226, ALL CLEAR.
KZZZT
I SWEAR, THAT KID...
NO WAY.
DOING?
THAT'S WHEN YOU GOTTA PUSH THE MEDIA TO—
KZZZT
THIS MEAT IS SO TENDER!
WHAT FLOOR ARE WE ON?
GO BUY THAT GIRL A DRINK.
AH, I'M SO TIRED.
KZZZT
NGH... I DRANK TOO MUCH.
HE'S GONE IN THE NEXT REORG.
CAN I GET SOME CHAMPAGNE?
HURRY UP ALREADY!
WE'LL DO IT TOMORROW FOR SURE.
LOOK AT THAT! WOW!
EW, GROSS!
HA HA HA! YOU CRACK ME UP, YOU KNOW THAT?
THEY TOOK ME TO THE SSS BUILDING AND...
IT'S TOO MUCH!
KZZZT
IT'S PRETTY COLD.
KZZZT

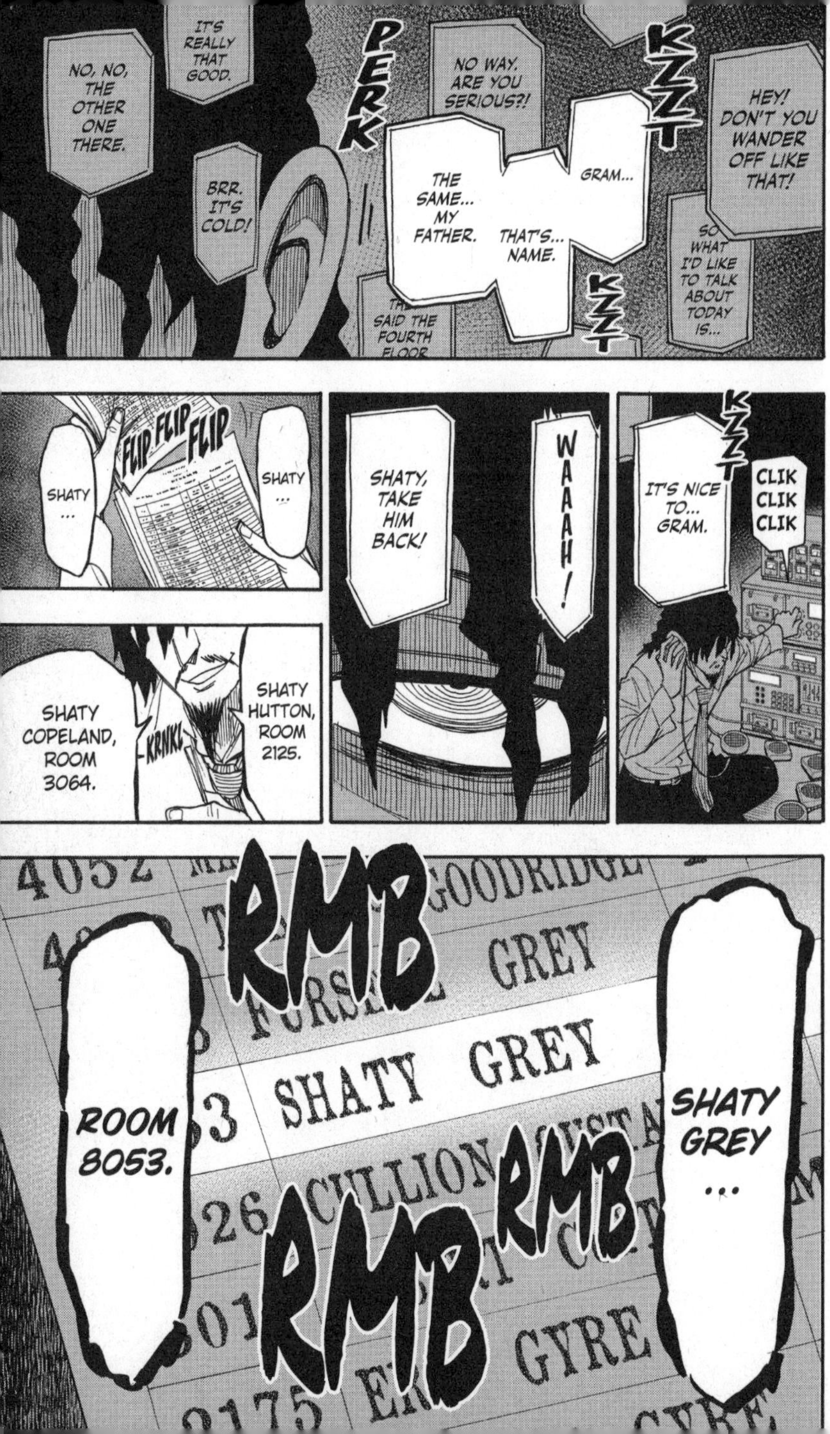
HEY! DON'T YOU WANDER OFF LIKE THAT!
KZZT
SO WHAT I'D LIKE TO TALK ABOUT TODAY IS...
NO WAY. ARE YOU SERIOUS?!
GRAM...
THAT'S... NAME.
THE SAME... MY FATHER.
KZZT
SAID THE FOURTH
PERK
IT'S REALLY THAT GOOD.
BRR. IT'S COLD!
NO, NO, THE OTHER ONE THERE.
KZZT
CLIK CLIK CLIK
IT'S NICE TO... GRAM.
WAAAAH!
SHATY, TAKE HIM BACK!
FLIP FLIP FLIP
SHATY...
SHATY...
SHATY HUTTON, ROOM 2125.
KRNKL
SHATY COPELAND, ROOM 3064.
SHATY GREY...
RMB
RMB
RMB
ROOM 8053.
4052
GOODRIDGE
GREY
SHATY GREY
CILLION
GYRE

SPY×FAMILY

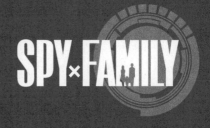

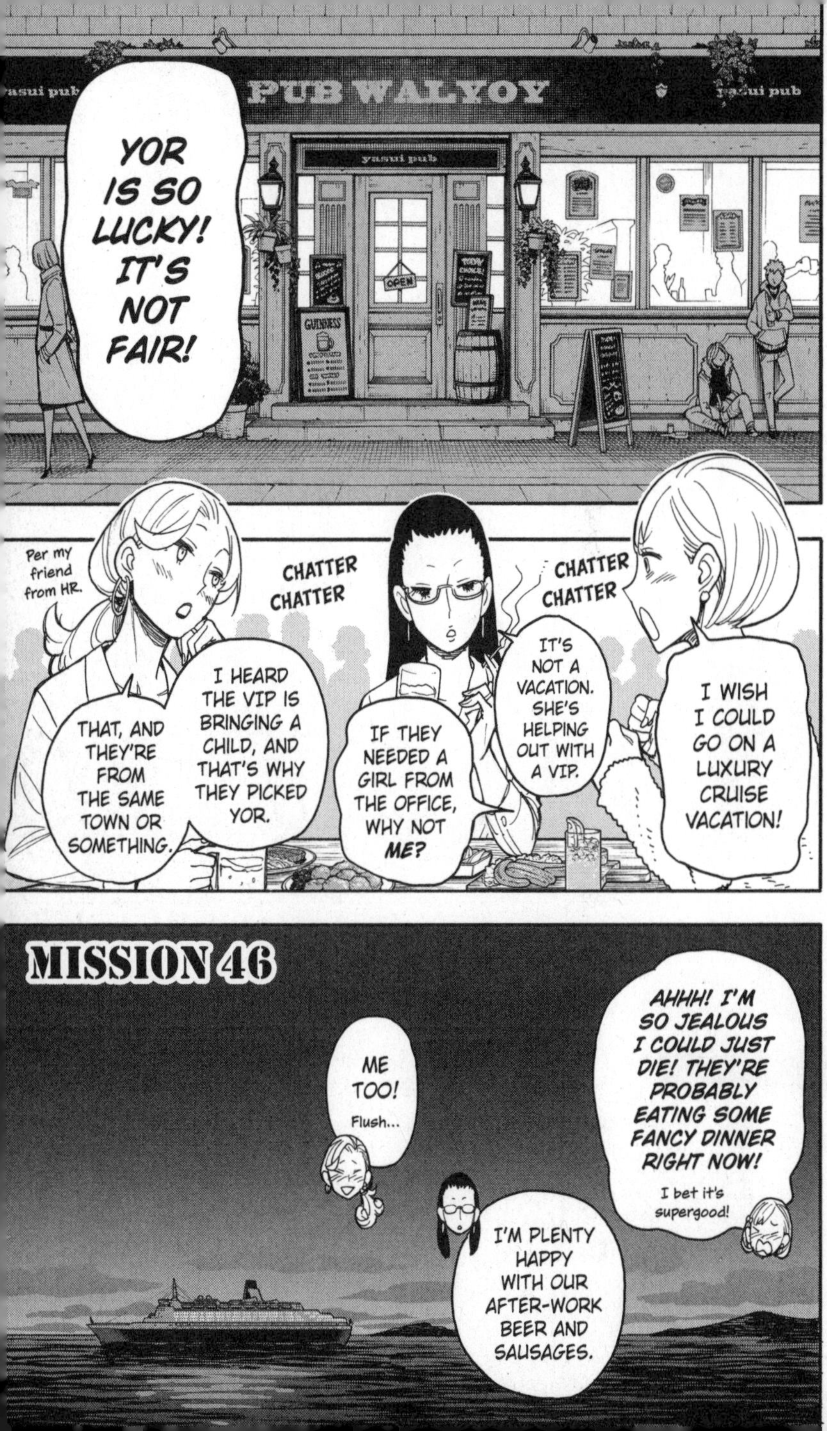
PUB WALYOY
yasui pub
yasui pub
yasui pub
OPEN
GUINNESS
YOR IS SO LUCKY! IT'S NOT FAIR!
CHATTER CHATTER
I WISH I COULD GO ON A LUXURY CRUISE VACATION!
IT'S NOT A VACATION. SHE'S HELPING OUT WITH A VIP.
CHATTER CHATTER
IF THEY NEEDED A GIRL FROM THE OFFICE, WHY NOT ME?
I HEARD THE VIP IS BRINGING A CHILD, AND THAT'S WHY THEY PICKED YOR.
Per my friend from HR.
THAT, AND THEY'RE FROM THE SAME TOWN OR SOMETHING.
MISSION 46
AHHH! I'M SO JEALOUS I COULD JUST DIE! THEY'RE PROBABLY EATING SOME FANCY DINNER RIGHT NOW!
I bet it's supergood!
ME TOO!
Flush...
I'M PLENTY HAPPY WITH OUR AFTER-WORK BEER AND SAUSAGES.

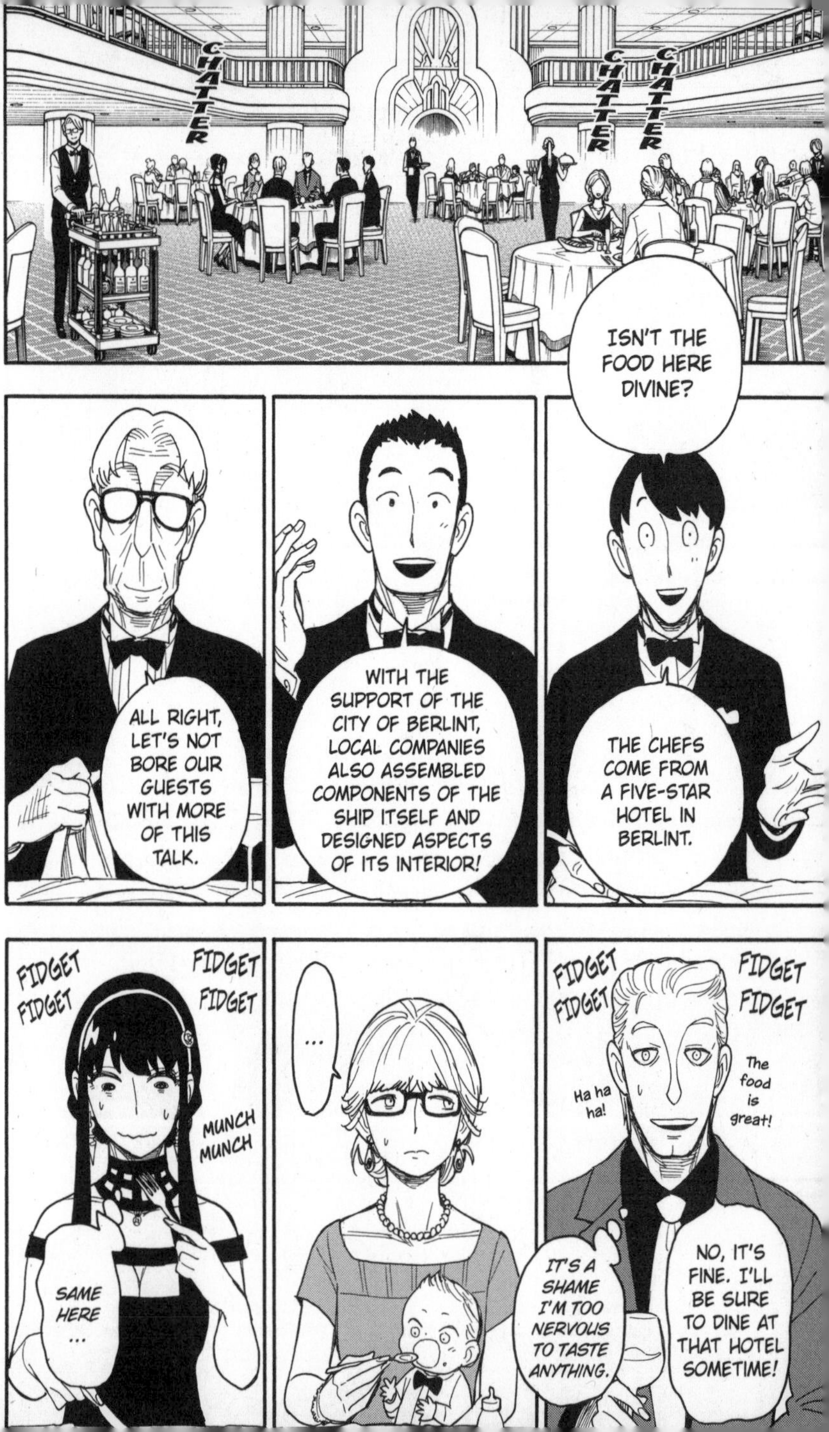

CHATTER CHATTER
CHATTER
ISN'T THE FOOD HERE DIVINE?
THE CHEFS COME FROM A FIVE-STAR HOTEL IN BERLINT.
WITH THE SUPPORT OF THE CITY OF BERLINT, LOCAL COMPANIES ALSO ASSEMBLED COMPONENTS OF THE SHIP ITSELF AND DESIGNED ASPECTS OF ITS INTERIOR!
ALL RIGHT, LET'S NOT BORE OUR GUESTS WITH MORE OF THIS TALK.
FIDGET FIDGET
FIDGET FIDGET
The food is great!
Ha ha ha!
NO, IT'S FINE. I'LL BE SURE TO DINE AT THAT HOTEL SOMETIME!
IT'S A SHAME I'M TOO NERVOUS TO TASTE ANYTHING.
...
FIDGET FIDGET
FIDGET FIDGET
MUNCH MUNCH
SAME HERE ...

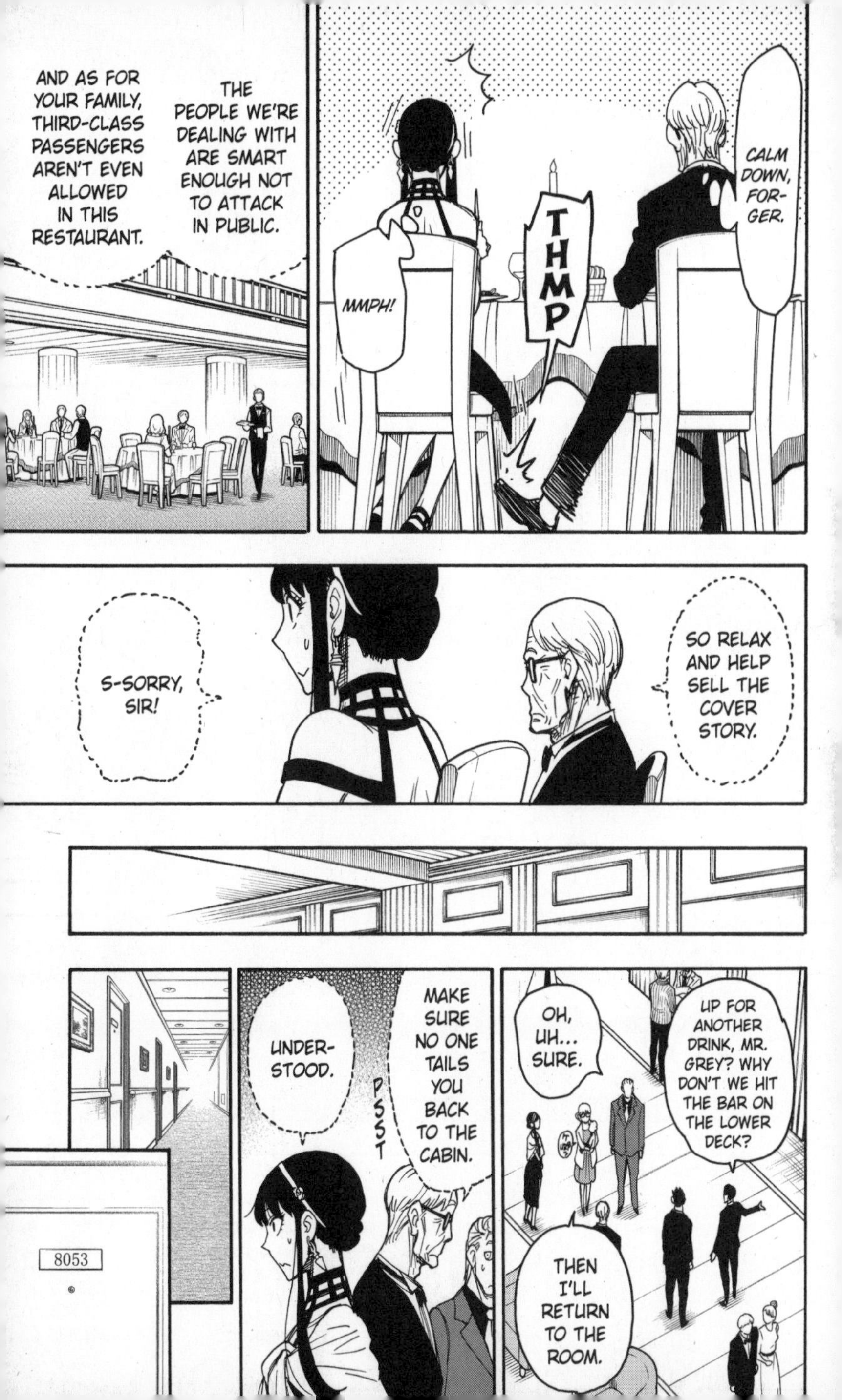
CALM DOWN, FOR-GER.
THMP
MMPH!
THE PEOPLE WE'RE DEALING WITH ARE SMART ENOUGH NOT TO ATTACK IN PUBLIC.
AND AS FOR YOUR FAMILY, THIRD-CLASS PASSENGERS AREN'T EVEN ALLOWED IN THIS RESTAURANT.
SO RELAX AND HELP SELL THE COVER STORY.
S-SORRY, SIR!
UP FOR ANOTHER DRINK, MR. GREY? WHY DON'T WE HIT THE BAR ON THE LOWER DECK?
OH, UH... SURE.
THEN I'LL RETURN TO THE ROOM.
MAKE SURE NO ONE TAILS YOU BACK TO THE CABIN.
PSST
UNDER-STOOD.
8053

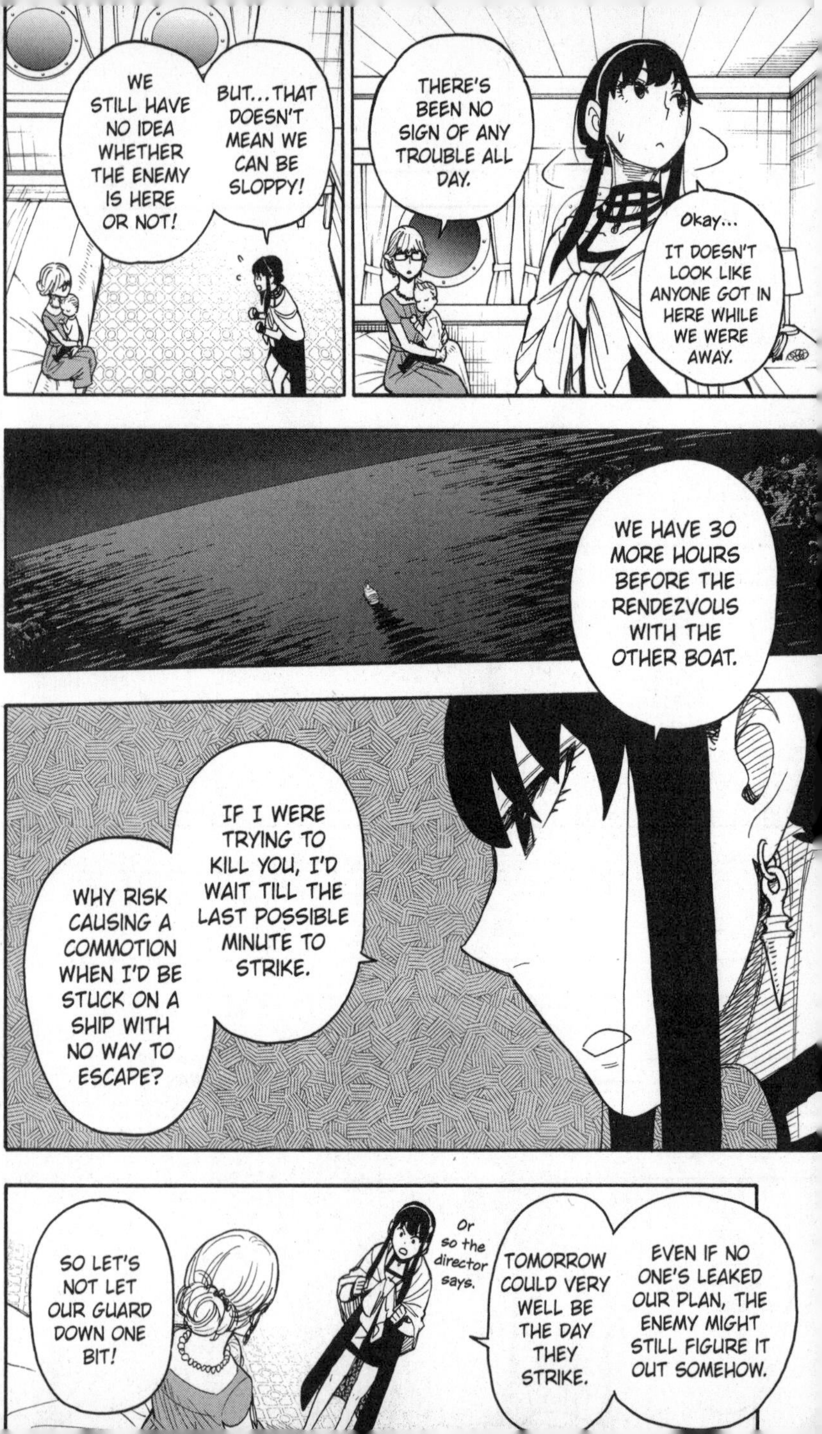
Okay... IT DOESN'T LOOK LIKE ANYONE GOT IN HERE WHILE WE WERE AWAY.
THERE'S BEEN NO SIGN OF ANY TROUBLE ALL DAY.
BUT...THAT DOESN'T MEAN WE CAN BE SLOPPY!
WE STILL HAVE NO IDEA WHETHER THE ENEMY IS HERE OR NOT!
WE HAVE 30 MORE HOURS BEFORE THE RENDEZVOUS WITH THE OTHER BOAT.
IF I WERE TRYING TO KILL YOU, I'D WAIT TILL THE LAST POSSIBLE MINUTE TO STRIKE.
WHY RISK CAUSING A COMMOTION WHEN I'D BE STUCK ON A SHIP WITH NO WAY TO ESCAPE?
EVEN IF NO ONE'S LEAKED OUR PLAN, THE ENEMY MIGHT STILL FIGURE IT OUT SOMEHOW.
TOMORROW COULD VERY WELL BE THE DAY THEY STRIKE.
Or so the director says.
SO LET'S NOT LET OUR GUARD DOWN ONE BIT!

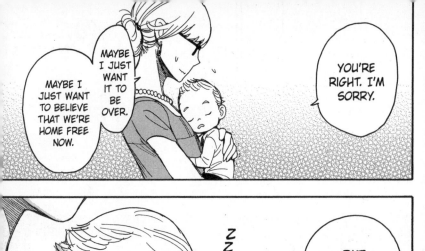

YOU'RE RIGHT. I'M SORRY.
MAYBE I JUST WANT IT TO BE OVER.
MAYBE I JUST WANT TO BELIEVE THAT WE'RE HOME FREE NOW.
ZZZ
BUT THIS ISN'T JUST MY PROBLEM.
I NEED TO BE STRONG.
THAT'S RIGHT!
AS SOON AS YOU ARRIVE AND WE CONFIRM IT'S SAFE, YOU CAN TAKE GRAM OUTSIDE TO PLAY AS MUCH AS HE WANTS!
Mmm...
POKE POKE
YOU KNOW, YOU REALLY DON'T SEEM TO BE THE UNDERWORLD TYPE. AT ALL.
OH, I'M SORRY. I'LL...TRY HARDER...?
UM...
IF WE MANAGE TO ESCAPE FROM HERE SAFELY...
...WHAT WILL YOU ALL DO NEXT?

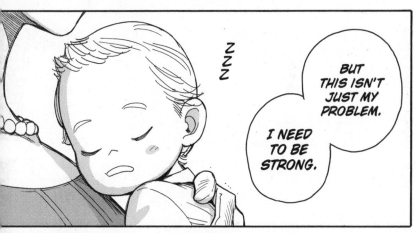

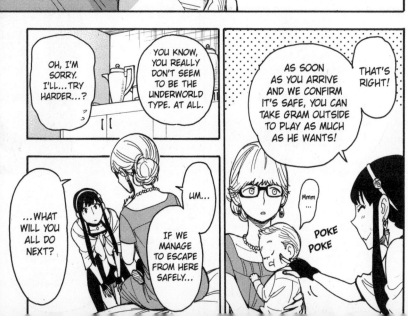

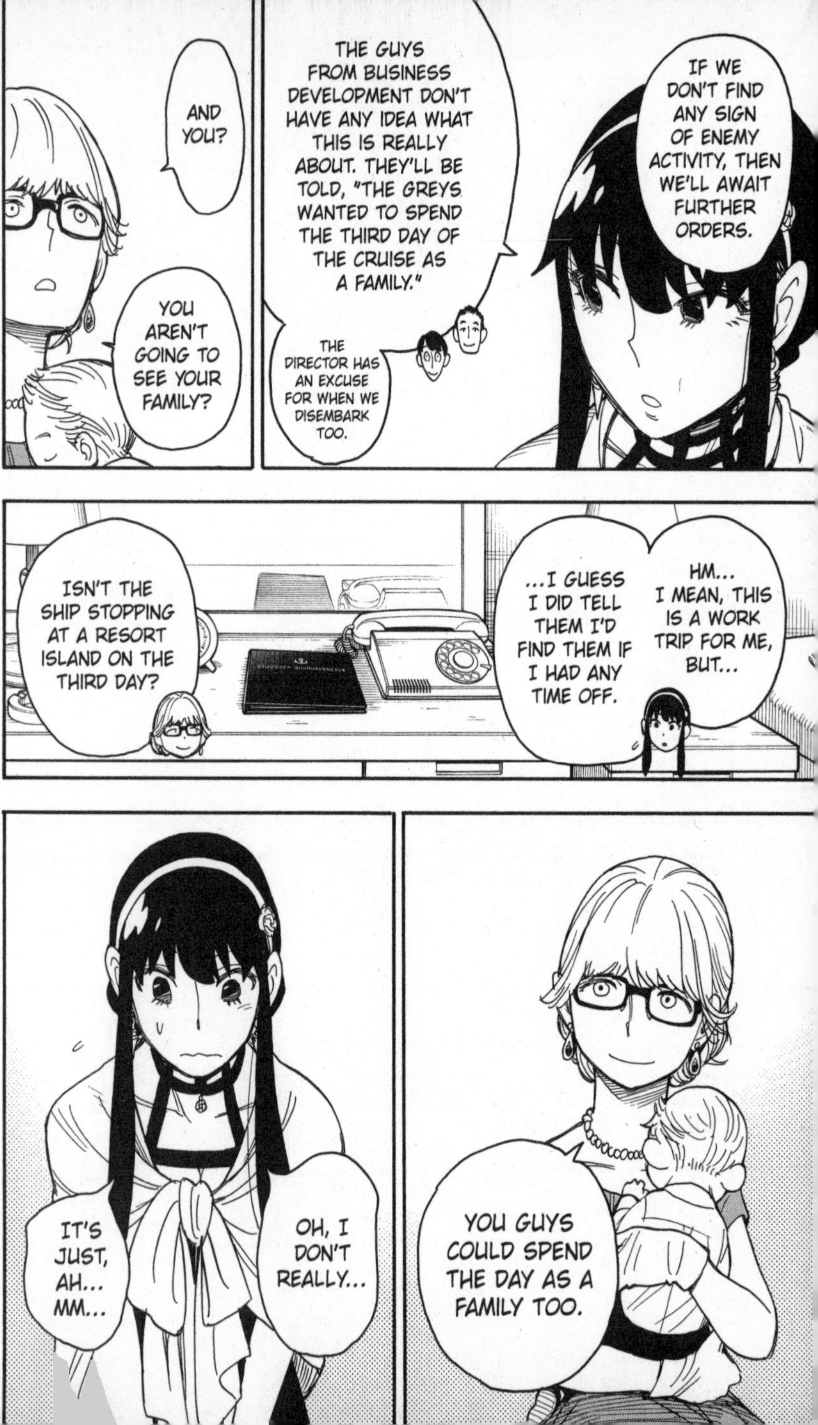
IF WE DON'T FIND ANY SIGN OF ENEMY ACTIVITY, THEN WE'LL AWAIT FURTHER ORDERS.
THE GUYS FROM BUSINESS DEVELOPMENT DON'T HAVE ANY IDEA WHAT THIS IS REALLY ABOUT. THEY'LL BE TOLD, "THE GREYS WANTED TO SPEND THE THIRD DAY OF THE CRUISE AS A FAMILY."
THE DIRECTOR HAS AN EXCUSE FOR WHEN WE DISEMBARK TOO.
AND YOU?
YOU AREN'T GOING TO SEE YOUR FAMILY?
HM... I MEAN, THIS IS A WORK TRIP FOR ME, BUT...
...I GUESS I DID TELL THEM I'D FIND THEM IF I HAD ANY TIME OFF.
ISN'T THE SHIP STOPPING AT A RESORT ISLAND ON THE THIRD DAY?
YOU GUYS COULD SPEND THE DAY AS A FAMILY TOO.
OH, I DON'T REALLY...
IT'S JUST, AH... MM...

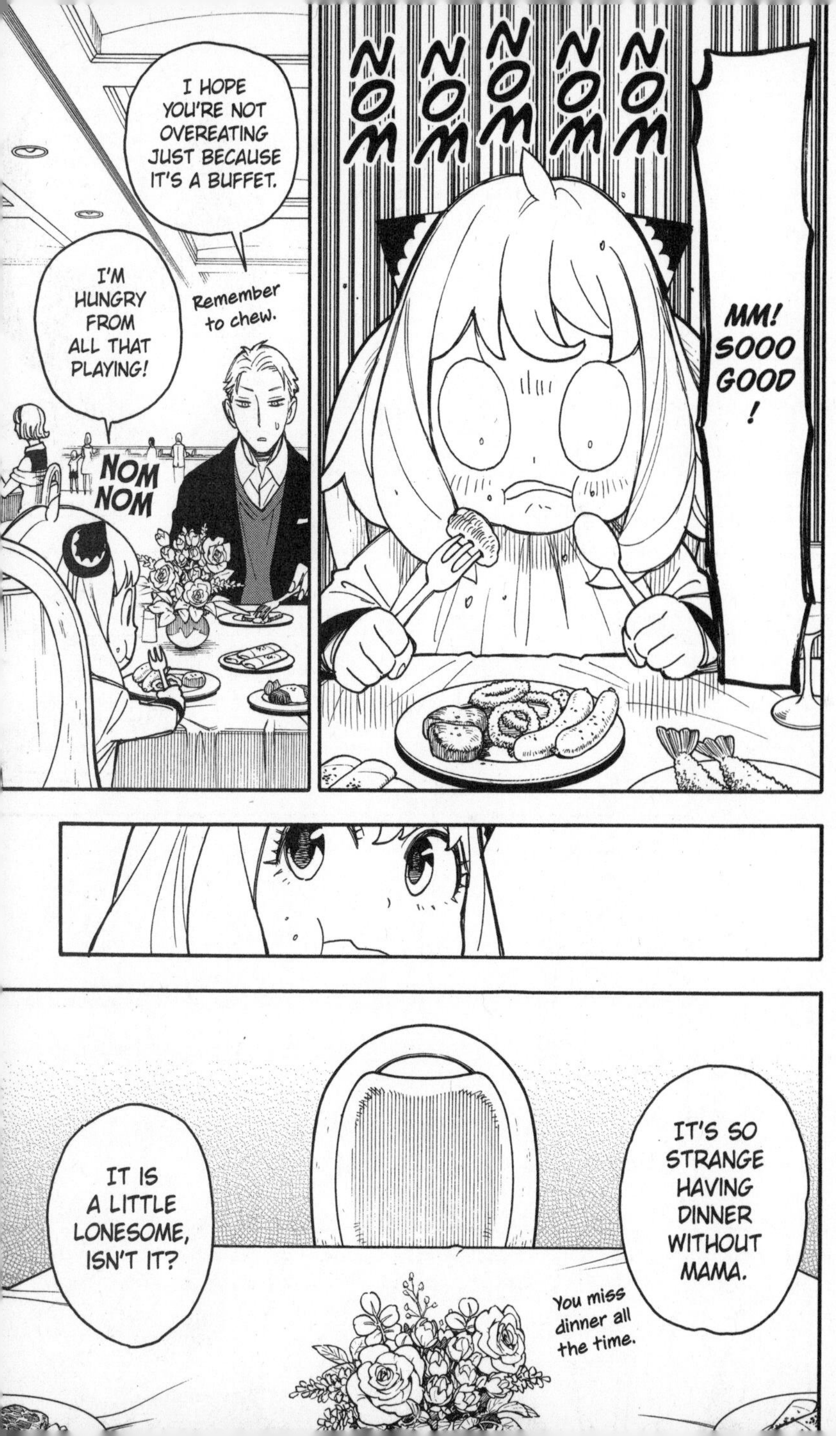
NOM NOM NOM NOM NOM NOM NOM NOM NOM NOM
MM! SOOO GOOD!
I HOPE YOU'RE NOT OVEREATING JUST BECAUSE IT'S A BUFFET.
Remember to chew.
I'M HUNGRY FROM ALL THAT PLAYING!
NOM NOM
IT'S SO STRANGE HAVING DINNER WITHOUT MAMA.
You miss dinner all the time.
IT IS A LITTLE LONESOME, ISN'T IT?

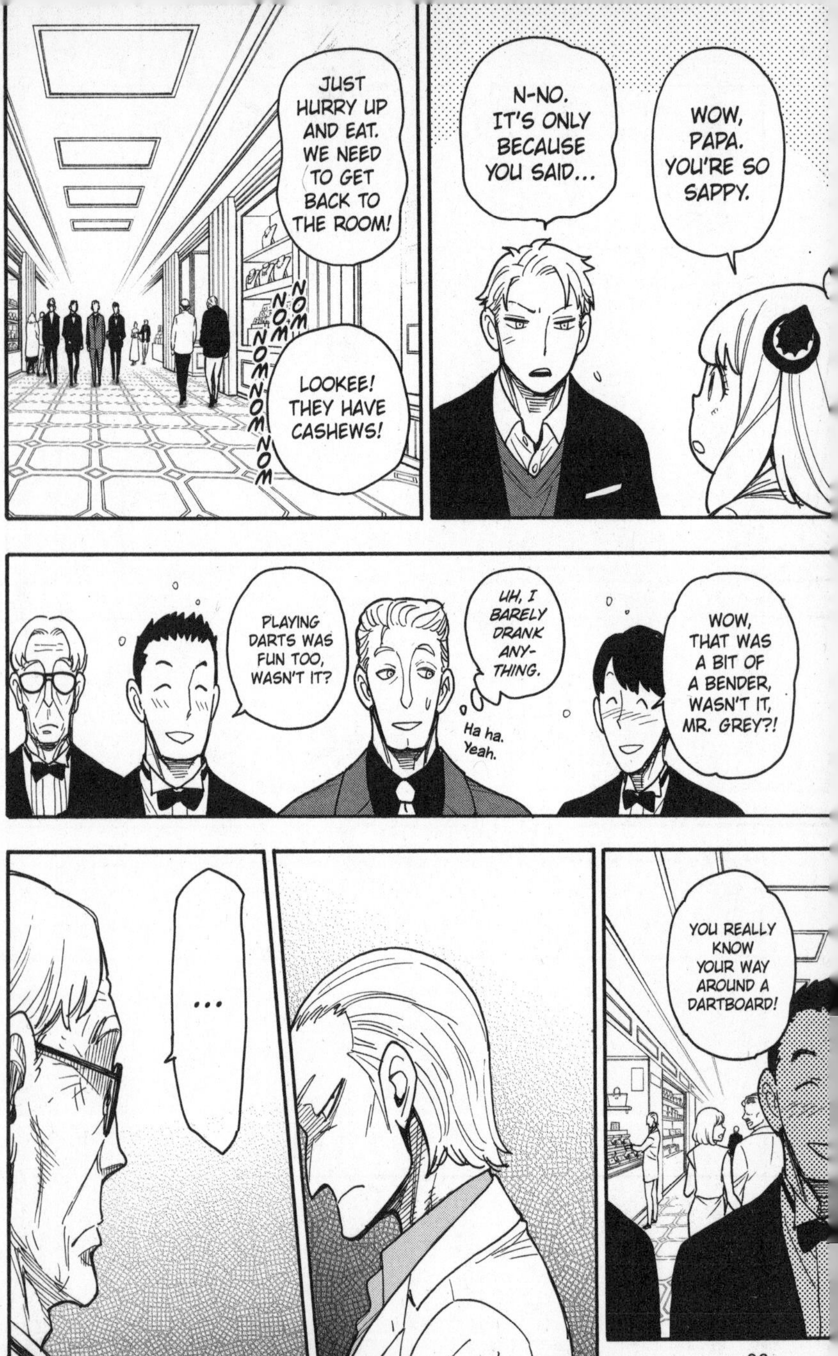
WOW, PAPA. YOU'RE SO SAPPY.
N-NO. IT'S ONLY BECAUSE YOU SAID...
JUST HURRY UP AND EAT. WE NEED TO GET BACK TO THE ROOM!
NOM NOM NOM NOM NOM
LOOKEE! THEY HAVE CASHEWS!
WOW, THAT WAS A BIT OF A BENDER, WASN'T IT, MR. GREY?!
UH, I BARELY DRANK ANYTHING.
Ha ha. Yeah.
PLAYING DARTS WAS FUN TOO, WASN'T IT?
YOU REALLY KNOW YOUR WAY AROUND A DARTBOARD!
...

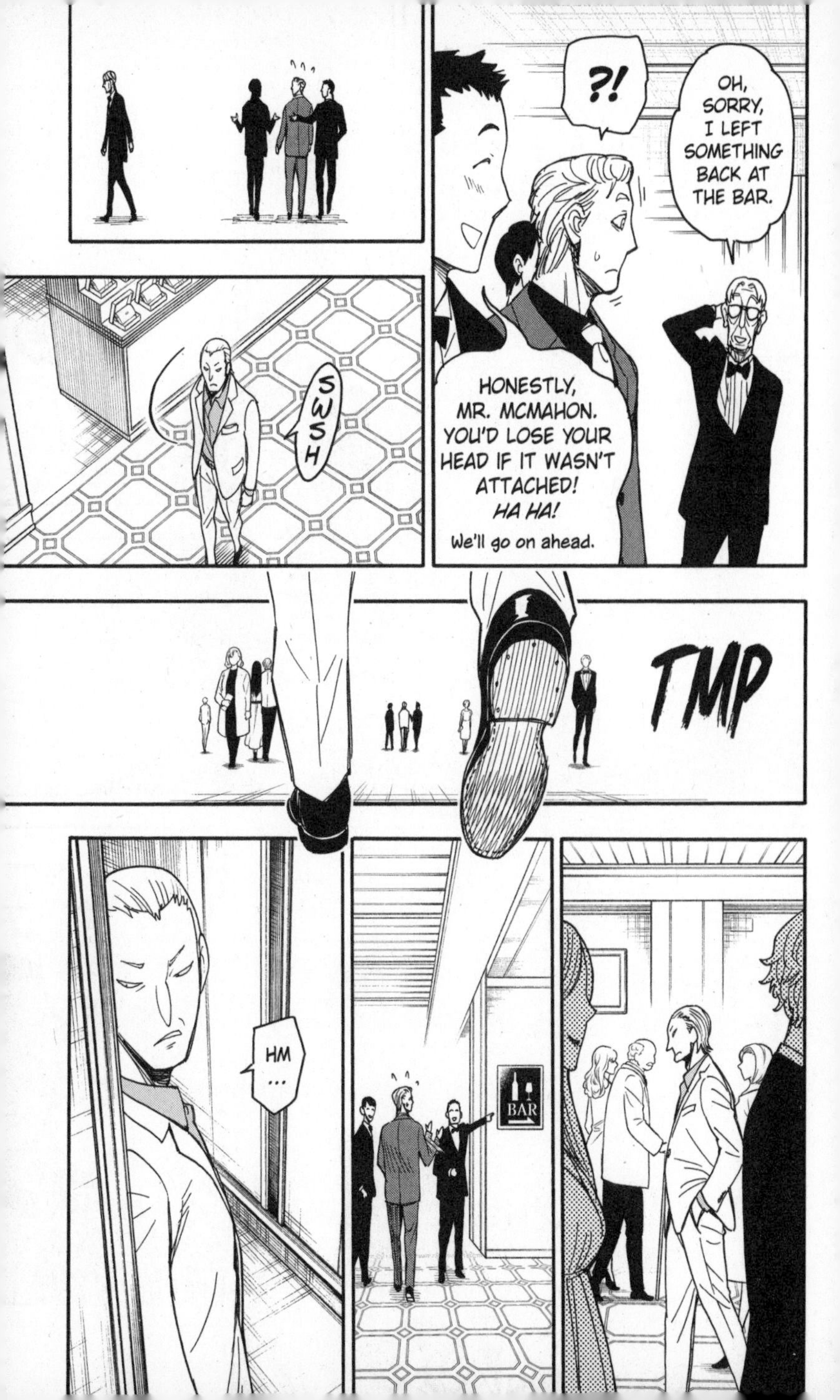
OH, SORRY, I LEFT SOMETHING BACK AT THE BAR.
?!
HONESTLY, MR. MCMAHON. YOU'D LOSE YOUR HEAD IF IT WASN'T ATTACHED! HA HA!
We'll go on ahead.
SWSH
TMP
BAR
HM ...

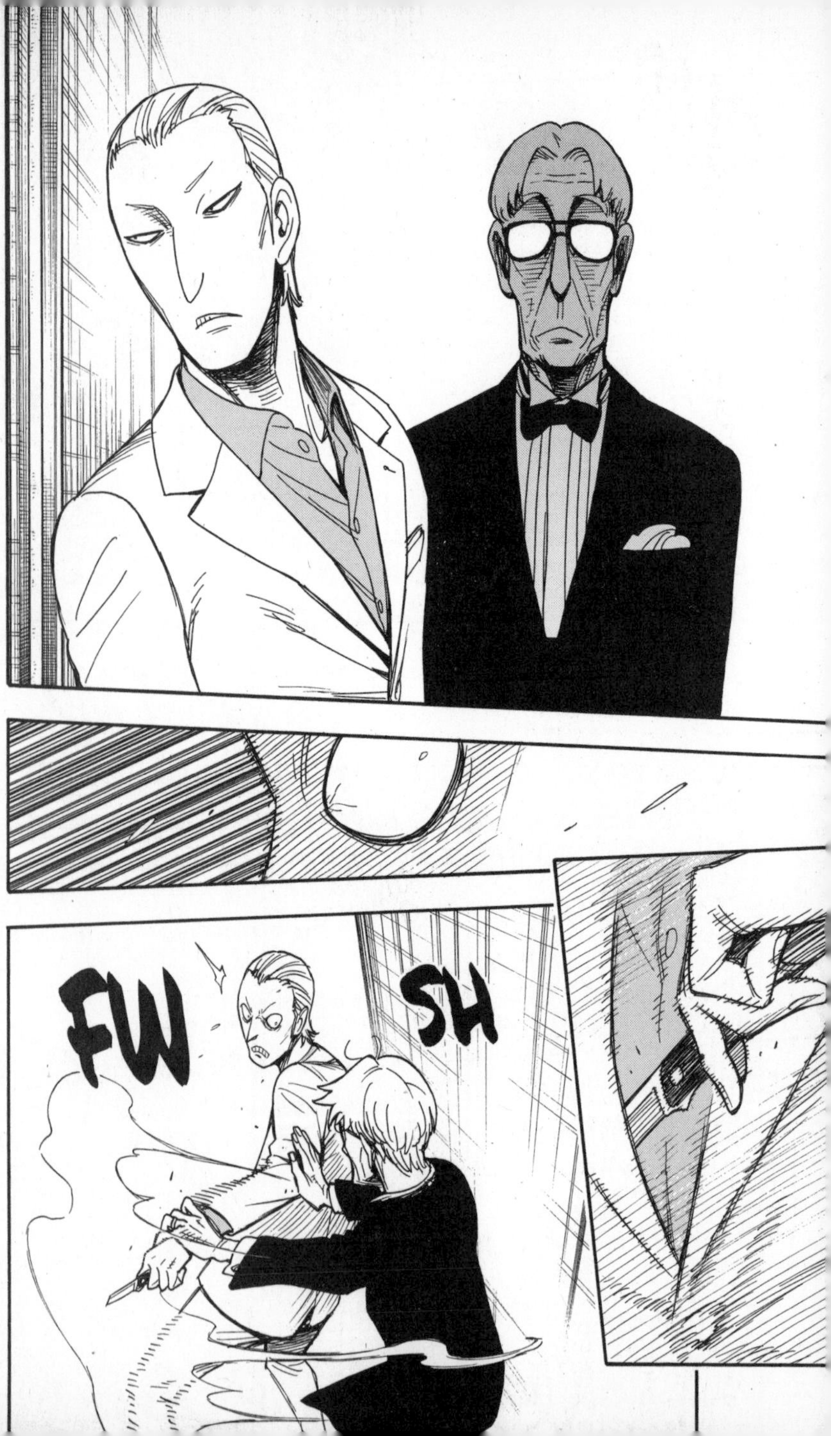
FW
SH

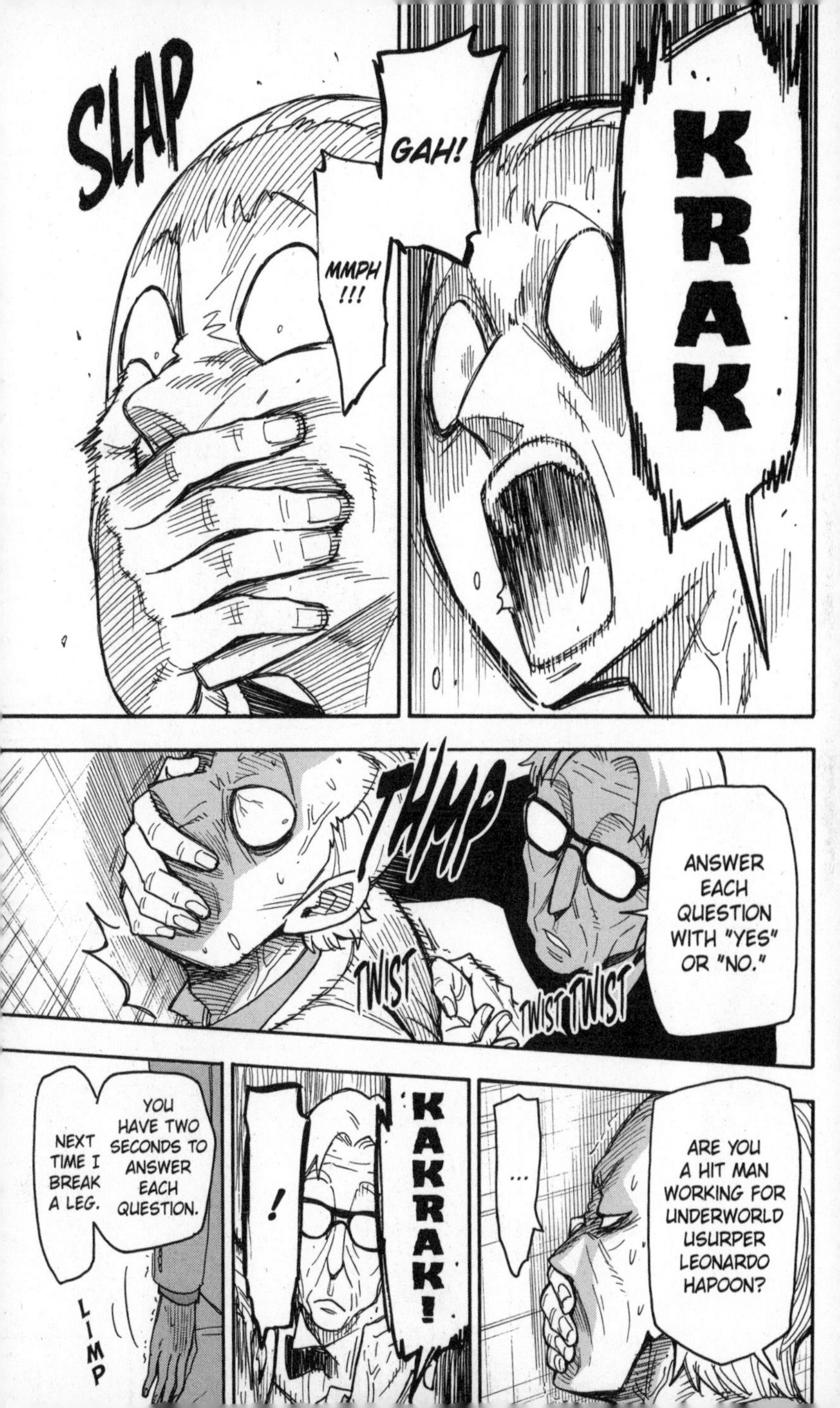
KRAK
GAH!
SLAP
MMPH !!!
ANSWER EACH QUESTION WITH "YES" OR "NO."
THMP
TWIST TWIST
TWIST
ARE YOU A HIT MAN WORKING FOR UNDERWORLD USURPER LEONARDO HAPOON?
...
KAKRAK!
!
YOU HAVE TWO SECONDS TO ANSWER EACH QUESTION.
NEXT TIME I BREAK A LEG.
LIMP

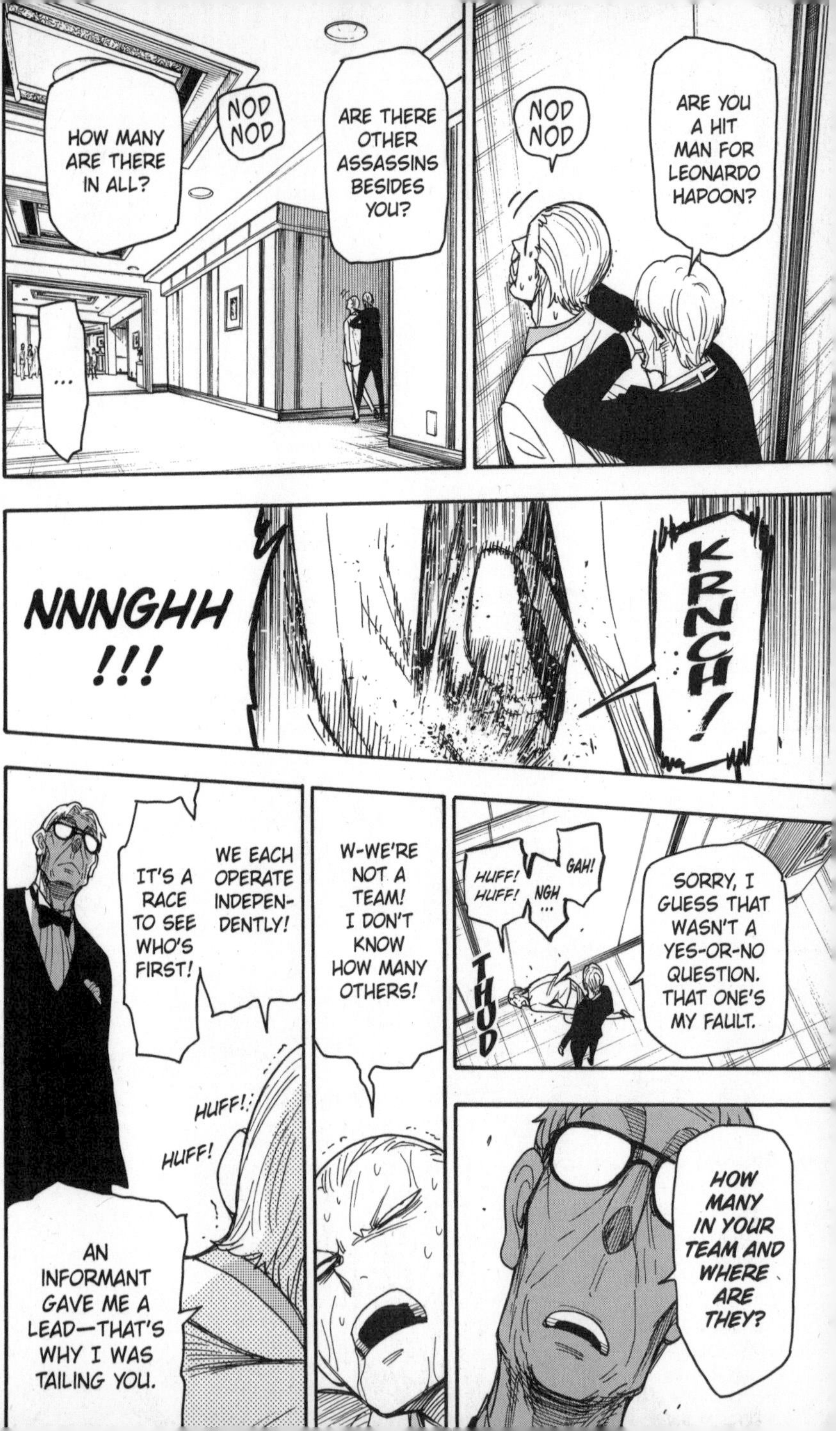
ARE YOU A HIT MAN FOR LEONARDO HAPOON?
NOD NOD
ARE THERE OTHER ASSASSINS BESIDES YOU?
NOD NOD
HOW MANY ARE THERE IN ALL?
...
KRNCH!
NNNGHH!!!
SORRY, I GUESS THAT WASN'T A YES-OR-NO QUESTION. THAT ONE'S MY FAULT.
GAH!
NGH...
HUFF! HUFF!
THUD
HOW MANY IN YOUR TEAM AND WHERE ARE THEY?
W-WE'RE NOT A TEAM! I DON'T KNOW HOW MANY OTHERS!
WE EACH OPERATE INDEPENDENTLY!
IT'S A RACE TO SEE WHO'S FIRST!
HUFF!
HUFF!
AN INFORMANT GAVE ME A LEAD—THAT'S WHY I WAS TAILING YOU.

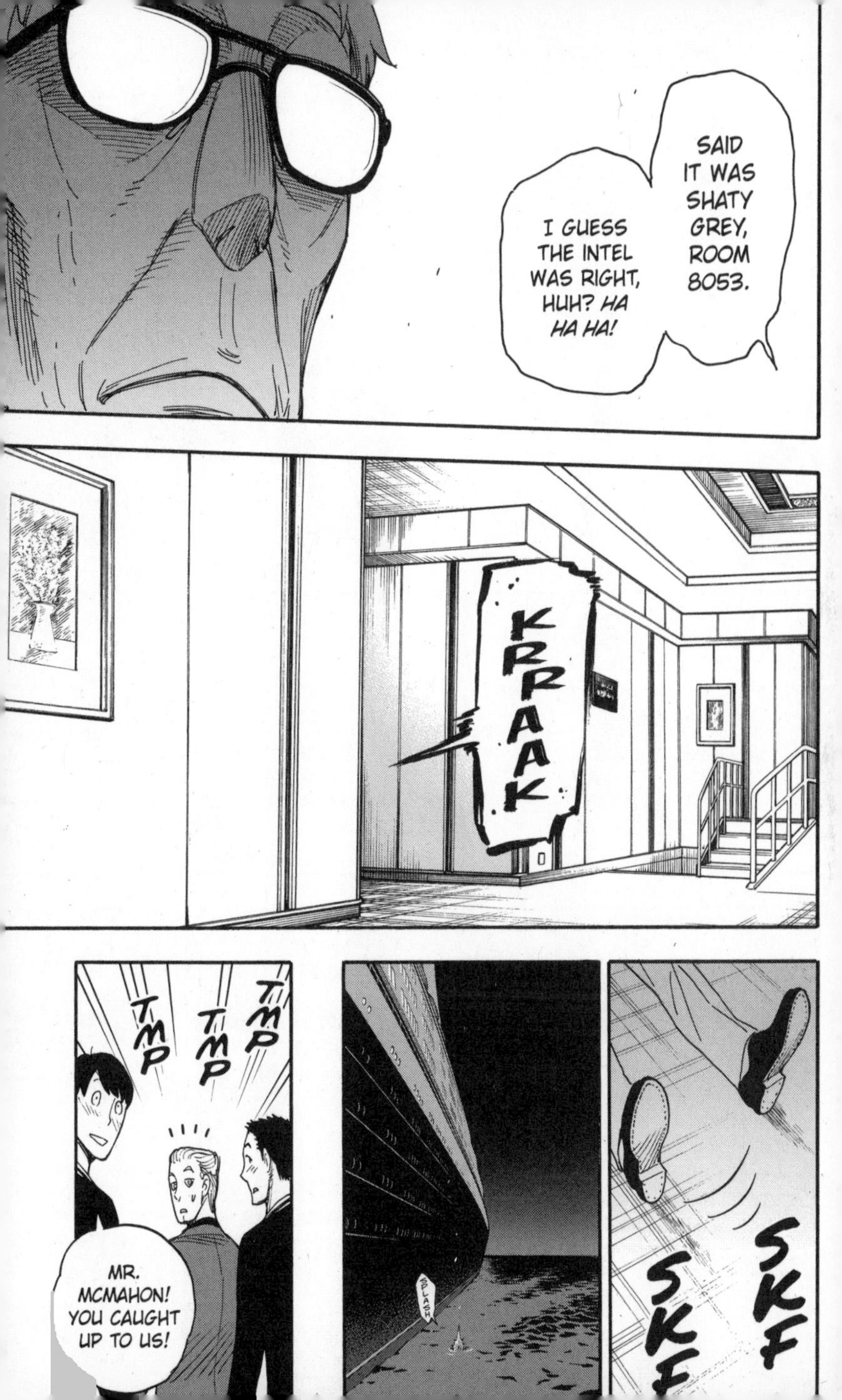
SAID IT WAS SHATY GREY, ROOM 8053.
I GUESS THE INTEL WAS RIGHT, HUH? HA HA HA!
KRRAAK
SKF SKF
SPLASH
TMP TMP TMP
MR. MCMAHON! YOU CAUGHT UP TO US!

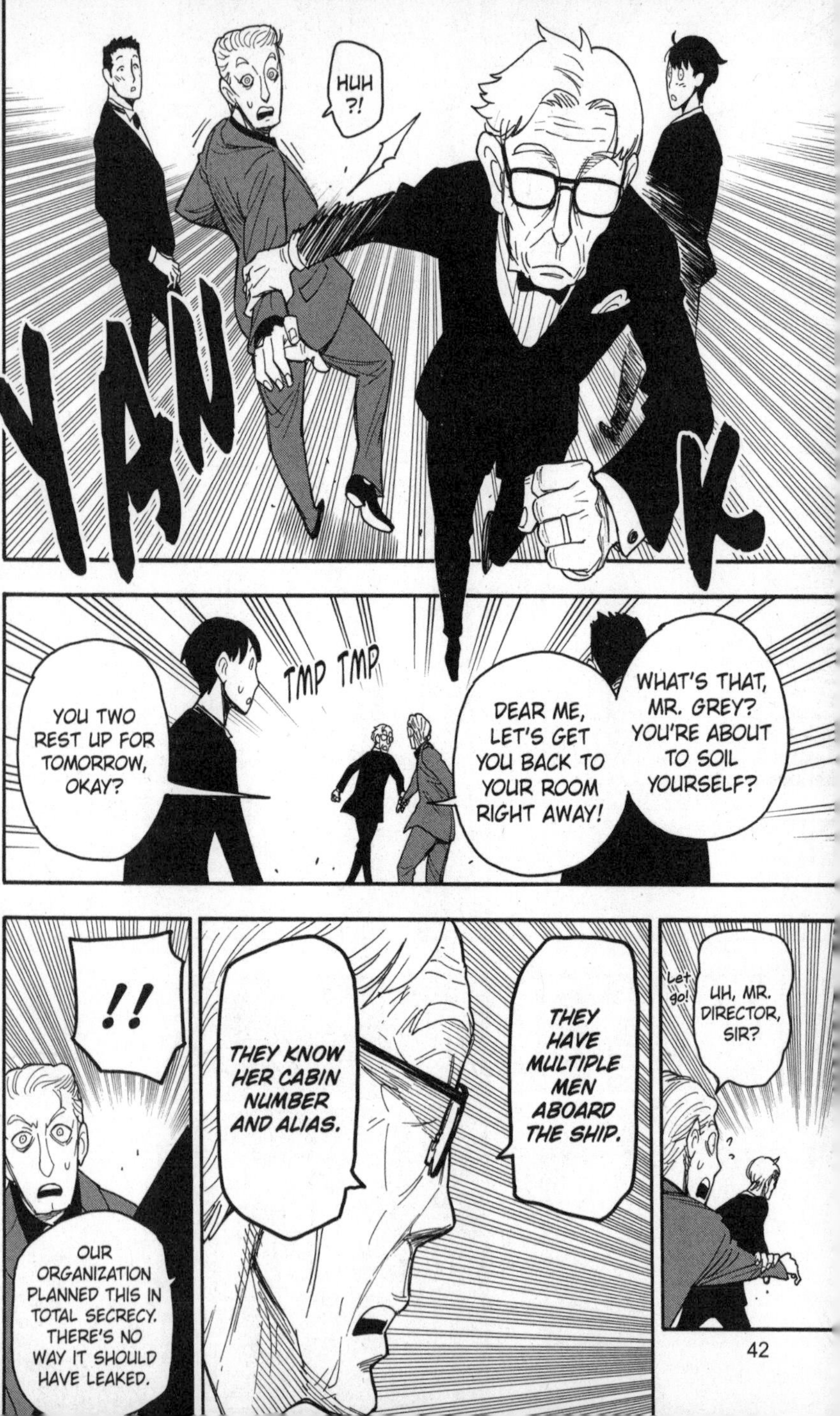
HUH ?!
YANK
WHAT'S THAT, MR. GREY? YOU'RE ABOUT TO SOIL YOURSELF?
DEAR ME, LET'S GET YOU BACK TO YOUR ROOM RIGHT AWAY!
TMP TMP
YOU TWO REST UP FOR TOMORROW, OKAY?
UH, MR. DIRECTOR, SIR?
Let go!
THEY HAVE MULTIPLE MEN ABOARD THE SHIP.
THEY KNOW HER CABIN NUMBER AND ALIAS.
!!
OUR ORGANIZATION PLANNED THIS IN TOTAL SECRECY. THERE'S NO WAY IT SHOULD HAVE LEAKED.

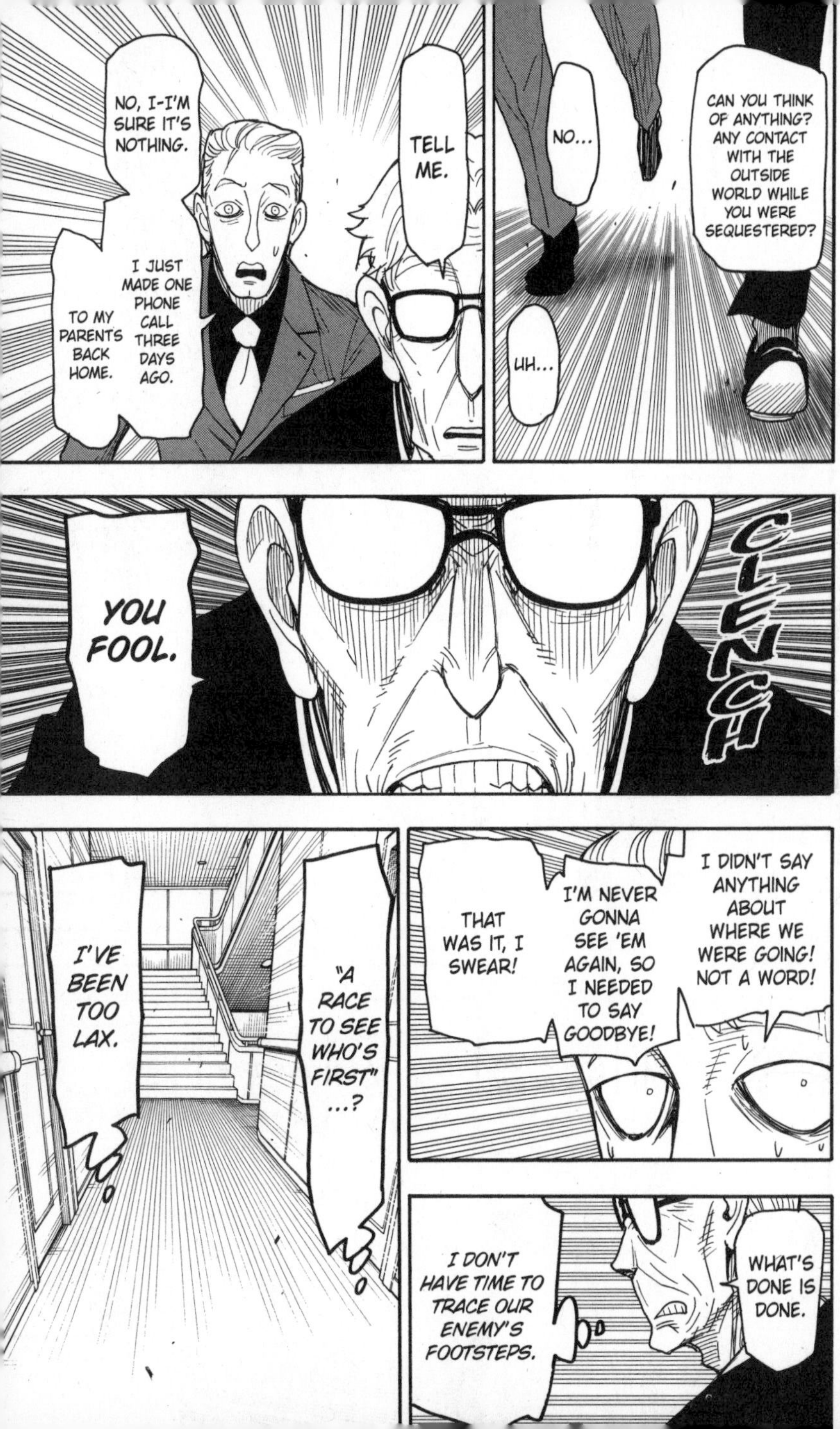
CAN YOU THINK OF ANYTHING? ANY CONTACT WITH THE OUTSIDE WORLD WHILE YOU WERE SEQUESTERED?
NO...
UH...
TELL ME.
NO, I-I'M SURE IT'S NOTHING.
I JUST MADE ONE PHONE CALL THREE DAYS AGO.
TO MY PARENTS BACK HOME.
CLENCH
YOU FOOL.
I DIDN'T SAY ANYTHING ABOUT WHERE WE WERE GOING! NOT A WORD!
I'M NEVER GONNA SEE 'EM AGAIN, SO I NEEDED TO SAY GOODBYE!
THAT WAS IT, I SWEAR!
WHAT'S DONE IS DONE.
I DON'T HAVE TIME TO TRACE OUR ENEMY'S FOOTSTEPS.
"A RACE TO SEE WHO'S FIRST"...?
I'VE BEEN TOO LAX.

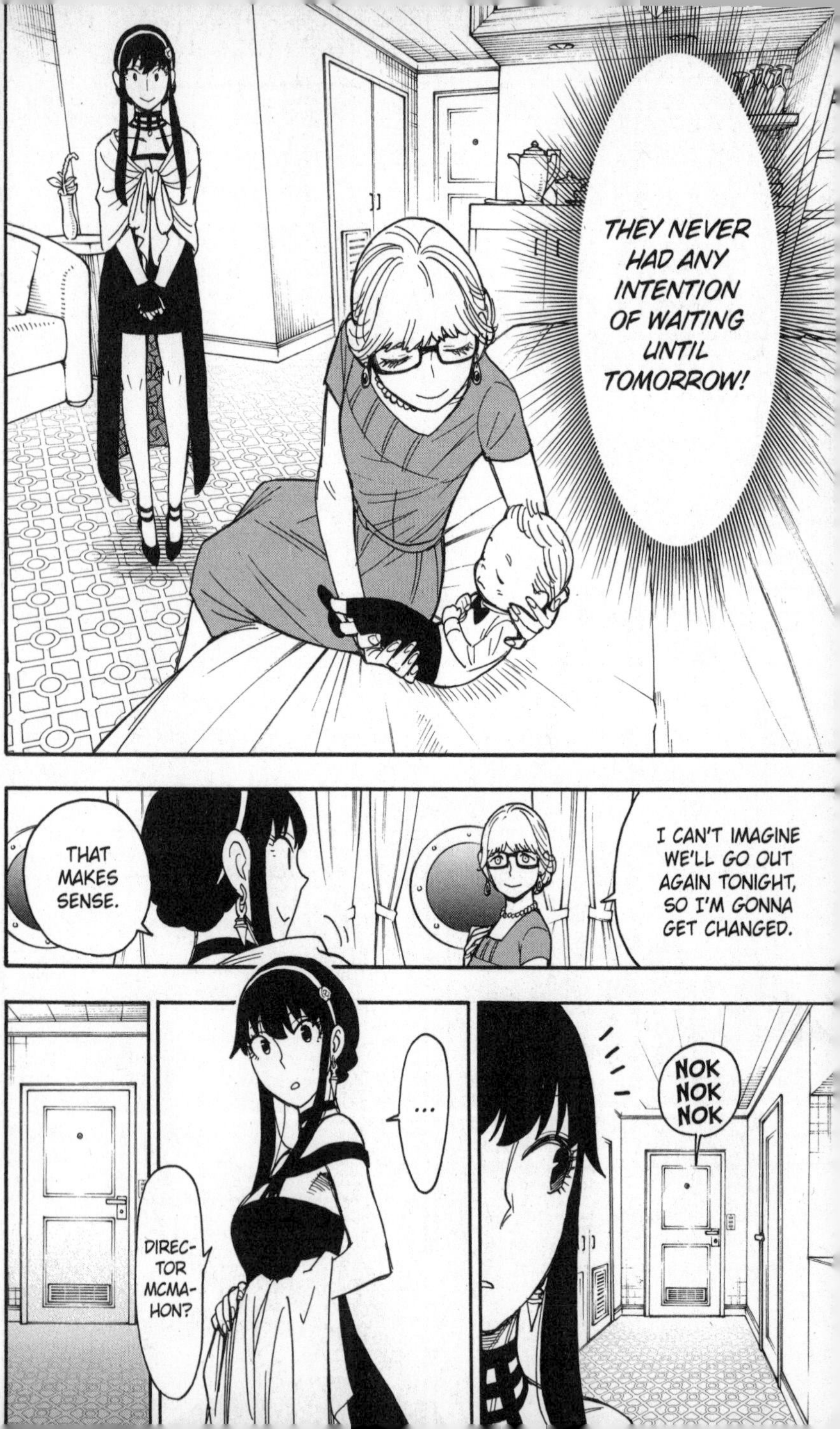
THEY NEVER HAD ANY INTENTION OF WAITING UNTIL TOMORROW!
I CAN'T IMAGINE WE'LL GO OUT AGAIN TONIGHT, SO I'M GONNA GET CHANGED.
THAT MAKES SENSE.
NOK NOK NOK
...
DIREC-TOR MCMA-HON?

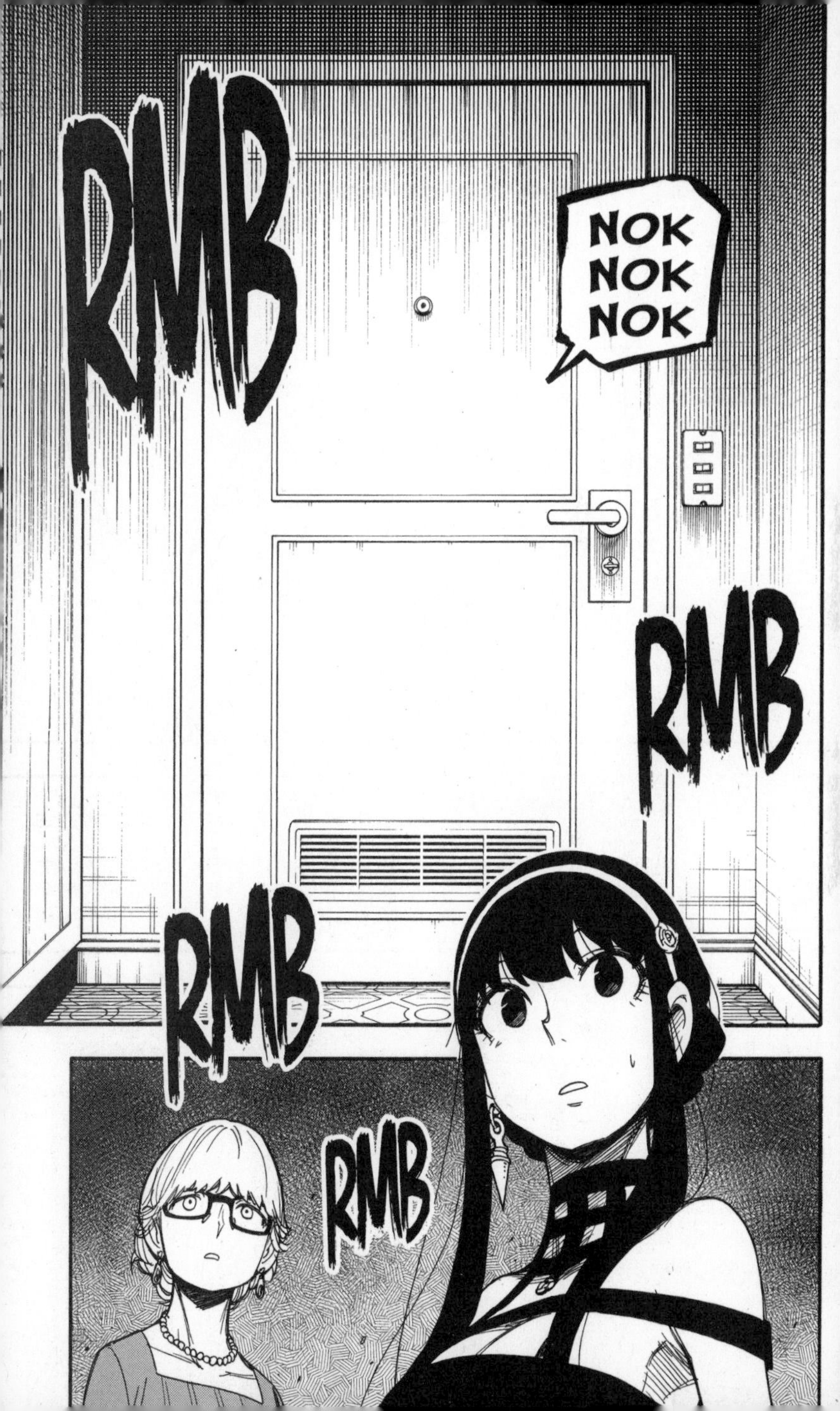
NOK NOK NOK
RMB
RMB
RMB
RMB

SPY×FAMILY

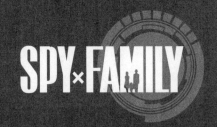

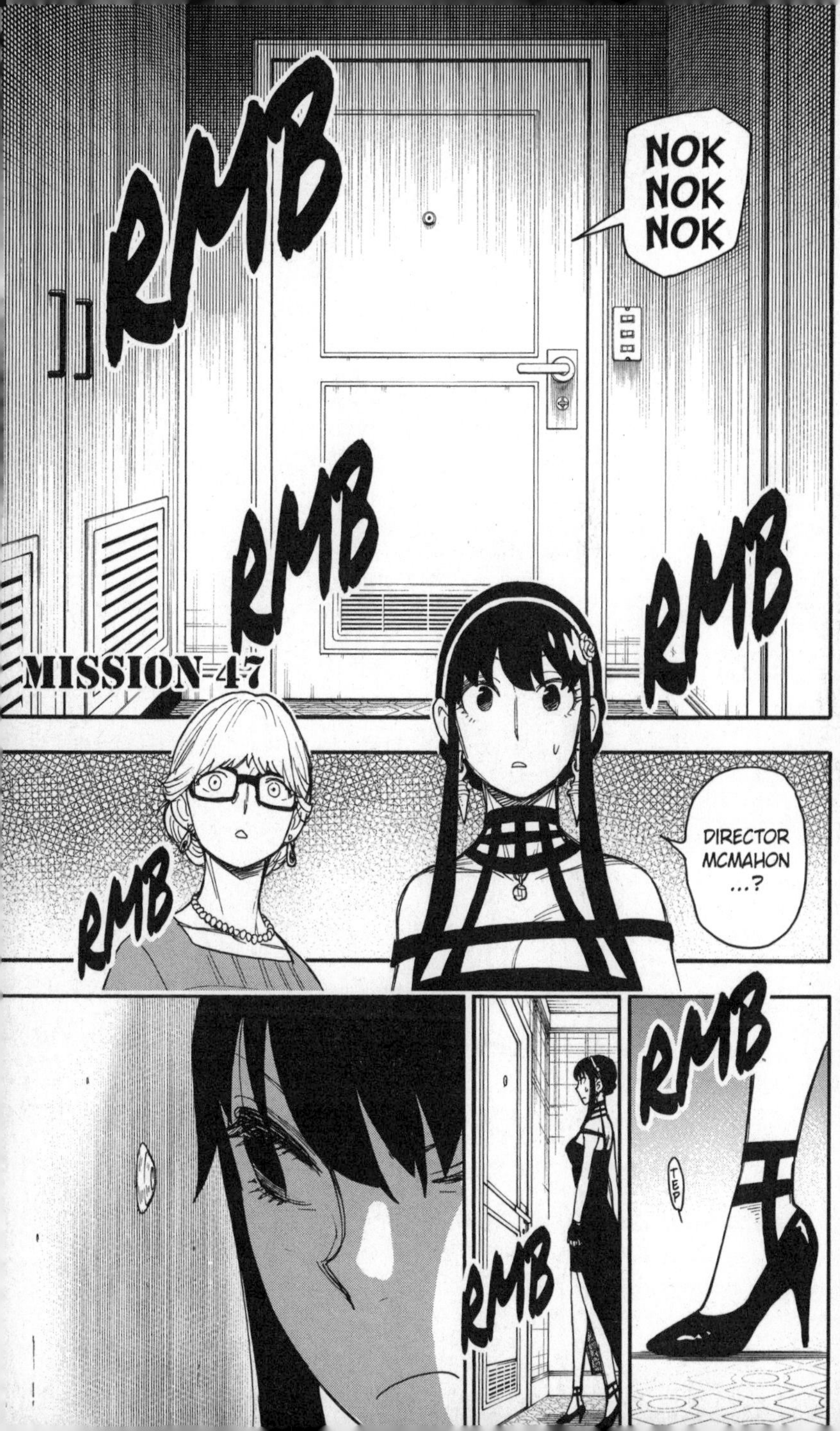
NOK NOK NOK
RMB
RMB
RMB
MISSION 47
DIRECTOR MCMAHON ...?
RMB
RMB
TEP
RMB

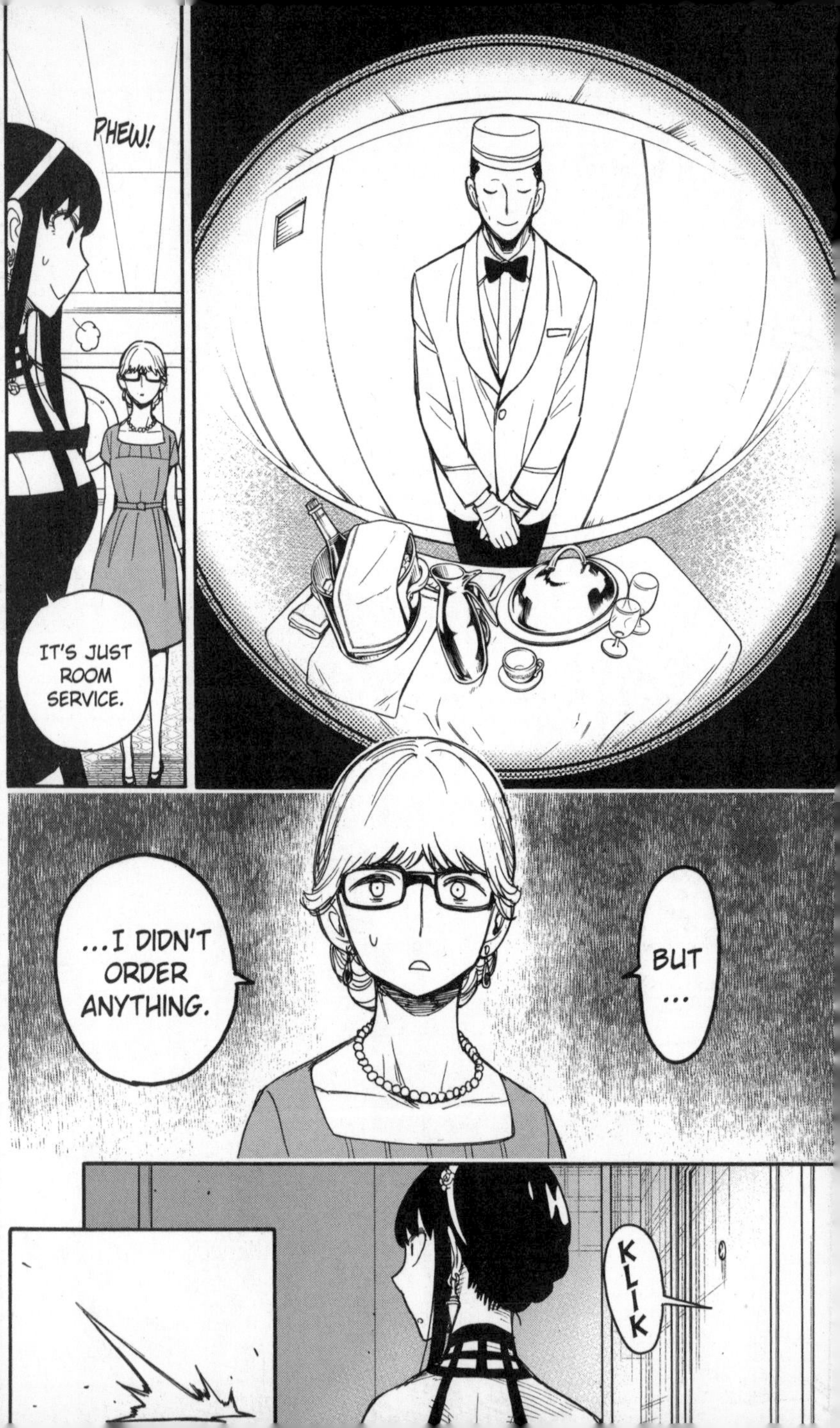
PHEW!
IT'S JUST ROOM SERVICE.
BUT...
...I DIDN'T ORDER ANYTHING.
KLIK

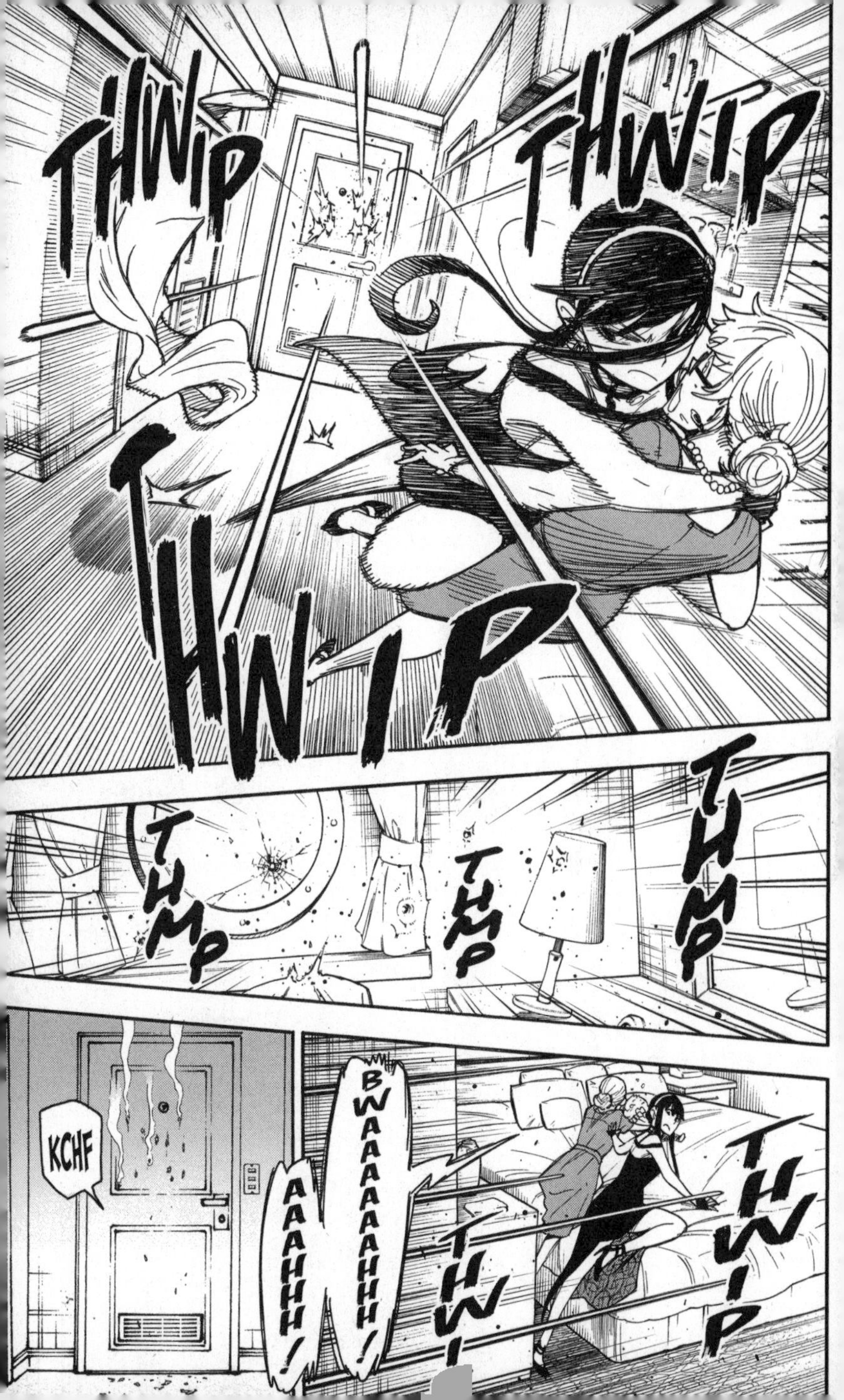
THWIP
THWIP
THWIP
THUMP
THMP
THUMP
THWIP
THWI
BWAAAAAAAAHHH!
AAAHHHH!
KCHF

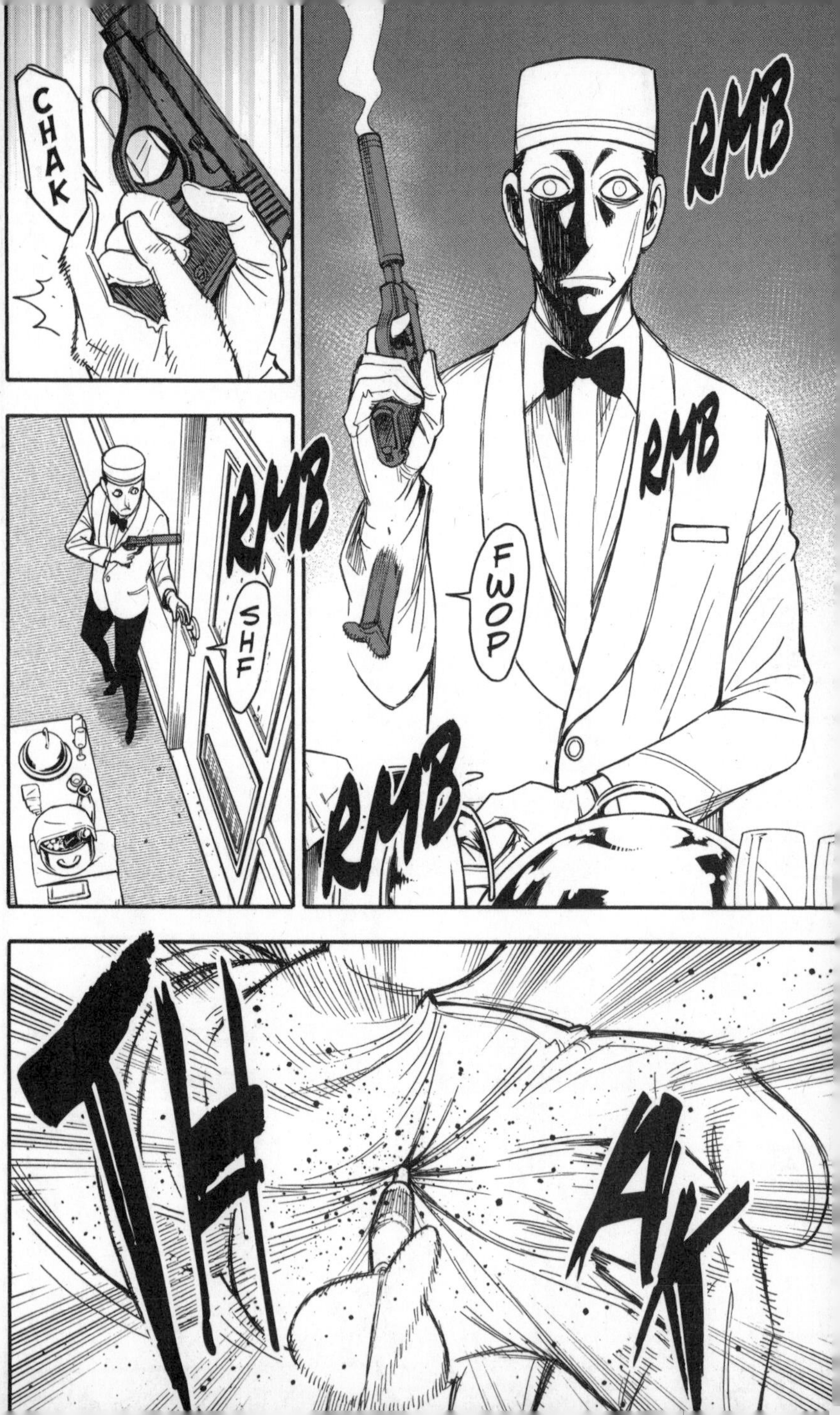
RMB
RMB
FWOP
RMB
CHAK
RMB
SHF
THAK

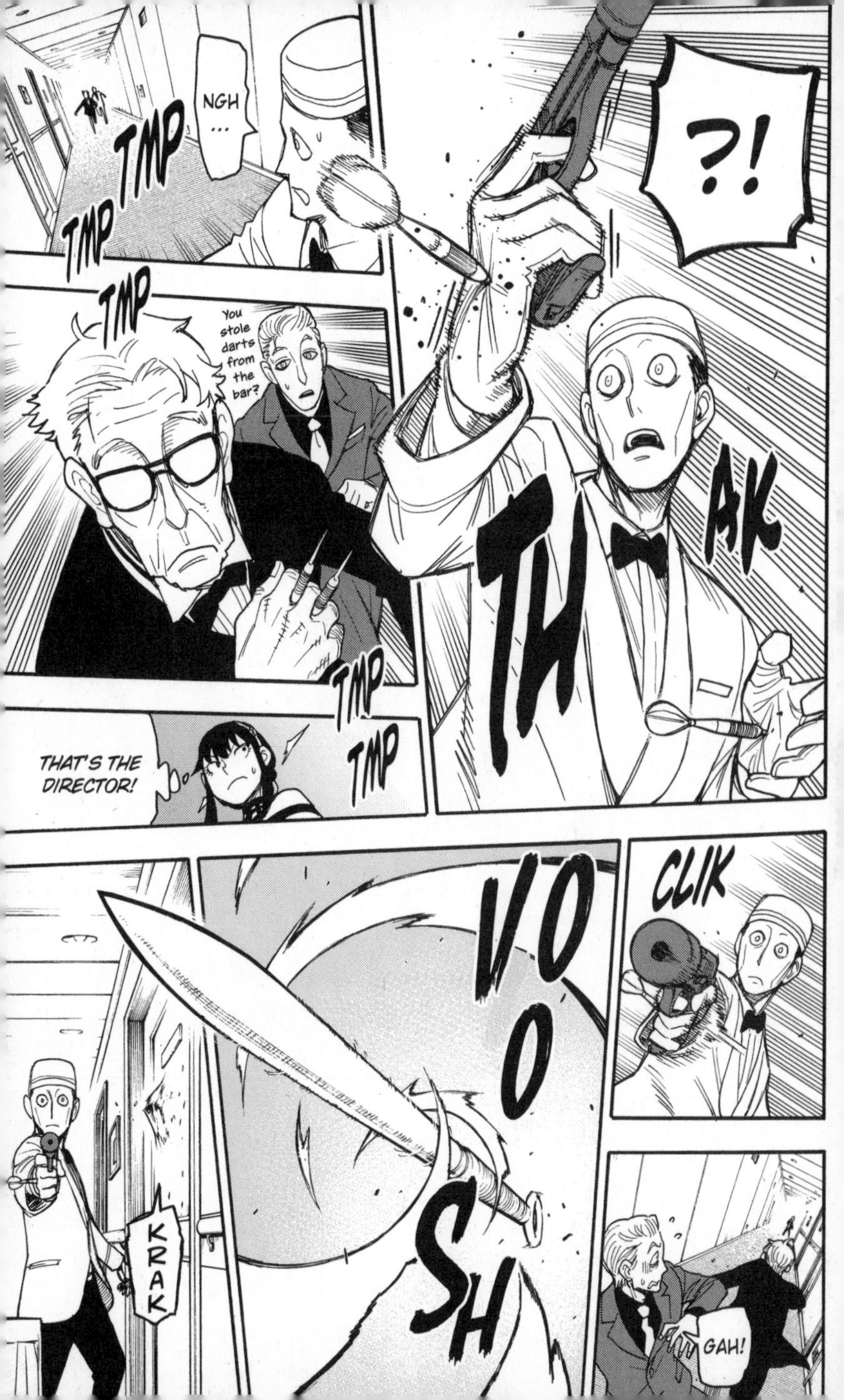
?!
TH AK
NGH ...
TMP TMP TMP
TMP
You stole darts from the bar?
TMP TMP
THAT'S THE DIRECTOR!
CLIK
GAH!
VO O SH
KRAK

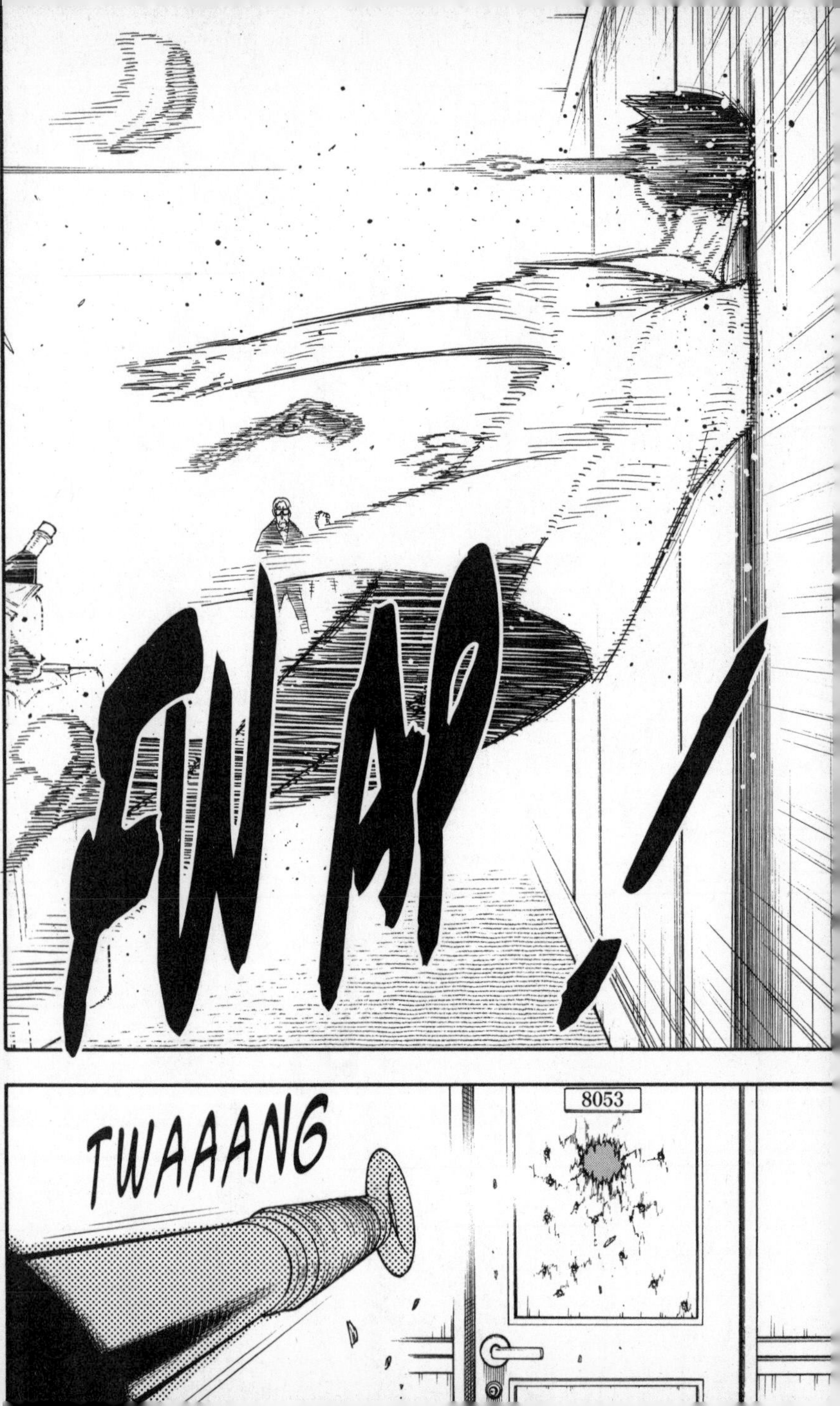
FWAP!
8053
TWAAANG

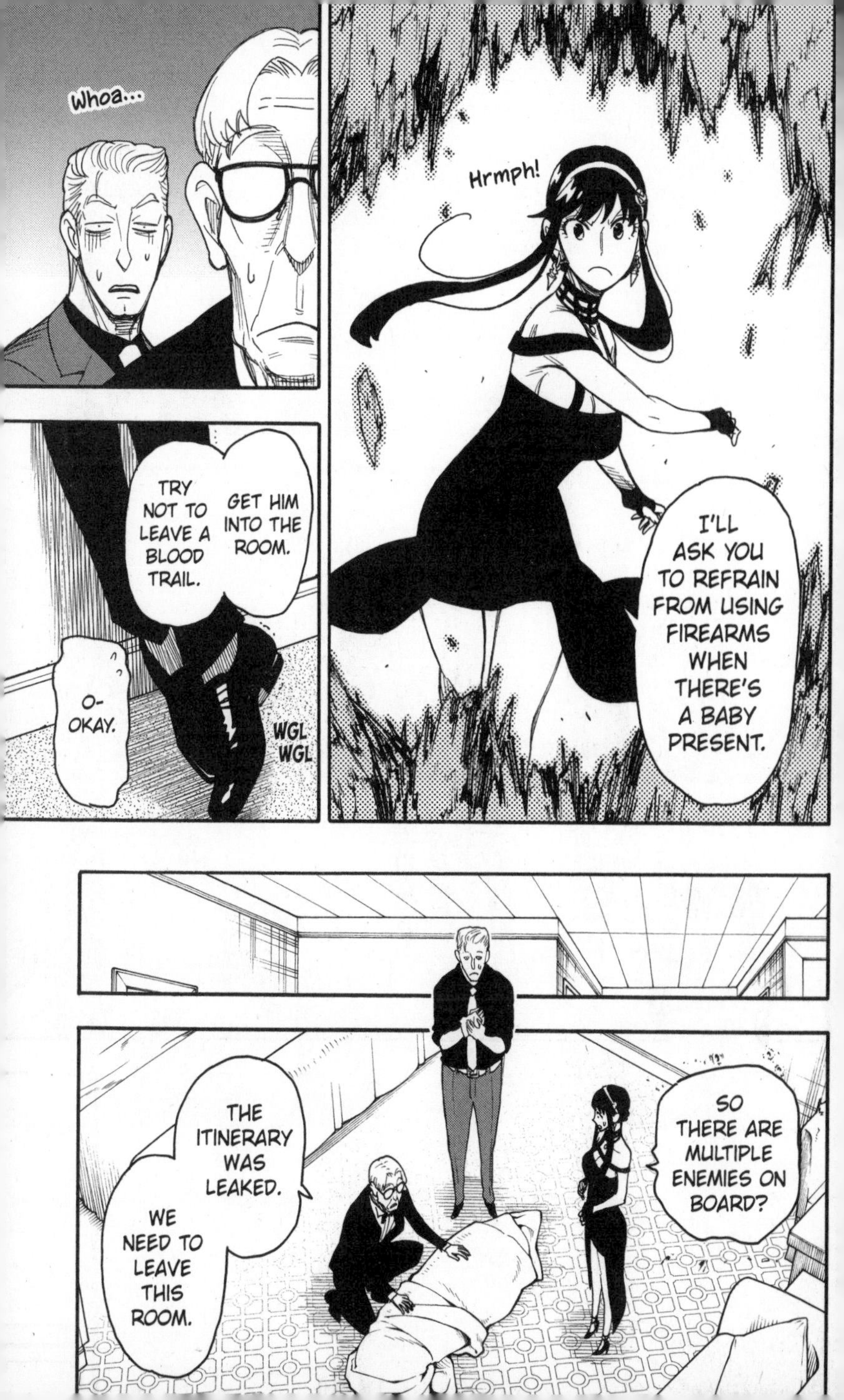
Hrmph!
I'LL ASK YOU TO REFRAIN FROM USING FIREARMS WHEN THERE'S A BABY PRESENT.
Whoa...
GET HIM INTO THE ROOM.
TRY NOT TO LEAVE A BLOOD TRAIL.
WGL WGL
O-OKAY.
SO THERE ARE MULTIPLE ENEMIES ON BOARD?
THE ITINERARY WAS LEAKED.
WE NEED TO LEAVE THIS ROOM.

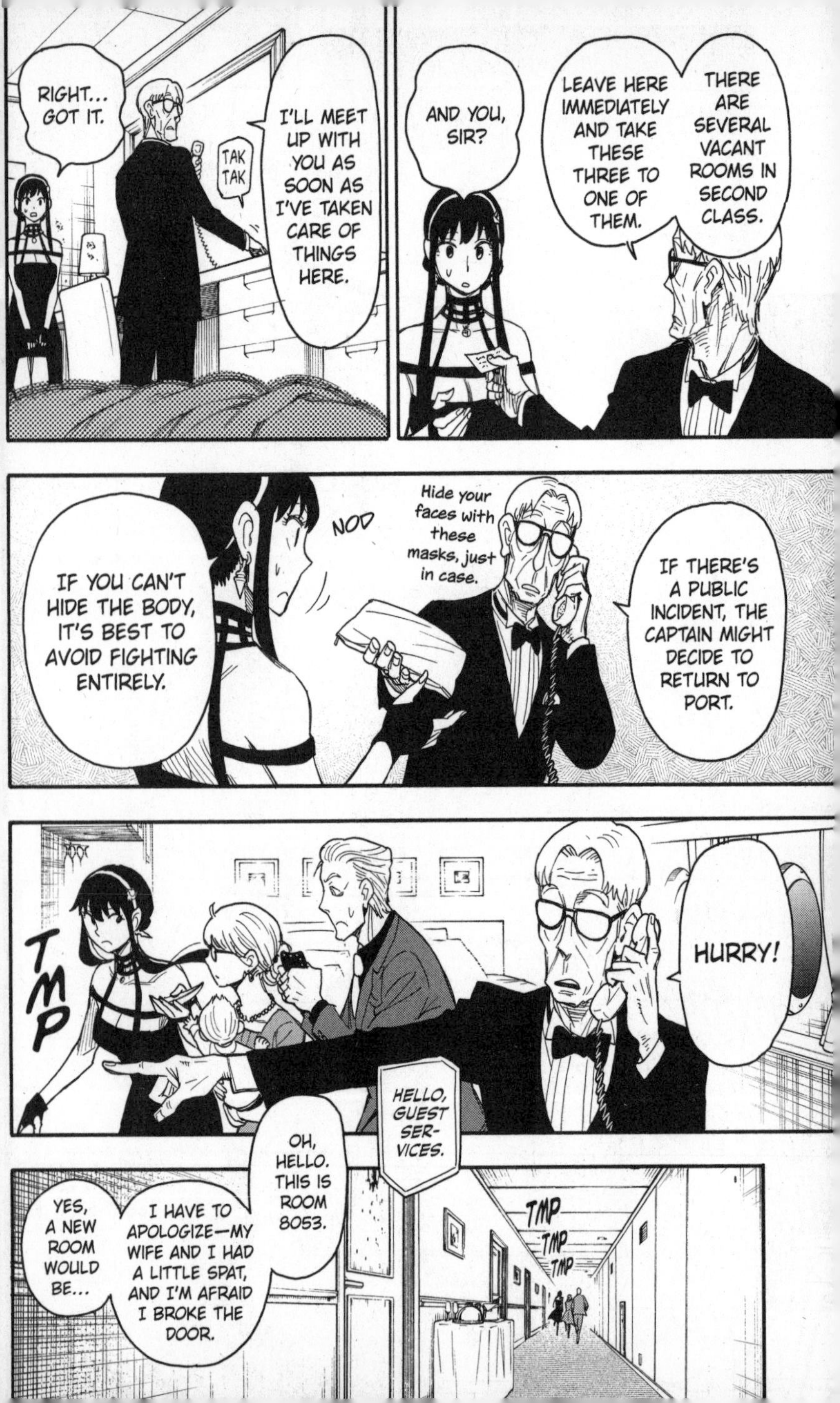
THERE ARE SEVERAL VACANT ROOMS IN SECOND CLASS.
LEAVE HERE IMMEDIATELY AND TAKE THESE THREE TO ONE OF THEM.
AND YOU, SIR?
I'LL MEET UP WITH YOU AS SOON AS I'VE TAKEN CARE OF THINGS HERE.
TAK TAK
RIGHT... GOT IT.
IF THERE'S A PUBLIC INCIDENT, THE CAPTAIN MIGHT DECIDE TO RETURN TO PORT.
Hide your faces with these masks, just in case.
NOD
IF YOU CAN'T HIDE THE BODY, IT'S BEST TO AVOID FIGHTING ENTIRELY.
HURRY!
TMP
HELLO, GUEST SERVICES.
OH, HELLO. THIS IS ROOM 8053.
TMP TMP TMP
I HAVE TO APOLOGIZE—MY WIFE AND I HAD A LITTLE SPAT, AND I'M AFRAID I BROKE THE DOOR.
YES, A NEW ROOM WOULD BE...

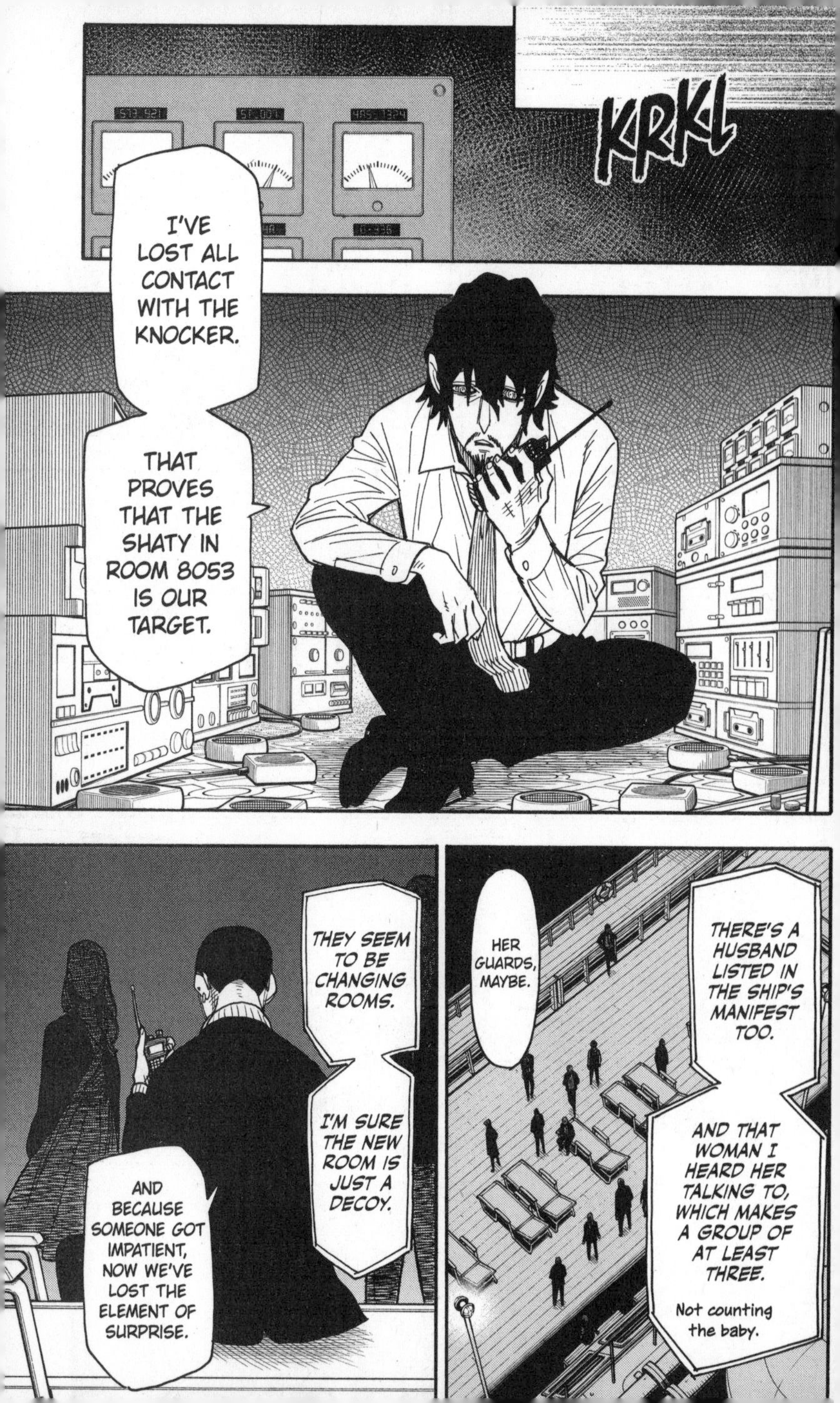
KRKL
I'VE LOST ALL CONTACT WITH THE KNOCKER.
THAT PROVES THAT THE SHATY IN ROOM 8053 IS OUR TARGET.
THERE'S A HUSBAND LISTED IN THE SHIP'S MANIFEST TOO.
HER GUARDS, MAYBE.
AND THAT WOMAN I HEARD HER TALKING TO, WHICH MAKES A GROUP OF AT LEAST THREE.
Not counting the baby.
THEY SEEM TO BE CHANGING ROOMS.
I'M SURE THE NEW ROOM IS JUST A DECOY.
AND BECAUSE SOMEONE GOT IMPATIENT, NOW WE'VE LOST THE ELEMENT OF SURPRISE.

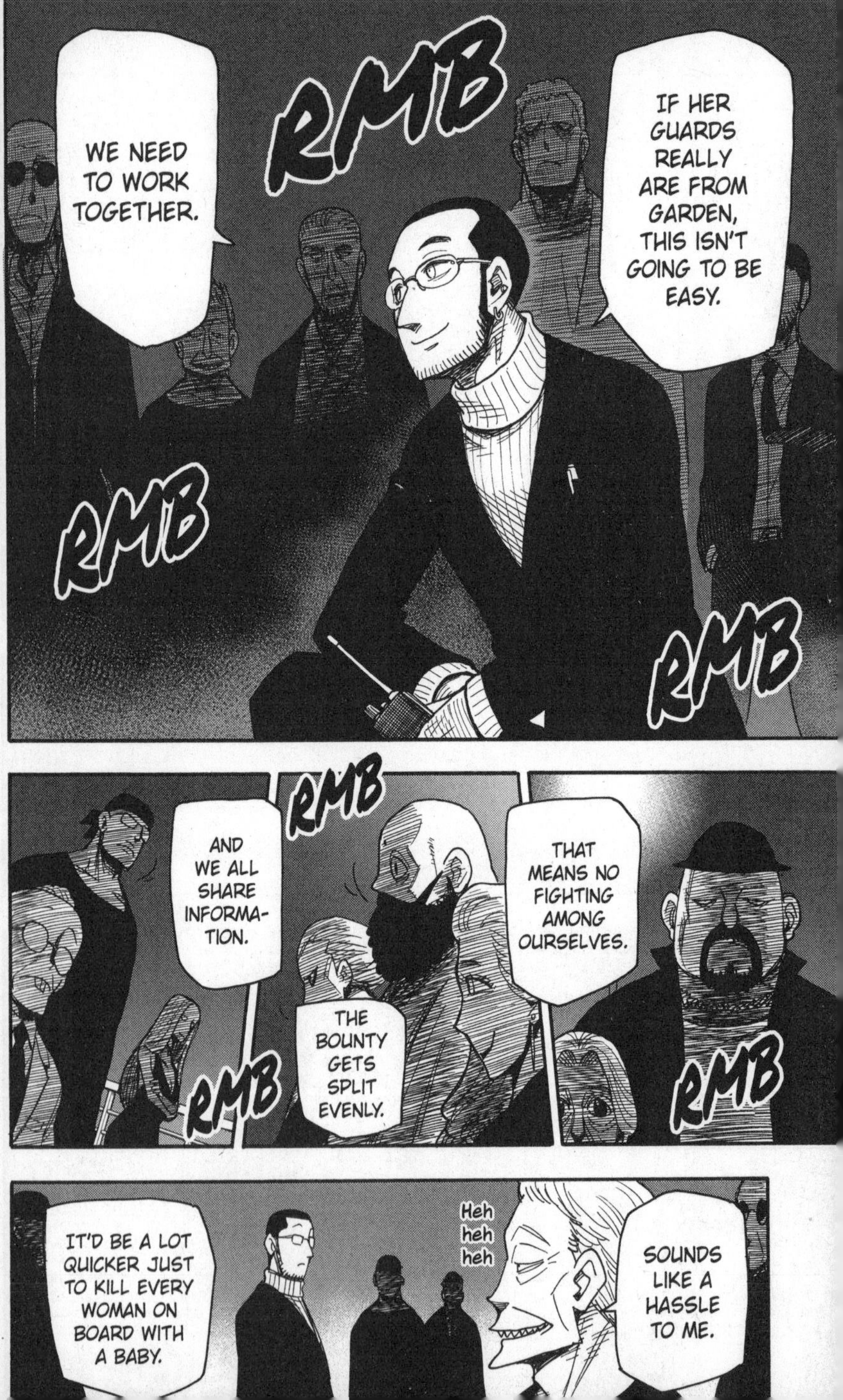
IF HER GUARDS REALLY ARE FROM GARDEN, THIS ISN'T GOING TO BE EASY.
RMB
WE NEED TO WORK TOGETHER.
RMB
RMB
THAT MEANS NO FIGHTING AMONG OURSELVES.
RMB
RMB
THE BOUNTY GETS SPLIT EVENLY.
AND WE ALL SHARE INFORMA-TION.
RMB
SOUNDS LIKE A HASSLE TO ME.
Heh heh heh
IT'D BE A LOT QUICKER JUST TO KILL EVERY WOMAN ON BOARD WITH A BABY.

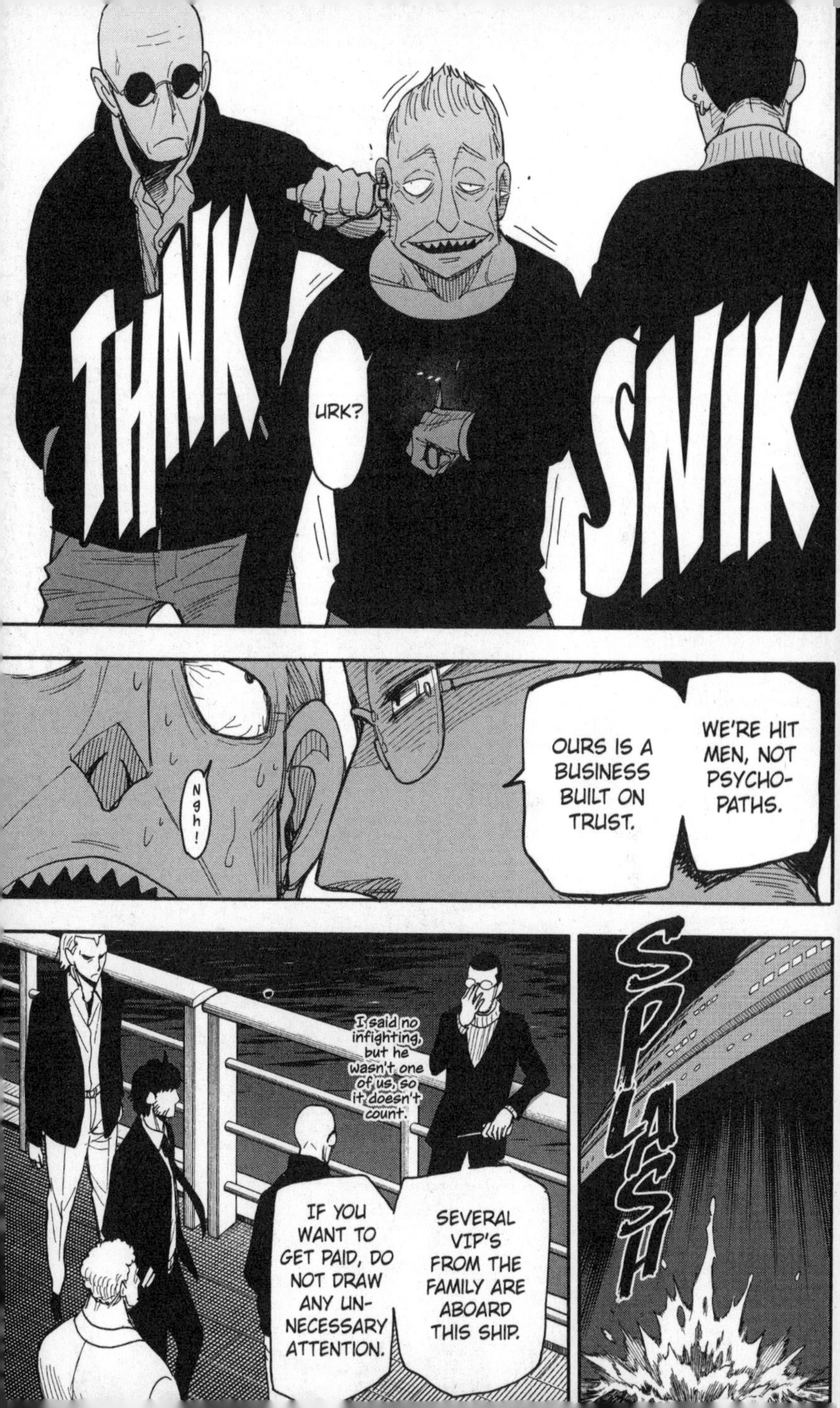
SNIK
URK?
THNK
WE'RE HIT MEN, NOT PSYCHO-PATHS.
OURS IS A BUSINESS BUILT ON TRUST.
Ngh!
SPLASH
I said no infighting, but he wasn't one of us, so it doesn't count.
SEVERAL VIP'S FROM THE FAMILY ARE ABOARD THIS SHIP.
IF YOU WANT TO GET PAID, DO NOT DRAW ANY UN-NECESSARY ATTENTION.

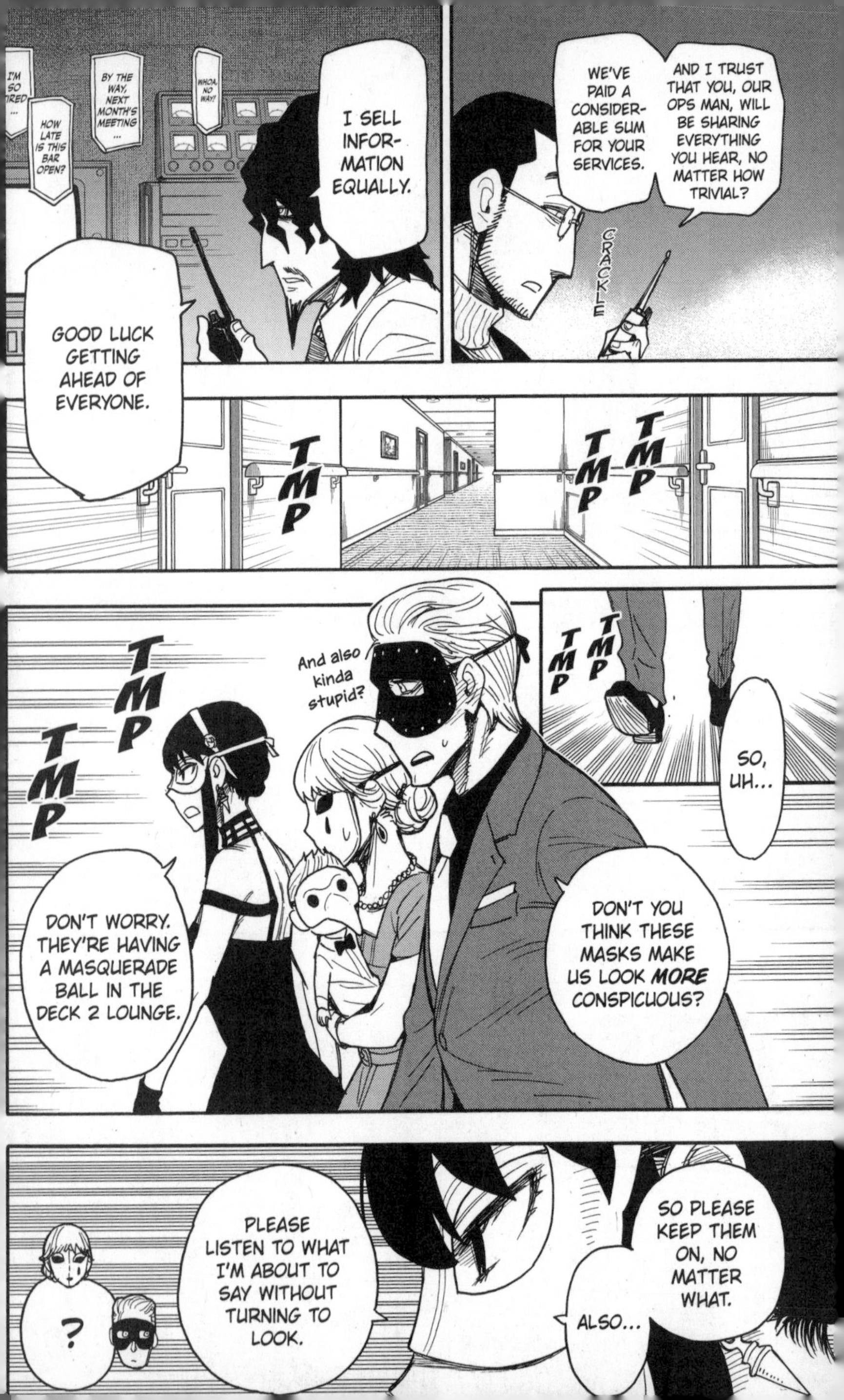

WE'VE PAID A CONSIDER-ABLE SUM FOR YOUR SERVICES.
AND I TRUST THAT YOU, OUR OPS MAN, WILL BE SHARING EVERYTHING YOU HEAR, NO MATTER HOW TRIVIAL?
CRACKLE
I SELL INFOR-MATION EQUALLY.
WHOA, NO WAY!
BY THE WAY, NEXT MONTH'S MEETING...
I'M SO TIRED...
HOW LATE IS THIS BAR OPEN?
GOOD LUCK GETTING AHEAD OF EVERYONE.
TMP TMP
TMP
TMP TMP
SO, UH...
DON'T YOU THINK THESE MASKS MAKE US LOOK MORE CONSPICUOUS?
And also kinda stupid?
TMP TMP
DON'T WORRY. THEY'RE HAVING A MASQUERADE BALL IN THE DECK 2 LOUNGE.
SO PLEASE KEEP THEM ON, NO MATTER WHAT.
ALSO...
PLEASE LISTEN TO WHAT I'M ABOUT TO SAY WITHOUT TURNING TO LOOK.
?

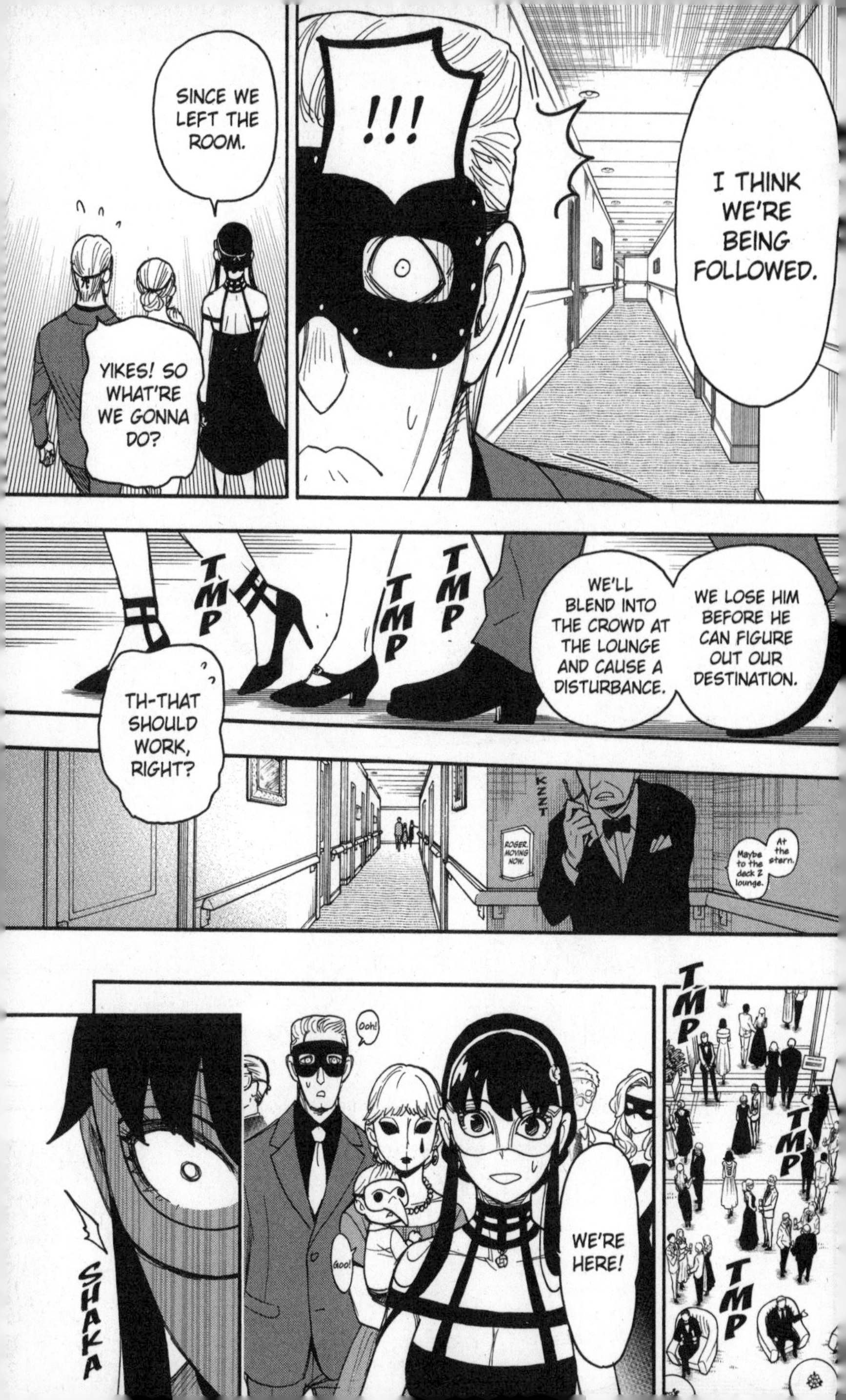
I THINK WE'RE BEING FOLLOWED.
!!!
SINCE WE LEFT THE ROOM.
YIKES! SO WHAT'RE WE GONNA DO?
WE LOSE HIM BEFORE HE CAN FIGURE OUT OUR DESTINATION.
WE'LL BLEND INTO THE CROWD AT THE LOUNGE AND CAUSE A DISTURBANCE.
TMP
TMP
TMP
TH-THAT SHOULD WORK, RIGHT?
At the stern.
Maybe to the deck 2 lounge.
KZZT
ROGER. MOVING NOW.
TMP
TMP
TMP
TMP
Ooh!
WE'RE HERE!
Goo!
SHAKA

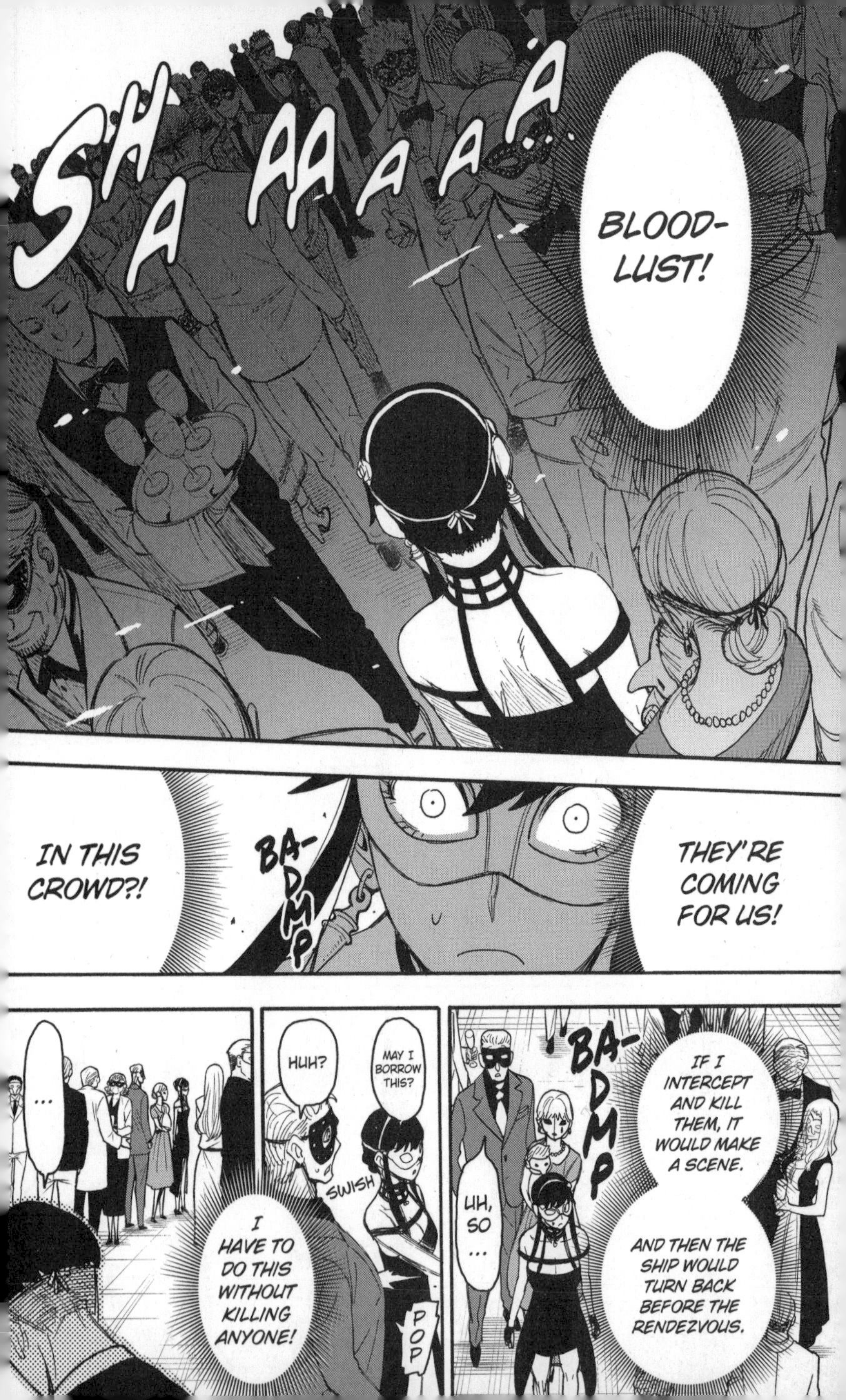
BLOOD-LUST!
SHAAAAAA
THEY'RE COMING FOR US!
BA-DUMP
IN THIS CROWD?!
BA-DUMP
IF I INTERCEPT AND KILL THEM, IT WOULD MAKE A SCENE.
AND THEN THE SHIP WOULD TURN BACK BEFORE THE RENDEZVOUS.
UH, SO...
MAY I BORROW THIS?
HUH?
SWISH
I HAVE TO DO THIS WITHOUT KILLING ANYONE!
POP
...

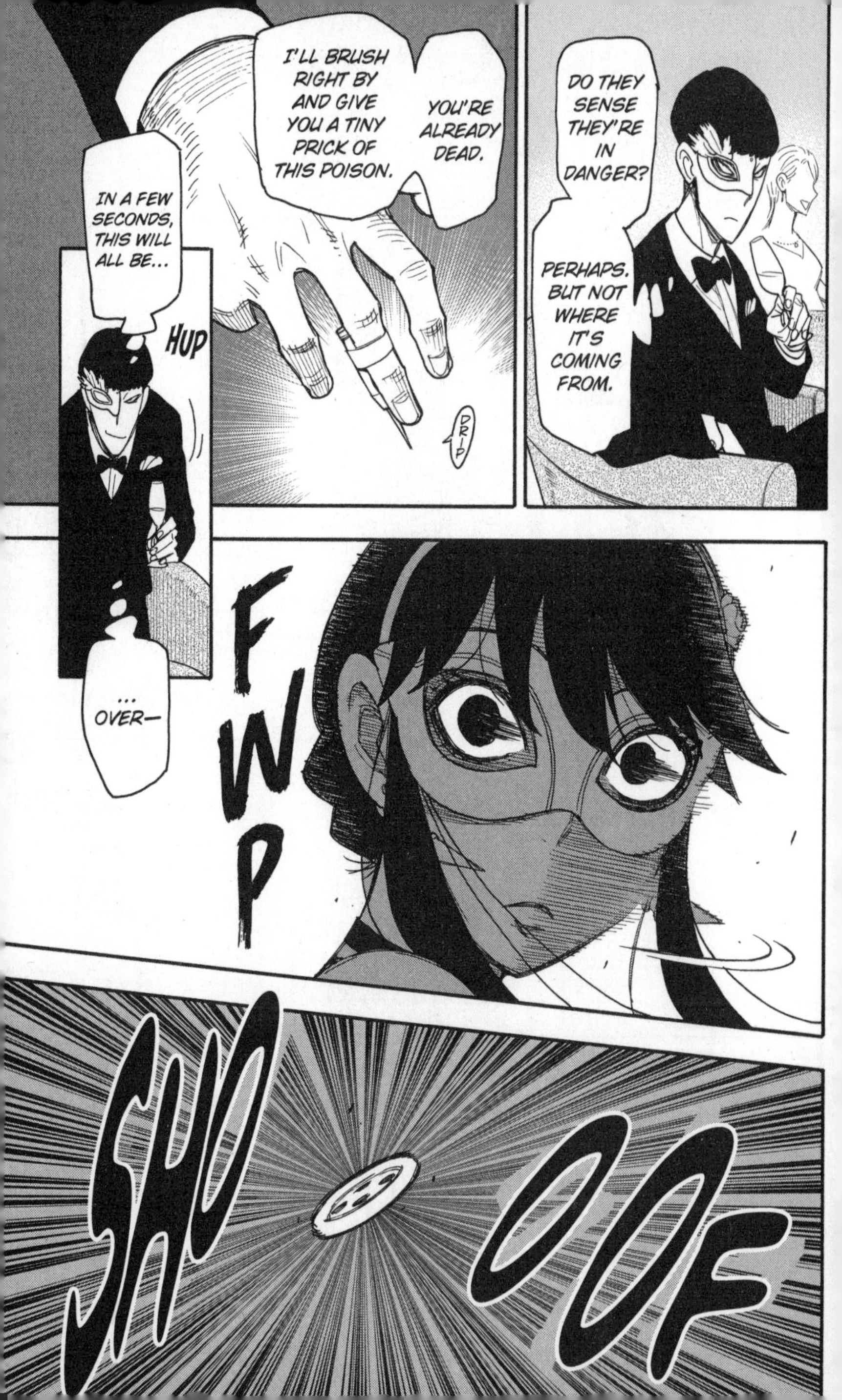
DO THEY SENSE THEY'RE IN DANGER?
PERHAPS. BUT NOT WHERE IT'S COMING FROM.
I'LL BRUSH RIGHT BY AND GIVE YOU A TINY PRICK OF THIS POISON.
YOU'RE ALREADY DEAD.
DRIP
IN A FEW SECONDS, THIS WILL ALL BE...
HUP
... OVER—
FWP
SHOOOF

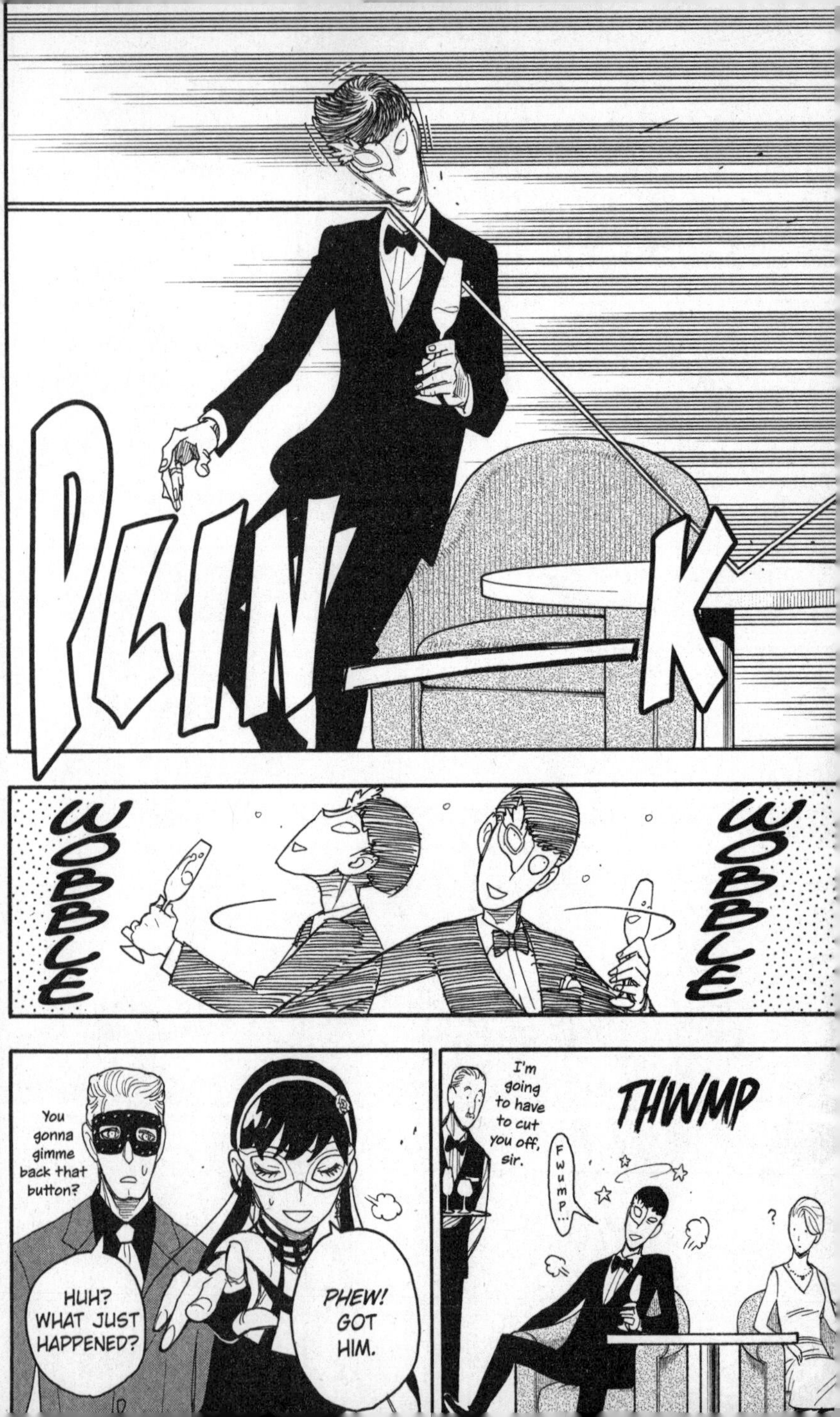
PLIN—K
WOBBLE
WOBBLE
THWMP
I'm going to have to cut you off, sir.
Fwump...
You gonna gimme back that button?
PHEW! GOT HIM.
HUH? WHAT JUST HAPPENED?

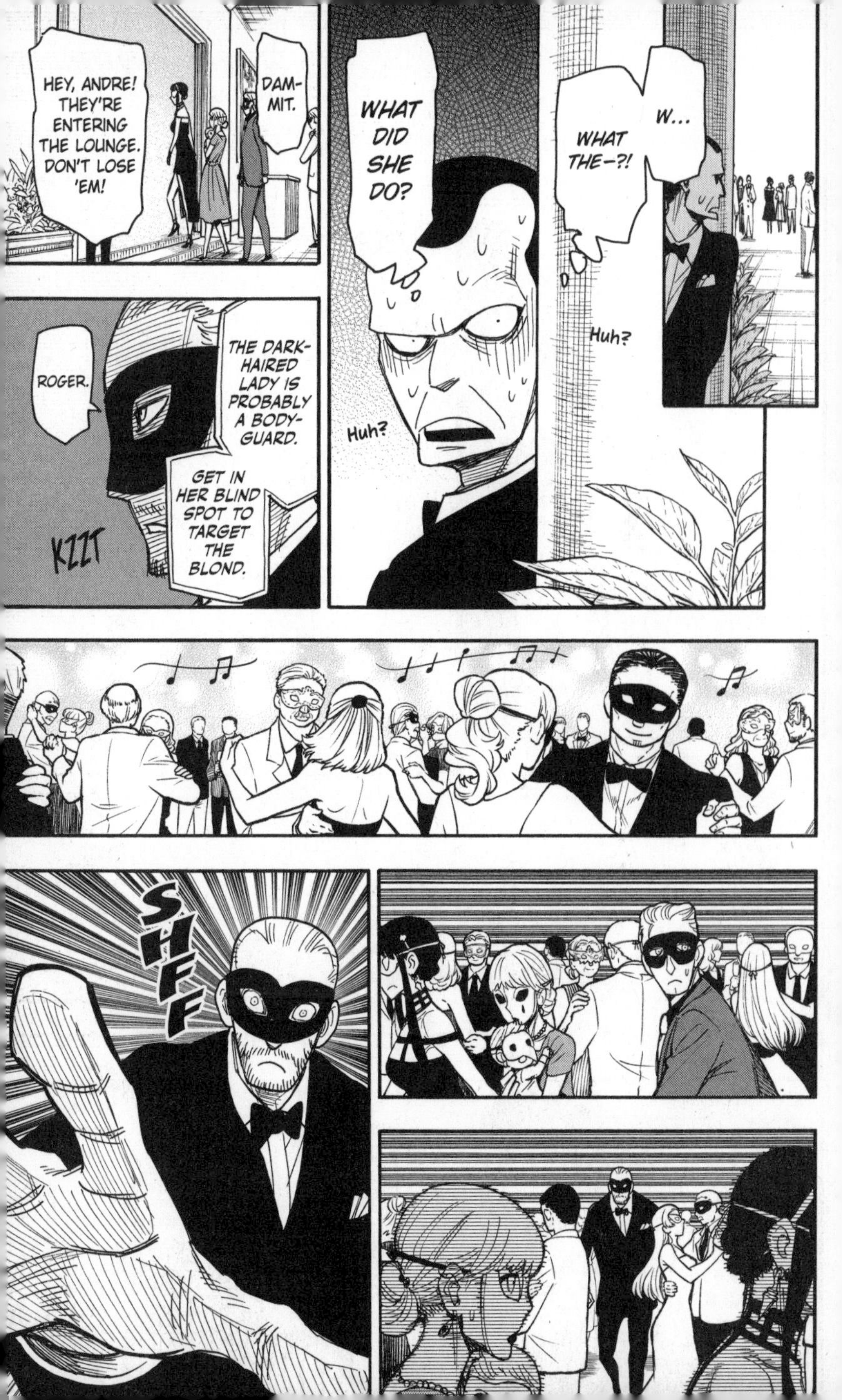
W...
WHAT THE-?!
Huh?
WHAT DID SHE DO?
Huh?
DAM-MIT.
HEY, ANDRE! THEY'RE ENTERING THE LOUNGE. DON'T LOSE 'EM!
THE DARK-HAIRED LADY IS PROBABLY A BODY-GUARD.
GET IN HER BLIND SPOT TO TARGET THE BLOND.
ROGER.
KZZT
SHFF

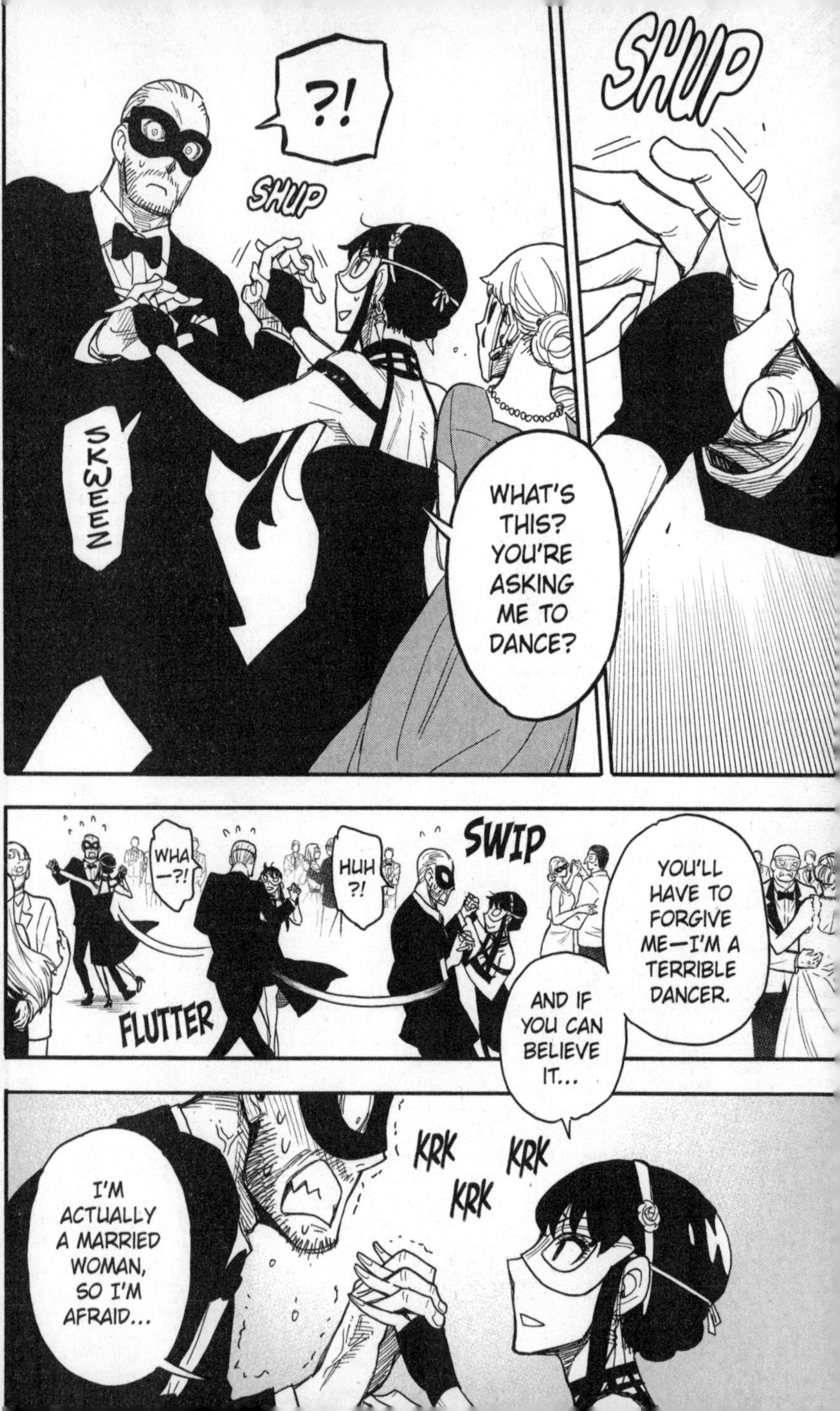
SHUP
?!
SHUP
WHAT'S THIS? YOU'RE ASKING ME TO DANCE?
SKWEEZ
YOU'LL HAVE TO FORGIVE ME—I'M A TERRIBLE DANCER.
SWIP
HUH ?!
WHA —?!
FLUTTER
AND IF YOU CAN BELIEVE IT...
KRK
KRK
KRK
I'M ACTUALLY A MARRIED WOMAN, SO I'M AFRAID...

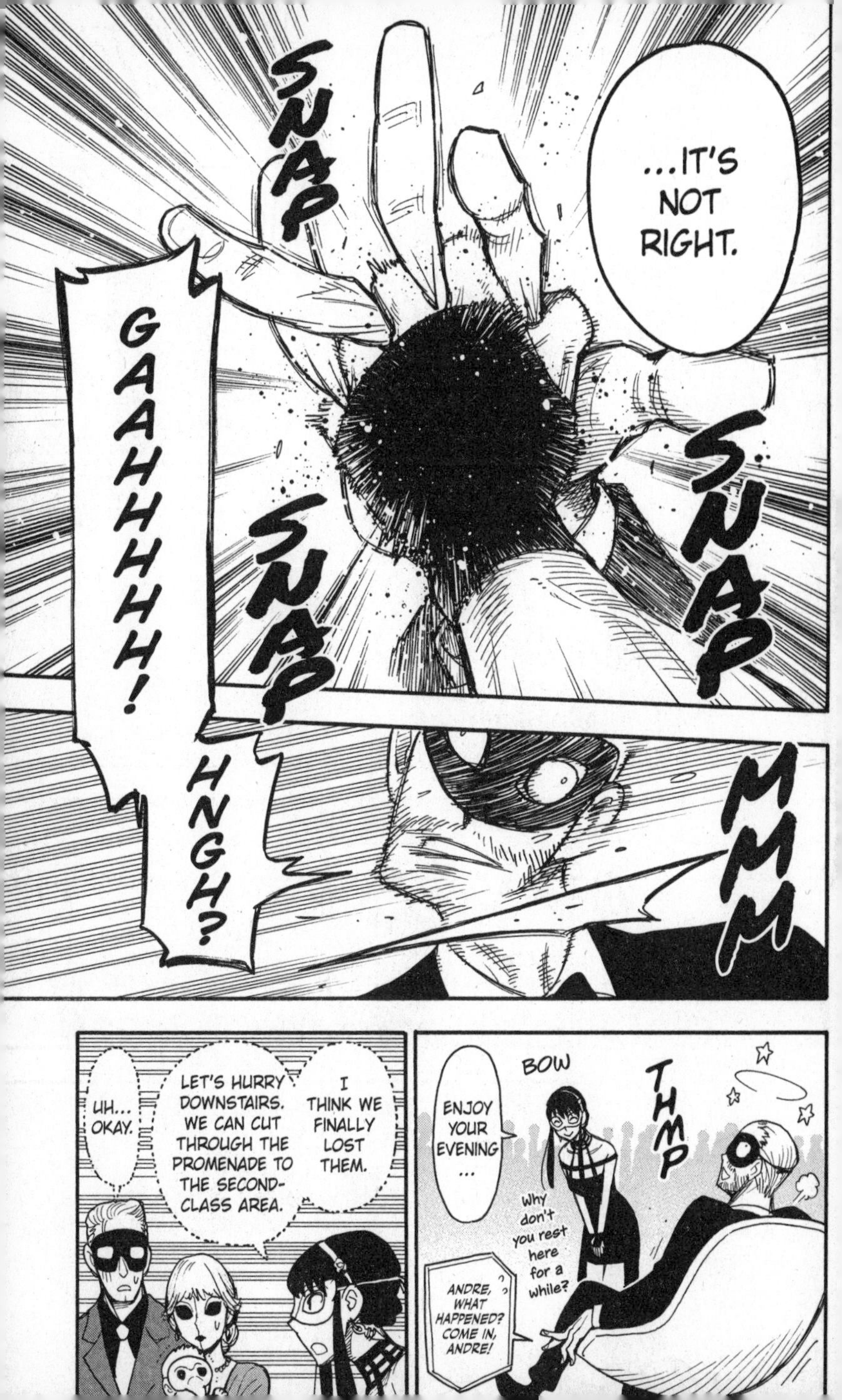
...IT'S NOT RIGHT.
SNAP
SNAP
SNAP
GAAHHHHHH!
MMMM
HNGH?
THMP
BOW
ENJOY YOUR EVENING...
Why don't you rest here for a while?
ANDRE, WHAT HAPPENED? COME IN, ANDRE!
I THINK WE FINALLY LOST THEM.
LET'S HURRY DOWNSTAIRS. WE CAN CUT THROUGH THE PROMENADE TO THE SECOND-CLASS AREA.
UH... OKAY.

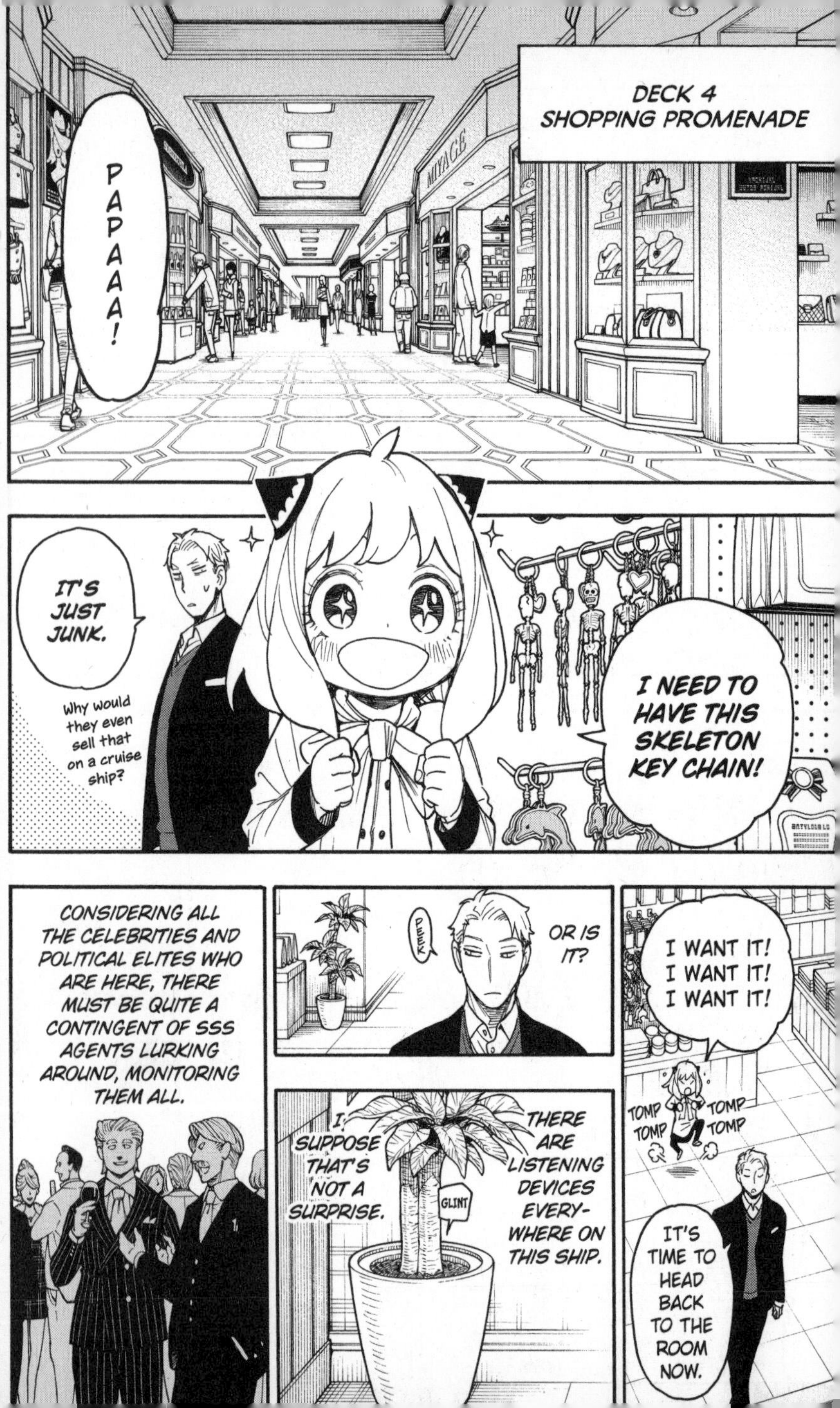
DECK 4 SHOPPING PROMENADE
PAPAAAA!
I NEED TO HAVE THIS SKELETON KEY CHAIN!
IT'S JUST JUNK.
Why would they even sell that on a cruise ship?
I WANT IT! I WANT IT! I WANT IT!
TOMP TOMP
TOMP TOMP
IT'S TIME TO HEAD BACK TO THE ROOM NOW.
OR IS IT?
PEEK
THERE ARE LISTENING DEVICES EVERYWHERE ON THIS SHIP.
GLINT
I SUPPOSE THAT'S NOT A SURPRISE.
CONSIDERING ALL THE CELEBRITIES AND POLITICAL ELITES WHO ARE HERE, THERE MUST BE QUITE A CONTINGENT OF SSS AGENTS LURKING AROUND, MONITORING THEM ALL.

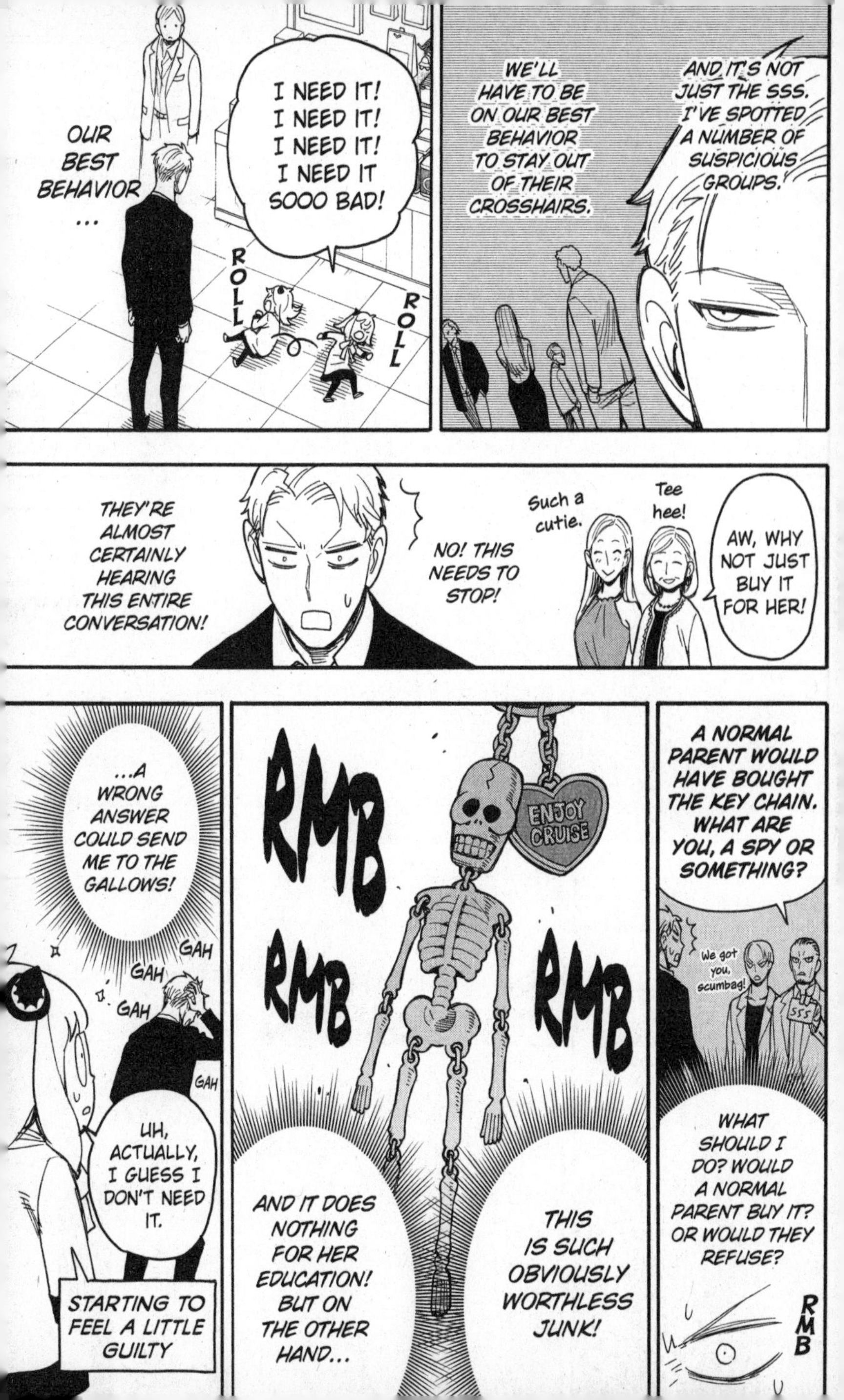
AND IT'S NOT JUST THE SSS. I'VE SPOTTED A NUMBER OF SUSPICIOUS GROUPS.
WE'LL HAVE TO BE ON OUR BEST BEHAVIOR TO STAY OUT OF THEIR CROSSHAIRS.
I NEED IT! I NEED IT! I NEED IT! I NEED IT SOOO BAD!
OUR BEST BEHAVIOR ...
ROLL
ROLL
AW, WHY NOT JUST BUY IT FOR HER!
Tee hee!
Such a cutie.
NO! THIS NEEDS TO STOP!
THEY'RE ALMOST CERTAINLY HEARING THIS ENTIRE CONVERSATION!
A NORMAL PARENT WOULD HAVE BOUGHT THE KEY CHAIN. WHAT ARE YOU, A SPY OR SOMETHING?
We got you, scumbag!
SSS
WHAT SHOULD I DO? WOULD A NORMAL PARENT BUY IT? OR WOULD THEY REFUSE?
RMB
RMB
ENJOY CRUISE
RMB
RMB
THIS IS SUCH OBVIOUSLY WORTHLESS JUNK!
AND IT DOES NOTHING FOR HER EDUCATION! BUT ON THE OTHER HAND...
...A WRONG ANSWER COULD SEND ME TO THE GALLOWS!
GAH
GAH
GAH
GAH
UH, ACTUALLY, I GUESS I DON'T NEED IT.
STARTING TO FEEL A LITTLE GUILTY

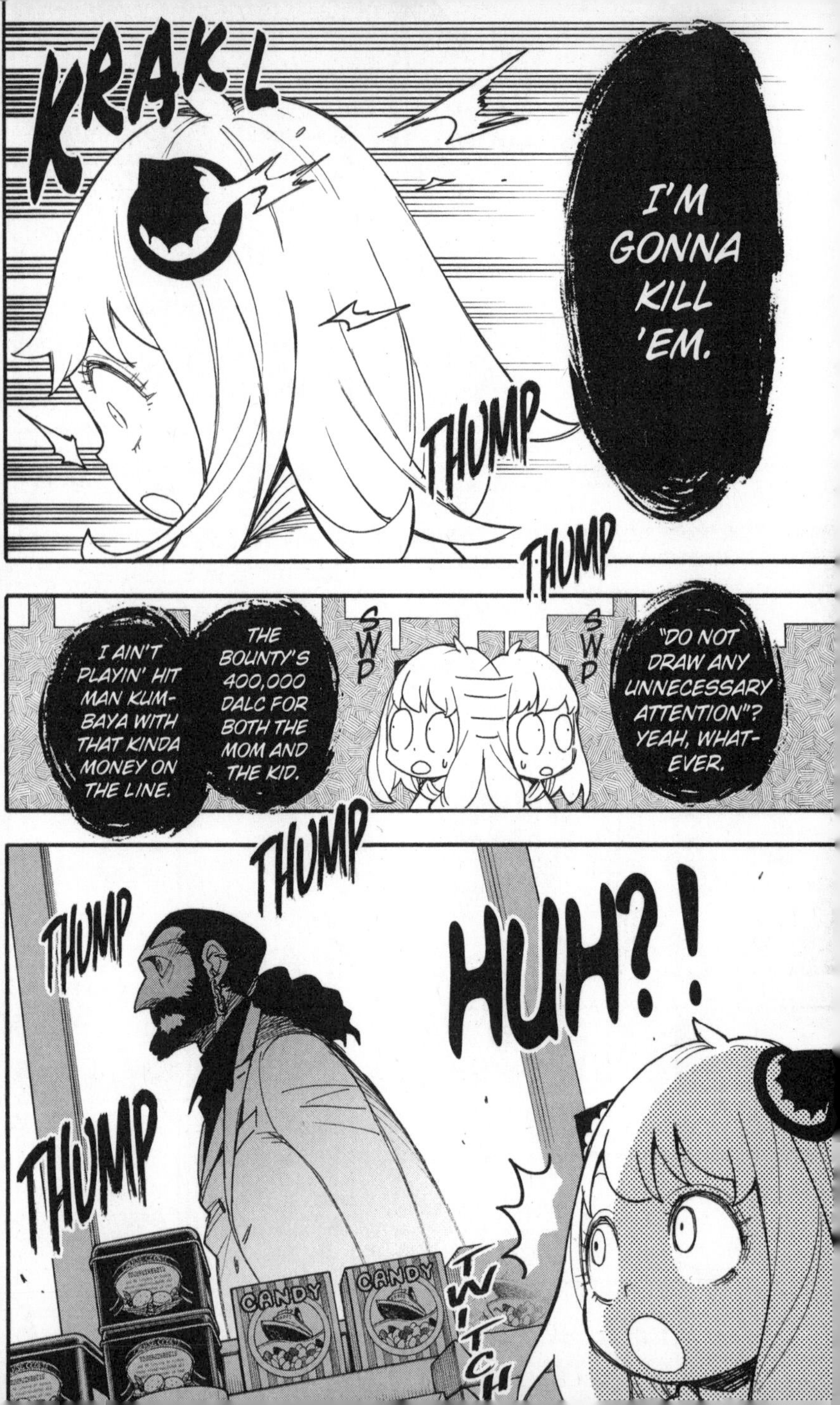
I'M GONNA KILL 'EM.
KRAKL
THUMP
THUMP
"DO NOT DRAW ANY UNNECESSARY ATTENTION"? YEAH, WHATEVER.
SWP
SWP
THE BOUNTY'S 400,000 DALC FOR BOTH THE MOM AND THE KID.
I AIN'T PLAYIN' HIT MAN KUM-BAYA WITH THAT KINDA MONEY ON THE LINE.
HUH?!
THUMP
THUMP
THUMP
TWITCH
CANDY
CANDY

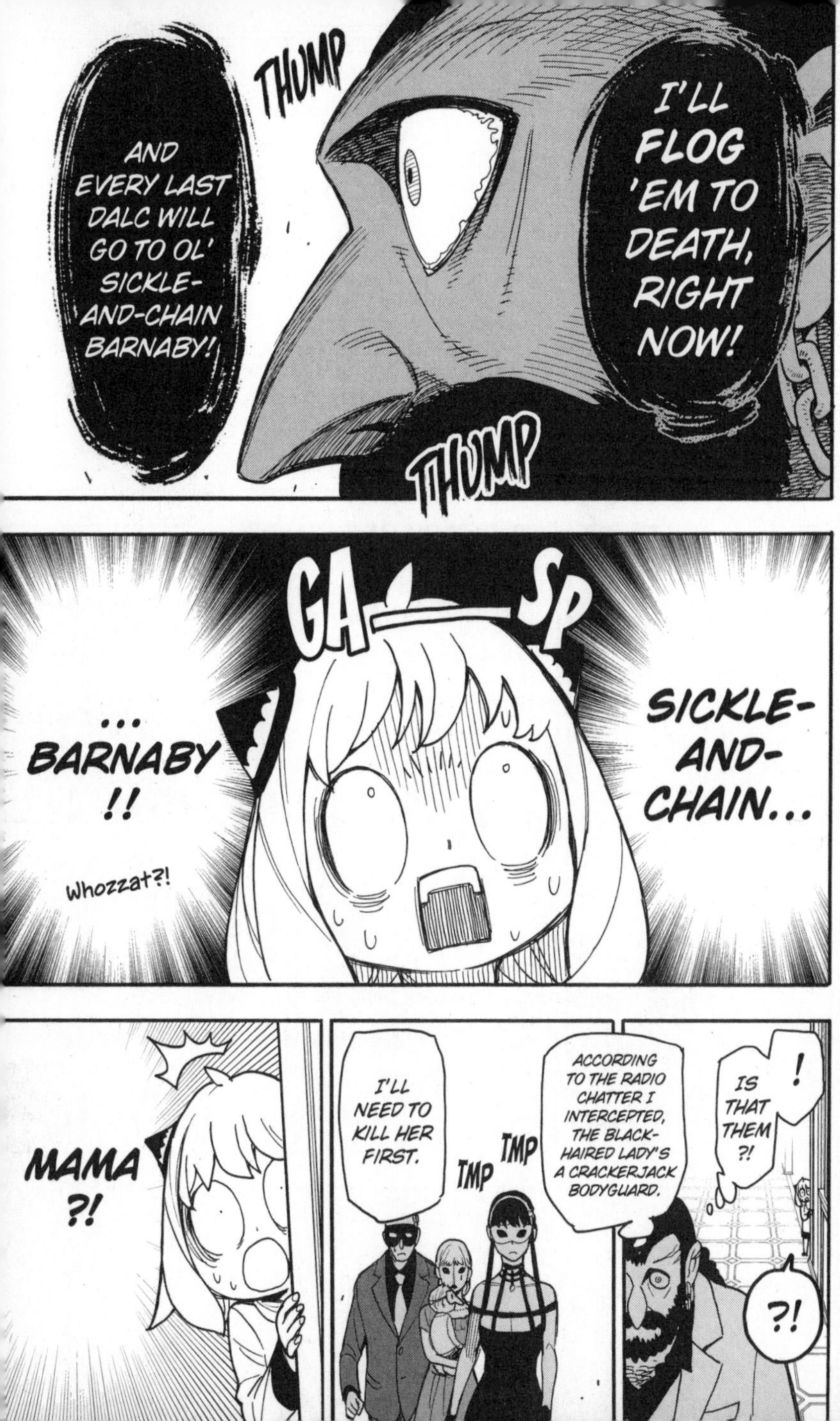
I'LL FLOG 'EM TO DEATH, RIGHT NOW!
THUMP
AND EVERY LAST DALC WILL GO TO OL' SICKLE-AND-CHAIN BARNABY!
THUMP
GASP
SICKLE-AND-CHAIN...
...BARNABY!!
Whozzat?!
!
IS THAT THEM?!
?!
ACCORDING TO THE RADIO CHATTER I INTERCEPTED, THE BLACK-HAIRED LADY'S A CRACKERJACK BODYGUARD.
TMP
TMP
I'LL NEED TO KILL HER FIRST.
MAMA?!

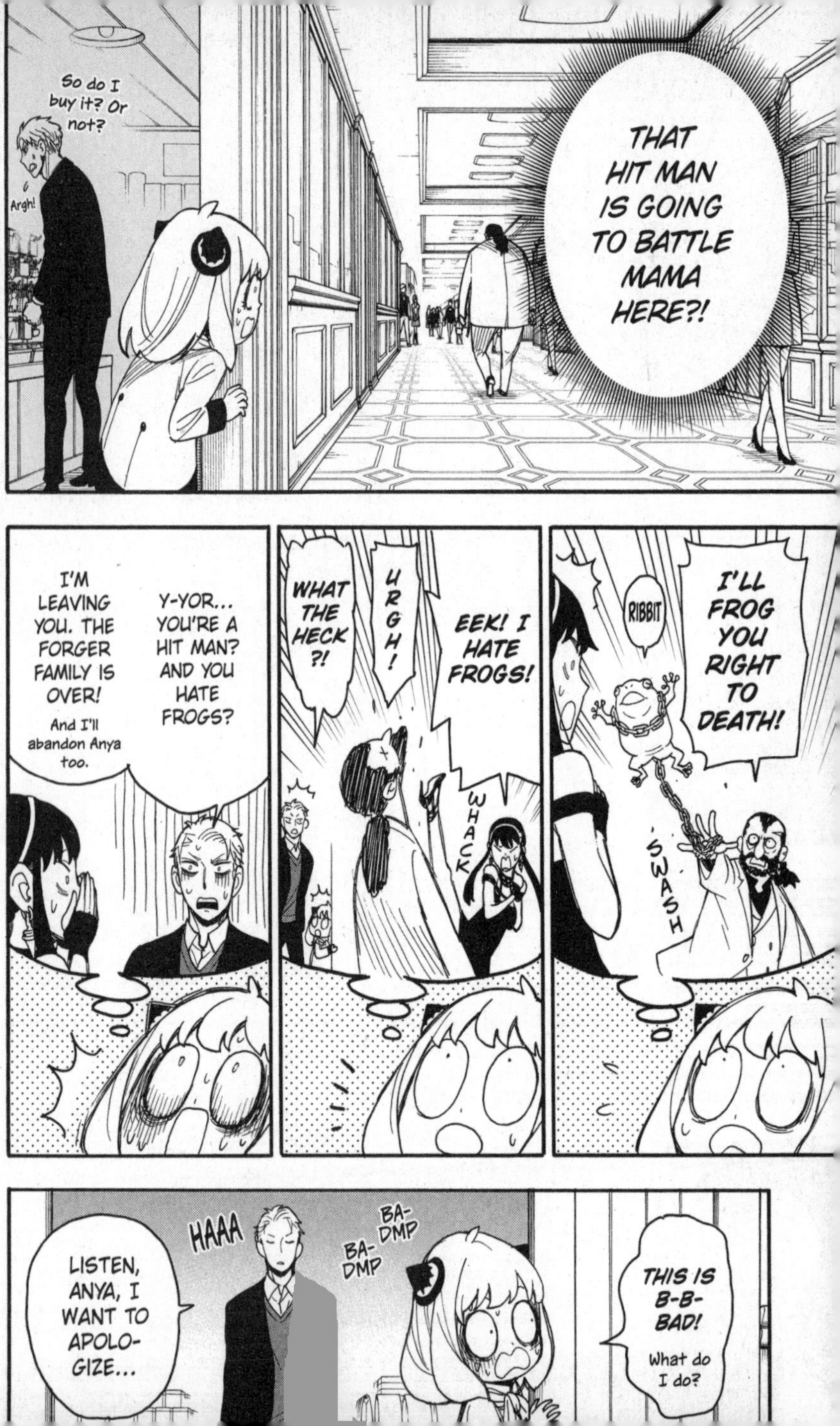
THAT HIT MAN IS GOING TO BATTLE MAMA HERE?!
So do I buy it? Or not?
Argh!
RIBBIT
I'LL FROG YOU RIGHT TO DEATH!
SWASH
EEK! I HATE FROGS!
URGH!
WHAT THE HECK?!
WHACK
Y-YOR... YOU'RE A HIT MAN? AND YOU HATE FROGS?
I'M LEAVING YOU. THE FORGER FAMILY IS OVER!
And I'll abandon Anya too.
THIS IS B-B-BAD!
What do I do?
BA-DMP
BA-DMP
HAAA
LISTEN, ANYA, I WANT TO APOLOGIZE...

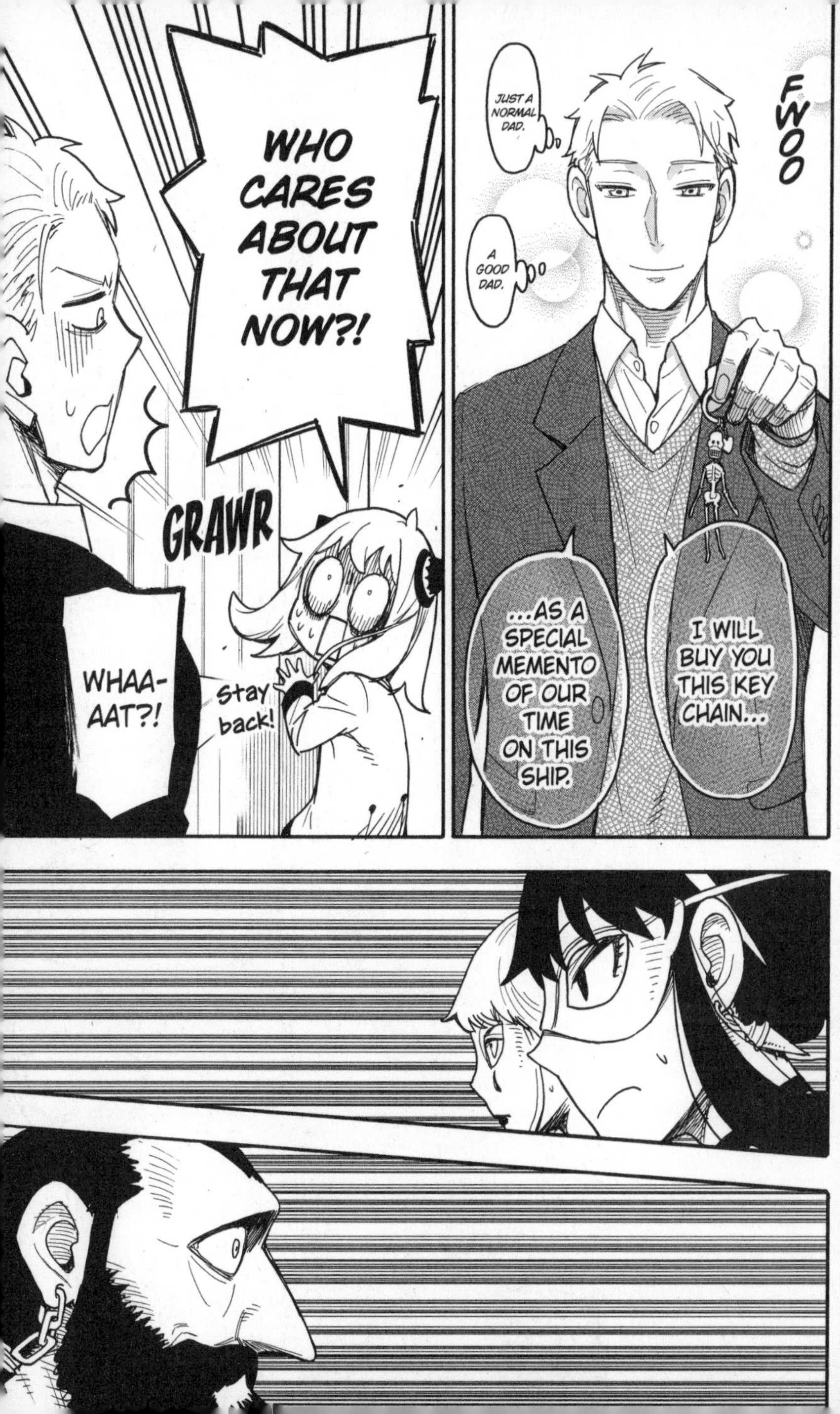
FWOO
JUST A NORMAL DAD.
A GOOD DAD.
I WILL BUY YOU THIS KEY CHAIN...
...AS A SPECIAL MEMENTO OF OUR TIME ON THIS SHIP.
WHO CARES ABOUT THAT NOW?!
GRAWR
Stay back!
WHAA-AAT?!

SPY×FAMILY

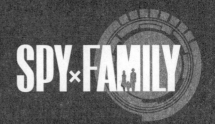

MISSION 48

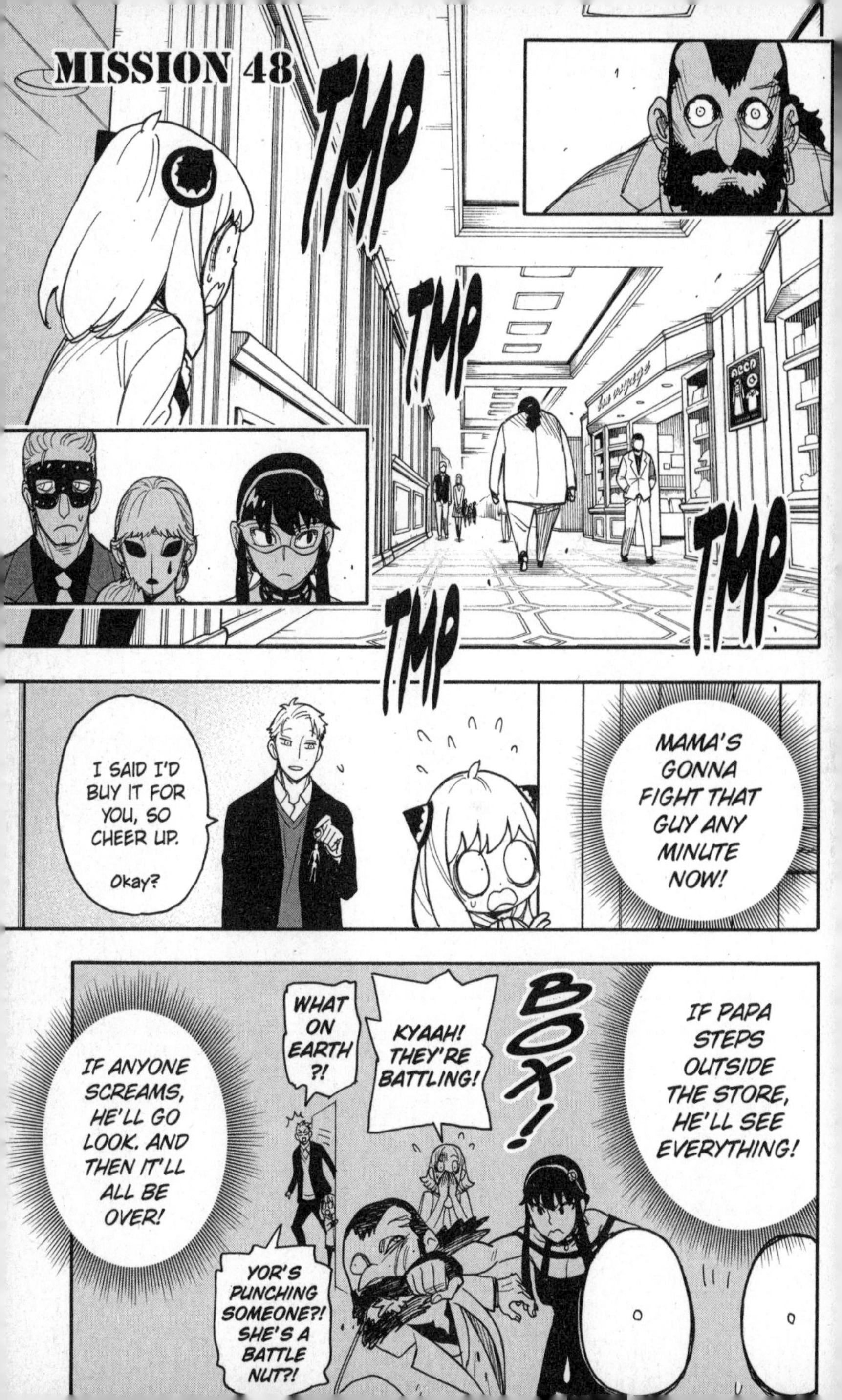

TMP
TMP
TMP
TMP
MAMA'S GONNA FIGHT THAT GUY ANY MINUTE NOW!
I SAID I'D BUY IT FOR YOU, SO CHEER UP.
Okay?
IF PAPA STEPS OUTSIDE THE STORE, HE'LL SEE EVERYTHING!
BOX!
KYAAH! THEY'RE BATTLING!
WHAT ON EARTH?!
IF ANYONE SCREAMS, HE'LL GO LOOK. AND THEN IT'LL ALL BE OVER!
YOR'S PUNCHING SOMEONE?! SHE'S A BATTLE NUT?!

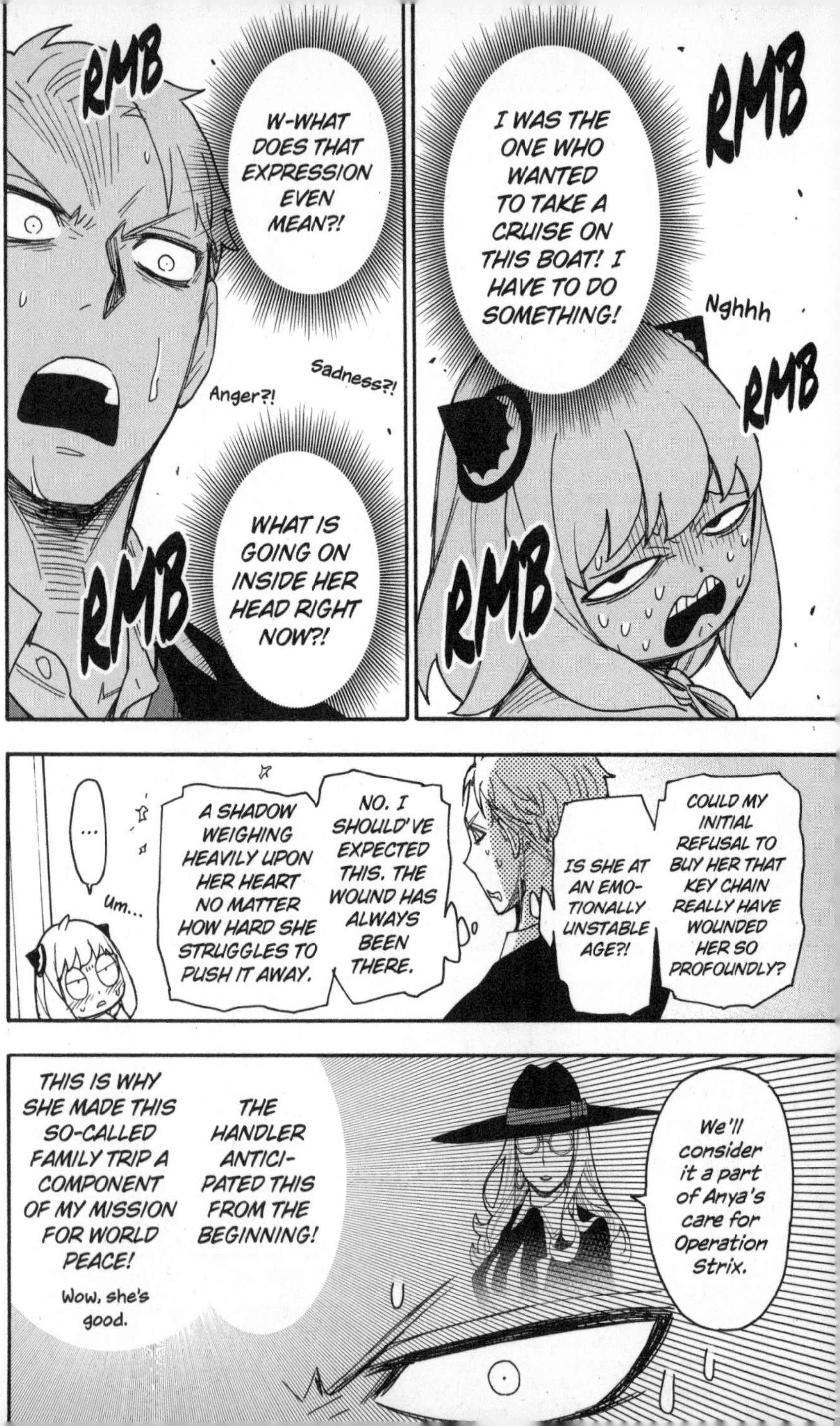
RMB
I WAS THE ONE WHO WANTED TO TAKE A CRUISE ON THIS BOAT! I HAVE TO DO SOMETHING!
Nghhh
RMB
RMB
RMB
W-WHAT DOES THAT EXPRESSION EVEN MEAN?!
Sadness?!
Anger?!
WHAT IS GOING ON INSIDE HER HEAD RIGHT NOW?!
RMB
COULD MY INITIAL REFUSAL TO BUY HER THAT KEY CHAIN REALLY HAVE WOUNDED HER SO PROFOUNDLY?
IS SHE AT AN EMOTIONALLY UNSTABLE AGE?!
NO. I SHOULD'VE EXPECTED THIS. THE WOUND HAS ALWAYS BEEN THERE.
A SHADOW WEIGHING HEAVILY UPON HER HEART NO MATTER HOW HARD SHE STRUGGLES TO PUSH IT AWAY.
...
Um...
We'll consider it a part of Anya's care for Operation Strix.
THE HANDLER ANTICIPATED THIS FROM THE BEGINNING!
THIS IS WHY SHE MADE THIS SO-CALLED FAMILY TRIP A COMPONENT OF MY MISSION FOR WORLD PEACE!
Wow, she's good.

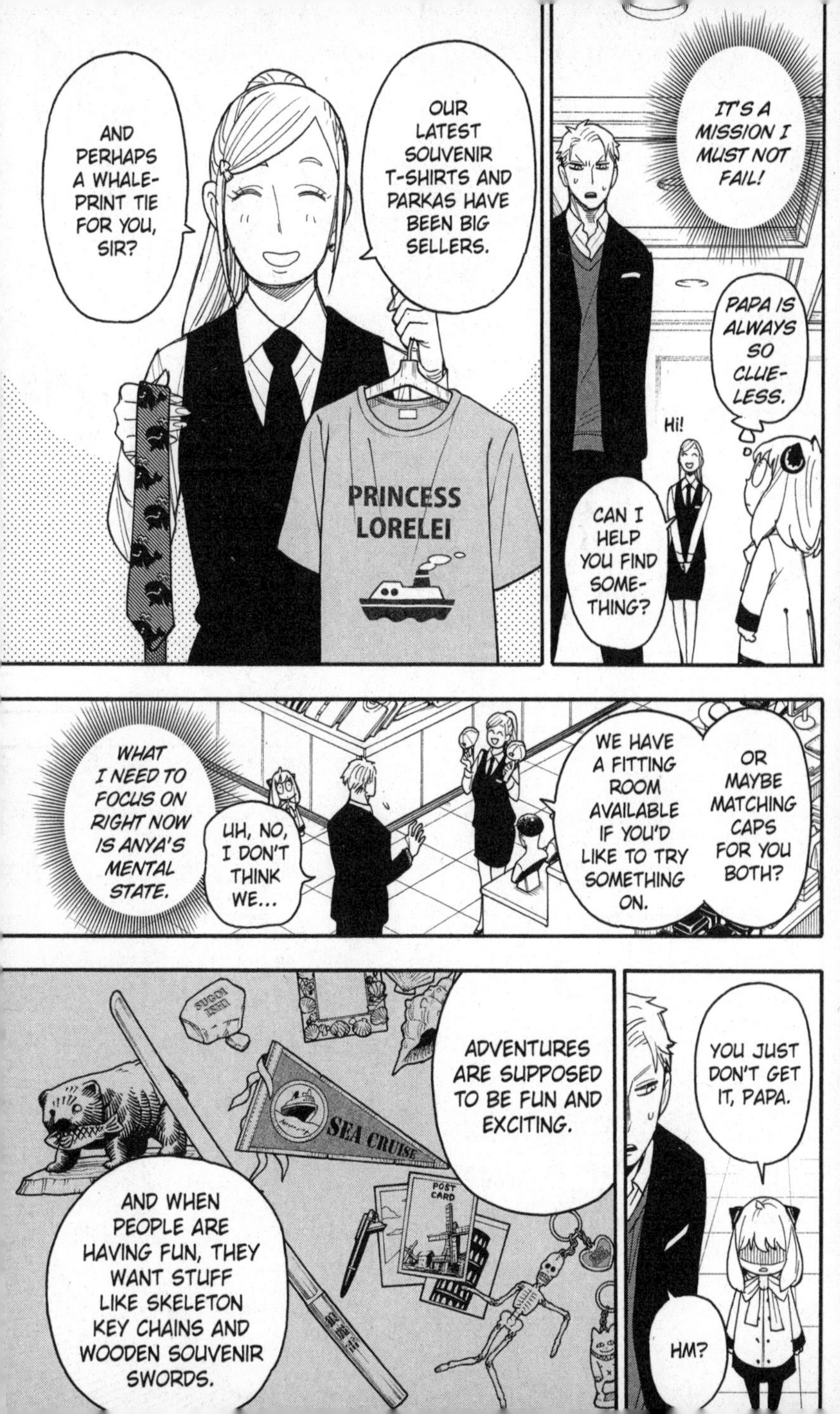
IT'S A MISSION I MUST NOT FAIL!
PAPA IS ALWAYS SO CLUELESS.
Hi!
CAN I HELP YOU FIND SOMETHING?
OUR LATEST SOUVENIR T-SHIRTS AND PARKAS HAVE BEEN BIG SELLERS.
AND PERHAPS A WHALE-PRINT TIE FOR YOU, SIR?
PRINCESS LORELEI
OR MAYBE MATCHING CAPS FOR YOU BOTH?
WE HAVE A FITTING ROOM AVAILABLE IF YOU'D LIKE TO TRY SOMETHING ON.
UH, NO, I DON'T THINK WE...
WHAT I NEED TO FOCUS ON RIGHT NOW IS ANYA'S MENTAL STATE.
YOU JUST DON'T GET IT, PAPA.
HM?
ADVENTURES ARE SUPPOSED TO BE FUN AND EXCITING.
SEA CRUISE
POST CARD
AND WHEN PEOPLE ARE HAVING FUN, THEY WANT STUFF LIKE SKELETON KEY CHAINS AND WOODEN SOUVENIR SWORDS.

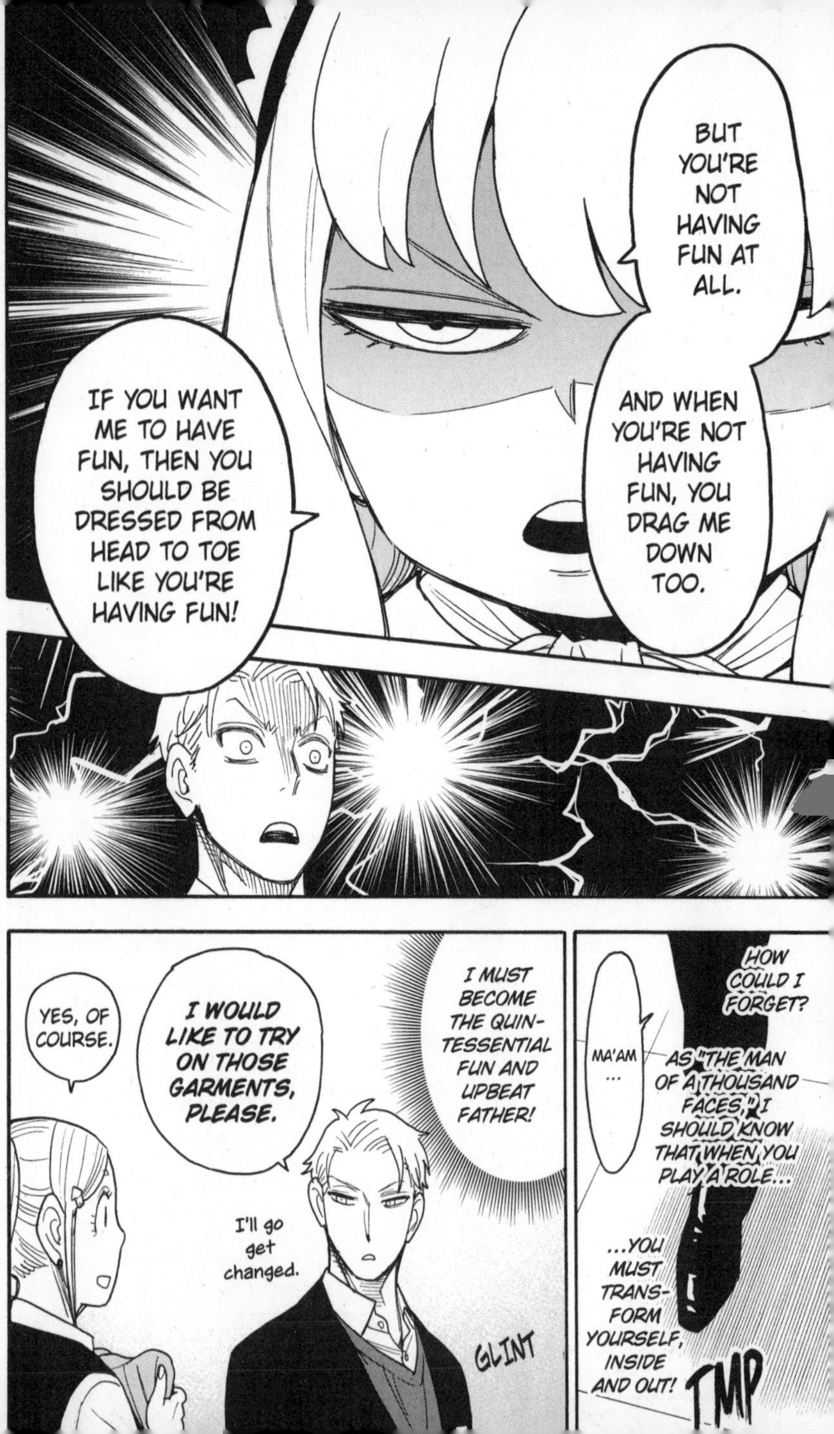
BUT YOU'RE NOT HAVING FUN AT ALL.
AND WHEN YOU'RE NOT HAVING FUN, YOU DRAG ME DOWN TOO.
IF YOU WANT ME TO HAVE FUN, THEN YOU SHOULD BE DRESSED FROM HEAD TO TOE LIKE YOU'RE HAVING FUN!
HOW COULD I FORGET?
MA'AM ...
AS "THE MAN OF A THOUSAND FACES," I SHOULD KNOW THAT WHEN YOU PLAY A ROLE...
...YOU MUST TRANSFORM YOURSELF, INSIDE AND OUT!
TMP
I MUST BECOME THE QUINTESSENTIAL FUN AND UPBEAT FATHER!
I WOULD LIKE TO TRY ON THOSE GARMENTS, PLEASE.
YES, OF COURSE.
I'll go get changed.
GLINT

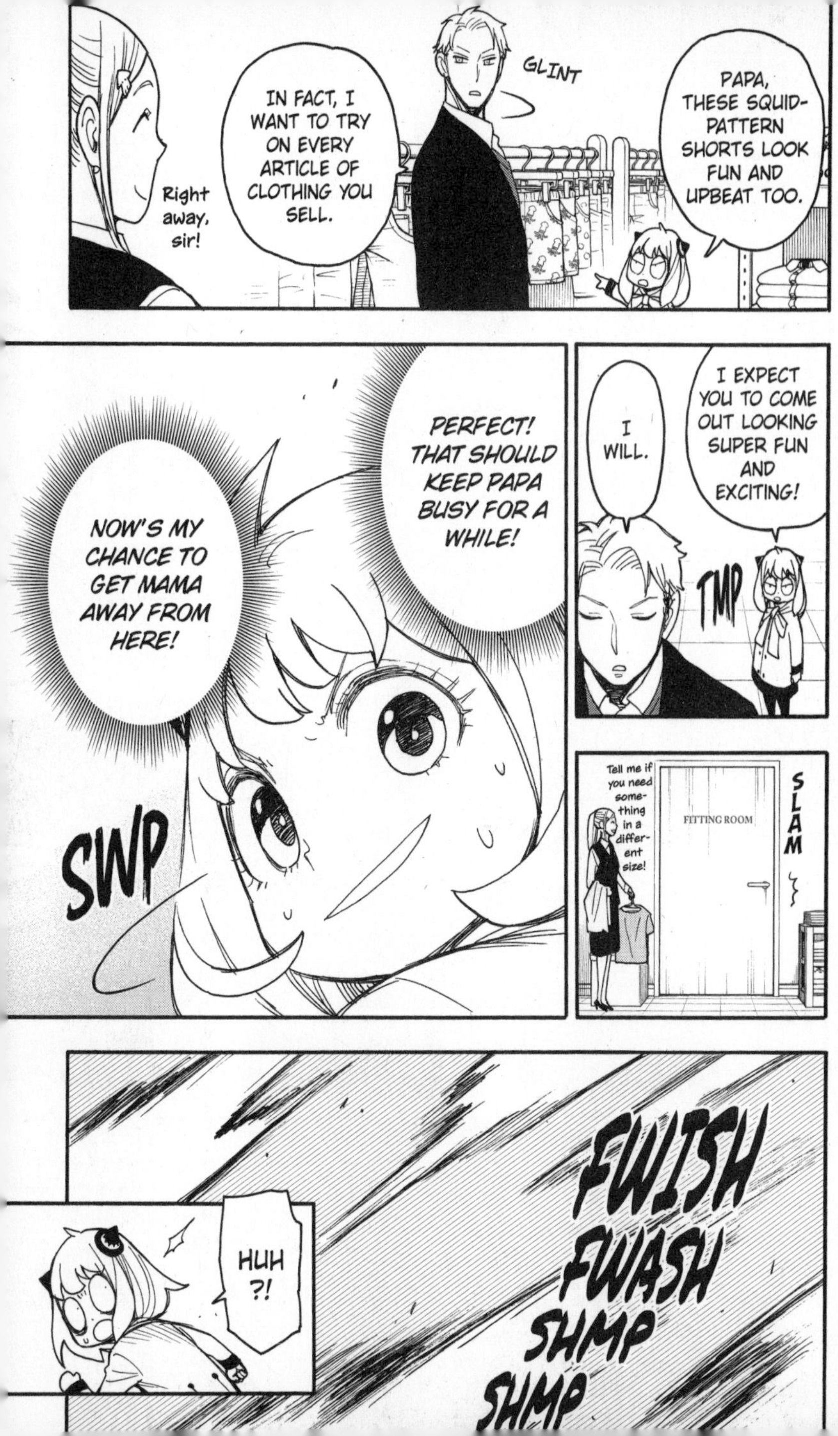
PAPA, THESE SQUID-PATTERN SHORTS LOOK FUN AND UPBEAT TOO.
GLINT
IN FACT, I WANT TO TRY ON EVERY ARTICLE OF CLOTHING YOU SELL.
Right away, sir!
I EXPECT YOU TO COME OUT LOOKING SUPER FUN AND EXCITING!
I WILL.
TMP
SLAM
FITTING ROOM
Tell me if you need something in a different size!
PERFECT! THAT SHOULD KEEP PAPA BUSY FOR A WHILE!
NOW'S MY CHANCE TO GET MAMA AWAY FROM HERE!
SWP
FWISH
FWASH
SHMP
SHMP
HUH ?!

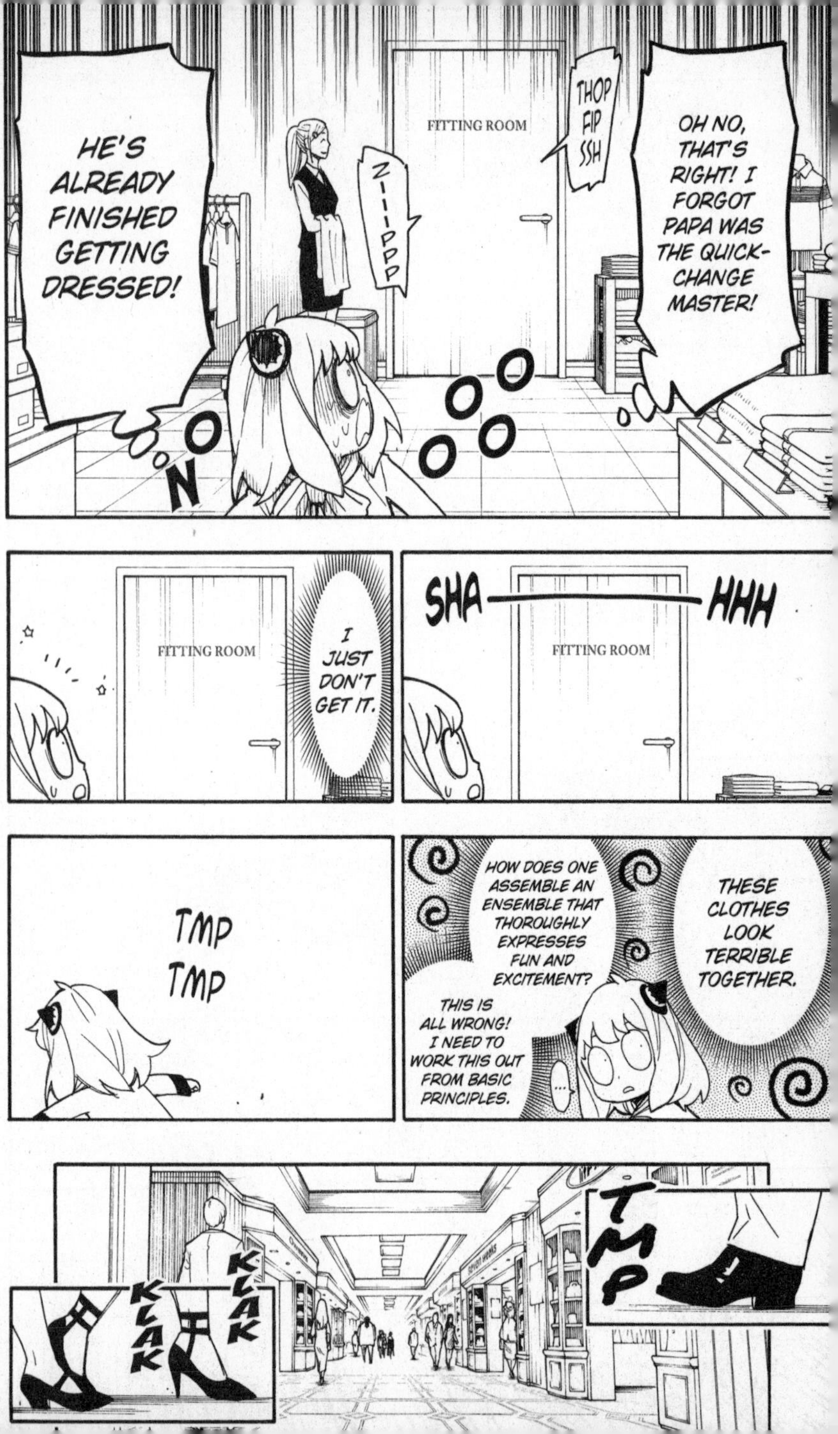
OH NO, THAT'S RIGHT! I FORGOT PAPA WAS THE QUICK-CHANGE MASTER!
THOP FIP SSH
FITTING ROOM
ZIIIPPP
HE'S ALREADY FINISHED GETTING DRESSED!
NOOOOOO
SHA———HHH
FITTING ROOM
I JUST DON'T GET IT.
FITTING ROOM
THESE CLOTHES LOOK TERRIBLE TOGETHER.
HOW DOES ONE ASSEMBLE AN ENSEMBLE THAT THOROUGHLY EXPRESSES FUN AND EXCITEMENT?
THIS IS ALL WRONG! I NEED TO WORK THIS OUT FROM BASIC PRINCIPLES.
...
TMP TMP
TMP
KLAK KLAK
KLAK KLAK

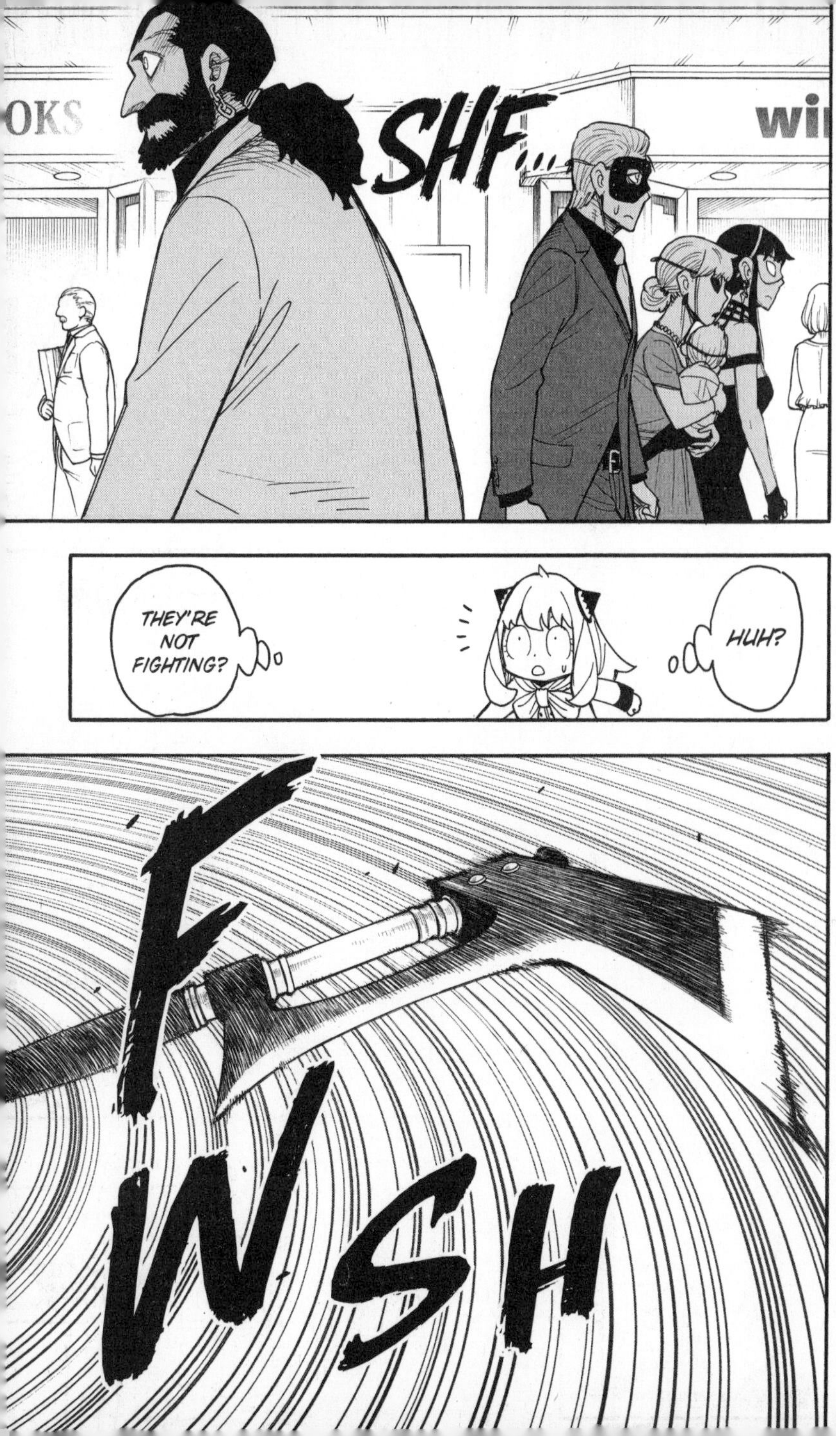
SHF...
HUH?
THEY'RE NOT FIGHTING?
FWSH

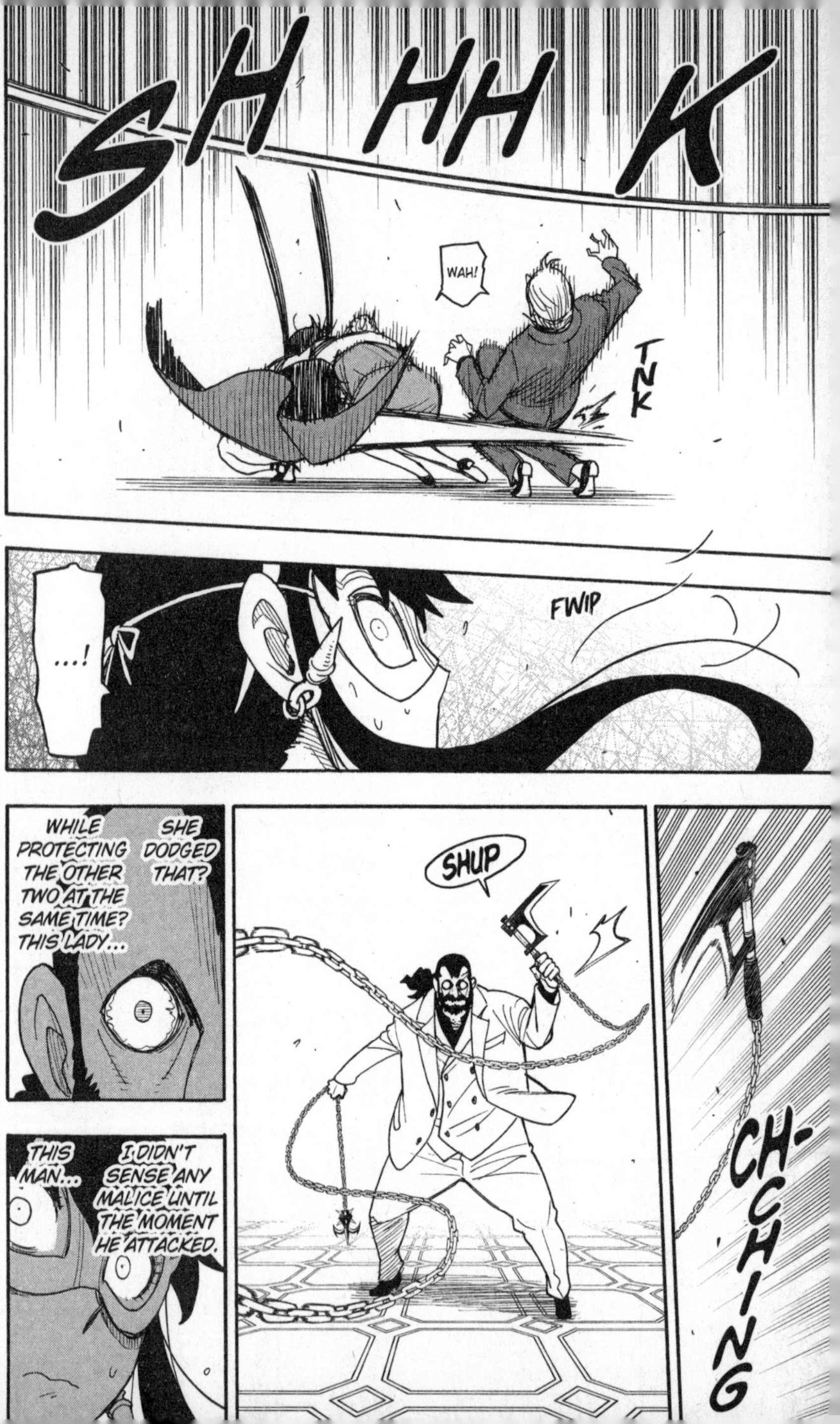
SHHHK
WAH!
TNK
FWIP
...!
CH-CHING
SHUP
SHE DODGED THAT?
WHILE PROTECTING THE OTHER TWO AT THE SAME TIME? THIS LADY...
I DIDN'T SENSE ANY MALICE UNTIL THE MOMENT HE ATTACKED.
THIS MAN...

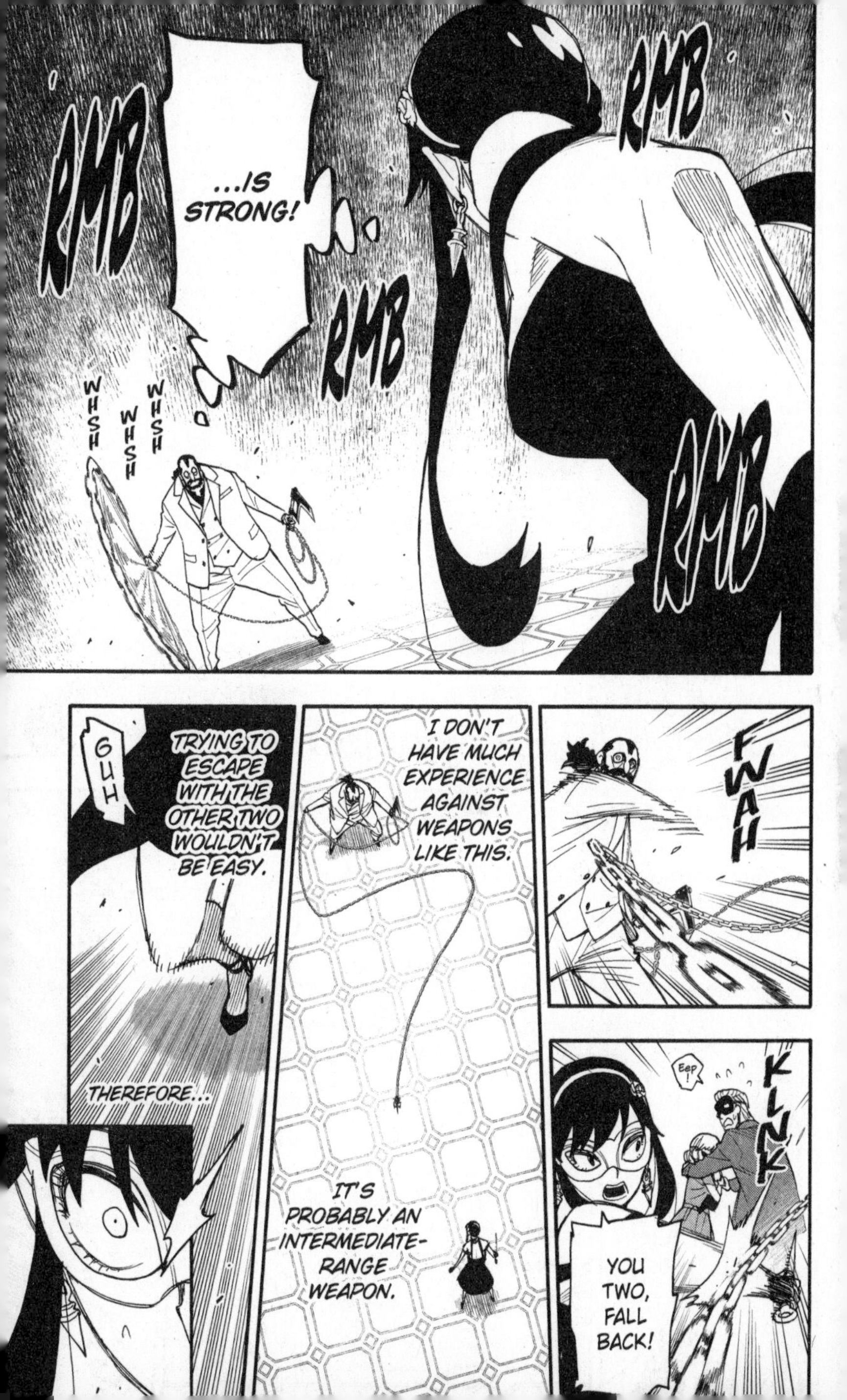
RMB
RMB
...IS STRONG!
RMB
RMB
WHSH WHSH WHSH
FWAH
Eep!
KLINK
YOU TWO, FALL BACK!
I DON'T HAVE MUCH EXPERIENCE AGAINST WEAPONS LIKE THIS.
IT'S PROBABLY AN INTERMEDIATE-RANGE WEAPON.
GUH
TRYING TO ESCAPE WITH THE OTHER TWO WOULDN'T BE EASY.
THEREFORE...

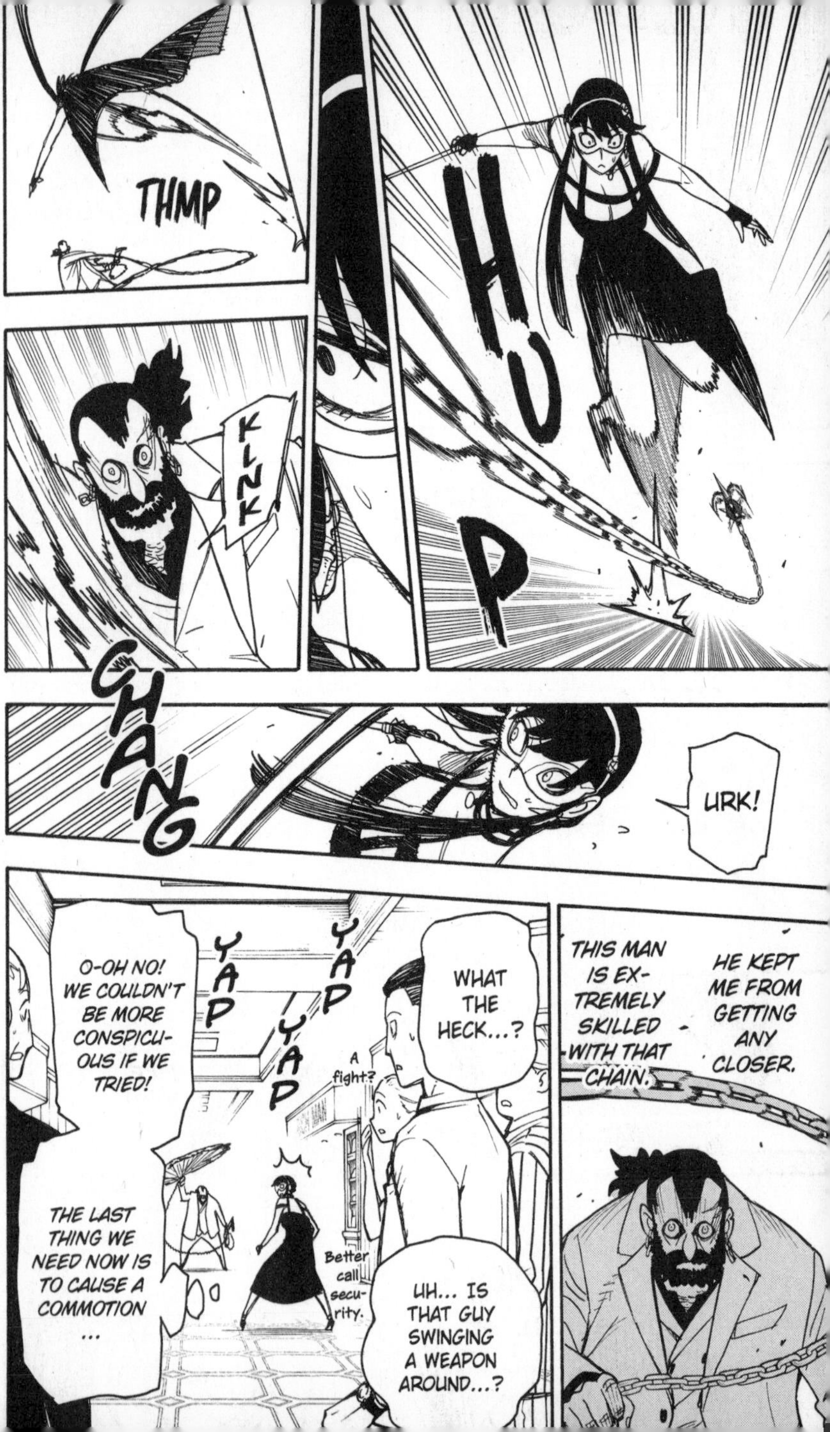
HUP
THMP
KLINK
CHANG
URK!
HE KEPT ME FROM GETTING ANY CLOSER.
THIS MAN IS EXTREMELY SKILLED WITH THAT CHAIN.
WHAT THE HECK...?
YAP YAP YAP YAP
A fight?
O-OH NO! WE COULDN'T BE MORE CONSPICUOUS IF WE TRIED!
UH... IS THAT GUY SWINGING A WEAPON AROUND...?
Better call security.
THE LAST THING WE NEED NOW IS TO CAUSE A COMMOTION...

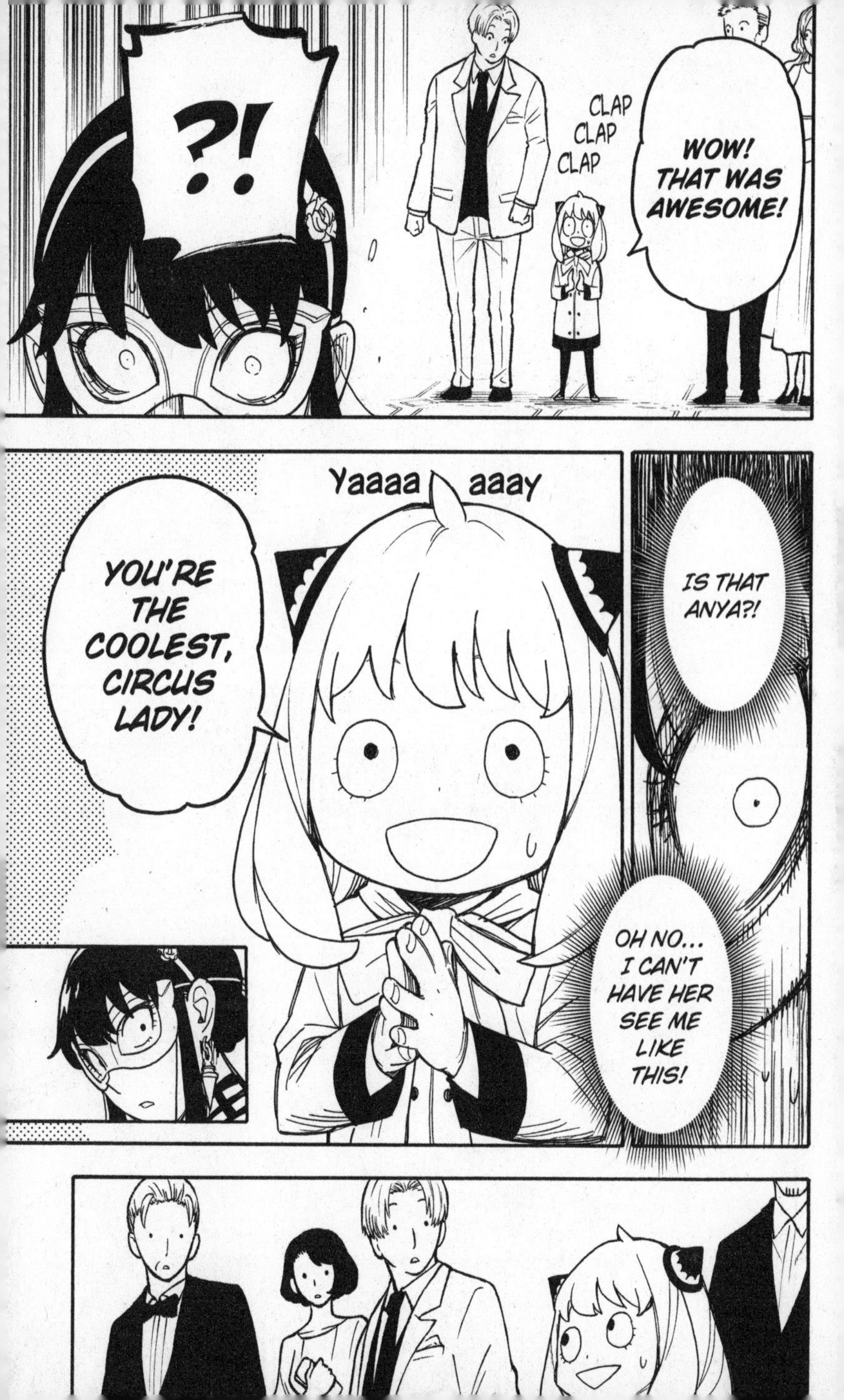
WOW! THAT WAS AWESOME!
CLAP CLAP CLAP
?!
IS THAT ANYA?!
OH NO... I CAN'T HAVE HER SEE ME LIKE THIS!
Yaaaa aaay
YOU'RE THE COOLEST, CIRCUS LADY!

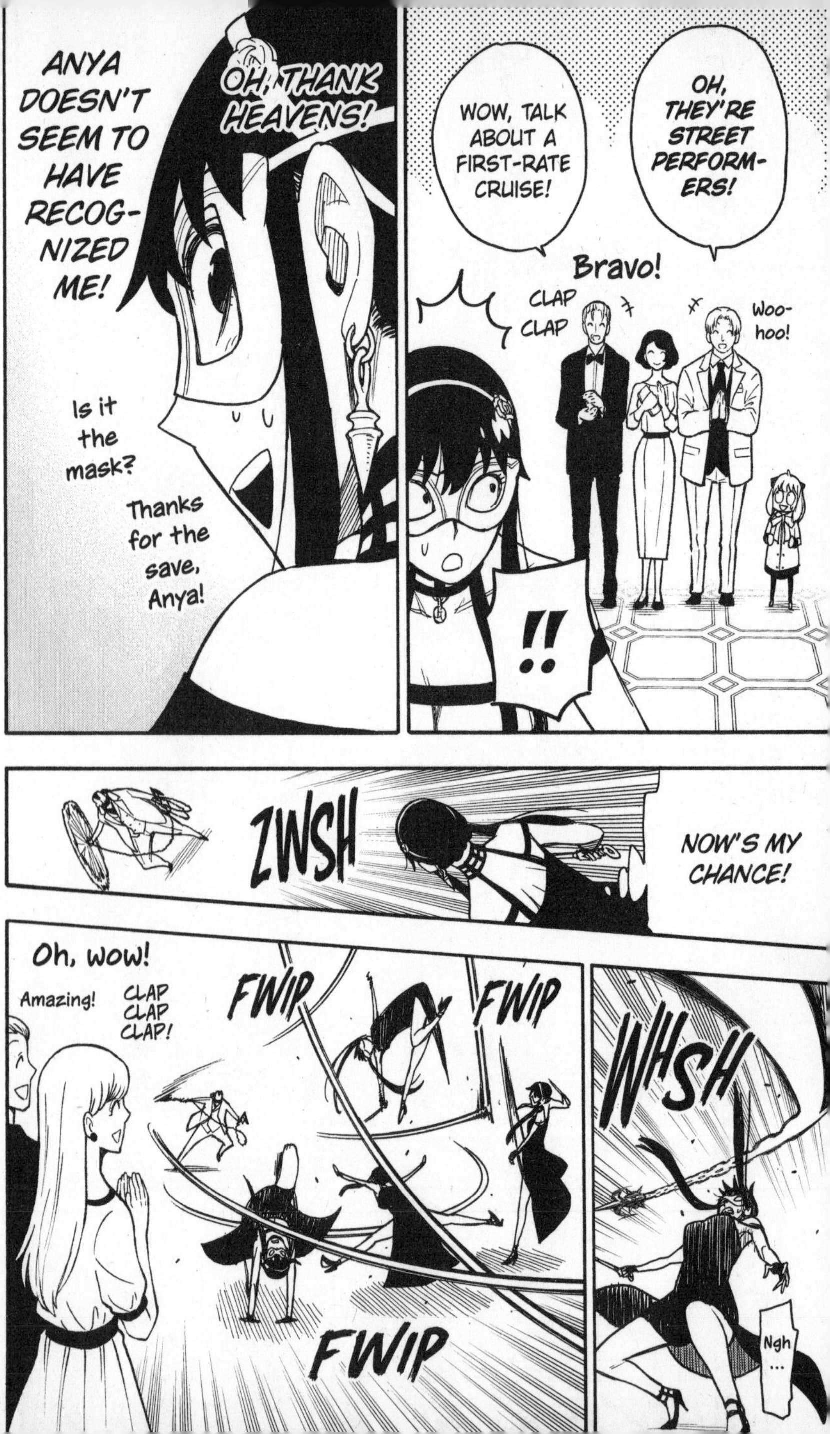
OH, THEY'RE STREET PERFORM-ERS!
WOW, TALK ABOUT A FIRST-RATE CRUISE!
Bravo!
Woo-hoo!
CLAP CLAP
!!
OH, THANK HEAVENS!
ANYA DOESN'T SEEM TO HAVE RECOG-NIZED ME!
Is it the mask?
Thanks for the save, Anya!
NOW'S MY CHANCE!
ZWSH
WHSH
Ngh...
Oh, wow!
Amazing!
CLAP CLAP CLAP!
FWIP
FWIP
FWIP

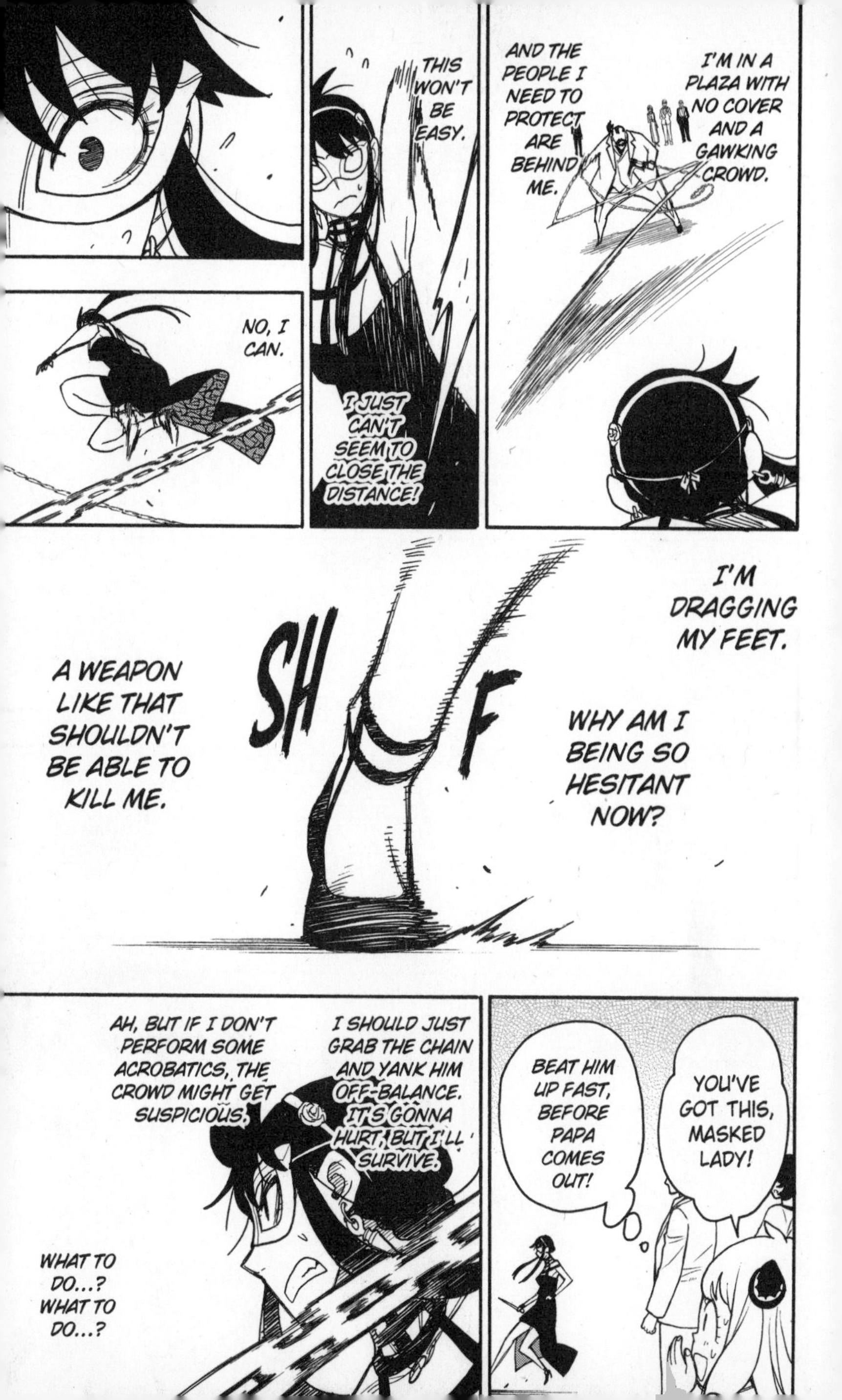
I'M IN A PLAZA WITH NO COVER AND A GAWKING CROWD.
AND THE PEOPLE I NEED TO PROTECT ARE BEHIND ME.
THIS WON'T BE EASY.
I JUST CAN'T SEEM TO CLOSE THE DISTANCE!
NO, I CAN.
I'M DRAGGING MY FEET.
WHY AM I BEING SO HESITANT NOW?
SHUF
A WEAPON LIKE THAT SHOULDN'T BE ABLE TO KILL ME.
YOU'VE GOT THIS, MASKED LADY!
BEAT HIM UP FAST, BEFORE PAPA COMES OUT!
I SHOULD JUST GRAB THE CHAIN AND YANK HIM OFF-BALANCE. IT'S GONNA HURT, BUT I'LL SURVIVE.
AH, BUT IF I DON'T PERFORM SOME ACROBATICS, THE CROWD MIGHT GET SUSPICIOUS.
WHAT TO DO...? WHAT TO DO...?

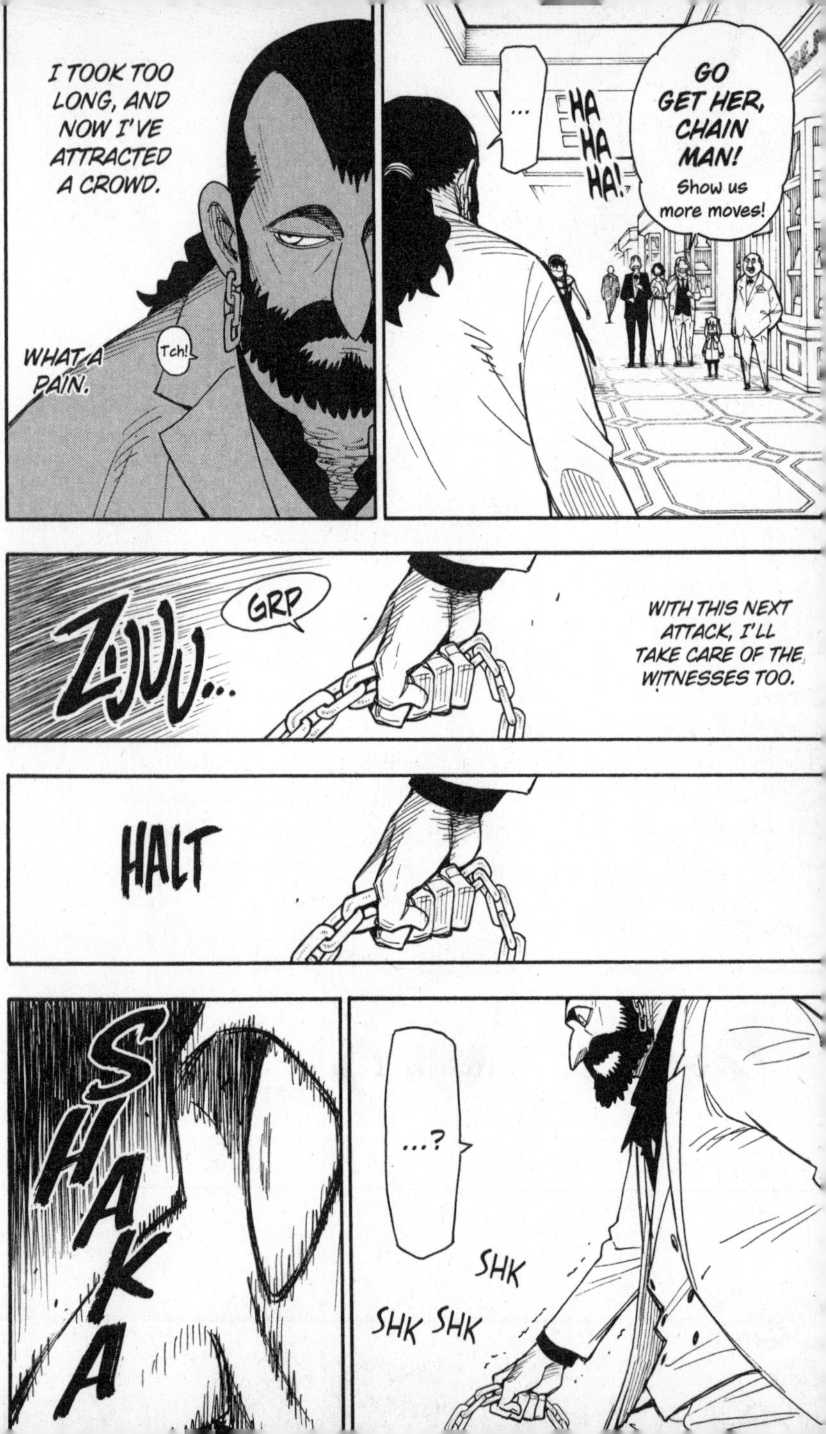
...
HA HA HA!
GO GET HER, CHAIN MAN! Show us more moves!
I TOOK TOO LONG, AND NOW I'VE ATTRACTED A CROWD.
Tch!
WHAT A PAIN.
WITH THIS NEXT ATTACK, I'LL TAKE CARE OF THE WITNESSES TOO.
GRP
ZJUU...
HALT
...?
SHK
SHK SHK
SHAKA

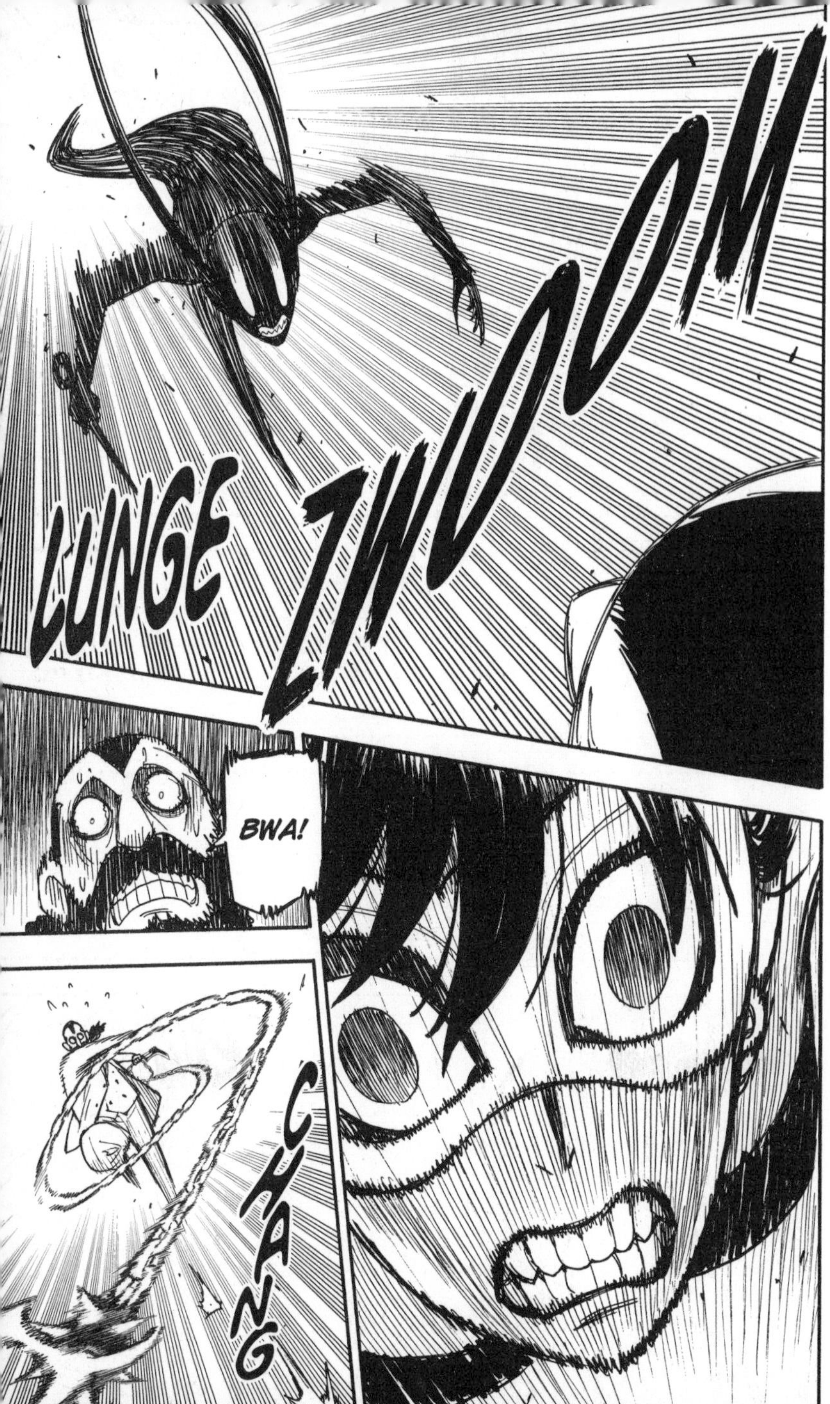
ZWOOM
LUNGE
BWA!
CHANG

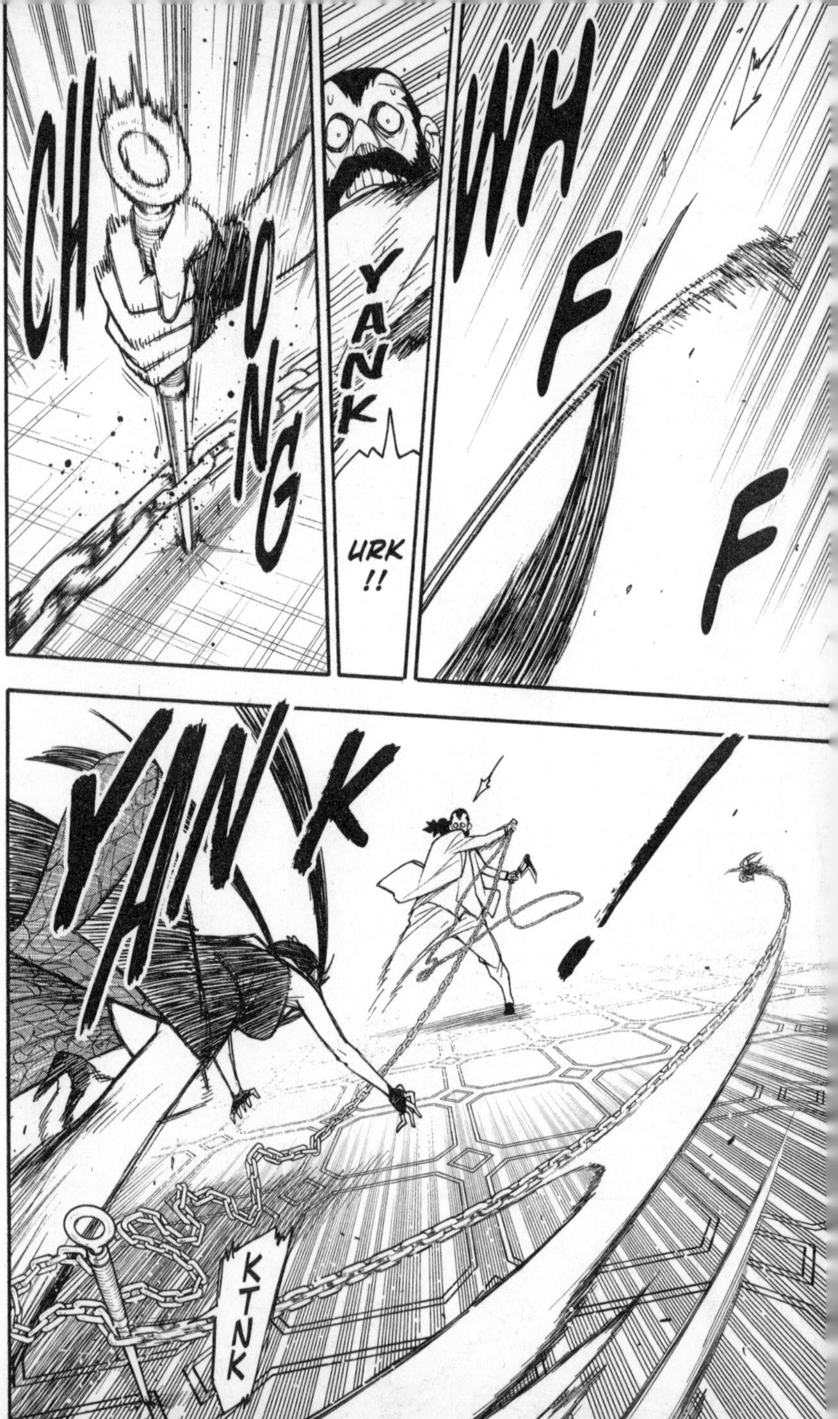

WHFF
YANK
URK!!
CHONG
YANK!
KTNK

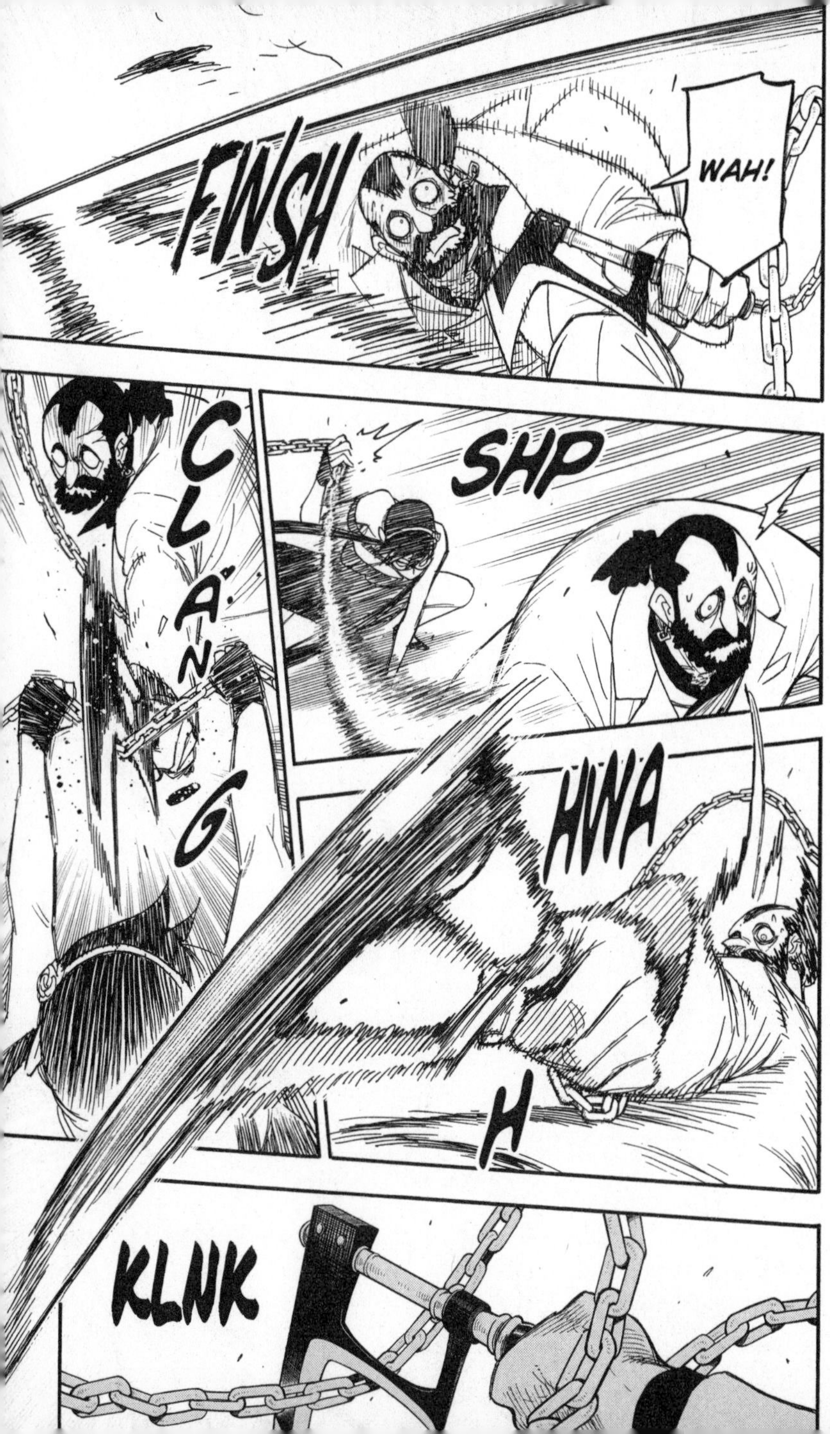
WAH!
FWSH
SHP
HWAH
CLANG
KLNK

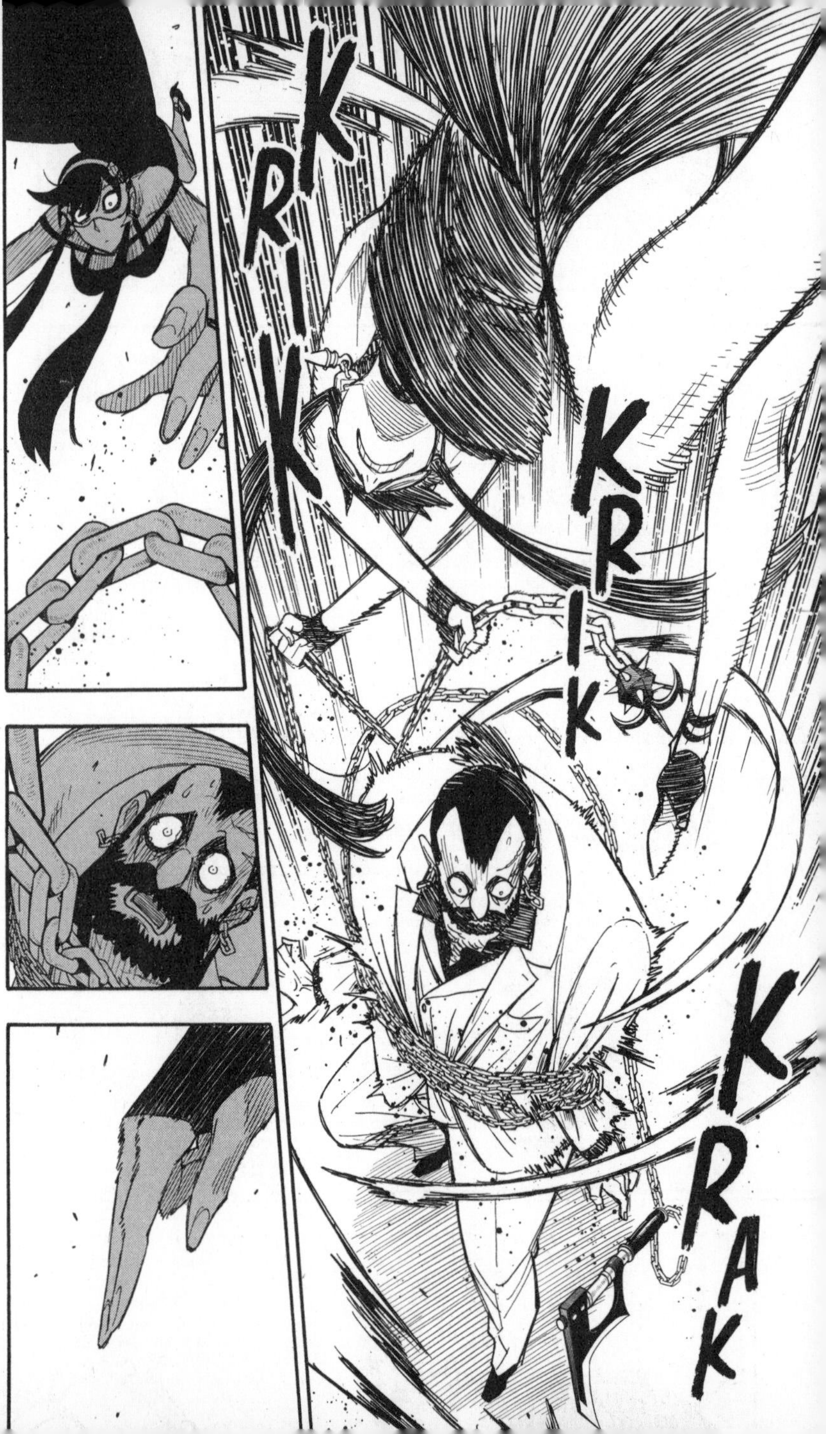
KRIK
KRIK
KRAK

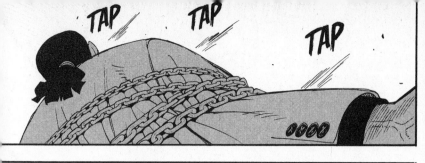

TAP TAP TAP

FWP

THMP

WORMP

BOW

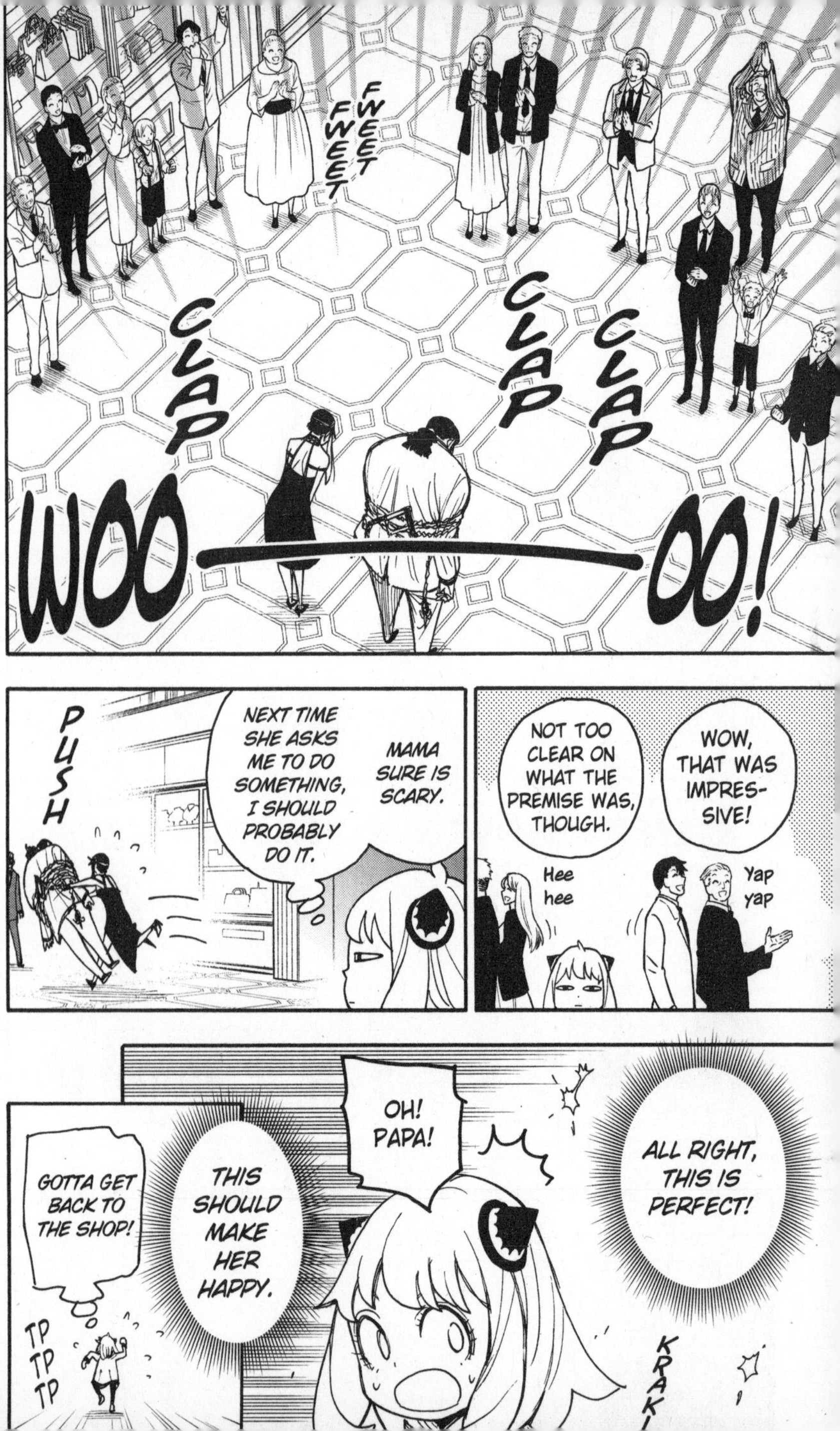
FWEET
FWEET
CLAP
CLAP
CLAP
WOO————OO!
WOW, THAT WAS IMPRES-SIVE!
NOT TOO CLEAR ON WHAT THE PREMISE WAS, THOUGH.
Yap yap
Hee hee
MAMA SURE IS SCARY.
NEXT TIME SHE ASKS ME TO DO SOMETHING, I SHOULD PROBABLY DO IT.
PUSH
ALL RIGHT, THIS IS PERFECT!
OH! PAPA!
KRAK
THIS SHOULD MAKE HER HAPPY.
GOTTA GET BACK TO THE SHOP!
TP TP TP

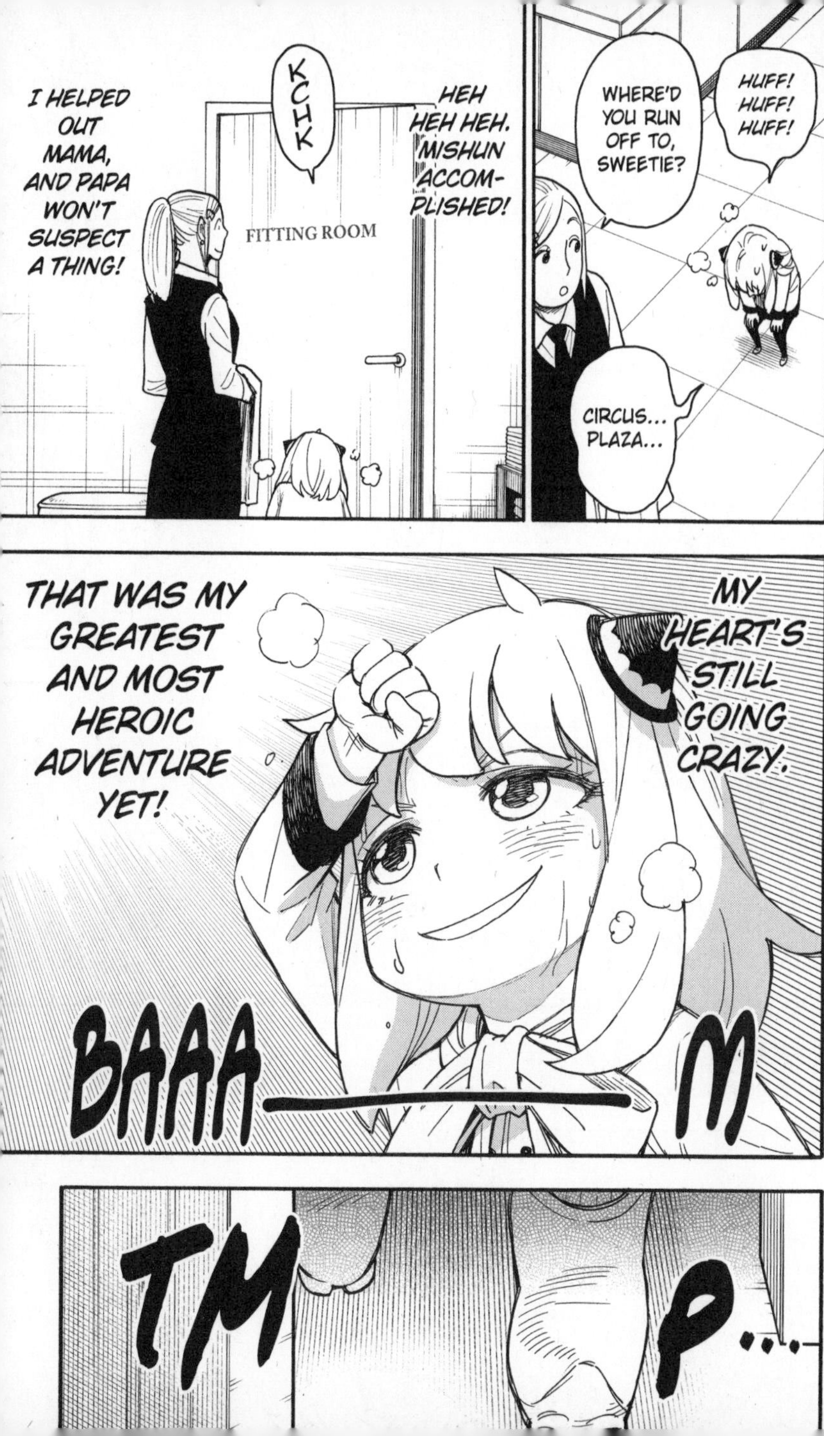
HUFF! HUFF! HUFF!
WHERE'D YOU RUN OFF TO, SWEETIE?
CIRCUS... PLAZA...
HEH HEH HEH. MISHUN ACCOM-PLISHED!
KCHK
I HELPED OUT MAMA, AND PAPA WON'T SUSPECT A THING!
FITTING ROOM
MY HEART'S STILL GOING CRAZY.
THAT WAS MY GREATEST AND MOST HEROIC ADVENTURE YET!
BAAA——M
TMP...

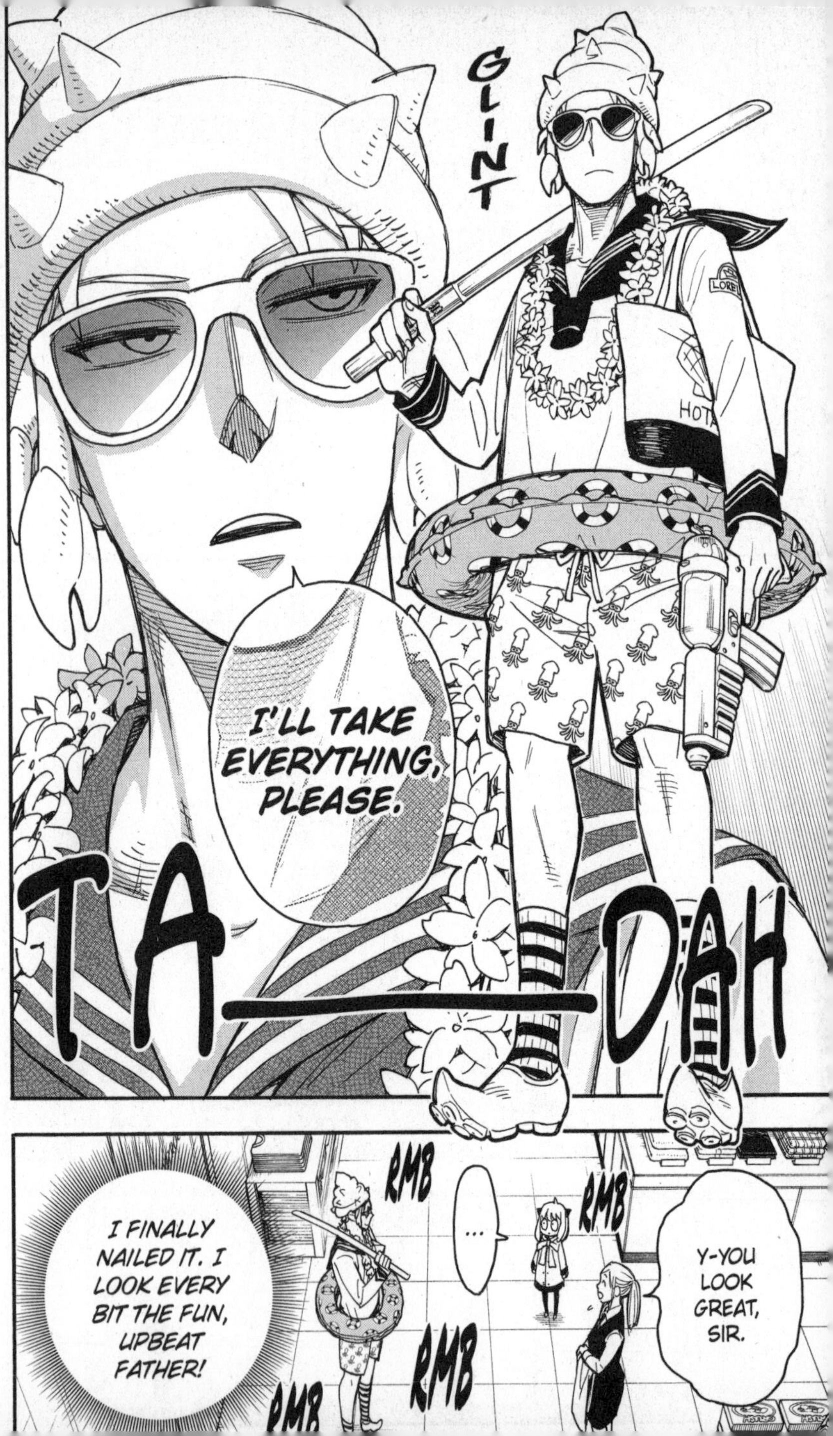
GLINT
I'LL TAKE EVERYTHING, PLEASE.
TA—DAH
Y-YOU LOOK GREAT, SIR.
RMB
...
RMB
I FINALLY NAILED IT. I LOOK EVERY BIT THE FUN, UPBEAT FATHER!
RMB
RMB

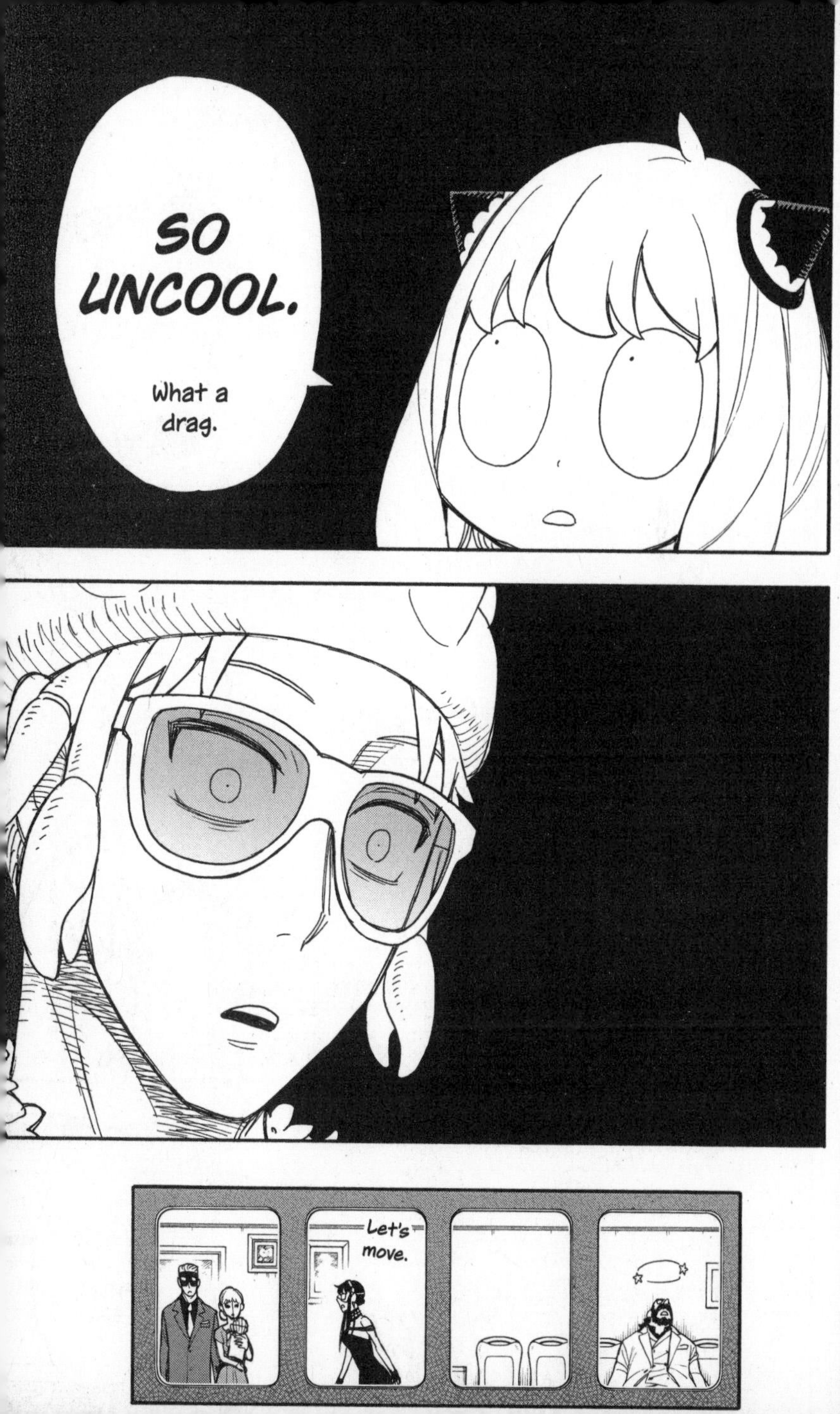
SO UNCOOL.
What a drag.
Let's move.

SPY×FAMILY

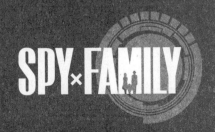

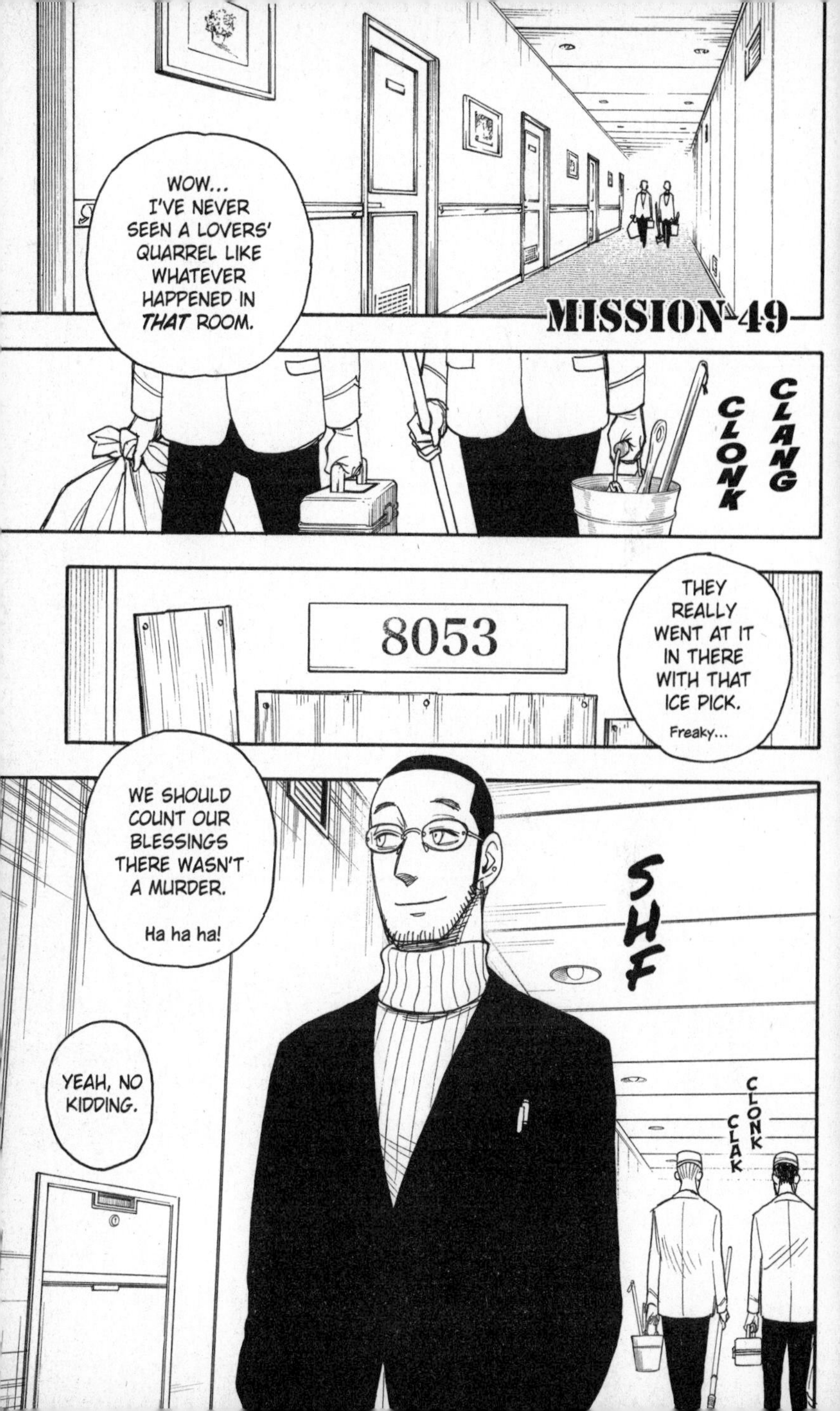
MISSION 49
WOW... I'VE NEVER SEEN A LOVERS' QUARREL LIKE WHATEVER HAPPENED IN *THAT* ROOM.
CLANG
CLONK
8053
THEY REALLY WENT AT IT IN THERE WITH THAT ICE PICK.
Freaky...
WE SHOULD COUNT OUR BLESSINGS THERE WASN'T A MURDER.
Ha ha ha!
SHF
CLONK
CLAK
YEAH, NO KIDDING.

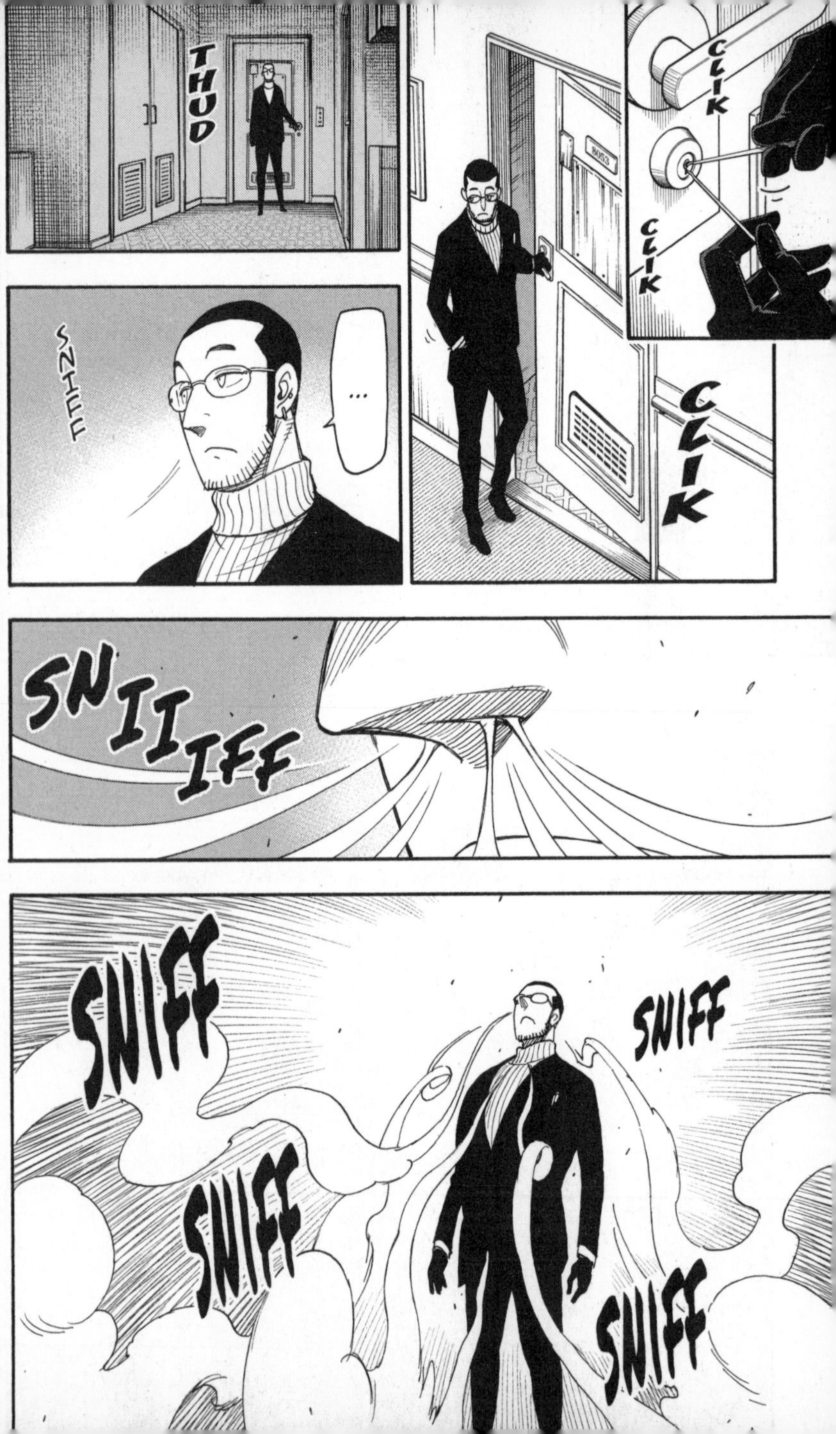

CLIK
CLIK
CLIK
CLIK
THUD
SNIFF
...
SNIIIFF
SNIFF
SNIFF
SNIFF
SNIFF

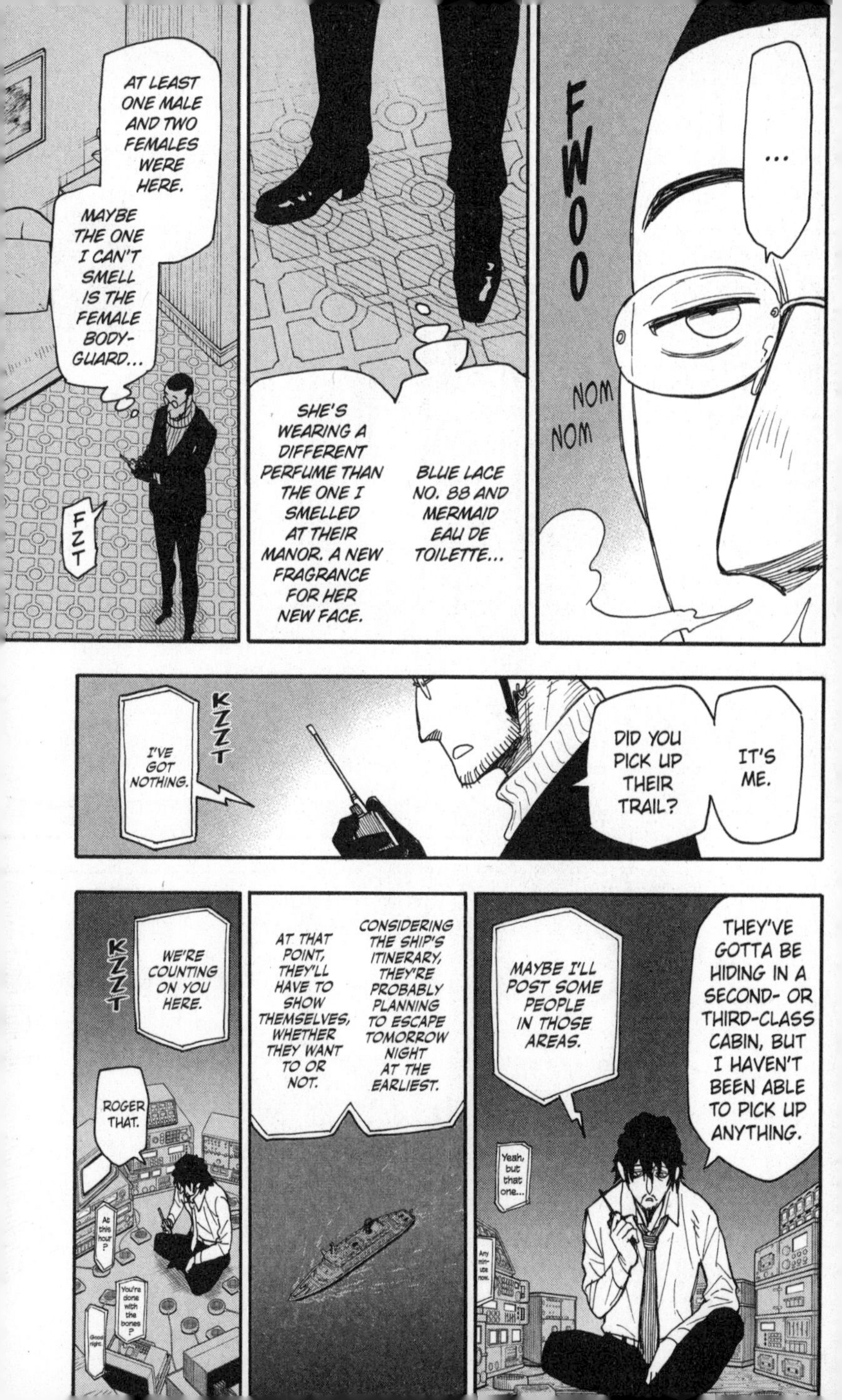
...
FWOO
NOM
NOM
BLUE LACE NO. 88 AND MERMAID EAU DE TOILETTE...
SHE'S WEARING A DIFFERENT PERFUME THAN THE ONE I SMELLED AT THEIR MANOR. A NEW FRAGRANCE FOR HER NEW FACE.
AT LEAST ONE MALE AND TWO FEMALES WERE HERE.
MAYBE THE ONE I CAN'T SMELL IS THE FEMALE BODY-GUARD...
FZT
IT'S ME.
DID YOU PICK UP THEIR TRAIL?
KZZT
I'VE GOT NOTHING.
THEY'VE GOTTA BE HIDING IN A SECOND- OR THIRD-CLASS CABIN, BUT I HAVEN'T BEEN ABLE TO PICK UP ANYTHING.
MAYBE I'LL POST SOME PEOPLE IN THOSE AREAS.
Yeah, but that one...
Any min-ute now.
CONSIDERING THE SHIP'S ITINERARY, THEY'RE PROBABLY PLANNING TO ESCAPE TOMORROW NIGHT AT THE EARLIEST.
AT THAT POINT, THEY'LL HAVE TO SHOW THEMSELVES, WHETHER THEY WANT TO OR NOT.
KZZT
WE'RE COUNTING ON YOU HERE.
ROGER THAT.
At this hour?
You're done with the bones?
Good night.

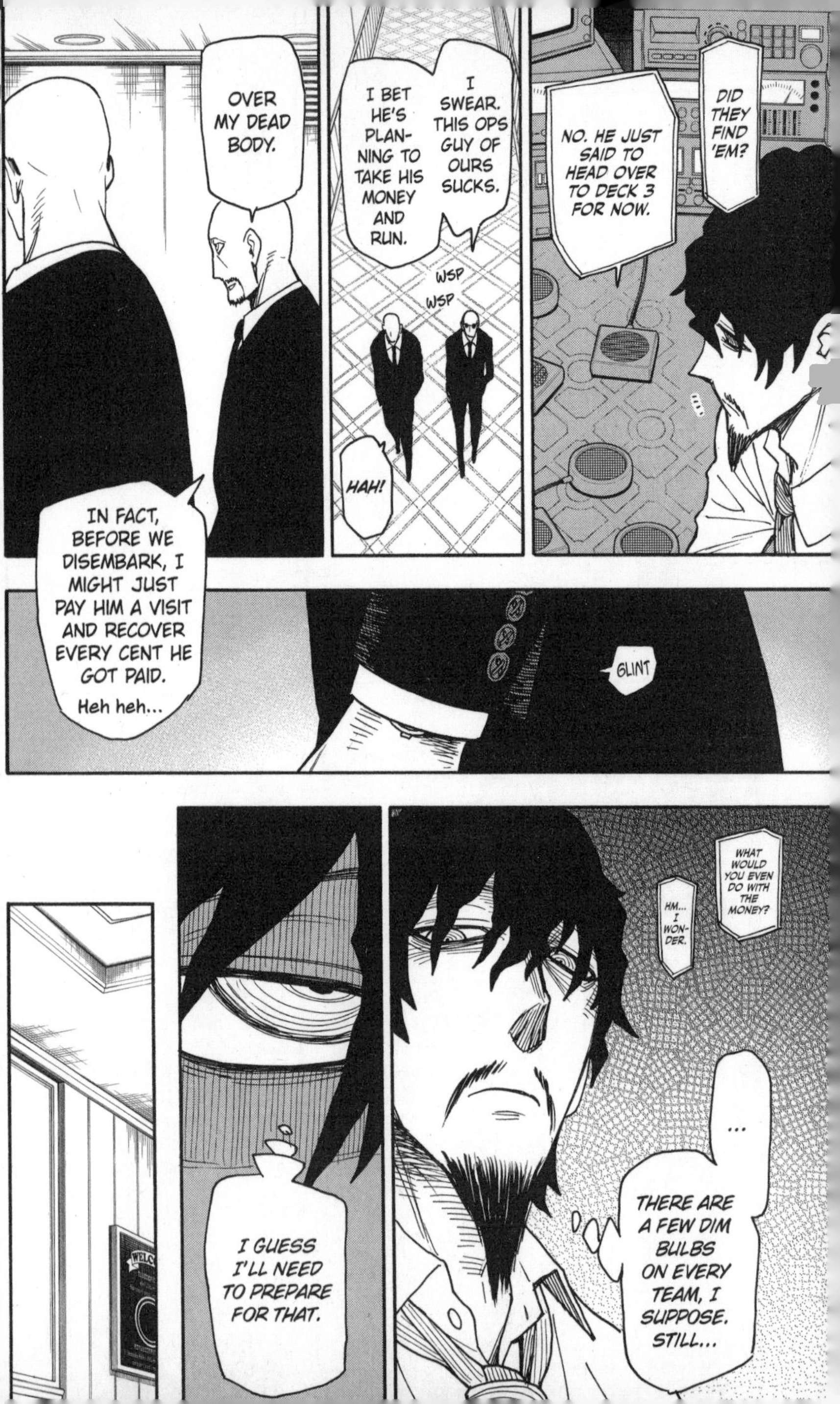
DID THEY FIND 'EM?
NO. HE JUST SAID TO HEAD OVER TO DECK 3 FOR NOW.
...
I SWEAR. THIS OPS GUY OF OURS SUCKS.
I BET HE'S PLAN-NING TO TAKE HIS MONEY AND RUN.
WSP
WSP
HAH!
OVER MY DEAD BODY.
IN FACT, BEFORE WE DISEMBARK, I MIGHT JUST PAY HIM A VISIT AND RECOVER EVERY CENT HE GOT PAID.
Heh heh...
GLINT
WHAT WOULD YOU EVEN DO WITH THE MONEY?
HM... I WON-DER.
...
THERE ARE A FEW DIM BULBS ON EVERY TEAM, I SUPPOSE. STILL...
I GUESS I'LL NEED TO PREPARE FOR THAT.

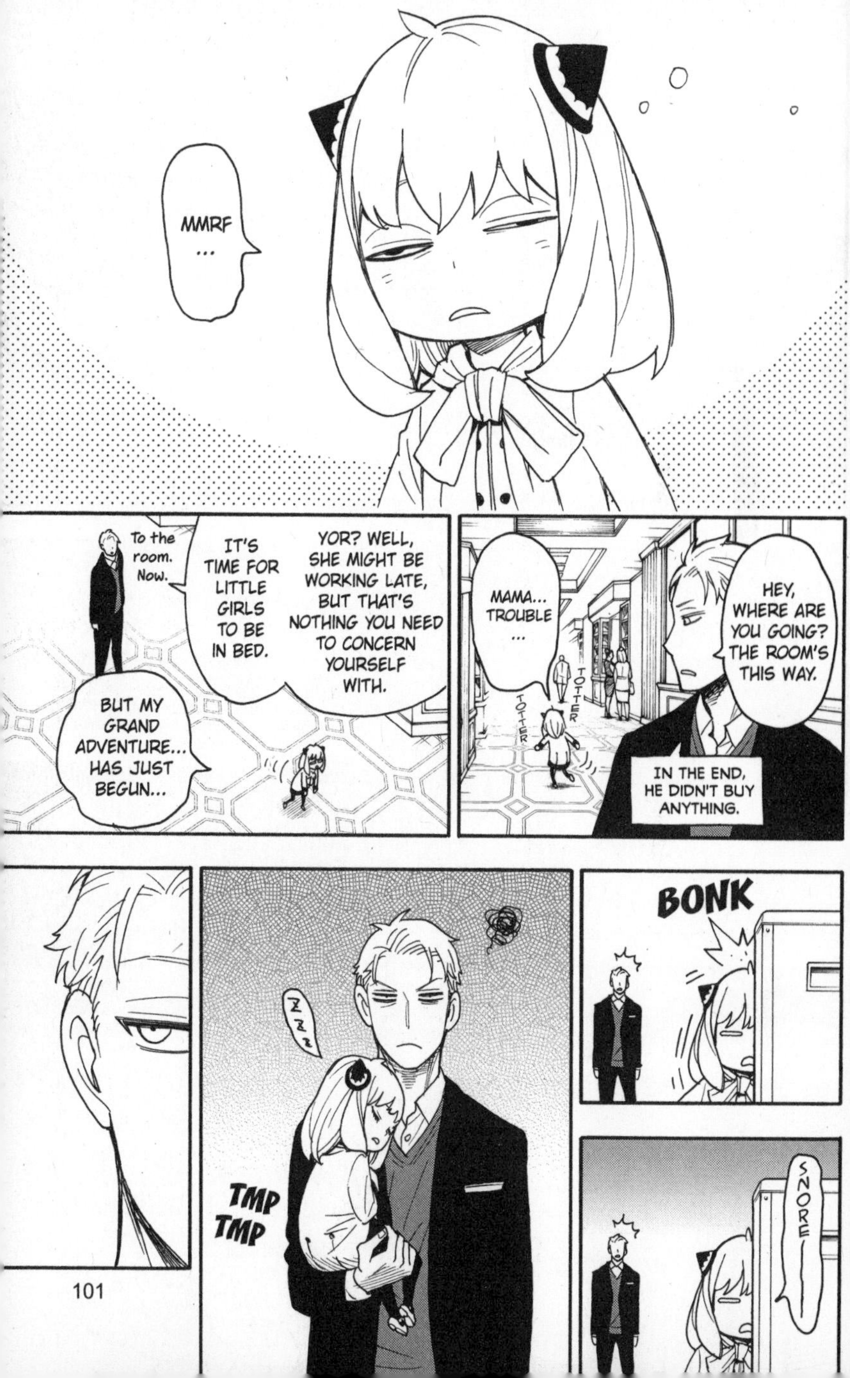
MMRF...
HEY, WHERE ARE YOU GOING? THE ROOM'S THIS WAY.
IN THE END, HE DIDN'T BUY ANYTHING.
MAMA... TROUBLE...
TOTTER
TOTTER
YOR? WELL, SHE MIGHT BE WORKING LATE, BUT THAT'S NOTHING YOU NEED TO CONCERN YOURSELF WITH.
IT'S TIME FOR LITTLE GIRLS TO BE IN BED.
To the room. Now.
BUT MY GRAND ADVENTURE... HAS JUST BEGUN...
BONK
SNORE—
ZZZ
TMP TMP

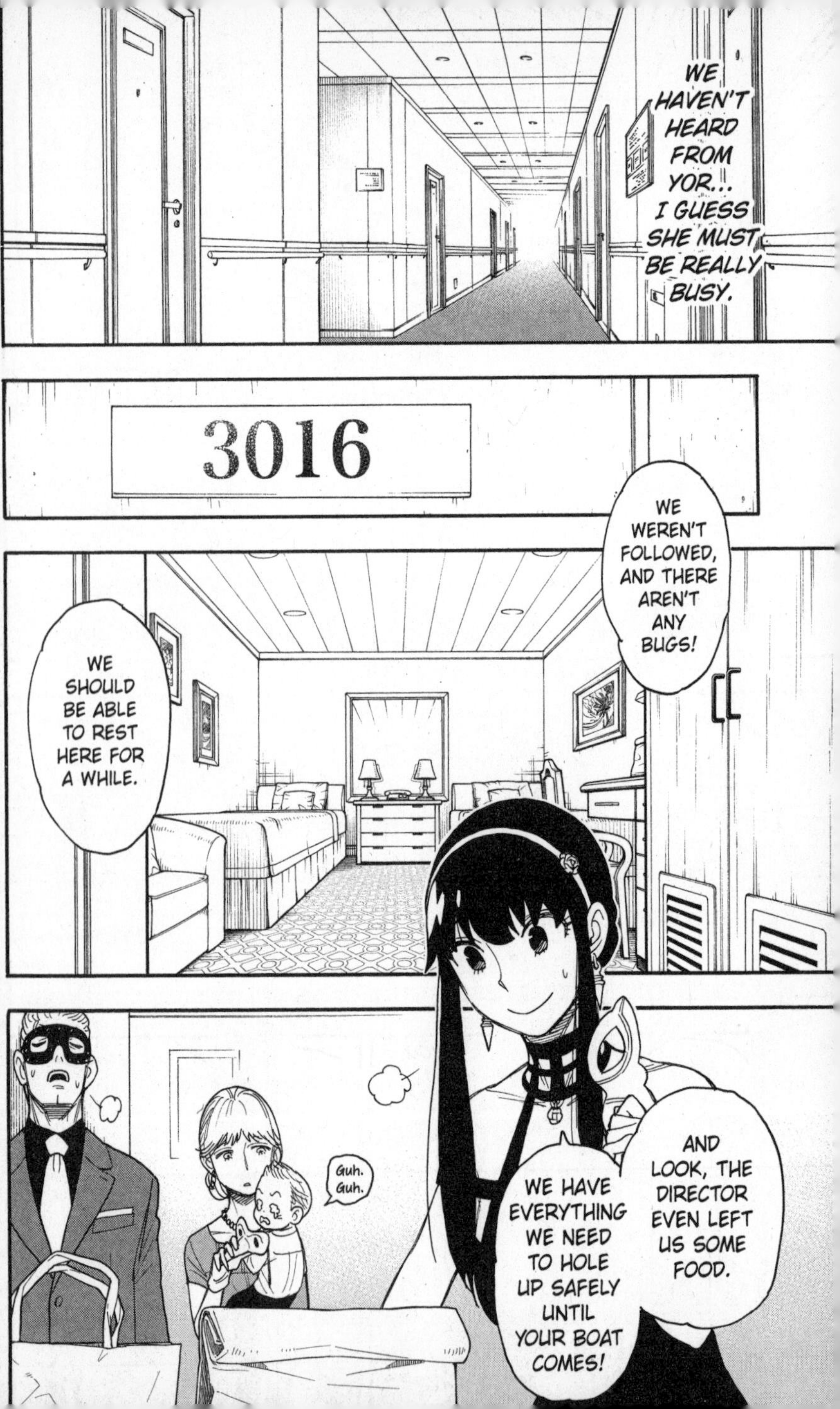
WE HAVEN'T HEARD FROM YOR... I GUESS SHE MUST BE REALLY BUSY.
3016
WE WEREN'T FOLLOWED, AND THERE AREN'T ANY BUGS!
WE SHOULD BE ABLE TO REST HERE FOR A WHILE.
AND LOOK, THE DIRECTOR EVEN LEFT US SOME FOOD.
WE HAVE EVERYTHING WE NEED TO HOLE UP SAFELY UNTIL YOUR BOAT COMES!
Guh. Guh.

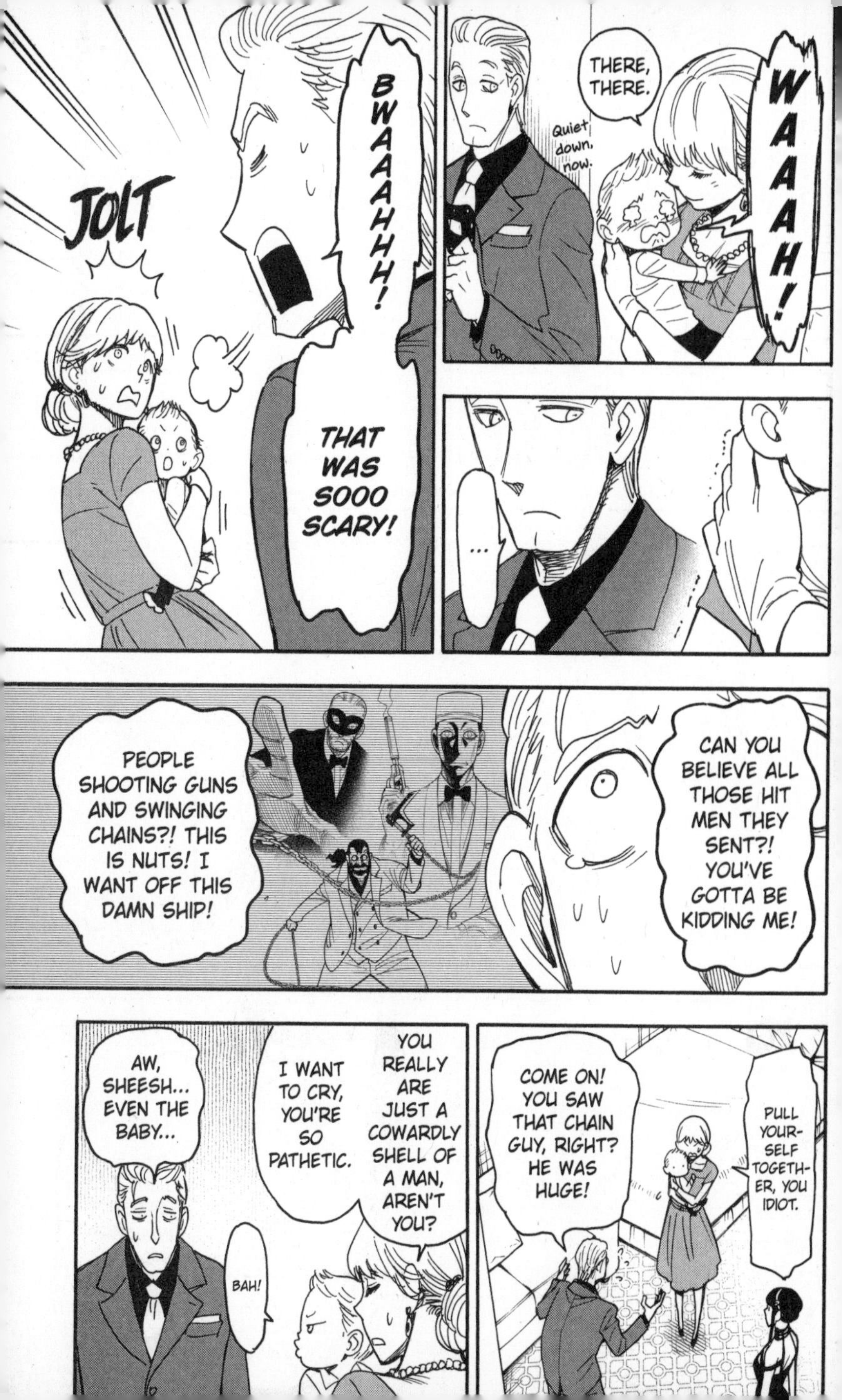
WAAAAH!
THERE, THERE.
Quiet down, now.
...
BWAAAAHHH!
JOLT
THAT WAS SOOO SCARY!
CAN YOU BELIEVE ALL THOSE HIT MEN THEY SENT?! YOU'VE GOTTA BE KIDDING ME!
PEOPLE SHOOTING GUNS AND SWINGING CHAINS?! THIS IS NUTS! I WANT OFF THIS DAMN SHIP!
PULL YOURSELF TOGETHER, YOU IDIOT.
COME ON! YOU SAW THAT CHAIN GUY, RIGHT? HE WAS HUGE!
YOU REALLY ARE JUST A COWARDLY SHELL OF A MAN, AREN'T YOU?
I WANT TO CRY, YOU'RE SO PATHETIC.
AW, SHEESH... EVEN THE BABY...
BAH!

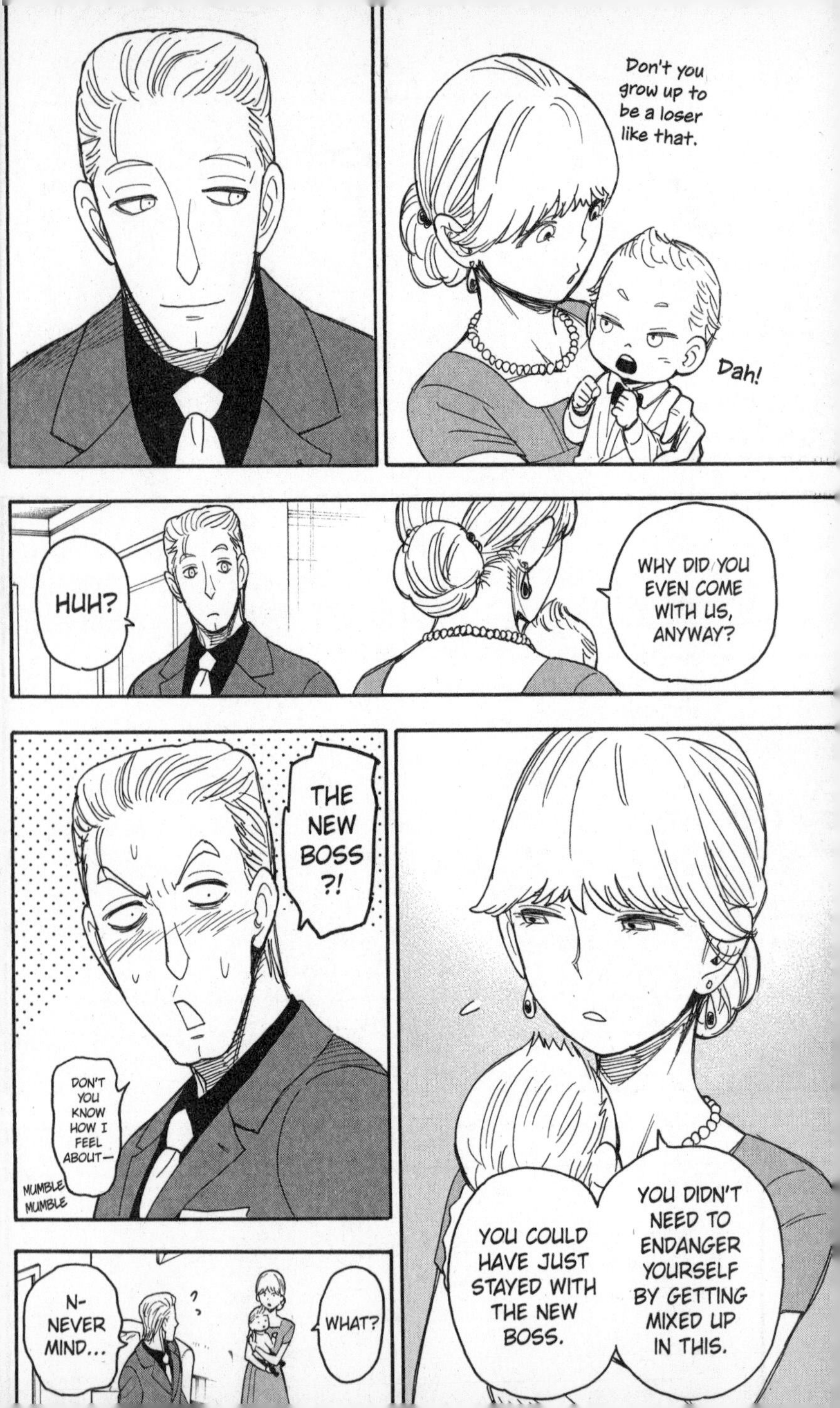
Don't you grow up to be a loser like that.
Dah!
WHY DID YOU EVEN COME WITH US, ANYWAY?
HUH?
YOU DIDN'T NEED TO ENDANGER YOURSELF BY GETTING MIXED UP IN THIS.
YOU COULD HAVE JUST STAYED WITH THE NEW BOSS.
THE NEW BOSS ?!
DON'T YOU KNOW HOW I FEEL ABOUT—
MUMBLE MUMBLE
WHAT?
N-NEVER MIND...

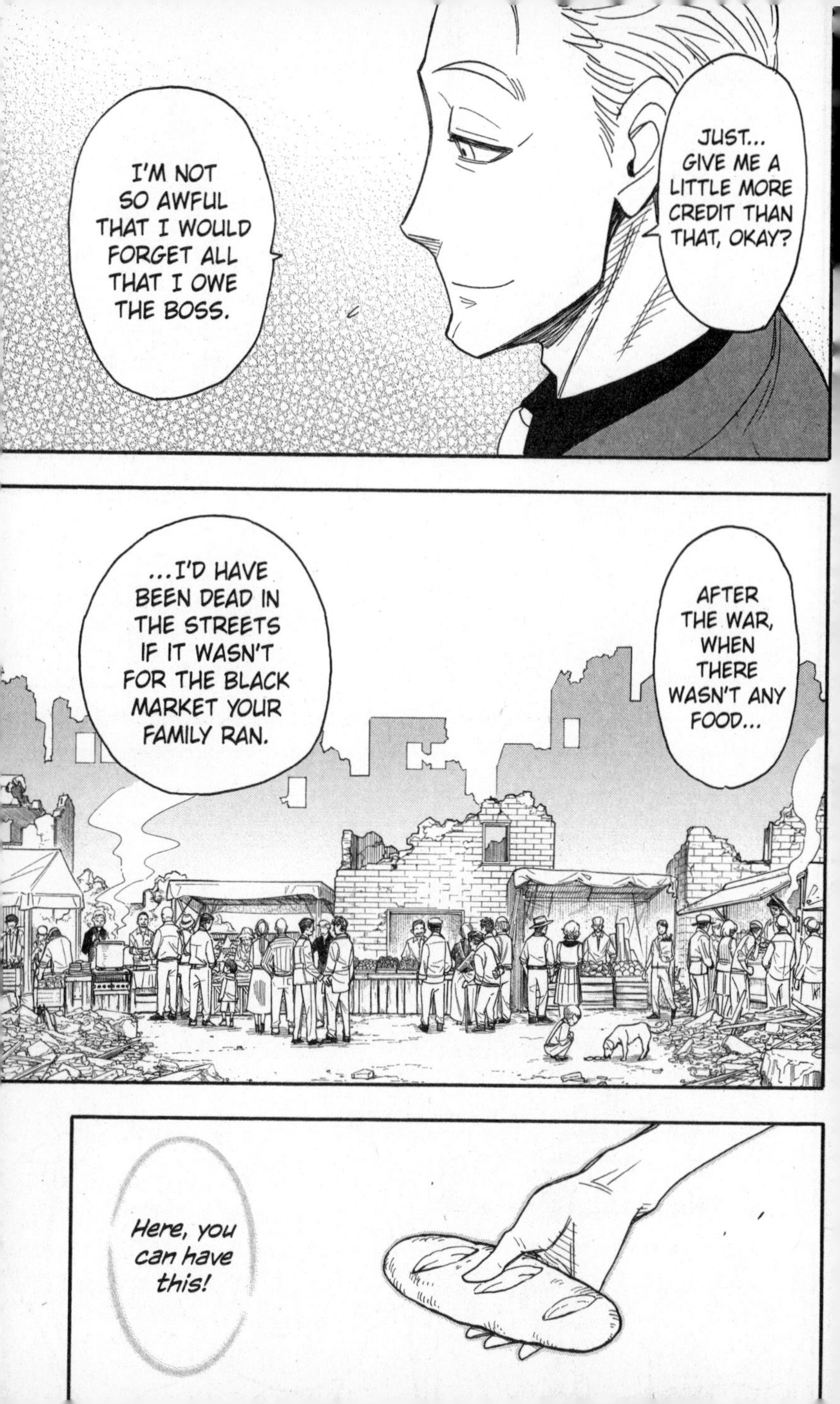
JUST... GIVE ME A LITTLE MORE CREDIT THAN THAT, OKAY?
I'M NOT SO AWFUL THAT I WOULD FORGET ALL THAT I OWE THE BOSS.
AFTER THE WAR, WHEN THERE WASN'T ANY FOOD...
...I'D HAVE BEEN DEAD IN THE STREETS IF IT WASN'T FOR THE BLACK MARKET YOUR FAMILY RAN.
Here, you can have this!

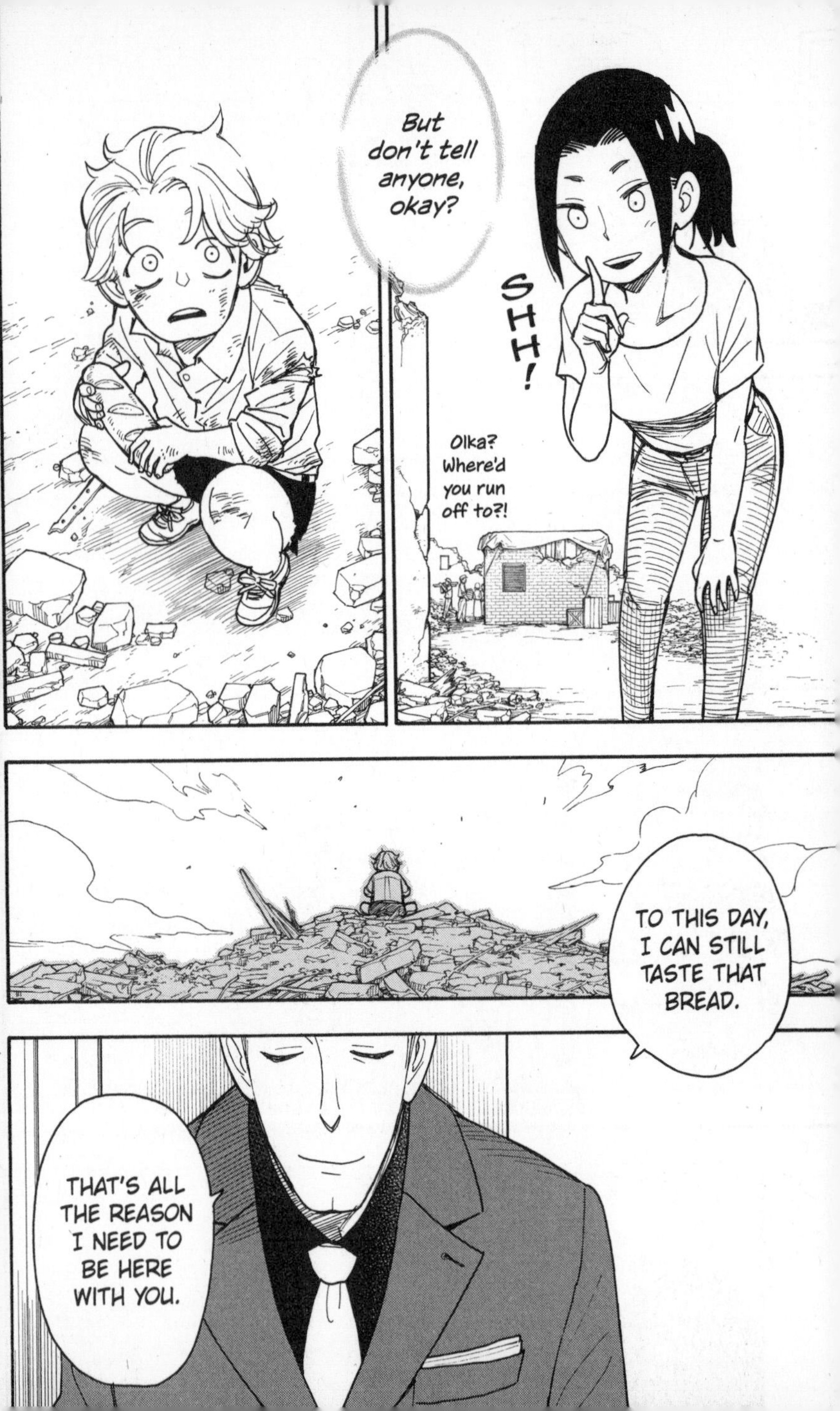
But don't tell anyone, okay?
SHH!
Olka? Where'd you run off to?!
TO THIS DAY, I CAN STILL TASTE THAT BREAD.
THAT'S ALL THE REASON I NEED TO BE HERE WITH YOU.

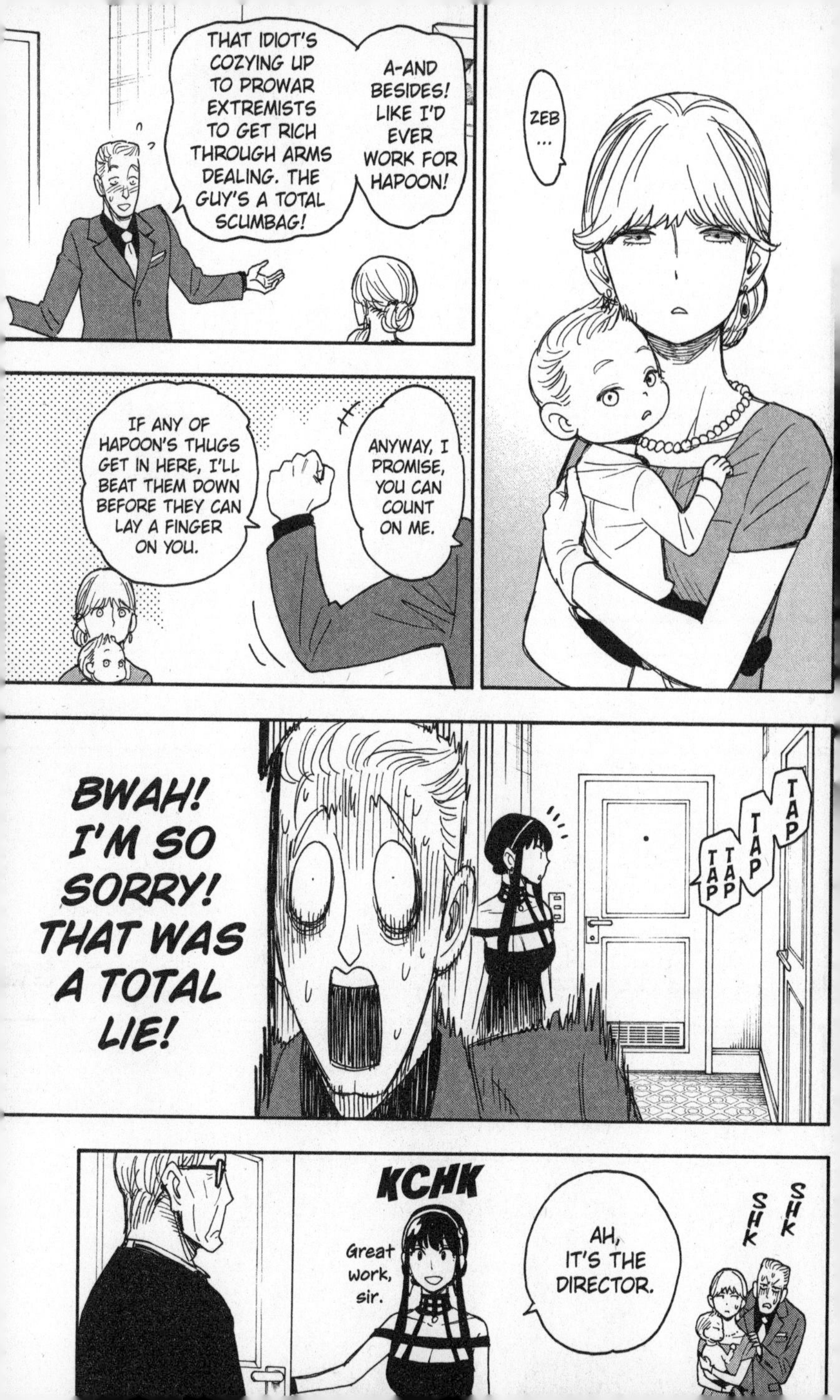
ZEB ...
A-AND BESIDES! LIKE I'D EVER WORK FOR HAPOON!
THAT IDIOT'S COZYING UP TO PROWAR EXTREMISTS TO GET RICH THROUGH ARMS DEALING. THE GUY'S A TOTAL SCUMBAG!
ANYWAY, I PROMISE, YOU CAN COUNT ON ME.
IF ANY OF HAPOON'S THUGS GET IN HERE, I'LL BEAT THEM DOWN BEFORE THEY CAN LAY A FINGER ON YOU.
TAP TAP TAP TAP
BWAH! I'M SO SORRY! THAT WAS A TOTAL LIE!
SHK SHK
AH, IT'S THE DIRECTOR.
KCHK
Great work, sir.

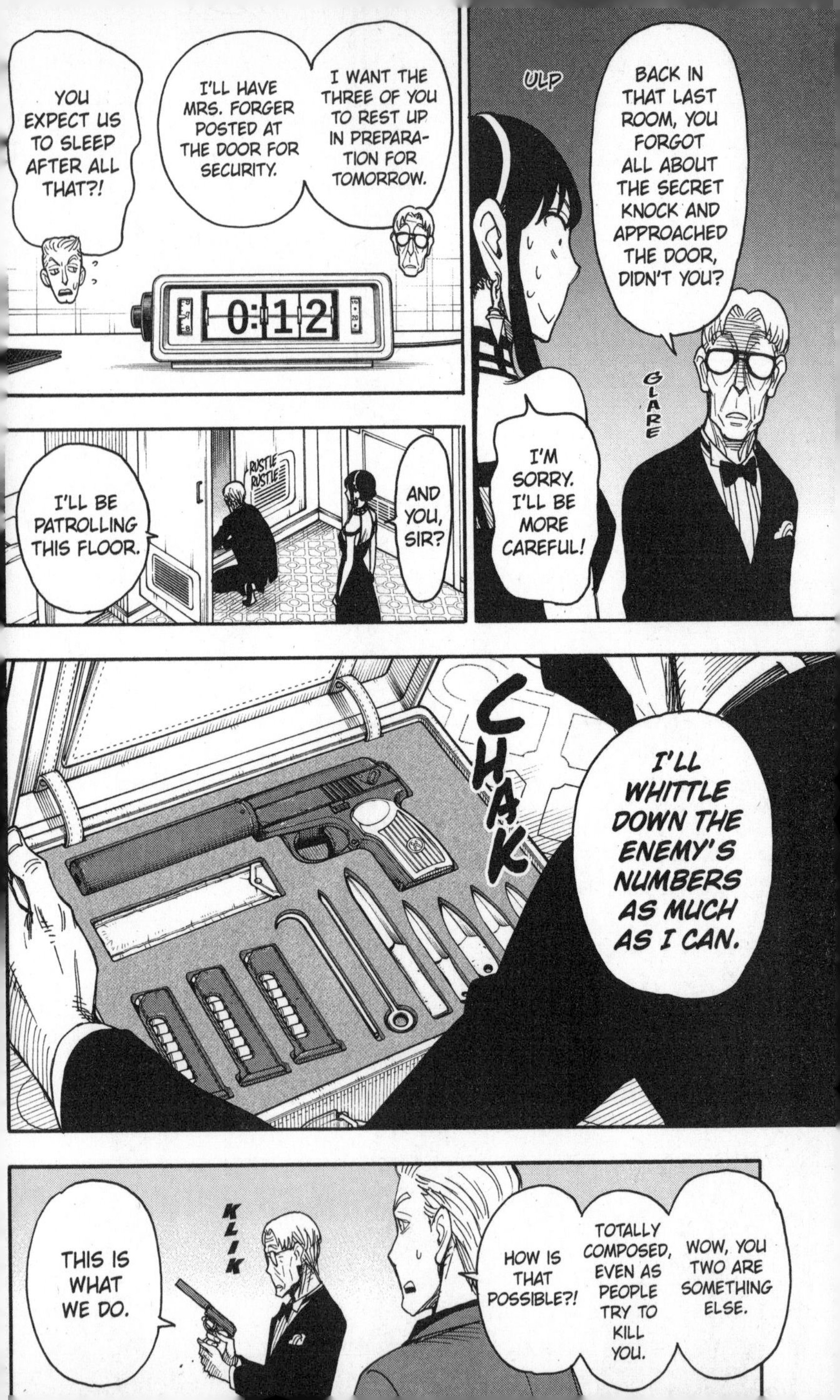
ULP
BACK IN THAT LAST ROOM, YOU FORGOT ALL ABOUT THE SECRET KNOCK AND APPROACHED THE DOOR, DIDN'T YOU?
GLARE
I'M SORRY. I'LL BE MORE CAREFUL!
I WANT THE THREE OF YOU TO REST UP IN PREPARATION FOR TOMORROW.
I'LL HAVE MRS. FORGER POSTED AT THE DOOR FOR SECURITY.
YOU EXPECT US TO SLEEP AFTER ALL THAT?!
0:12
AND YOU, SIR?
RUSTLE RUSTLE
I'LL BE PATROLLING THIS FLOOR.
CHAK
I'LL WHITTLE DOWN THE ENEMY'S NUMBERS AS MUCH AS I CAN.
WOW, YOU TWO ARE SOMETHING ELSE.
TOTALLY COMPOSED, EVEN AS PEOPLE TRY TO KILL YOU.
HOW IS THAT POSSIBLE?!
KLIK
THIS IS WHAT WE DO.

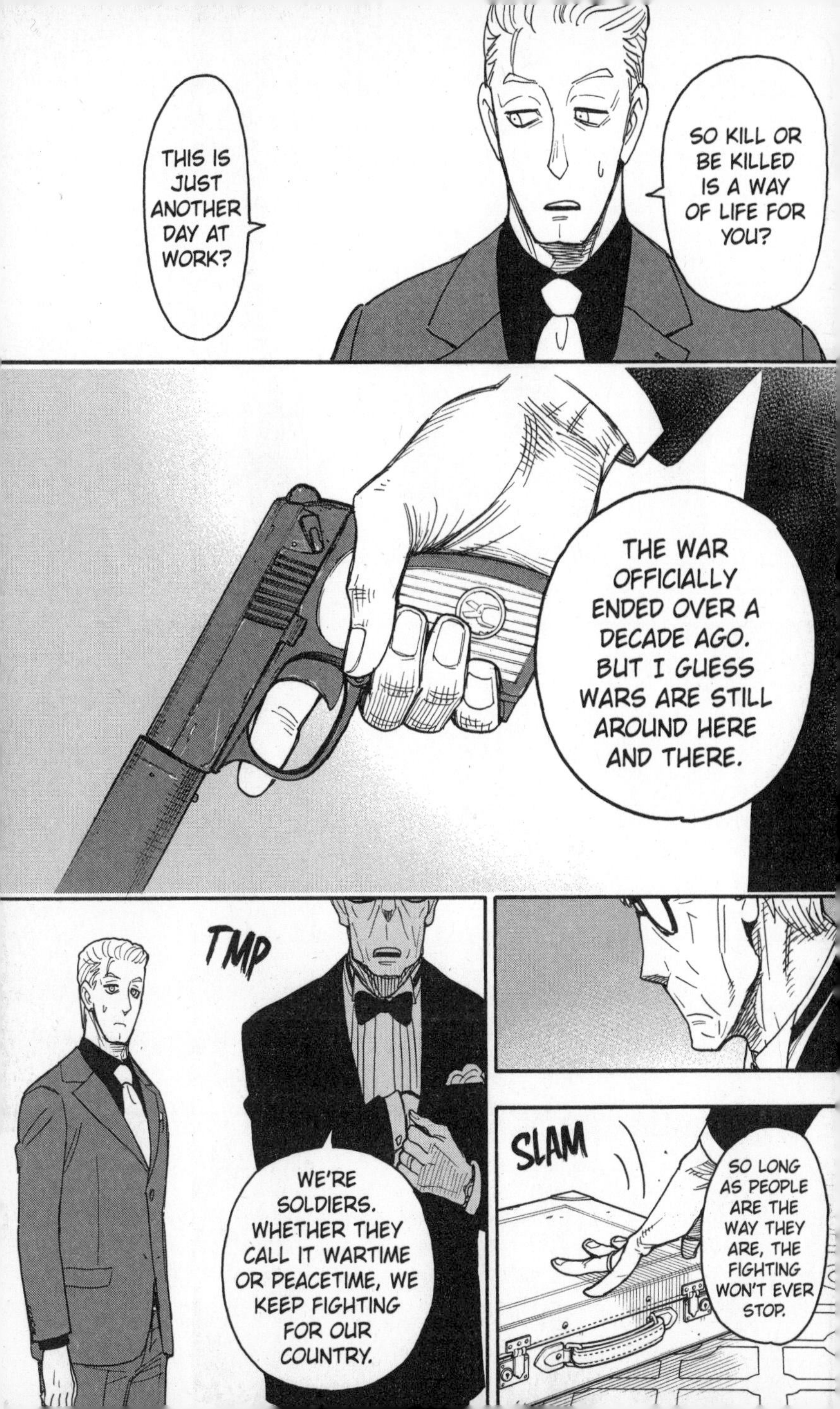
SO KILL OR BE KILLED IS A WAY OF LIFE FOR YOU?
THIS IS JUST ANOTHER DAY AT WORK?
THE WAR OFFICIALLY ENDED OVER A DECADE AGO. BUT I GUESS WARS ARE STILL AROUND HERE AND THERE.
SLAM
SO LONG AS PEOPLE ARE THE WAY THEY ARE, THE FIGHTING WON'T EVER STOP.
TMP
WE'RE SOLDIERS. WHETHER THEY CALL IT WARTIME OR PEACETIME, WE KEEP FIGHTING FOR OUR COUNTRY.

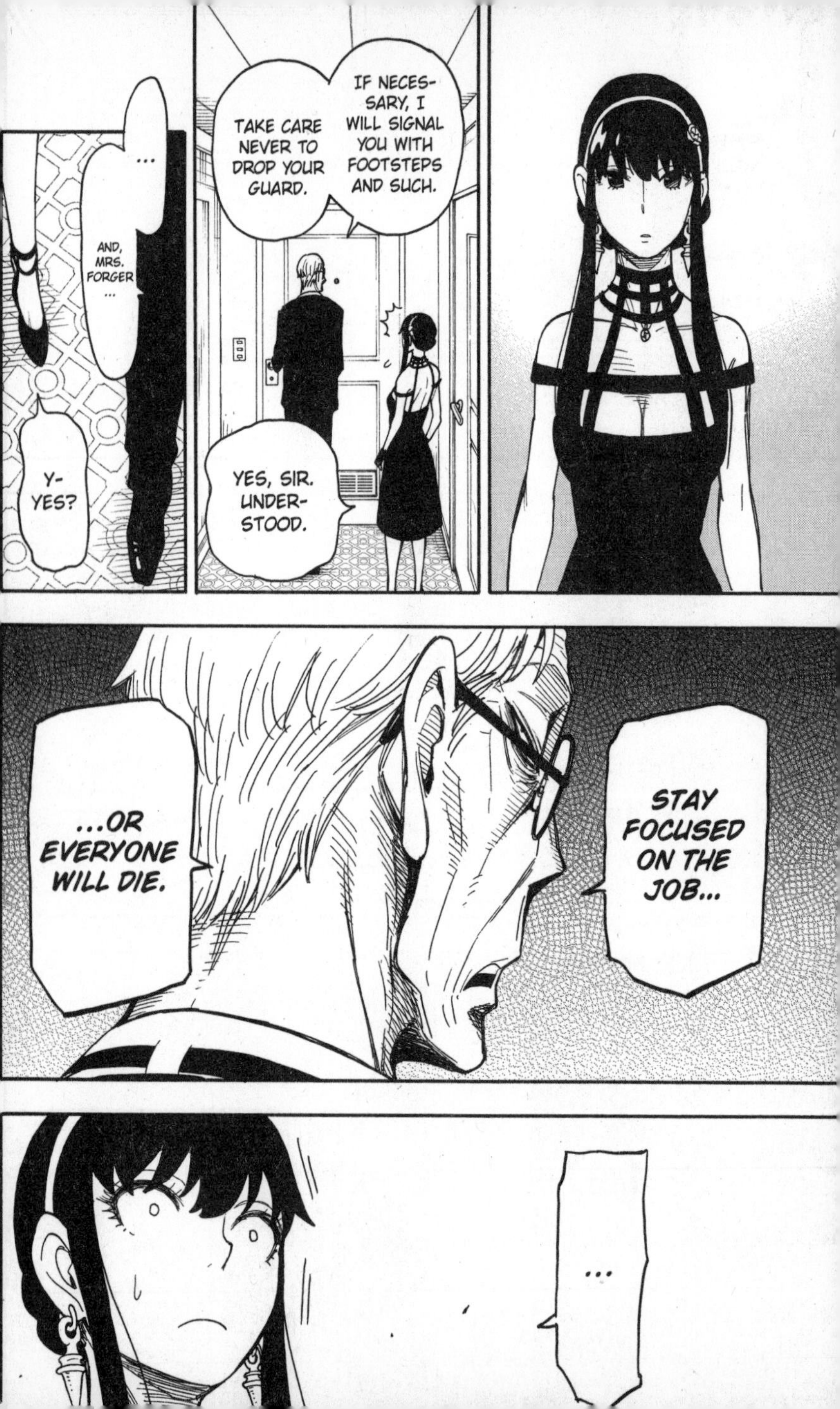
IF NECES-SARY, I WILL SIGNAL YOU WITH FOOTSTEPS AND SUCH.
TAKE CARE NEVER TO DROP YOUR GUARD.
YES, SIR. UNDER-STOOD.
...
AND, MRS. FORGER ...
Y-YES?
STAY FOCUSED ON THE JOB...
...OR EVERYONE WILL DIE.
...

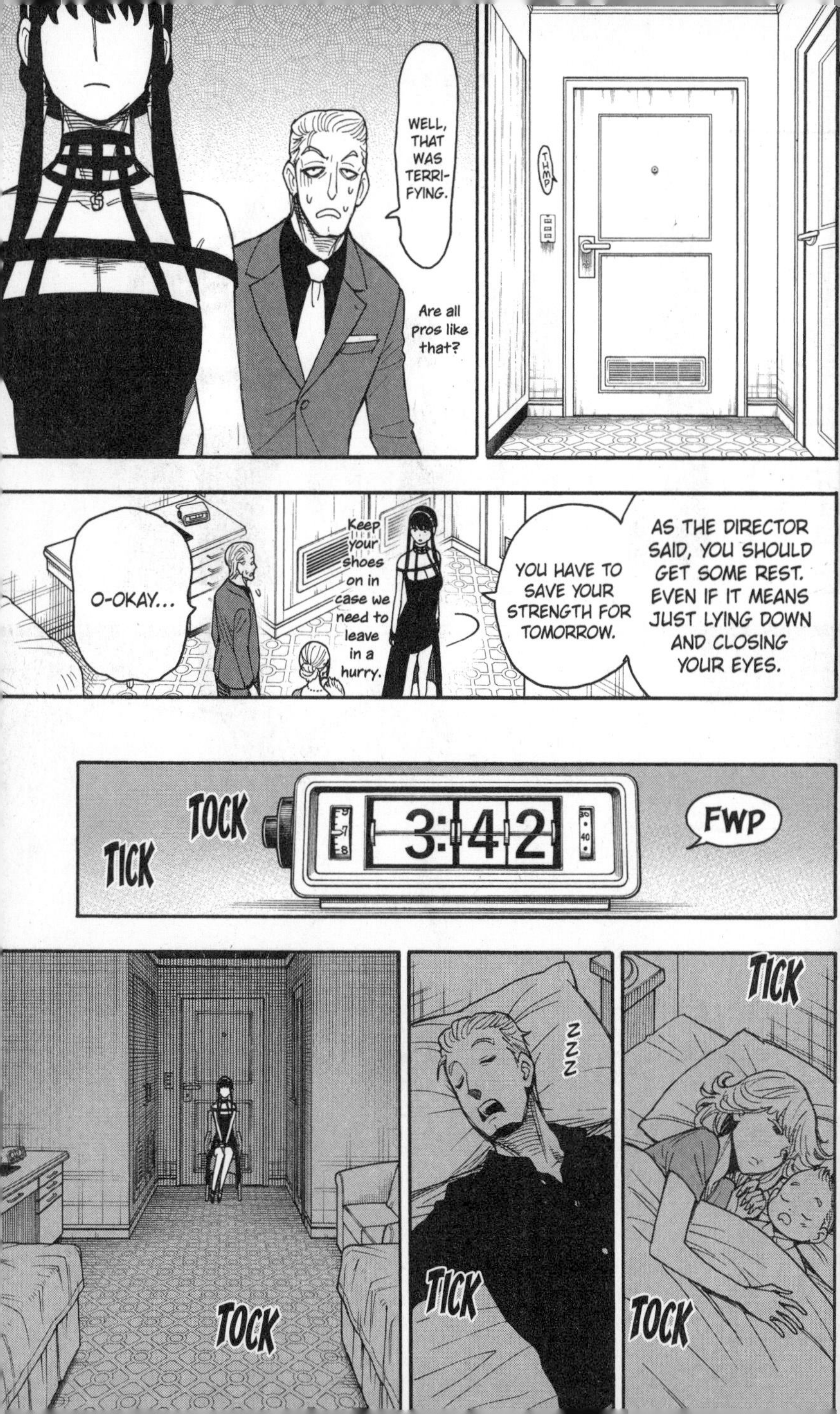

THMP
WELL, THAT WAS TERRI-FYING.
Are all pros like that?
AS THE DIRECTOR SAID, YOU SHOULD GET SOME REST. EVEN IF IT MEANS JUST LYING DOWN AND CLOSING YOUR EYES.
YOU HAVE TO SAVE YOUR STRENGTH FOR TOMORROW.
Keep your shoes on in case we need to leave in a hurry.
O-OKAY...
FWP
3:42
TOCK
TICK
TICK
TOCK
ZZZ
TICK
TOCK

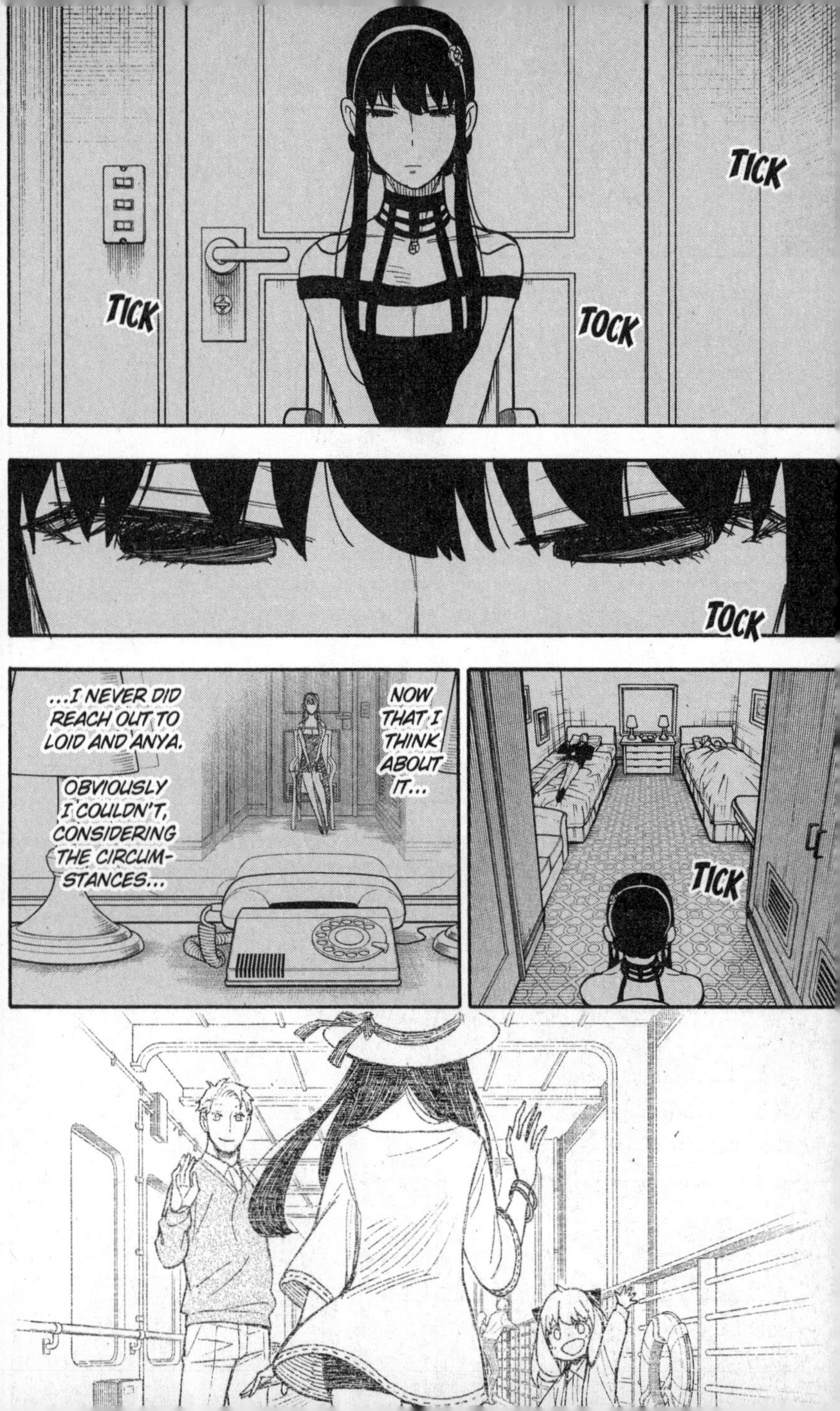
TICK
TOCK
TICK
TOCK
TICK
NOW THAT I THINK ABOUT IT...
...I NEVER DID REACH OUT TO LOID AND ANYA.
OBVIOUSLY I COULDN'T, CONSIDERING THE CIRCUM-STANCES...

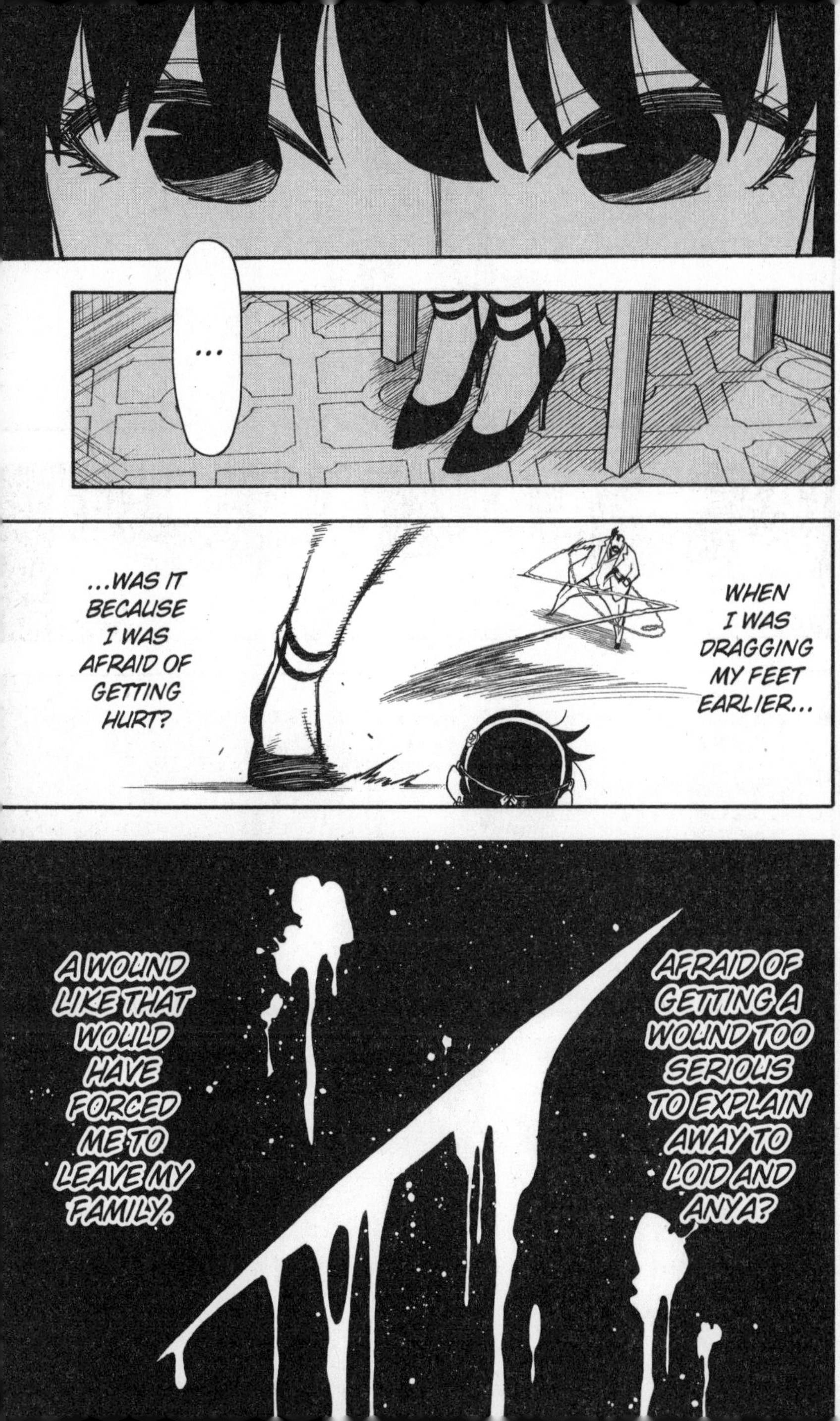
...
WHEN I WAS DRAGGING MY FEET EARLIER...
...WAS IT BECAUSE I WAS AFRAID OF GETTING HURT?
AFRAID OF GETTING A WOUND TOO SERIOUS TO EXPLAIN AWAY TO LOID AND ANYA?
A WOUND LIKE THAT WOULD HAVE FORCED ME TO LEAVE MY FAMILY.

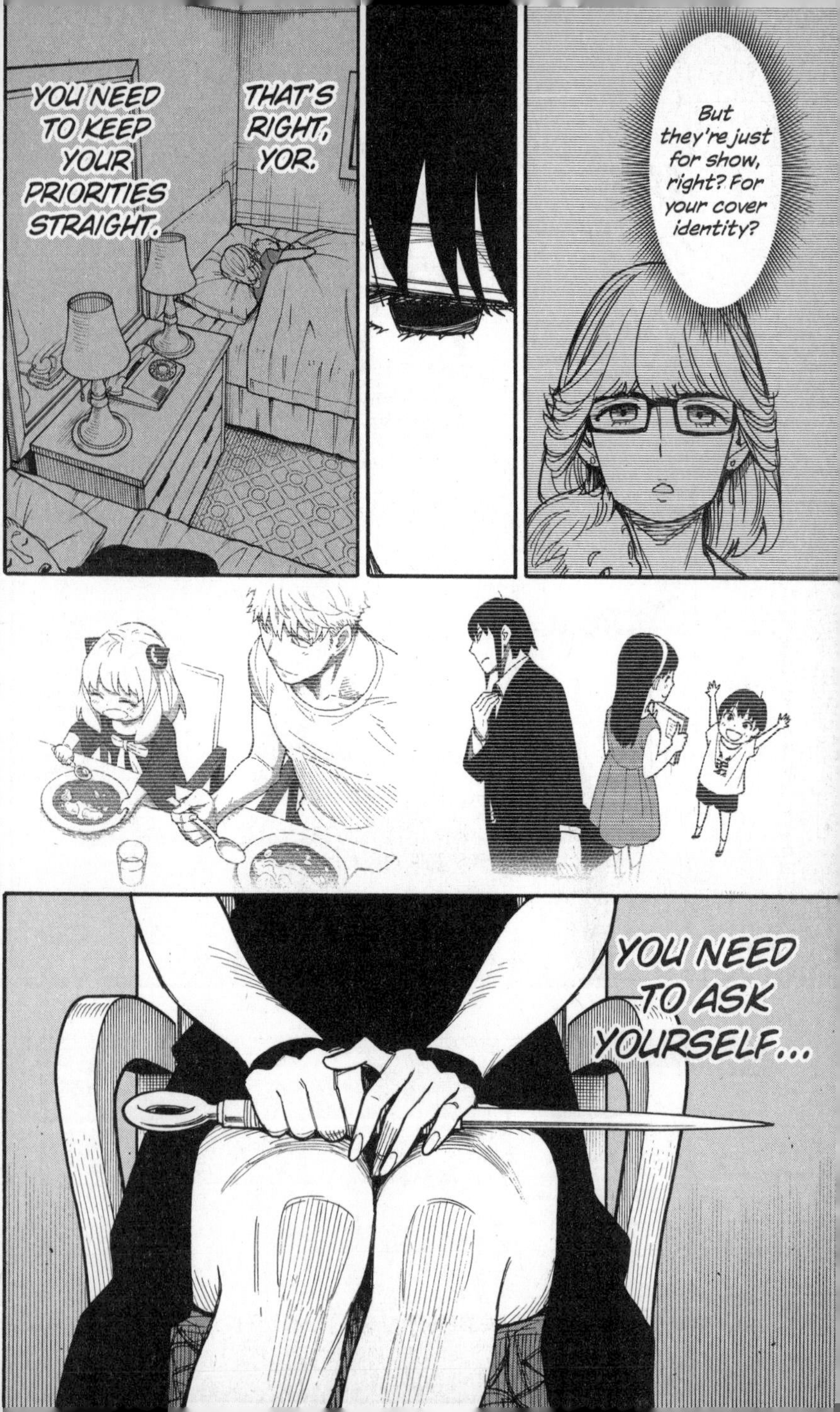
But they're just for show, right? For your cover identity?
THAT'S RIGHT, YOR.
YOU NEED TO KEEP YOUR PRIORITIES STRAIGHT.
YOU NEED TO ASK YOURSELF...

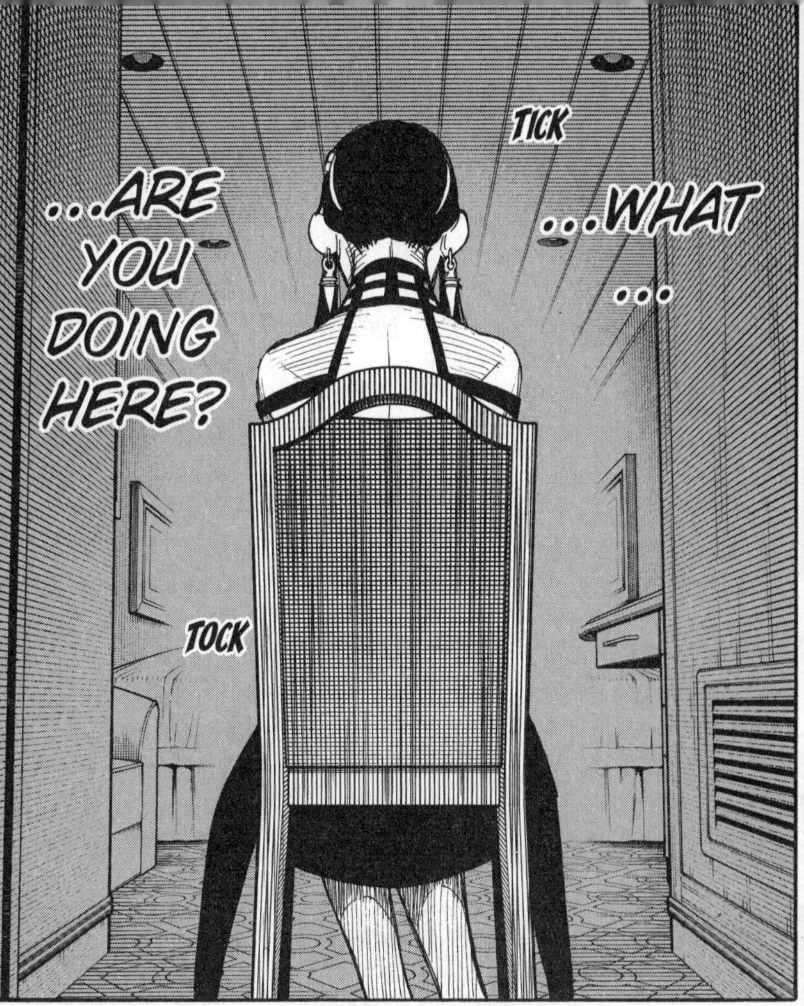
TICK
...WHAT...
...ARE YOU DOING HERE?
TOCK

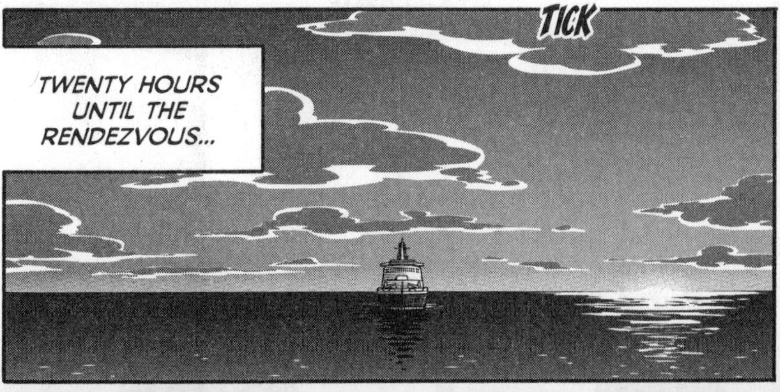
TICK
TWENTY HOURS UNTIL THE RENDEZVOUS...

SPY×FAMILY

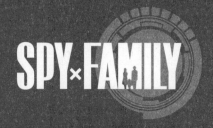

MISSION 50

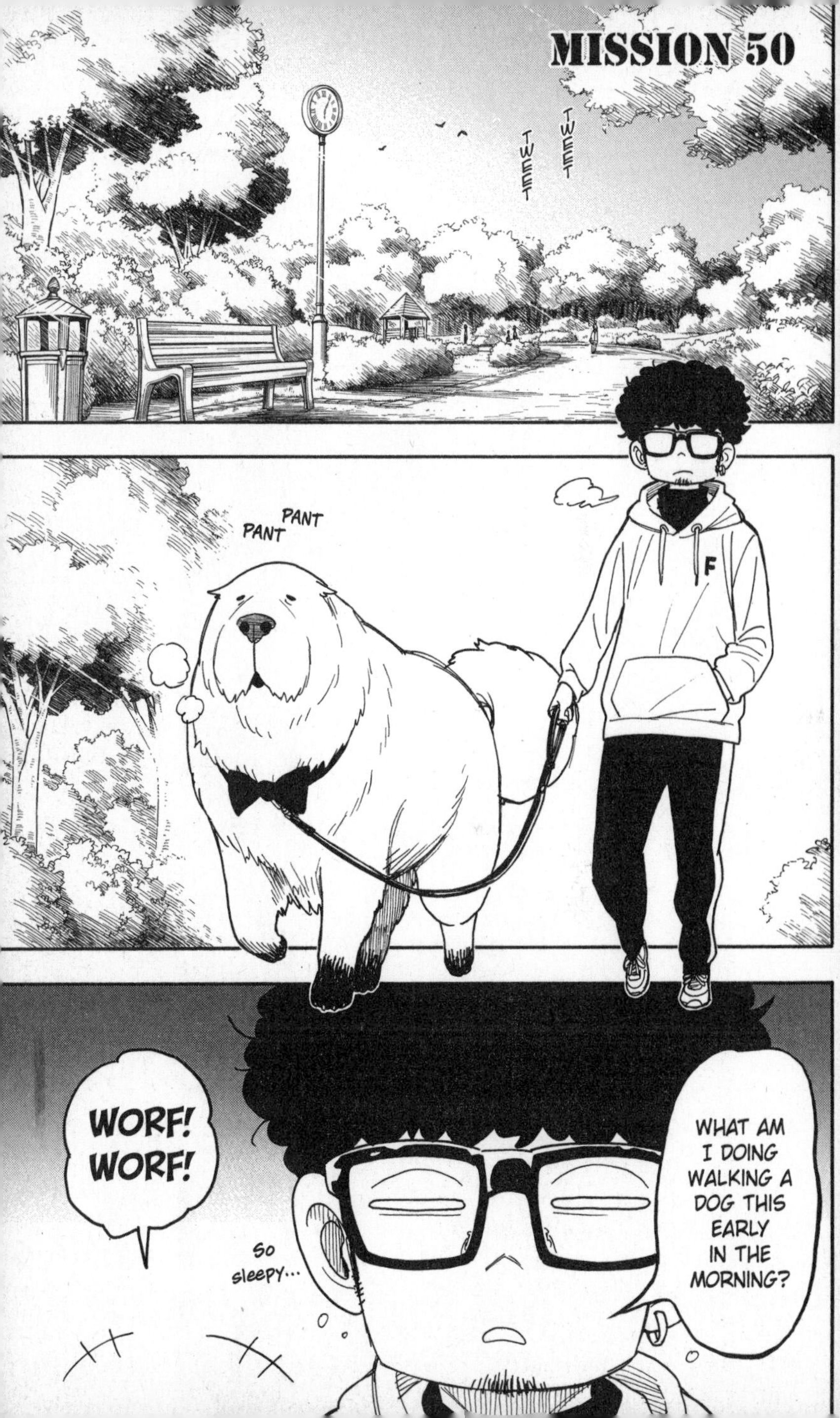
TWEET
TWEET
PANT
PANT
WHAT AM I DOING WALKING A DOG THIS EARLY IN THE MORNING?
So sleepy...
WORF! WORF!

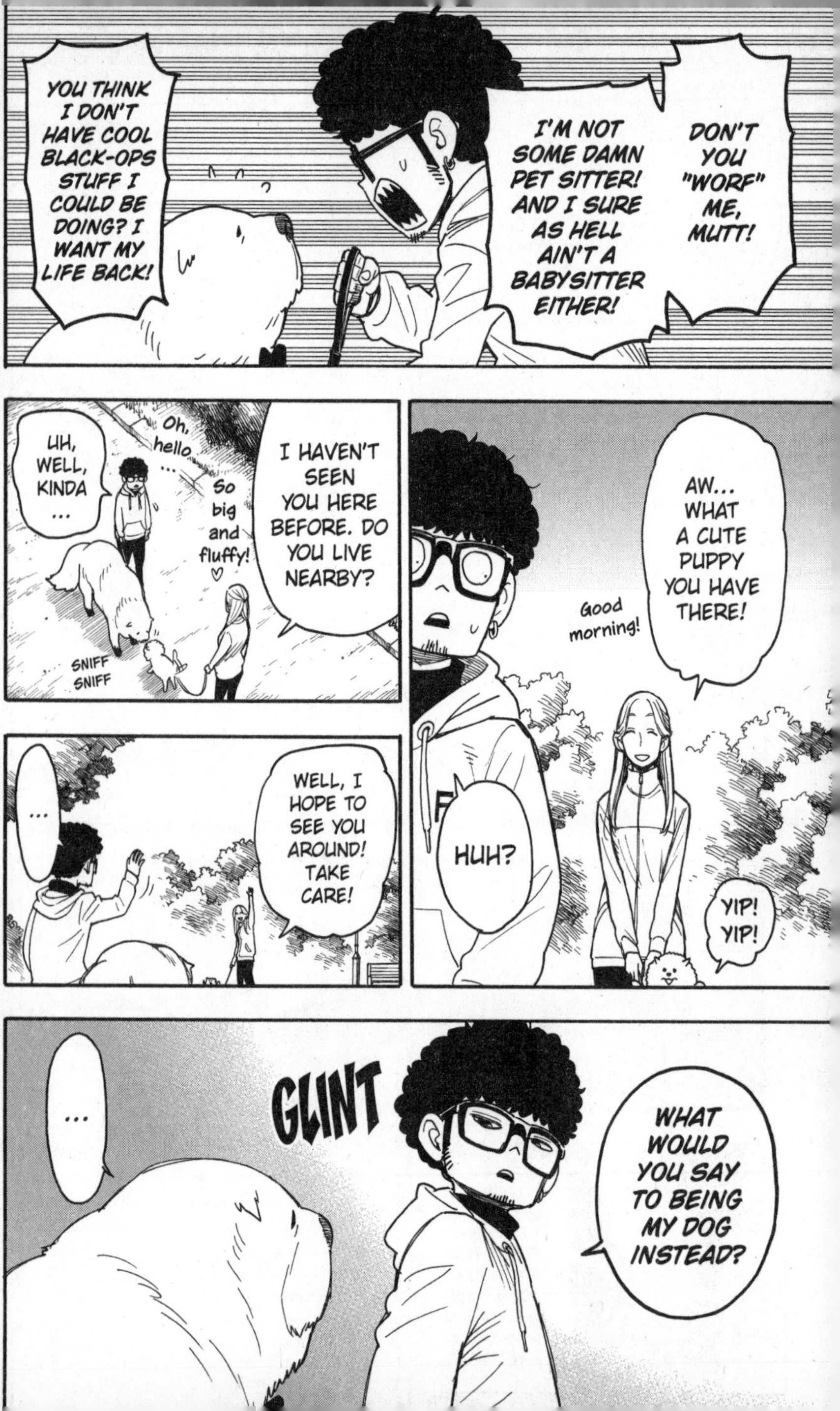

DON'T YOU "WORF" ME, MUTT!
I'M NOT SOME DAMN PET SITTER! AND I SURE AS HELL AIN'T A BABYSITTER EITHER!
YOU THINK I DON'T HAVE COOL BLACK-OPS STUFF I COULD BE DOING? I WANT MY LIFE BACK!
AW... WHAT A CUTE PUPPY YOU HAVE THERE!
Good morning!
HUH?
YIP! YIP!
I HAVEN'T SEEN YOU HERE BEFORE. DO YOU LIVE NEARBY?
So big and fluffy! ♡
Oh, hello ...
UH, WELL, KINDA ...
SNIFF SNIFF
WELL, I HOPE TO SEE YOU AROUND! TAKE CARE!
...
WHAT WOULD YOU SAY TO BEING MY DOG INSTEAD?
GLINT
...

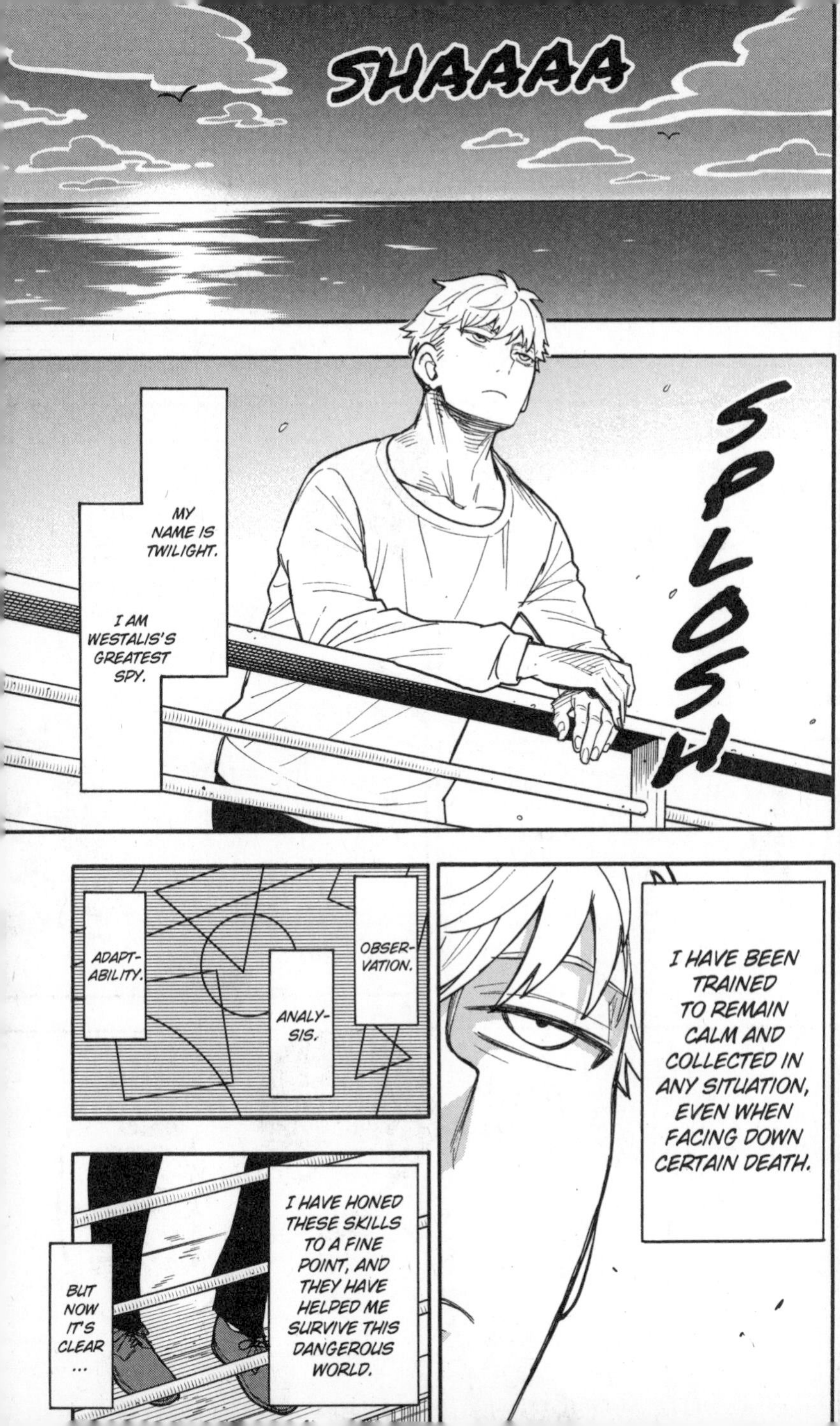
SHAAAA
SPLOSH
MY NAME IS TWILIGHT.
I AM WESTALIS'S GREATEST SPY.
I HAVE BEEN TRAINED TO REMAIN CALM AND COLLECTED IN ANY SITUATION, EVEN WHEN FACING DOWN CERTAIN DEATH.
OBSERVATION.
ANALYSIS.
ADAPTABILITY.
I HAVE HONED THESE SKILLS TO A FINE POINT, AND THEY HAVE HELPED ME SURVIVE THIS DANGEROUS WORLD.
BUT NOW IT'S CLEAR ...

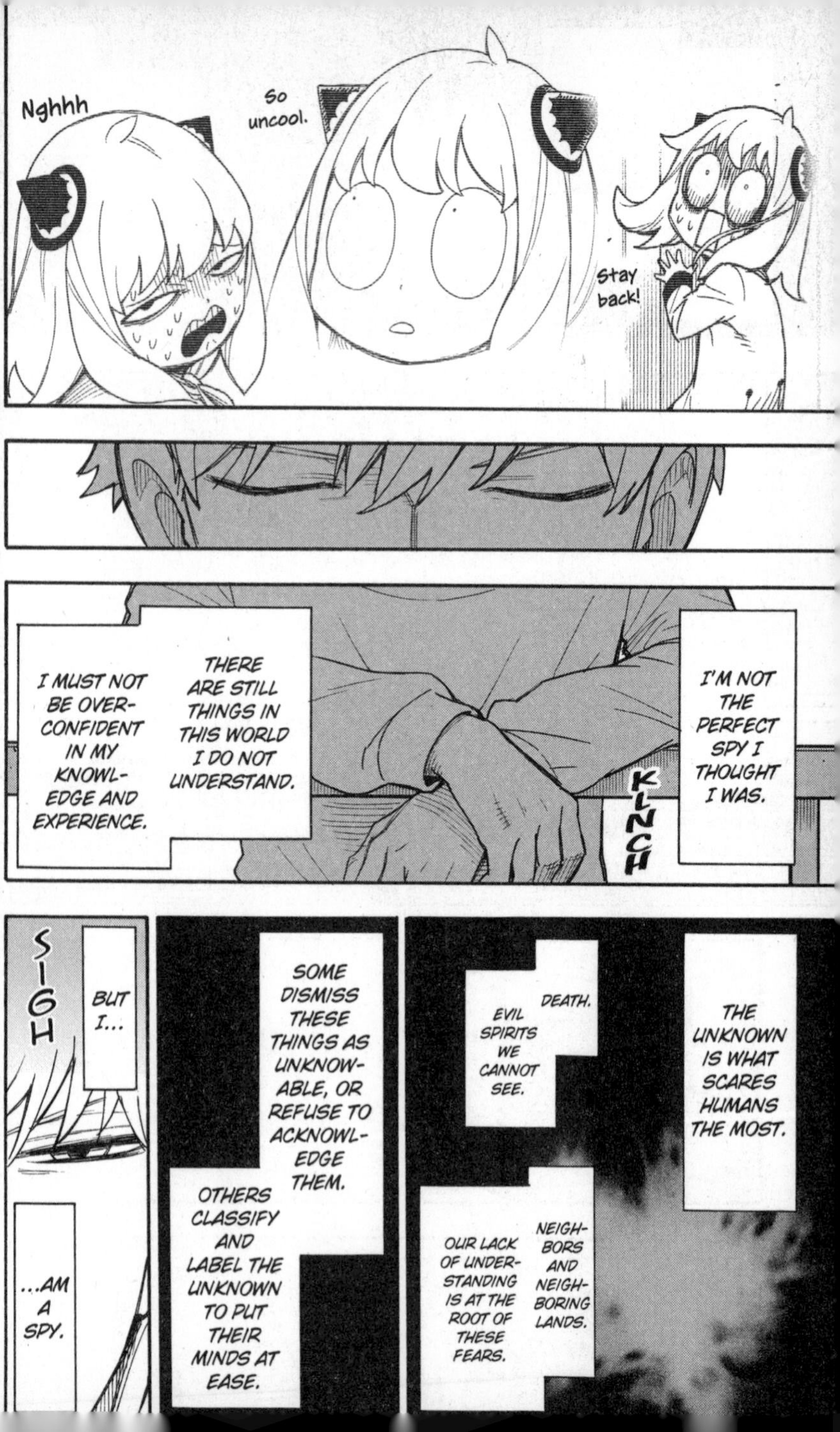

Stay back!
So uncool.
Nghhh
I'M NOT THE PERFECT SPY I THOUGHT I WAS.
KLINCH
THERE ARE STILL THINGS IN THIS WORLD I DO NOT UNDERSTAND.
I MUST NOT BE OVER-CONFIDENT IN MY KNOWL-EDGE AND EXPERIENCE.
THE UNKNOWN IS WHAT SCARES HUMANS THE MOST.
DEATH.
EVIL SPIRITS WE CANNOT SEE.
NEIGH-BORS AND NEIGH-BORING LANDS.
OUR LACK OF UNDER-STANDING IS AT THE ROOT OF THESE FEARS.
SOME DISMISS THESE THINGS AS UNKNOW-ABLE, OR REFUSE TO ACKNOWL-EDGE THEM.
OTHERS CLASSIFY AND LABEL THE UNKNOWN TO PUT THEIR MINDS AT EASE.
BUT I...
SIGH
...AM A SPY.

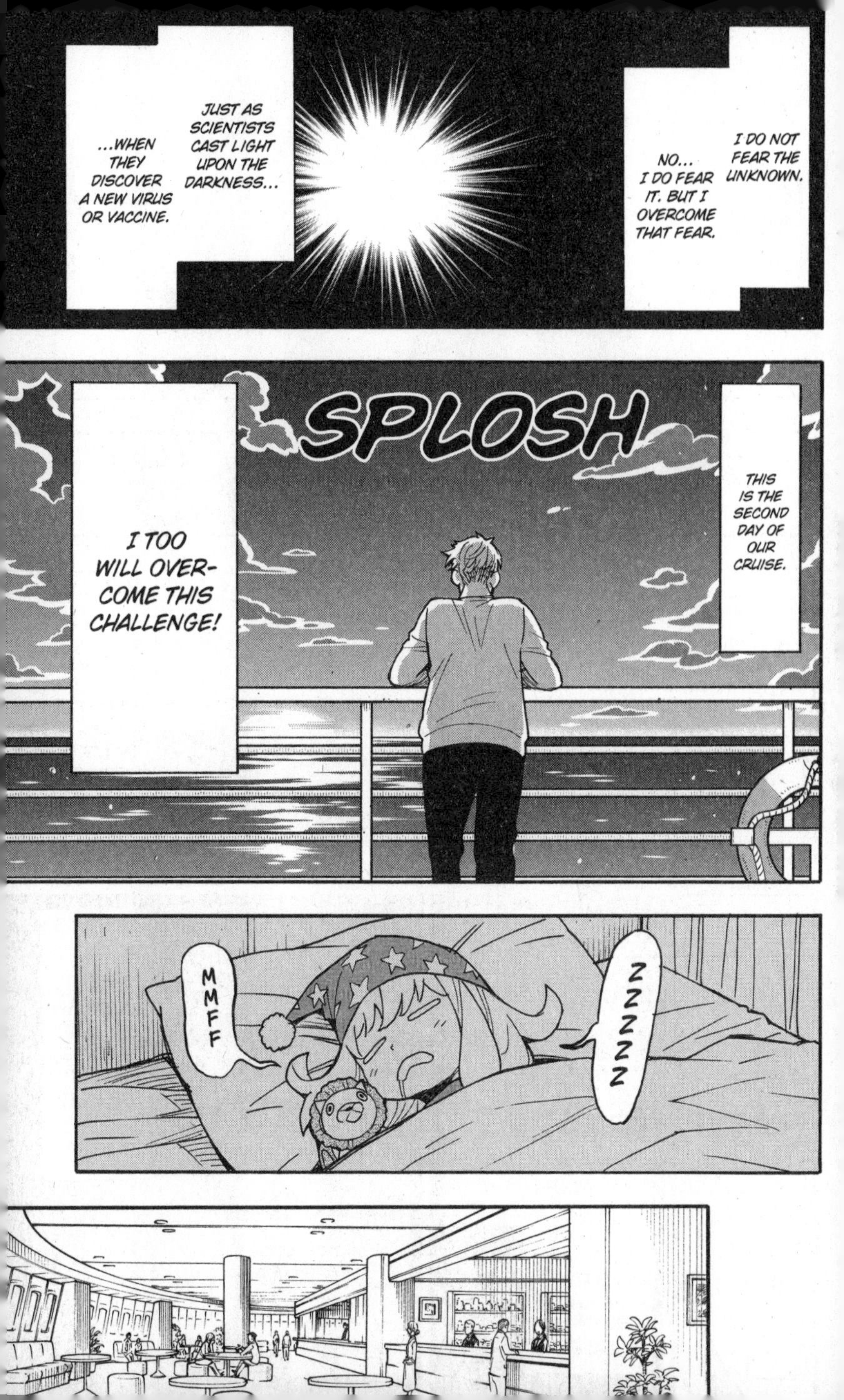
I DO NOT FEAR THE UNKNOWN.
NO... I DO FEAR IT. BUT I OVERCOME THAT FEAR.
JUST AS SCIENTISTS CAST LIGHT UPON THE DARKNESS...
...WHEN THEY DISCOVER A NEW VIRUS OR VACCINE.
THIS IS THE SECOND DAY OF OUR CRUISE.
SPLOSH
I TOO WILL OVER-COME THIS CHALLENGE!
ZZZZZ
MMFF

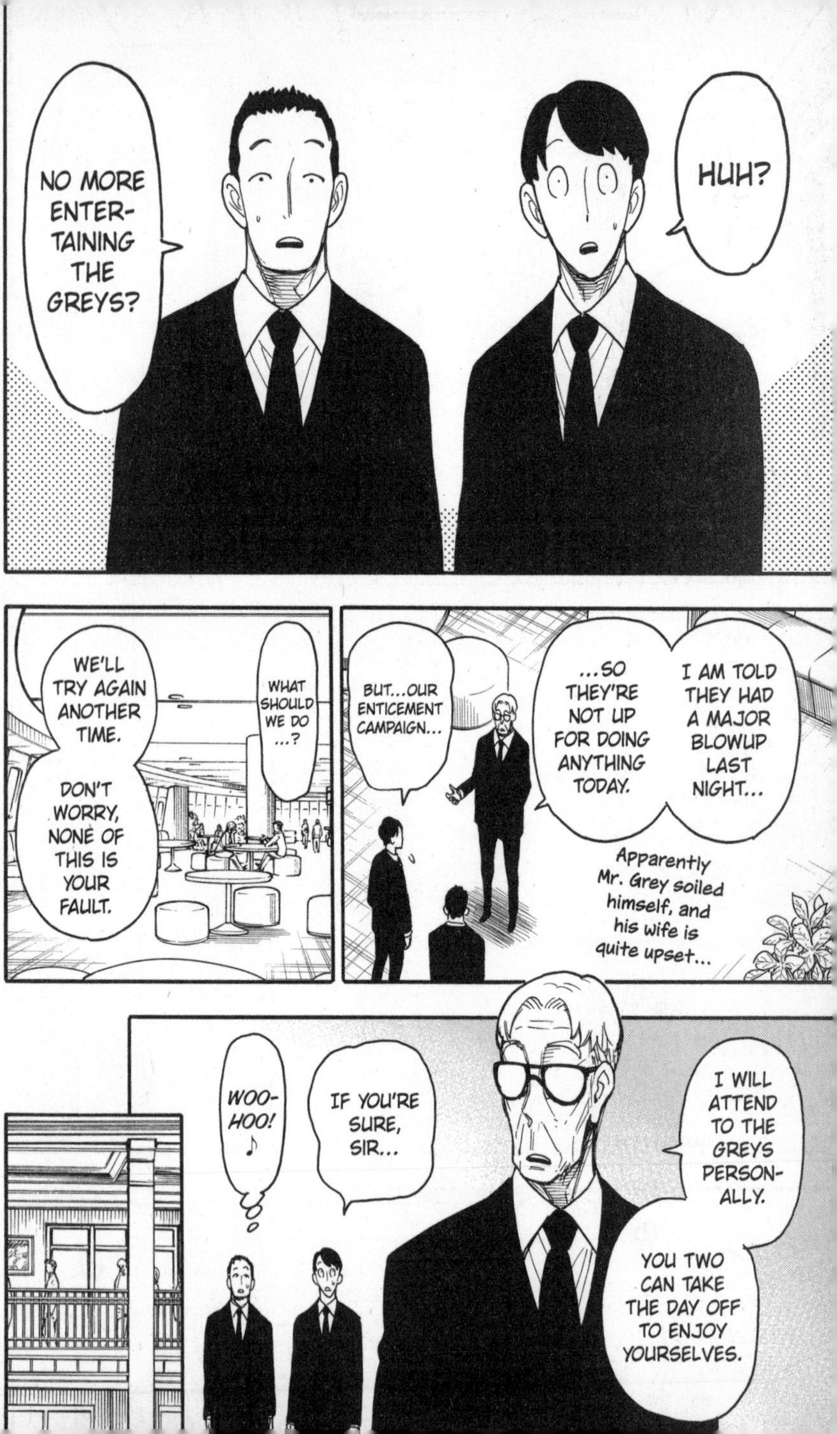
HUH?
NO MORE ENTERTAINING THE GREYS?
I AM TOLD THEY HAD A MAJOR BLOWUP LAST NIGHT...
...SO THEY'RE NOT UP FOR DOING ANYTHING TODAY.
Apparently Mr. Grey soiled himself, and his wife is quite upset...
BUT...OUR ENTICEMENT CAMPAIGN...
WHAT SHOULD WE DO ...?
WE'LL TRY AGAIN ANOTHER TIME.
DON'T WORRY, NONE OF THIS IS YOUR FAULT.
I WILL ATTEND TO THE GREYS PERSONALLY.
YOU TWO CAN TAKE THE DAY OFF TO ENJOY YOURSELVES.
IF YOU'RE SURE, SIR...
WOO-HOO! ♪

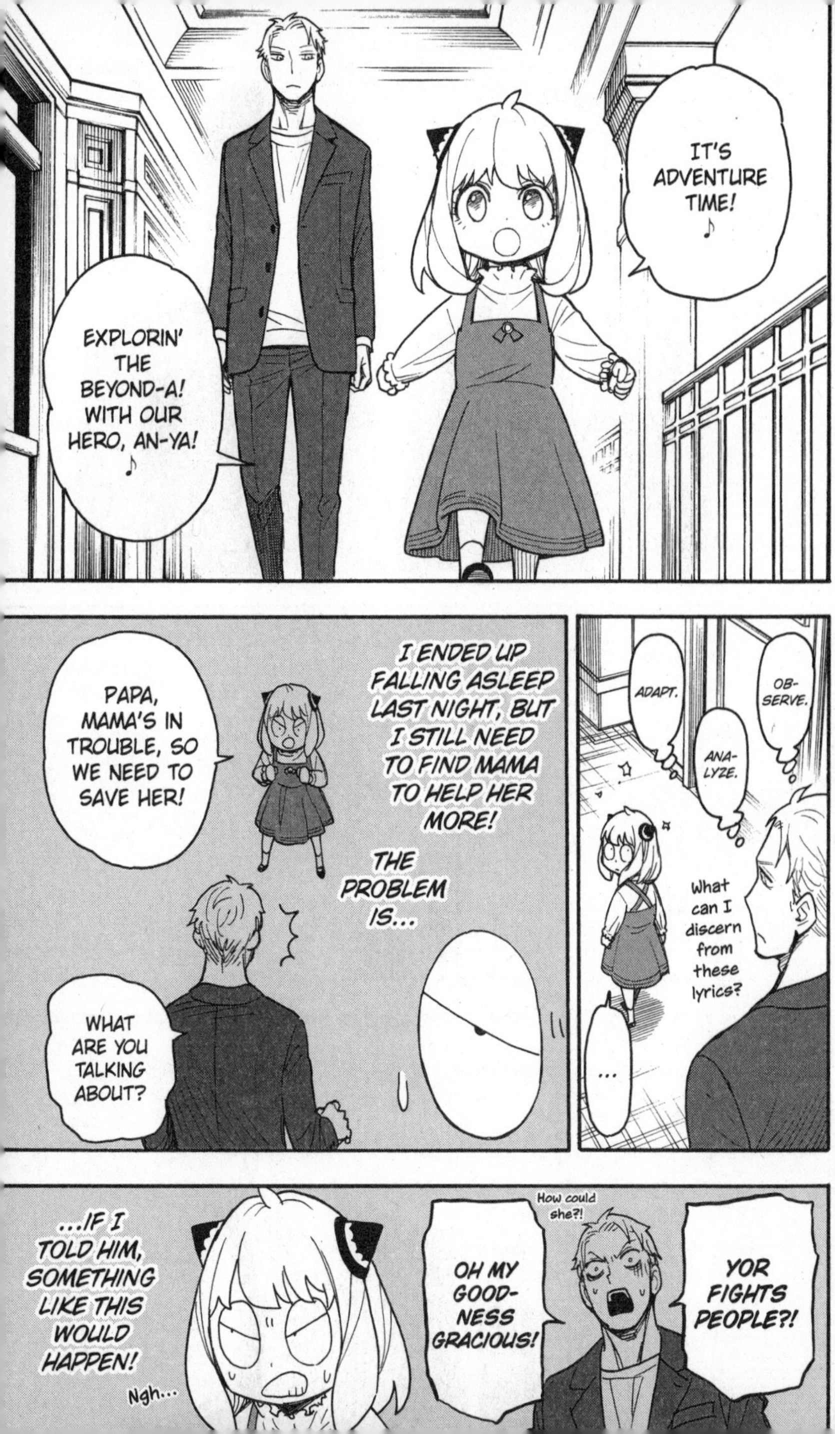
IT'S ADVENTURE TIME! ♪
EXPLORIN' THE BEYOND-A! WITH OUR HERO, AN-YA! ♪
OB-SERVE.
ADAPT.
ANA-LYZE.
What can I discern from these lyrics?
...
I ENDED UP FALLING ASLEEP LAST NIGHT, BUT I STILL NEED TO FIND MAMA TO HELP HER MORE!
PAPA, MAMA'S IN TROUBLE, SO WE NEED TO SAVE HER!
THE PROBLEM IS...
WHAT ARE YOU TALKING ABOUT?
YOR FIGHTS PEOPLE?!
How could she?!
OH MY GOOD-NESS GRACIOUS!
...IF I TOLD HIM, SOMETHING LIKE THIS WOULD HAPPEN!
Ngh...

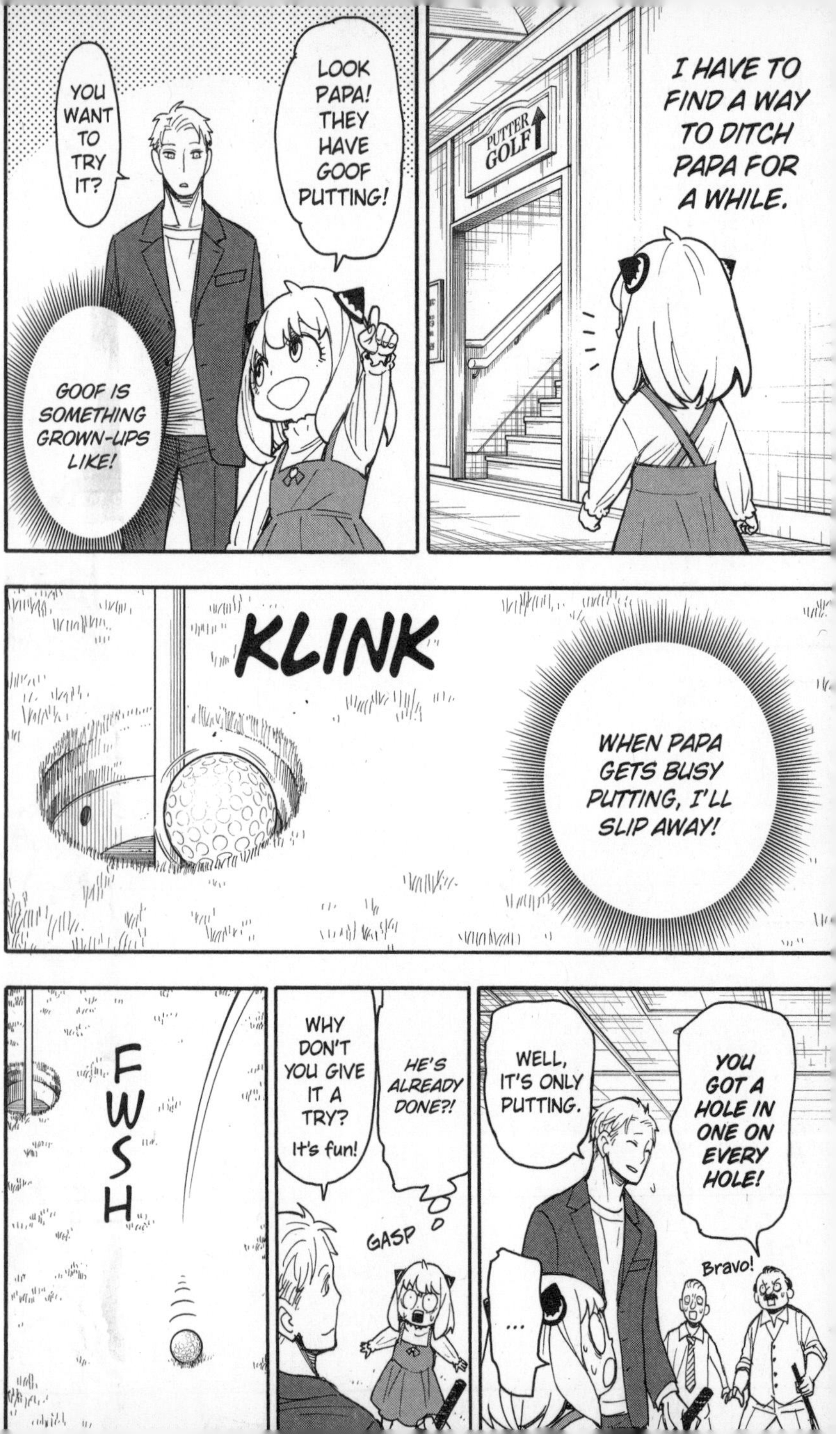
I HAVE TO FIND A WAY TO DITCH PAPA FOR A WHILE.
PUTTER GOLF
LOOK PAPA! THEY HAVE GOOF PUTTING!
YOU WANT TO TRY IT?
GOOF IS SOMETHING GROWN-UPS LIKE!
WHEN PAPA GETS BUSY PUTTING, I'LL SLIP AWAY!
KLINK
YOU GOT A HOLE IN ONE ON EVERY HOLE!
WELL, IT'S ONLY PUTTING.
Bravo!
...
HE'S ALREADY DONE?!
WHY DON'T YOU GIVE IT A TRY?
It's fun!
GASP
FWSH

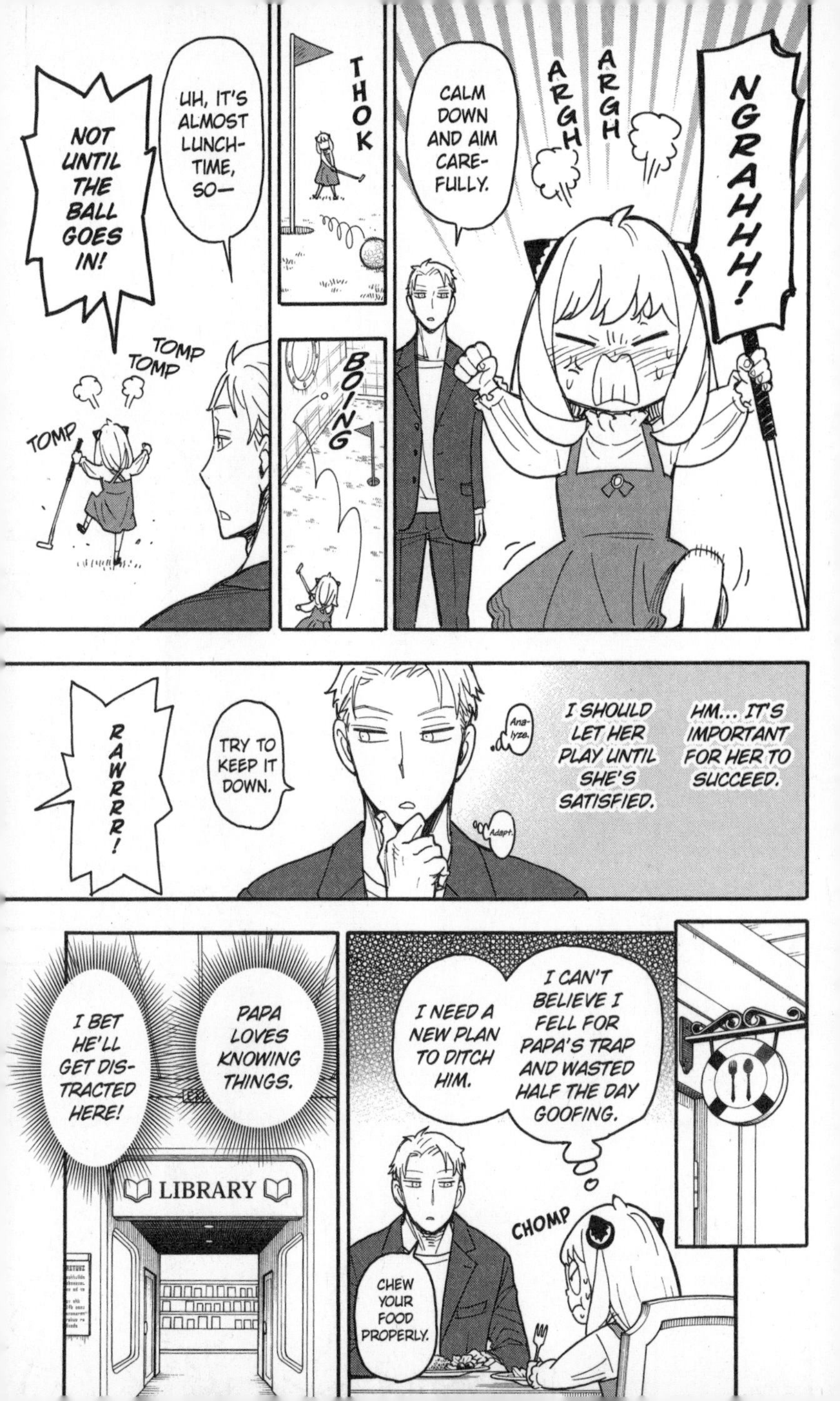
NGRAHHHH!
ARGH
ARGH
CALM DOWN AND AIM CARE-FULLY.
THOK
BOING
UH, IT'S ALMOST LUNCH-TIME, SO—
NOT UNTIL THE BALL GOES IN!
TOMP
TOMP
TOMP
HM... IT'S IMPORTANT FOR HER TO SUCCEED.
I SHOULD LET HER PLAY UNTIL SHE'S SATISFIED.
Ana-lyze.
Adapt.
TRY TO KEEP IT DOWN.
RAWRRR!
I CAN'T BELIEVE I FELL FOR PAPA'S TRAP AND WASTED HALF THE DAY GOOFING.
I NEED A NEW PLAN TO DITCH HIM.
CHOMP
CHEW YOUR FOOD PROPERLY.
PAPA LOVES KNOWING THINGS.
I BET HE'LL GET DIS-TRACTED HERE!
LIBRARY

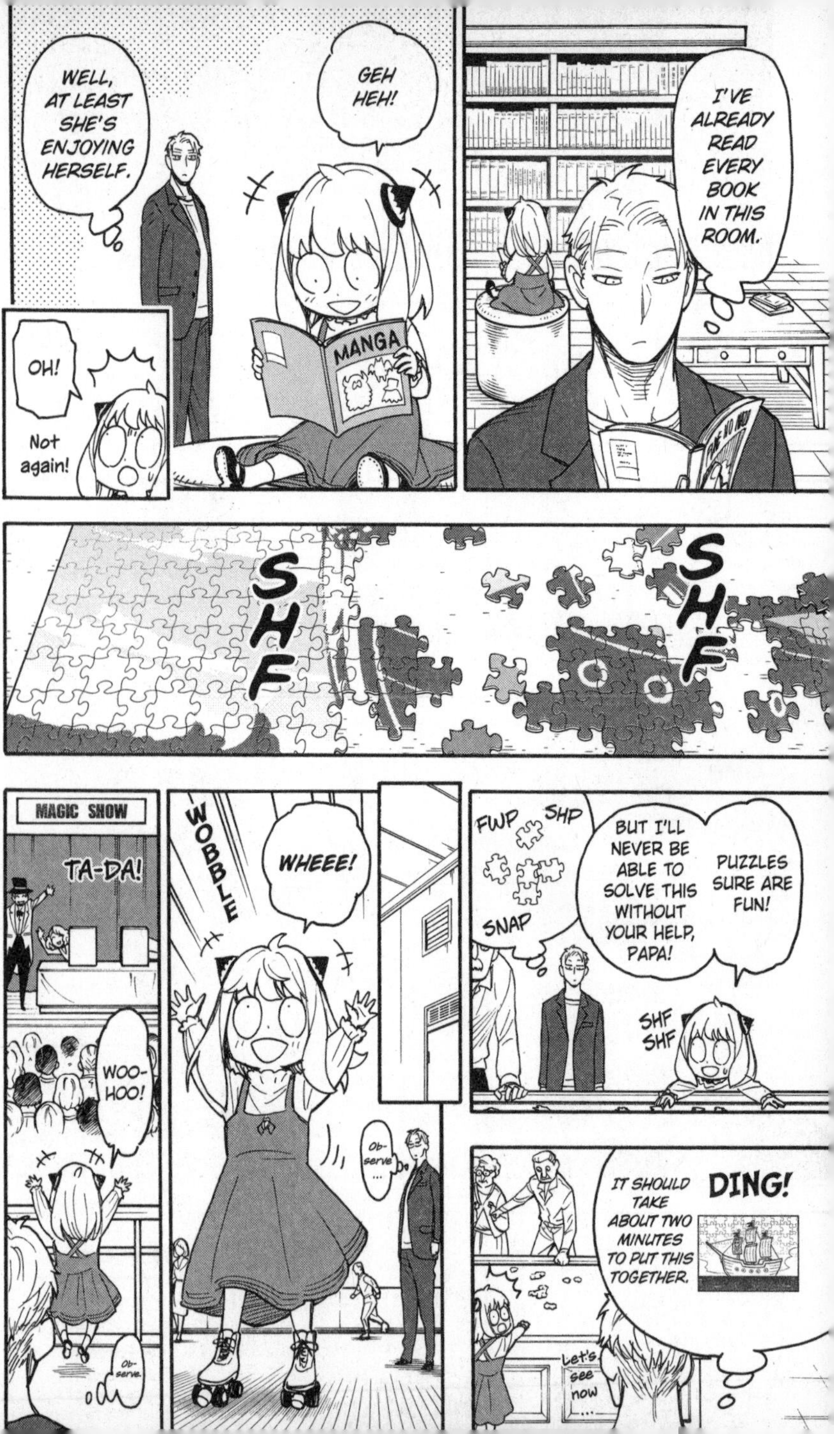
I'VE ALREADY READ EVERY BOOK IN THIS ROOM.
GEH HEH!
WELL, AT LEAST SHE'S ENJOYING HERSELF.
MANGA
OH!
Not again!
SHF
SHF
SHP
FWP
PUZZLES SURE ARE FUN!
BUT I'LL NEVER BE ABLE TO SOLVE THIS WITHOUT YOUR HELP, PAPA!
SNAP
SHF SHF
DING!
IT SHOULD TAKE ABOUT TWO MINUTES TO PUT THIS TOGETHER.
Let's see now ...
WHEEE!
WOBBLE
Ob-serve ...
MAGIC SHOW
TA-DA!
WOO-HOO!
Ob-serve.

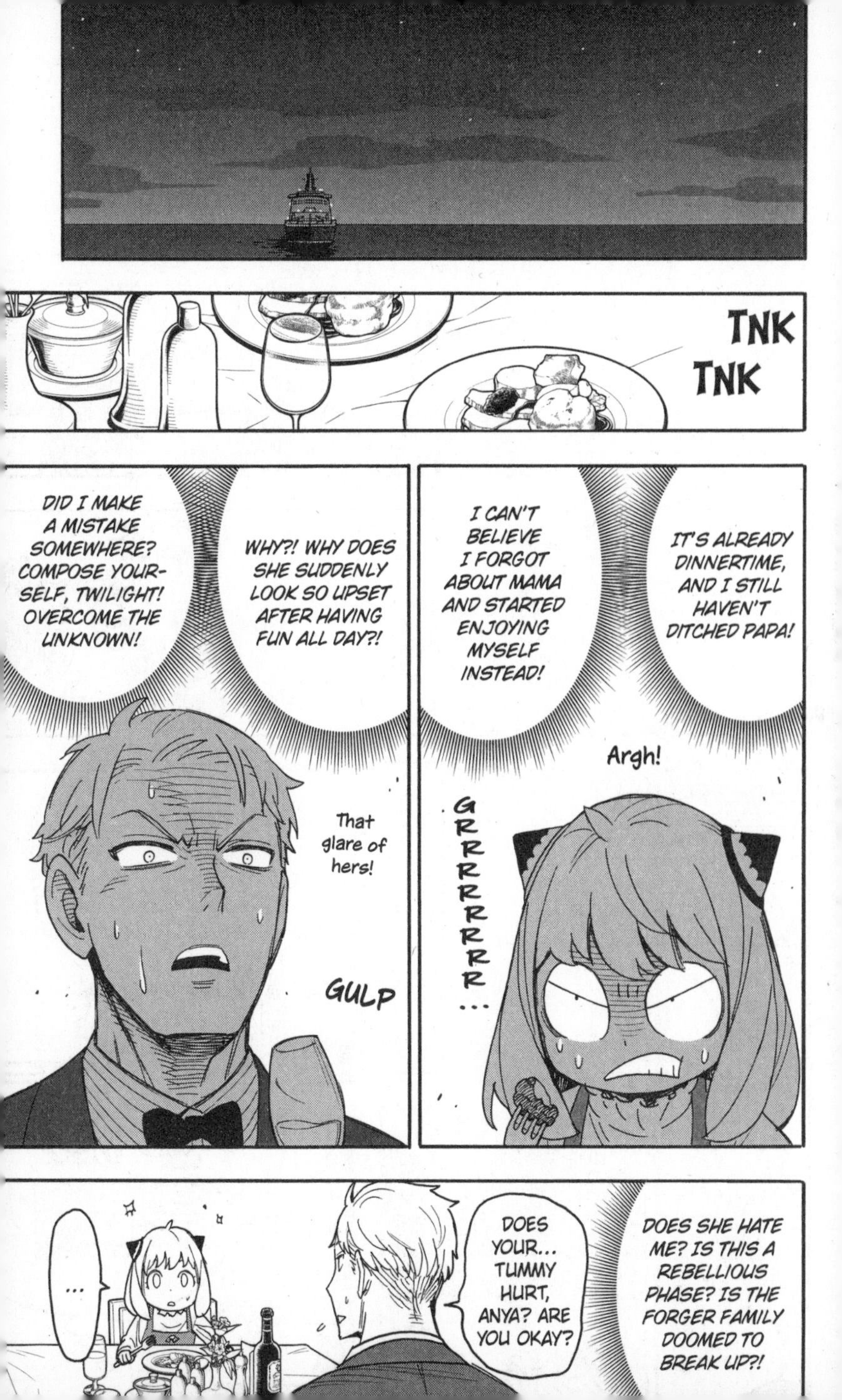
TNK
TNK
IT'S ALREADY DINNERTIME, AND I STILL HAVEN'T DITCHED PAPA!
I CAN'T BELIEVE I FORGOT ABOUT MAMA AND STARTED ENJOYING MYSELF INSTEAD!
Argh!
GRRRRRRRR...
WHY?! WHY DOES SHE SUDDENLY LOOK SO UPSET AFTER HAVING FUN ALL DAY?!
DID I MAKE A MISTAKE SOMEWHERE? COMPOSE YOURSELF, TWILIGHT! OVERCOME THE UNKNOWN!
That glare of hers!
GULP
DOES SHE HATE ME? IS THIS A REBELLIOUS PHASE? IS THE FORGER FAMILY DOOMED TO BREAK UP?!
DOES YOUR... TUMMY HURT, ANYA? ARE YOU OKAY?
...

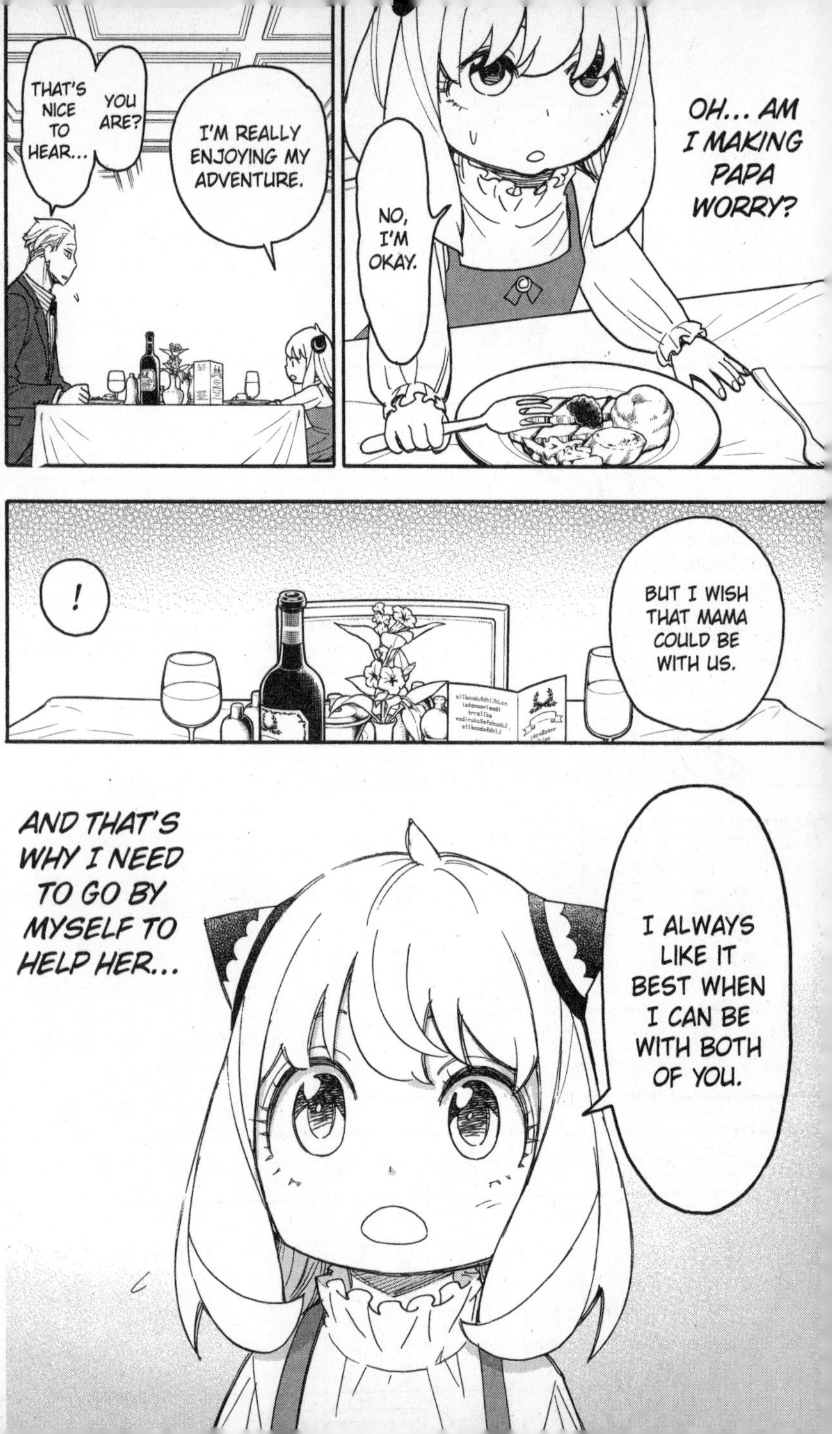
OH... AM I MAKING PAPA WORRY?
NO, I'M OKAY.
I'M REALLY ENJOYING MY ADVENTURE.
YOU ARE?
THAT'S NICE TO HEAR...
BUT I WISH THAT MAMA COULD BE WITH US.
!
I ALWAYS LIKE IT BEST WHEN I CAN BE WITH BOTH OF YOU.
AND THAT'S WHY I NEED TO GO BY MYSELF TO HELP HER...

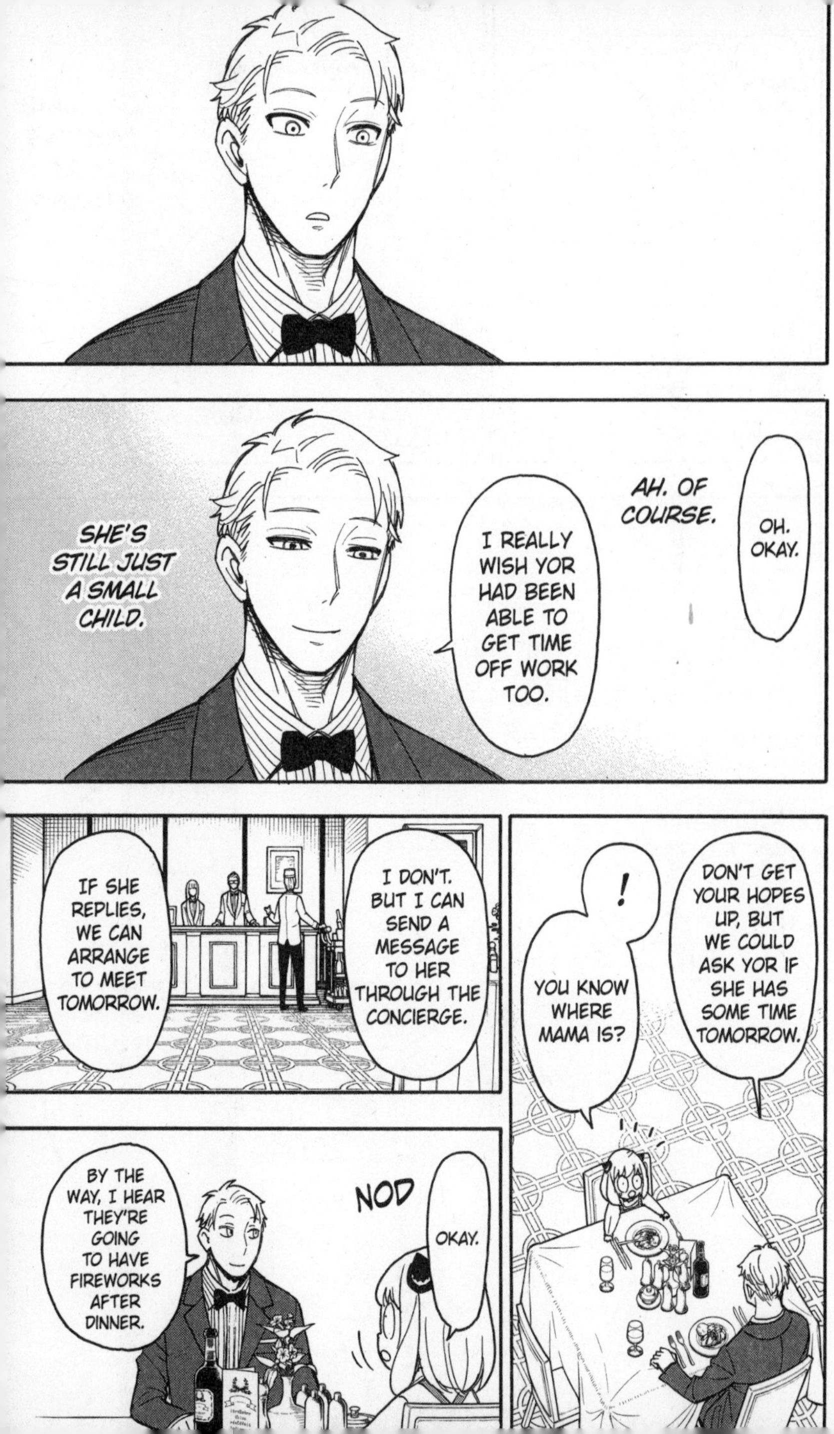
OH. OKAY.
AH. OF COURSE.
I REALLY WISH YOR HAD BEEN ABLE TO GET TIME OFF WORK TOO.
SHE'S STILL JUST A SMALL CHILD.
DON'T GET YOUR HOPES UP, BUT WE COULD ASK YOR IF SHE HAS SOME TIME TOMORROW.
!
YOU KNOW WHERE MAMA IS?
I DON'T. BUT I CAN SEND A MESSAGE TO HER THROUGH THE CONCIERGE.
IF SHE REPLIES, WE CAN ARRANGE TO MEET TOMORROW.
OKAY.
NOD
BY THE WAY, I HEAR THEY'RE GOING TO HAVE FIREWORKS AFTER DINNER.

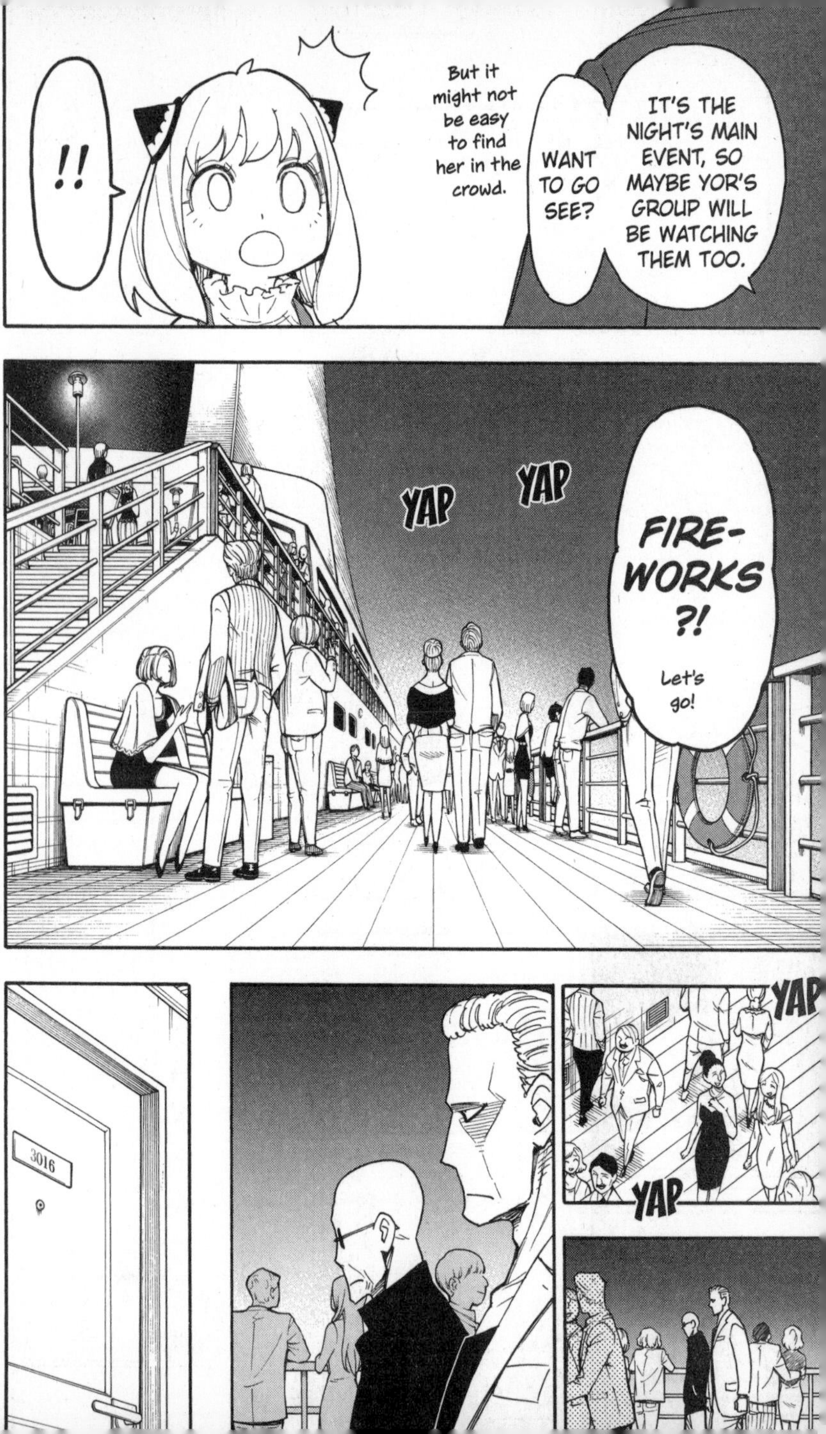
IT'S THE NIGHT'S MAIN EVENT, SO MAYBE YOR'S GROUP WILL BE WATCHING THEM TOO.
WANT TO GO SEE?
But it might not be easy to find her in the crowd.
!!
FIRE-WORKS?!
Let's go!
YAP
YAP
YAP
YAP
3016

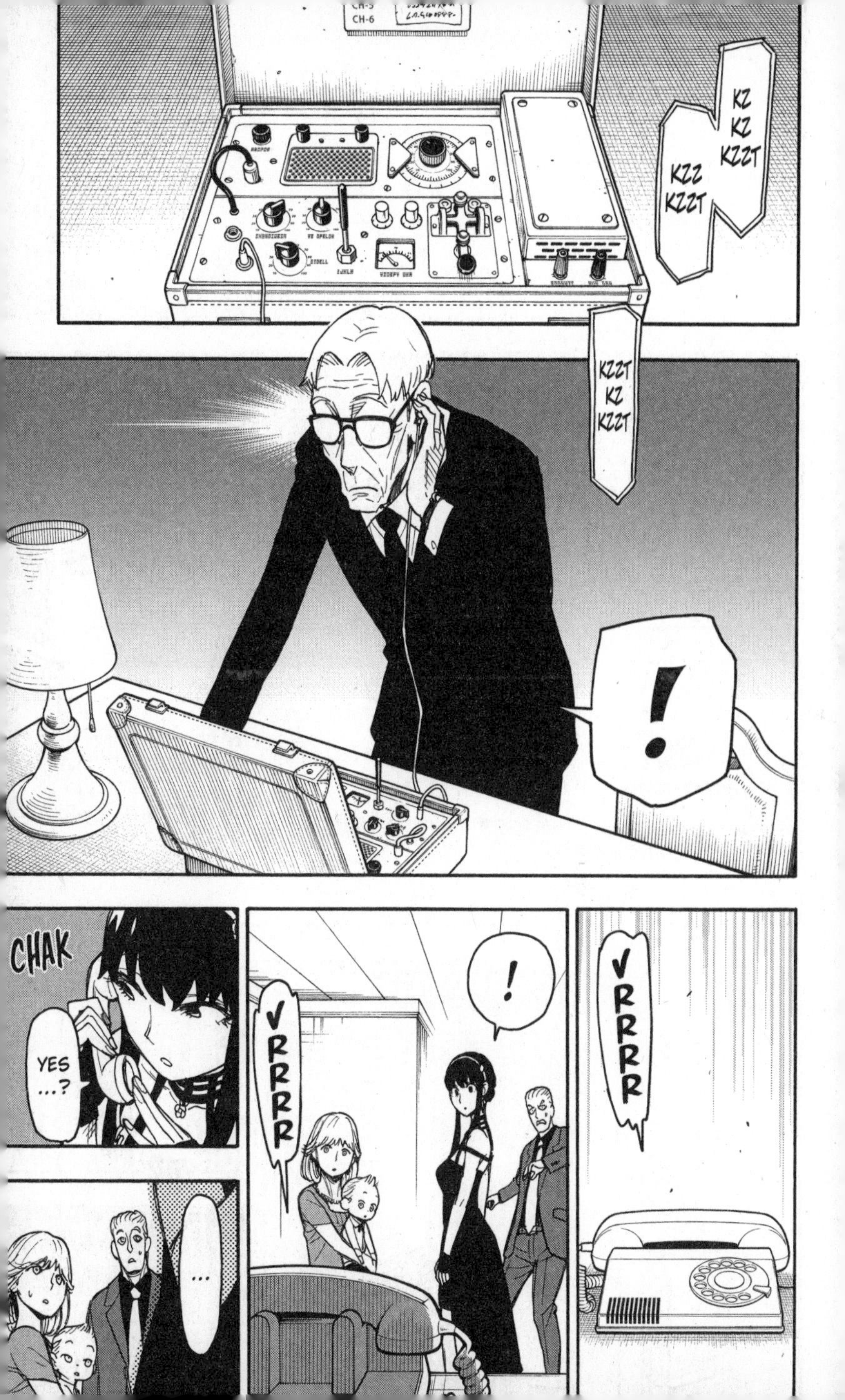
CH-6
KZ KZ KZZT
KZZ KZZT
KZZT KZ KZZT
!
VRRRR
!
VRRRR
CHAK
YES ...?
...

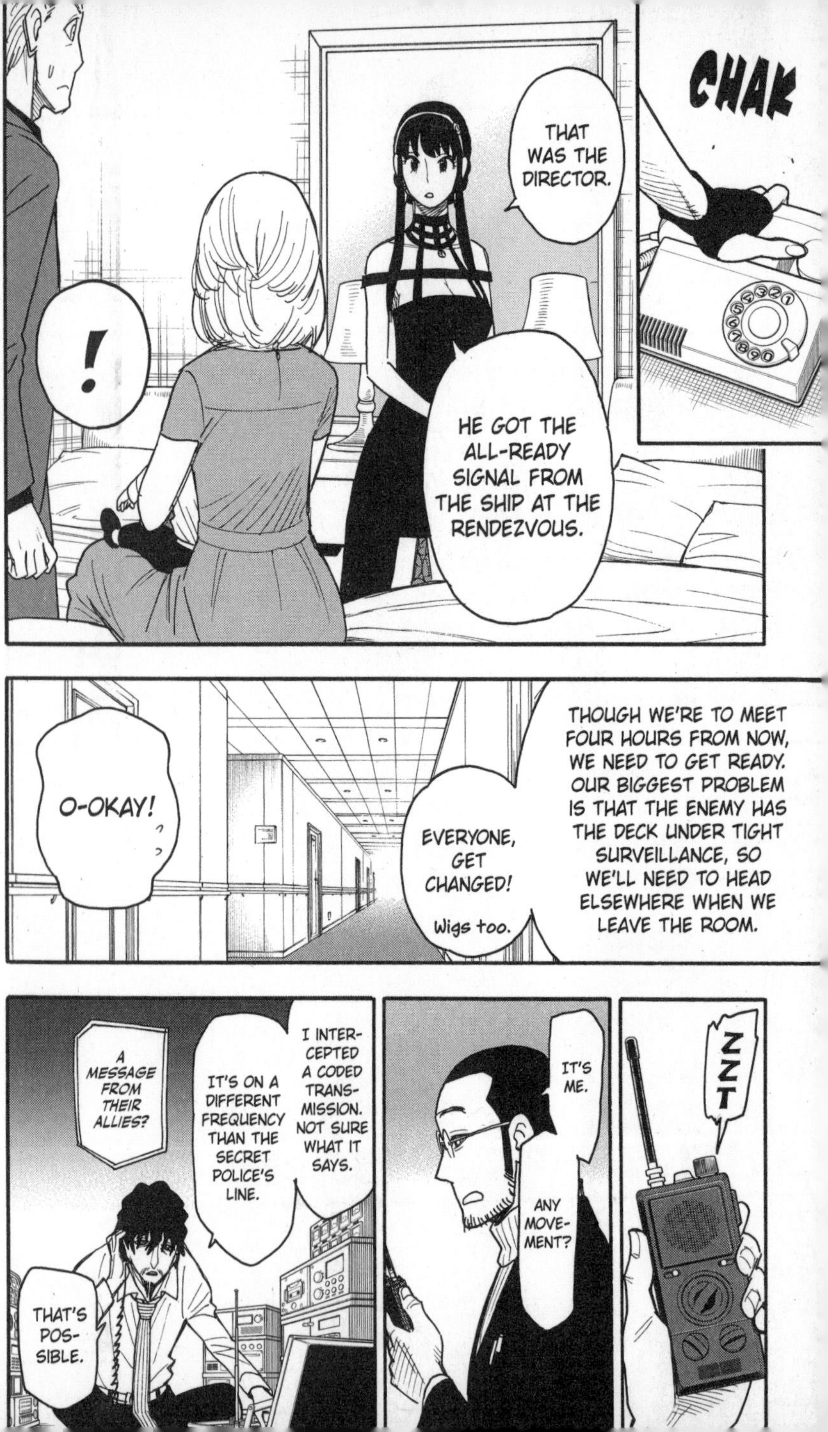
CHAK
THAT WAS THE DIRECTOR.
HE GOT THE ALL-READY SIGNAL FROM THE SHIP AT THE RENDEZVOUS.
!
THOUGH WE'RE TO MEET FOUR HOURS FROM NOW, WE NEED TO GET READY. OUR BIGGEST PROBLEM IS THAT THE ENEMY HAS THE DECK UNDER TIGHT SURVEILLANCE, SO WE'LL NEED TO HEAD ELSEWHERE WHEN WE LEAVE THE ROOM.
EVERYONE, GET CHANGED!
Wigs too.
O-OKAY!
ZZT
IT'S ME.
ANY MOVE-MENT?
I INTER-CEPTED A CODED TRANS-MISSION. NOT SURE WHAT IT SAYS.
IT'S ON A DIFFERENT FREQUENCY THAN THE SECRET POLICE'S LINE.
A MESSAGE FROM THEIR ALLIES?
THAT'S POS-SIBLE.

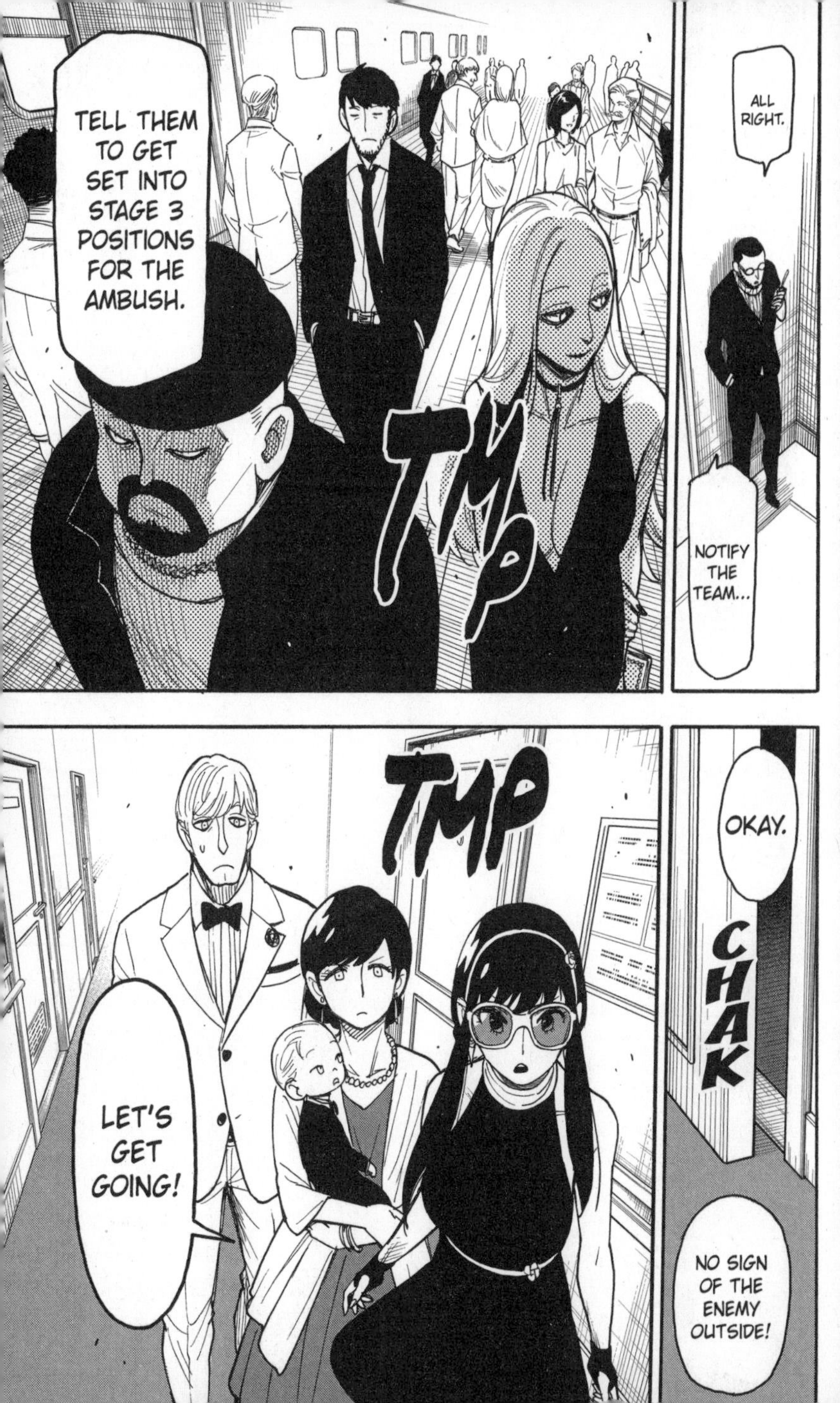
ALL RIGHT.
NOTIFY THE TEAM...
TELL THEM TO GET SET INTO STAGE 3 POSITIONS FOR THE AMBUSH.
TMP
OKAY.
CHAK
NO SIGN OF THE ENEMY OUTSIDE!
TMP
LET'S GET GOING!

SPY×FAMILY

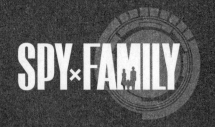

MISSION 51

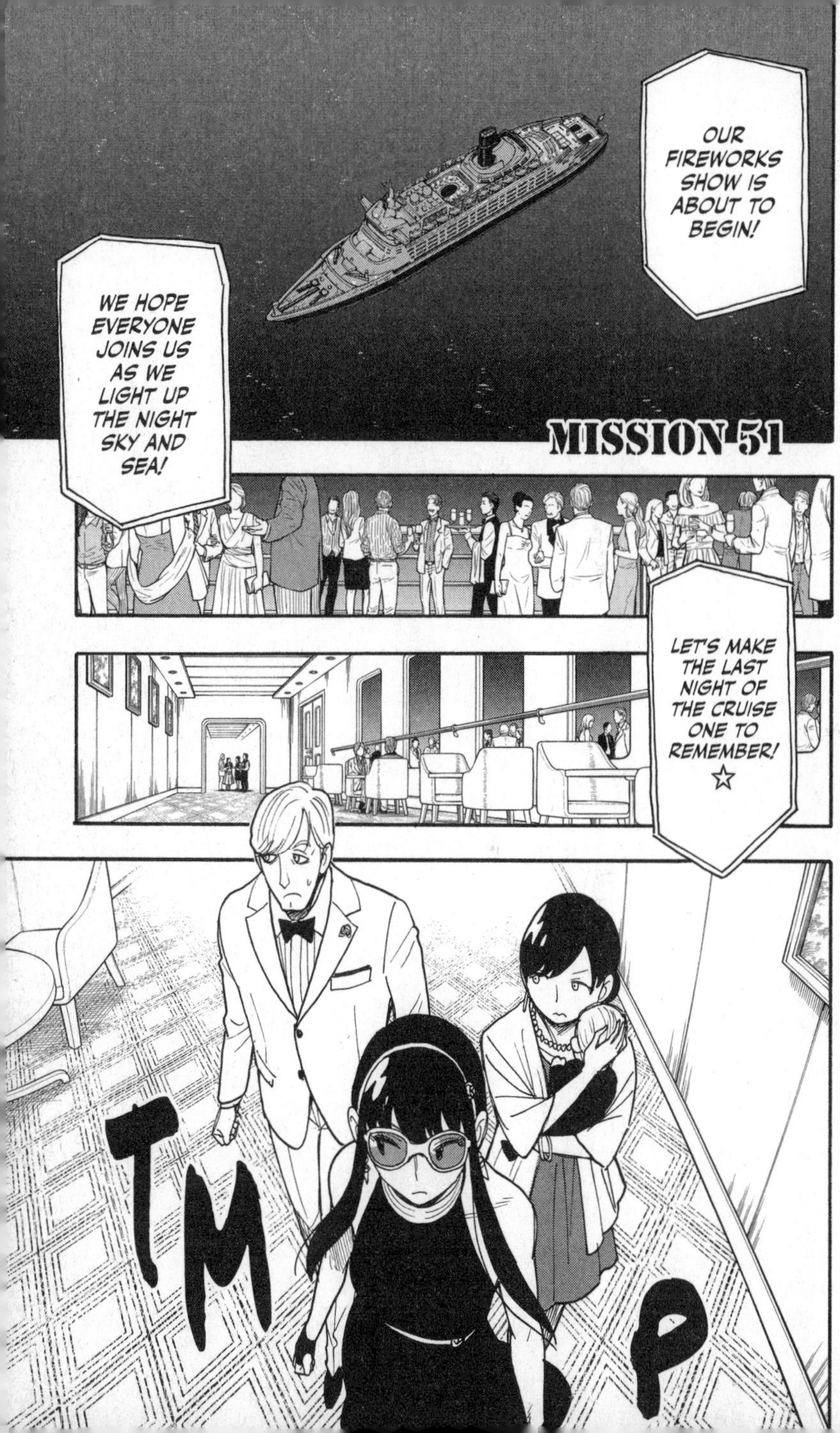
OUR FIREWORKS SHOW IS ABOUT TO BEGIN!
WE HOPE EVERYONE JOINS US AS WE LIGHT UP THE NIGHT SKY AND SEA!
MISSION 51
LET'S MAKE THE LAST NIGHT OF THE CRUISE ONE TO REMEMBER! ☆
TMP

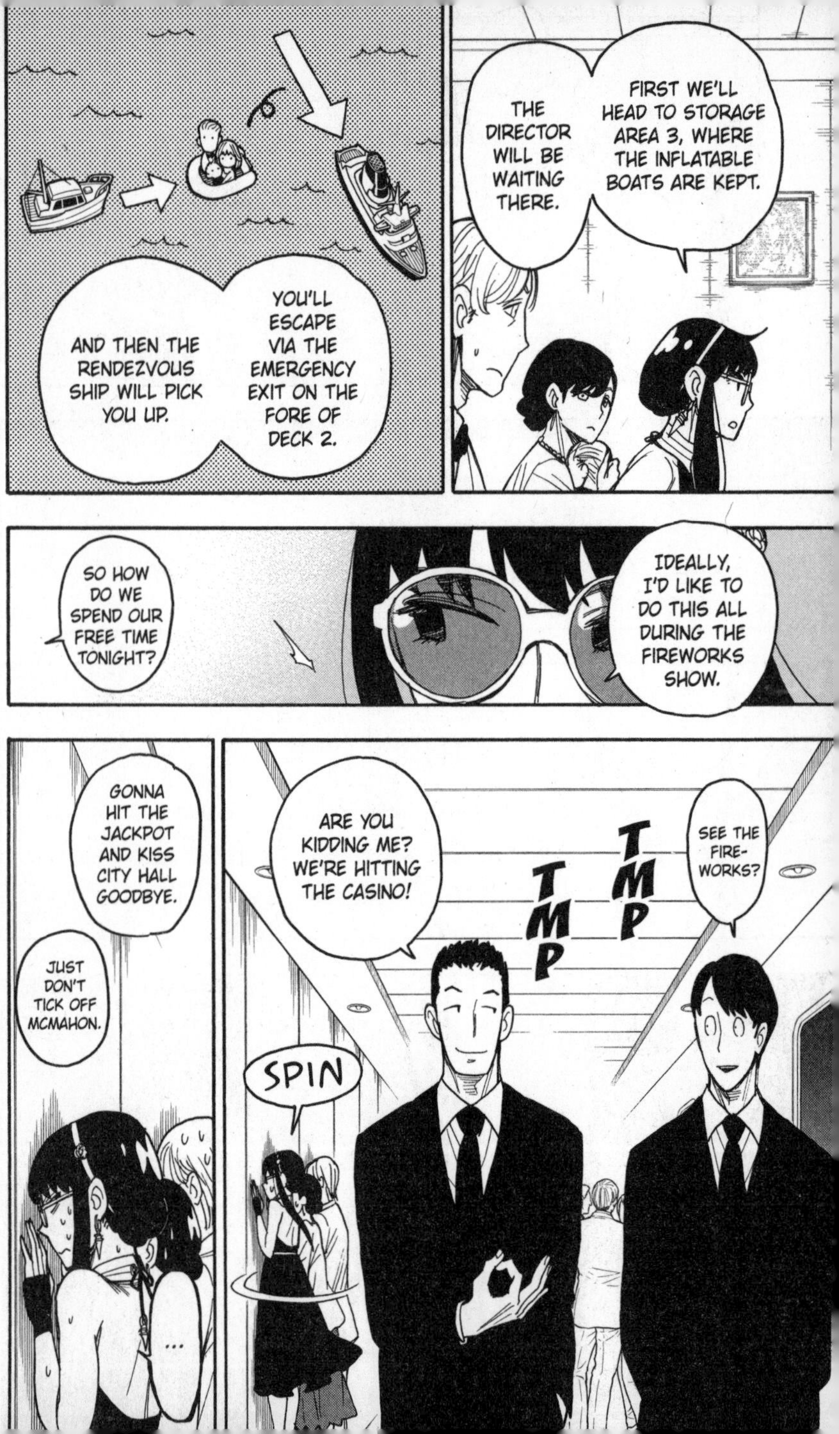
FIRST WE'LL HEAD TO STORAGE AREA 3, WHERE THE INFLATABLE BOATS ARE KEPT.
THE DIRECTOR WILL BE WAITING THERE.
YOU'LL ESCAPE VIA THE EMERGENCY EXIT ON THE FORE OF DECK 2.
AND THEN THE RENDEZVOUS SHIP WILL PICK YOU UP.
IDEALLY, I'D LIKE TO DO THIS ALL DURING THE FIREWORKS SHOW.
SO HOW DO WE SPEND OUR FREE TIME TONIGHT?
SEE THE FIRE-WORKS?
TMP
TMP
ARE YOU KIDDING ME? WE'RE HITTING THE CASINO!
SPIN
GONNA HIT THE JACKPOT AND KISS CITY HALL GOODBYE.
JUST DON'T TICK OFF MCMAHON.
...

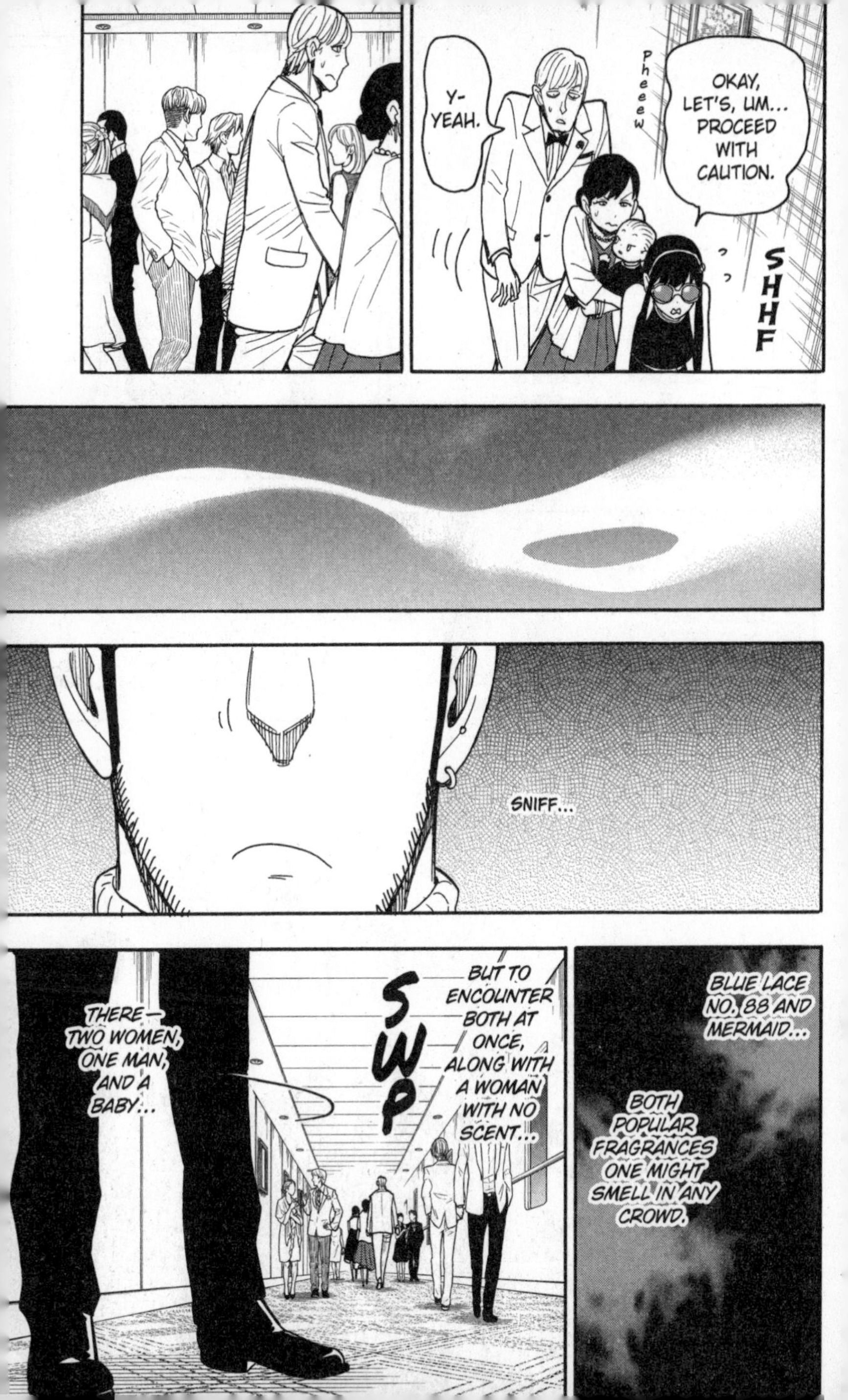
OKAY, LET'S, UM... PROCEED WITH CAUTION.
SHHF
Pheeew
Y-YEAH.
SNIFF...
BLUE LACE NO. 88 AND MERMAID...
BOTH POPULAR FRAGRANCES ONE MIGHT SMELL IN ANY CROWD.
BUT TO ENCOUNTER BOTH AT ONCE, ALONG WITH A WOMAN WITH NO SCENT...
SWP
THERE— TWO WOMEN, ONE MAN, AND A BABY...

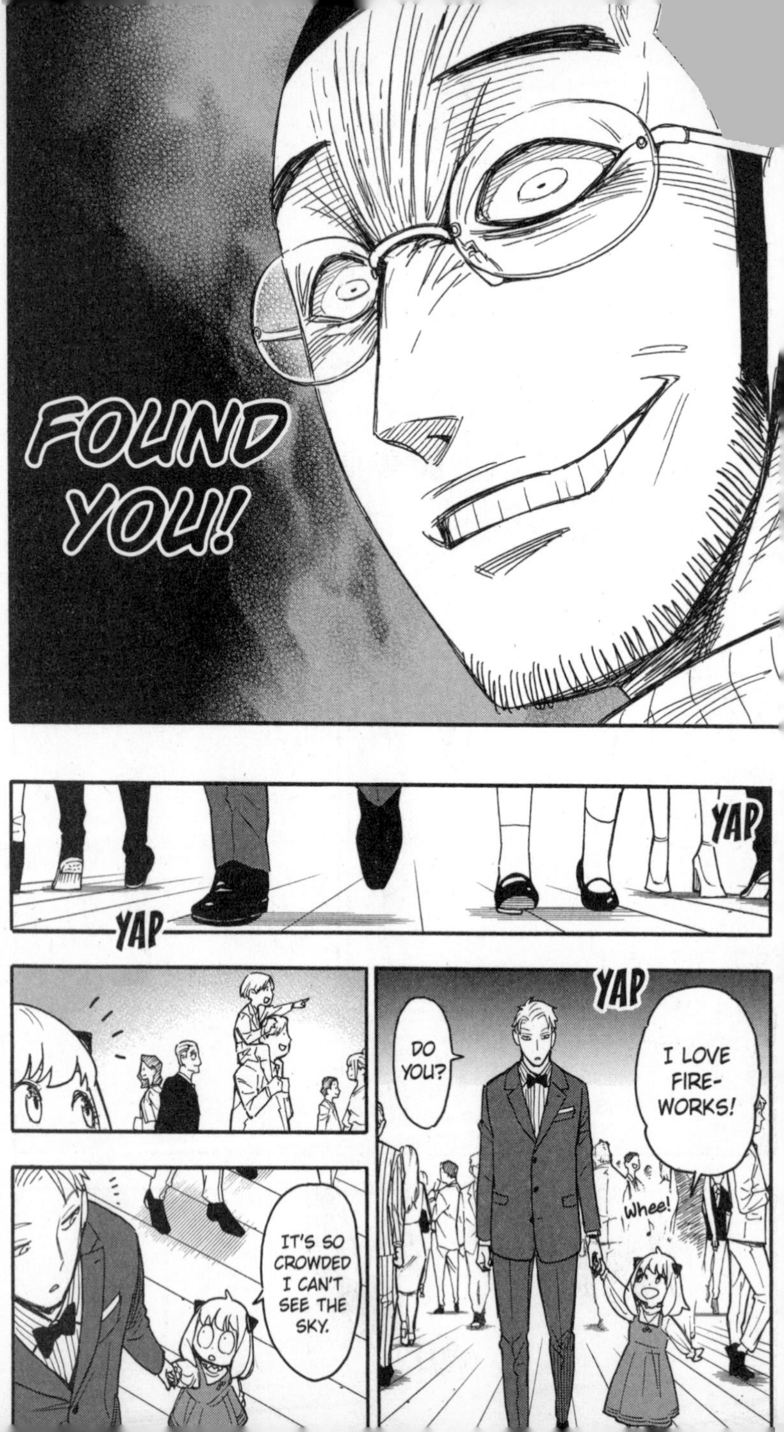
FOUND YOU!
YAP
YAP
YAP
I LOVE FIRE-WORKS!
DO YOU?
Whee!
IT'S SO CROWDED I CAN'T SEE THE SKY.

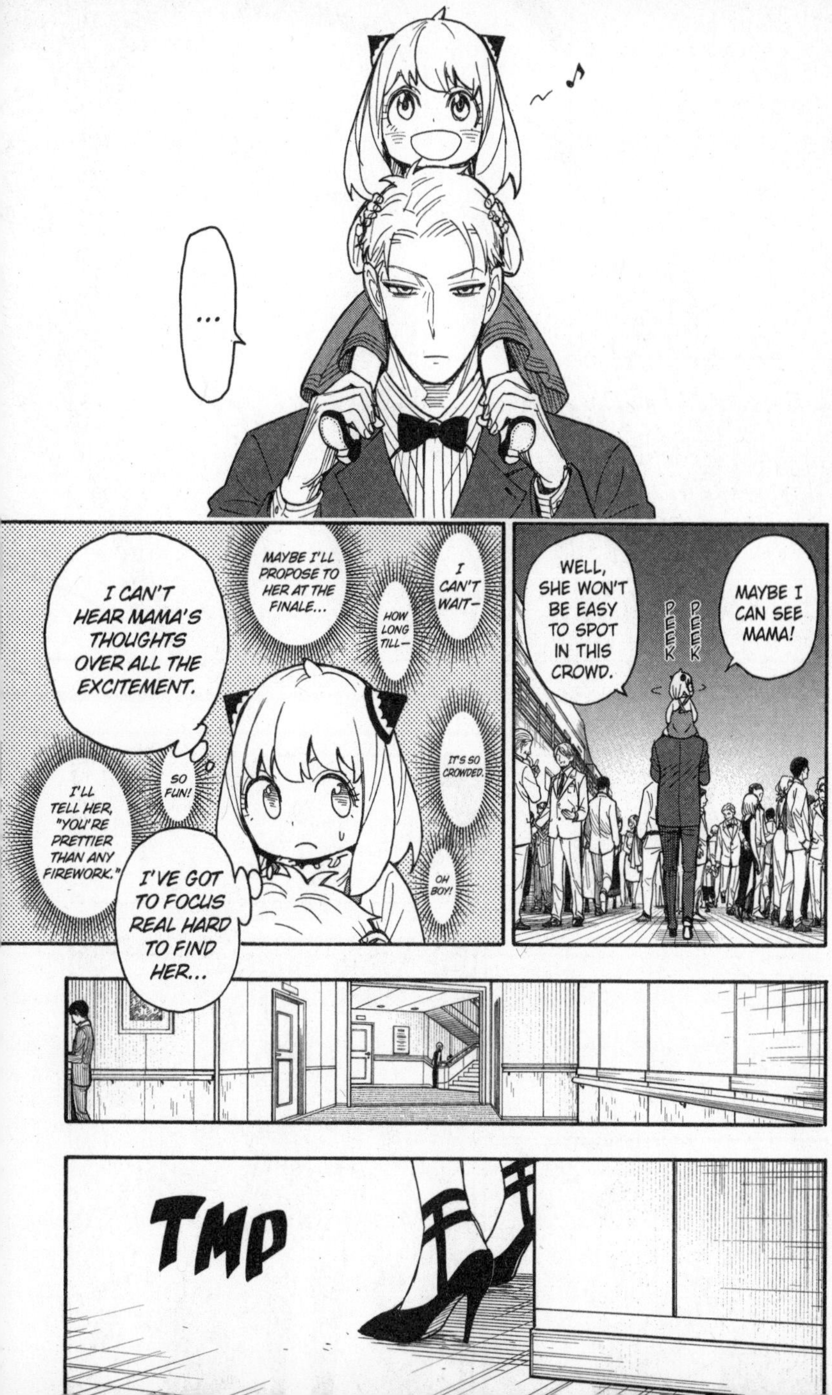

~♪
...
MAYBE I CAN SEE MAMA!
PEEK
PEEK
WELL, SHE WON'T BE EASY TO SPOT IN THIS CROWD.
I CAN'T WAIT—
MAYBE I'LL PROPOSE TO HER AT THE FINALE...
HOW LONG TILL—
I CAN'T HEAR MAMA'S THOUGHTS OVER ALL THE EXCITEMENT.
IT'S SO CROWDED.
OH BOY!
SO FUN!
I'LL TELL HER, "YOU'RE PRETTIER THAN ANY FIREWORK."
I'VE GOT TO FOCUS REAL HARD TO FIND HER...
TMP

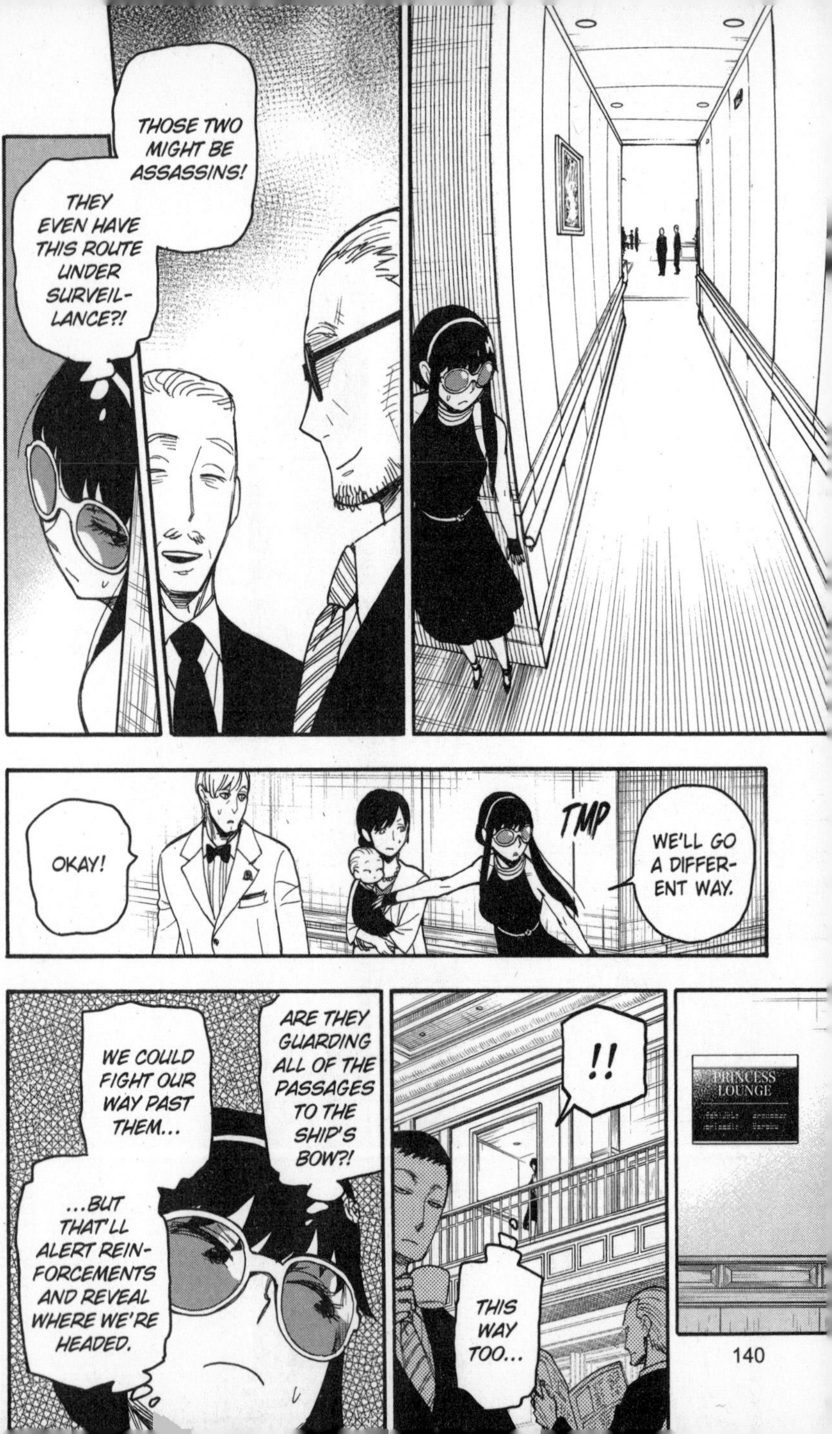
THOSE TWO MIGHT BE ASSASSINS!
THEY EVEN HAVE THIS ROUTE UNDER SURVEIL-LANCE?!
WE'LL GO A DIFFER-ENT WAY.
TMP
OKAY!
PRINCESS LOUNGE
!!
THIS WAY TOO...
ARE THEY GUARDING ALL OF THE PASSAGES TO THE SHIP'S BOW?!
WE COULD FIGHT OUR WAY PAST THEM...
...BUT THAT'LL ALERT REIN-FORCEMENTS AND REVEAL WHERE WE'RE HEADED.

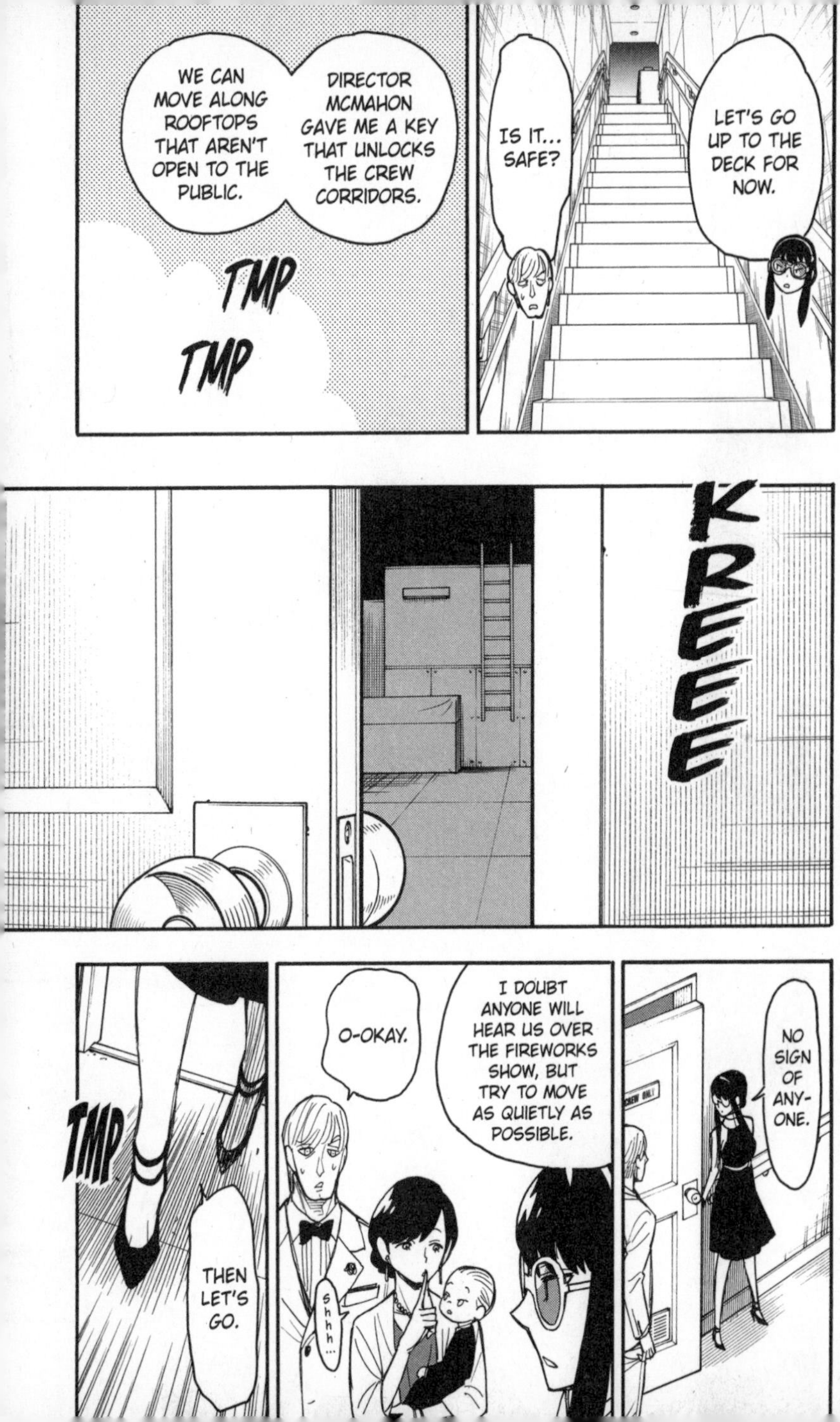
LET'S GO UP TO THE DECK FOR NOW.
IS IT... SAFE?
DIRECTOR MCMAHON GAVE ME A KEY THAT UNLOCKS THE CREW CORRIDORS.
WE CAN MOVE ALONG ROOFTOPS THAT AREN'T OPEN TO THE PUBLIC.
TMP
TMP
KREEE
NO SIGN OF ANY-ONE.
I DOUBT ANYONE WILL HEAR US OVER THE FIREWORKS SHOW, BUT TRY TO MOVE AS QUIETLY AS POSSIBLE.
O-OKAY.
Shhh...
TMP
THEN LET'S GO.

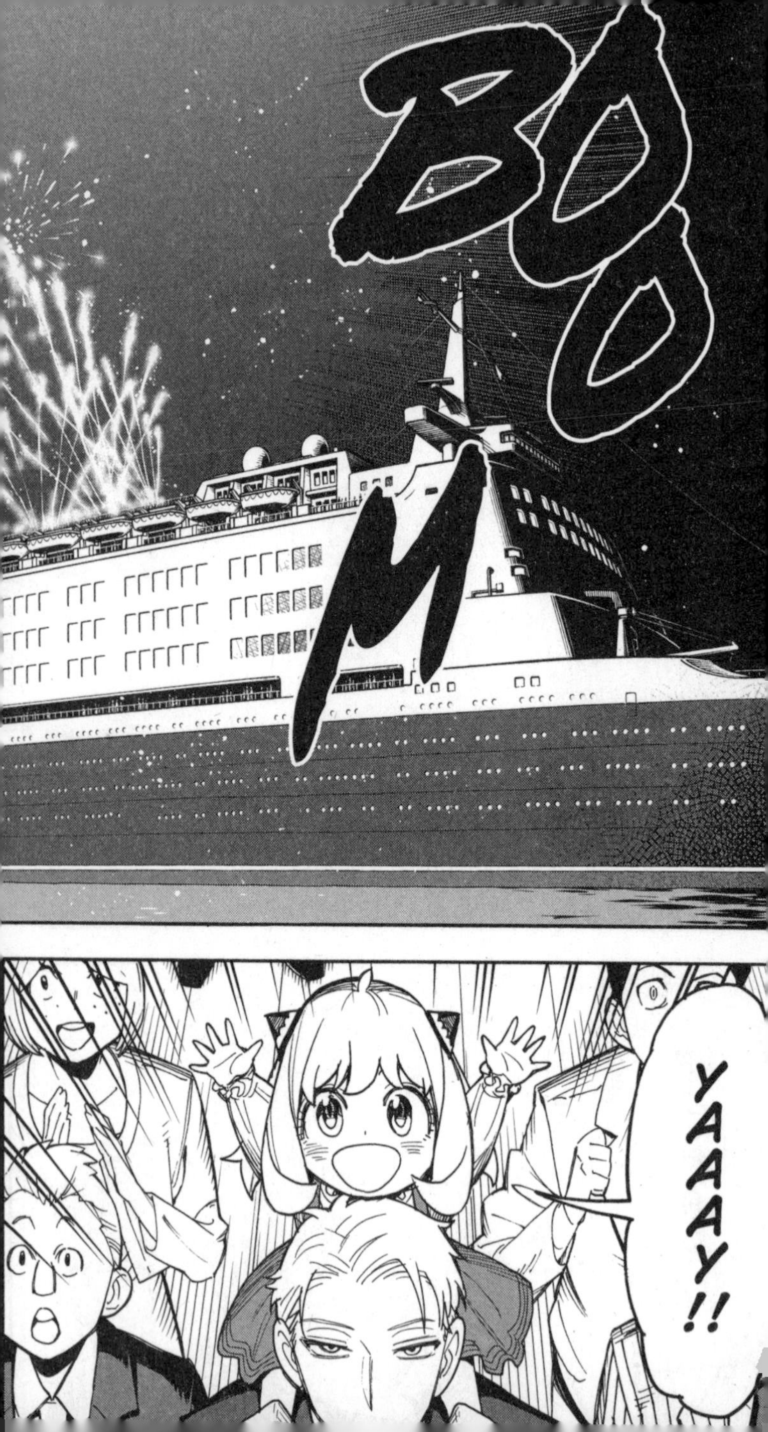
BOOM
YAAAY!!

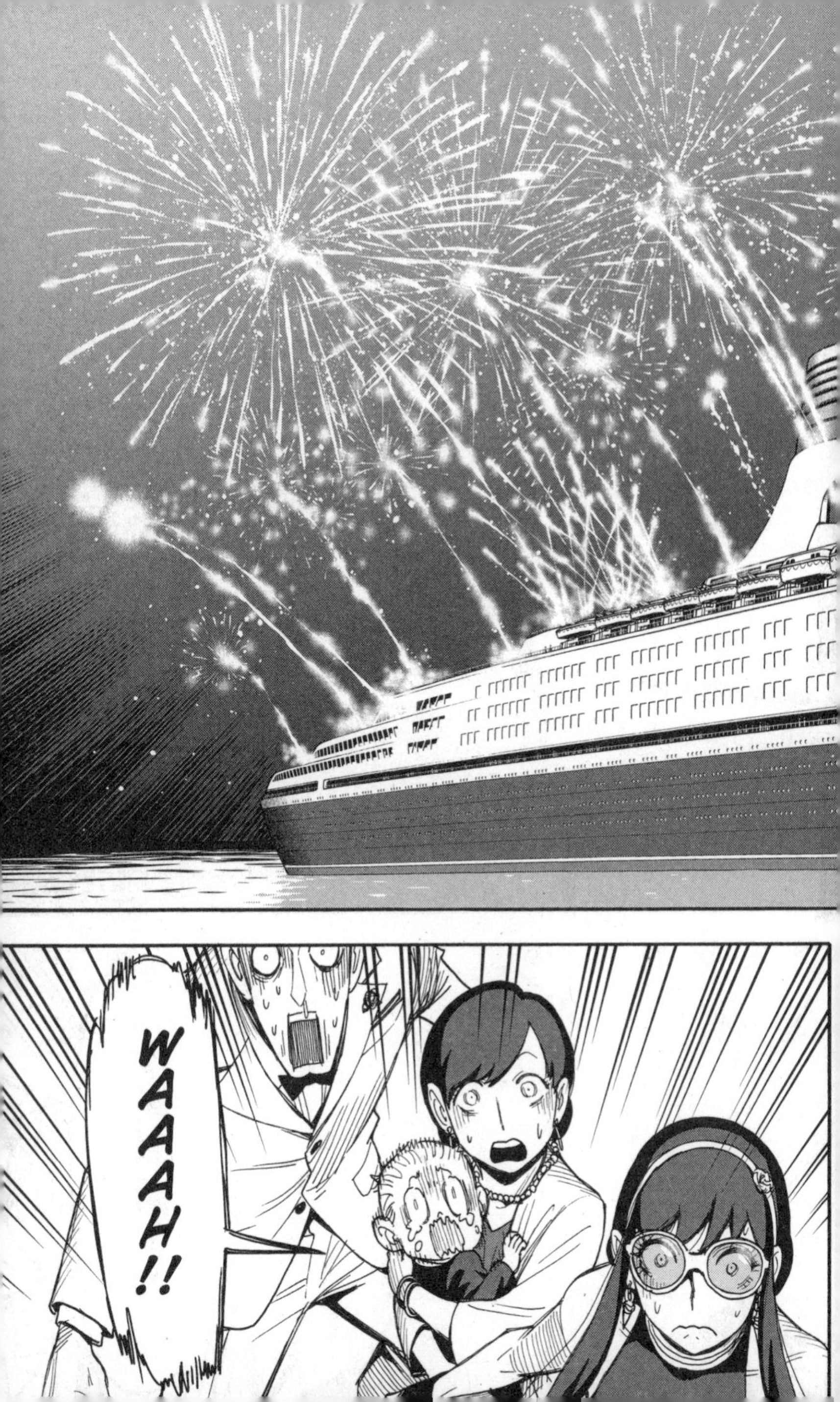
WAAAAH!!

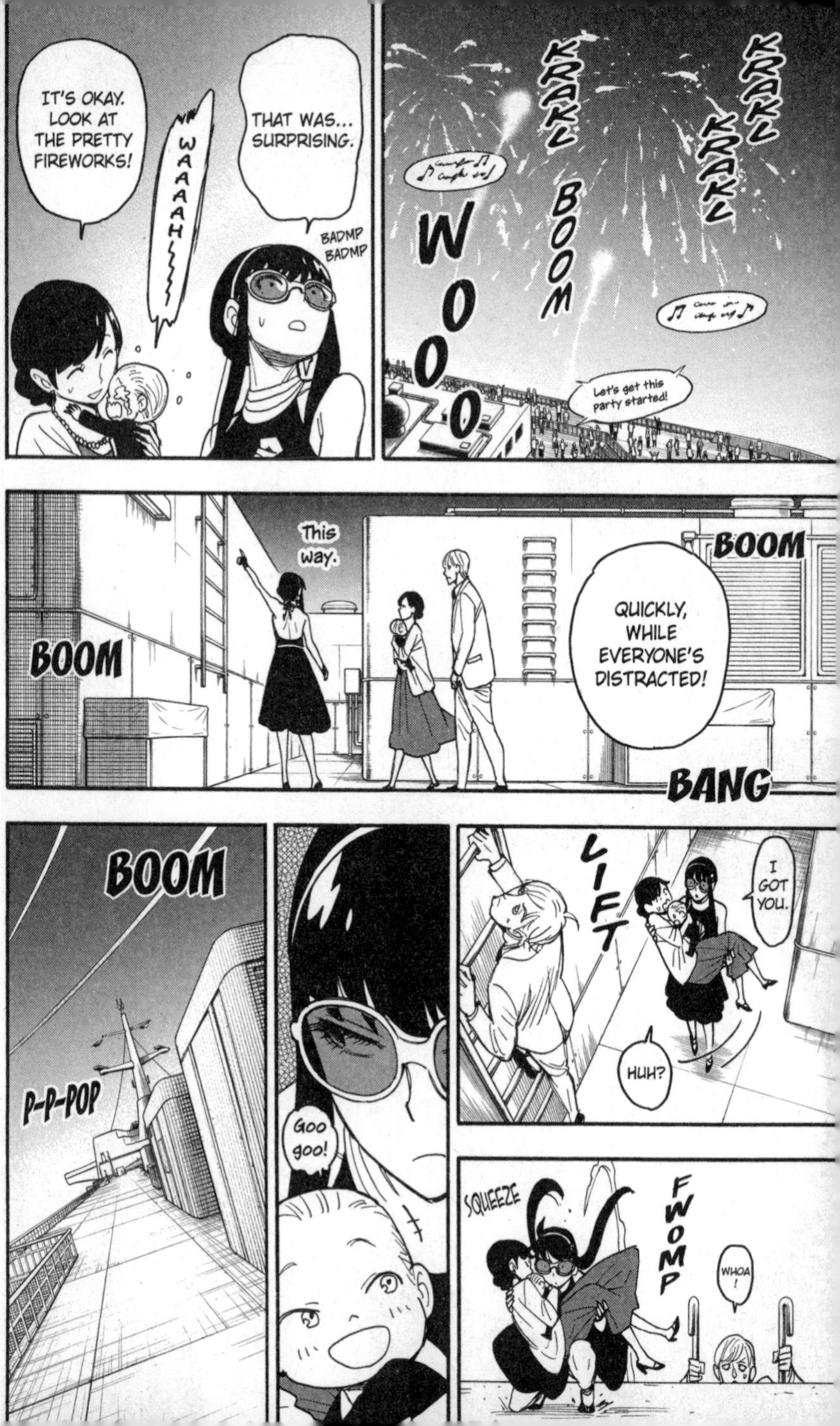
KRAKL
KRAKL
KRAKL
BOOM
WOOO
Let's get this party started!
THAT WAS... SURPRISING.
BADMP BADMP
WAAAAAH
IT'S OKAY. LOOK AT THE PRETTY FIREWORKS!
BOOM
QUICKLY, WHILE EVERYONE'S DISTRACTED!
BANG
This way.
BOOM
I GOT YOU.
LIFT
HUH?
FWOMP
WHOA!
SQUEEZE
Goo goo!
BOOM
P-P-POP

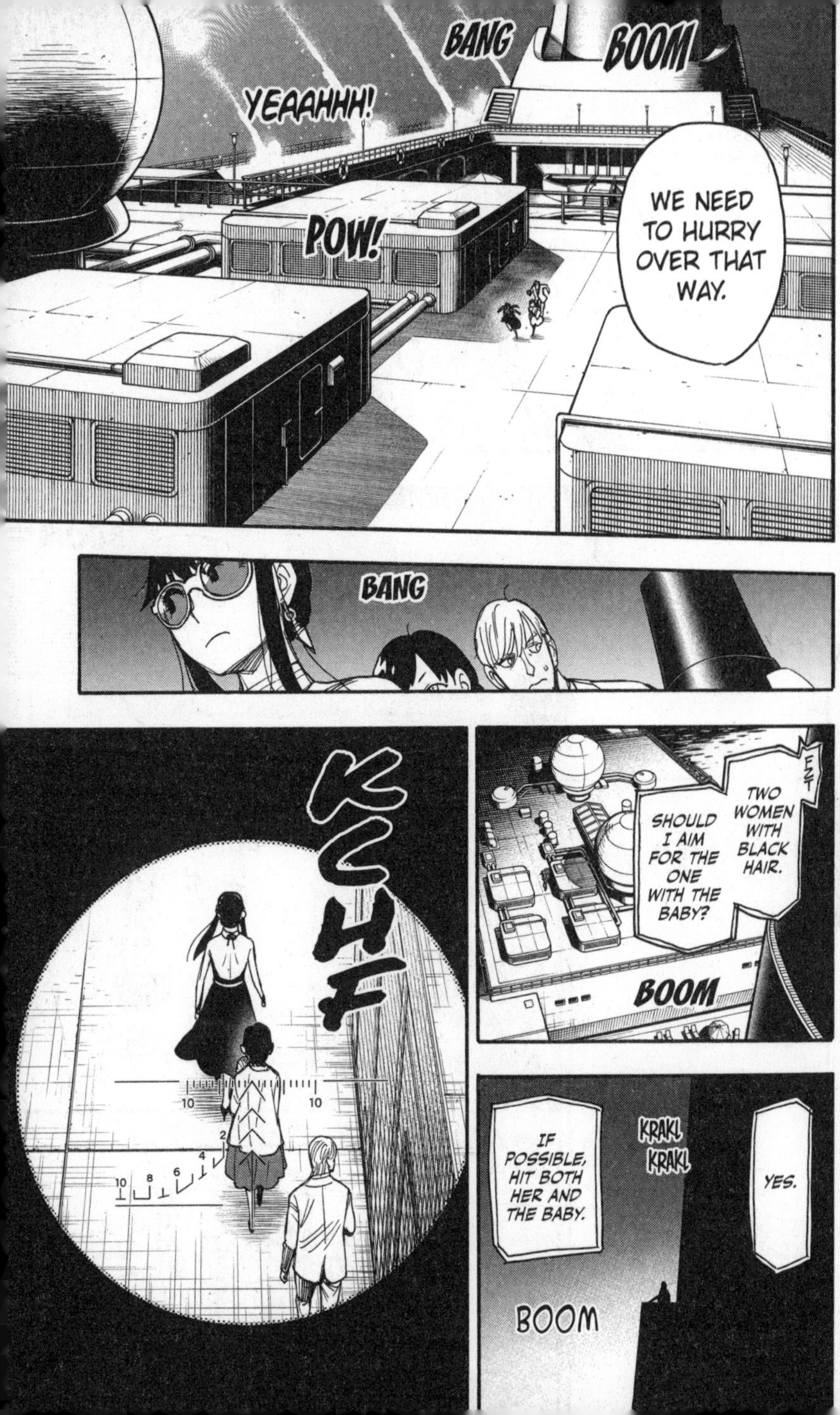

BOOM
BANG
YEAAHHH!
WE NEED TO HURRY OVER THAT WAY.
POW!
BANG
EZT
TWO WOMEN WITH BLACK HAIR.
SHOULD I AIM FOR THE ONE WITH THE BABY?
BOOM
YES.
KRAKL KRAKL
IF POSSIBLE, HIT BOTH HER AND THE BABY.
BOOM
10
10
2
4
6
8
10

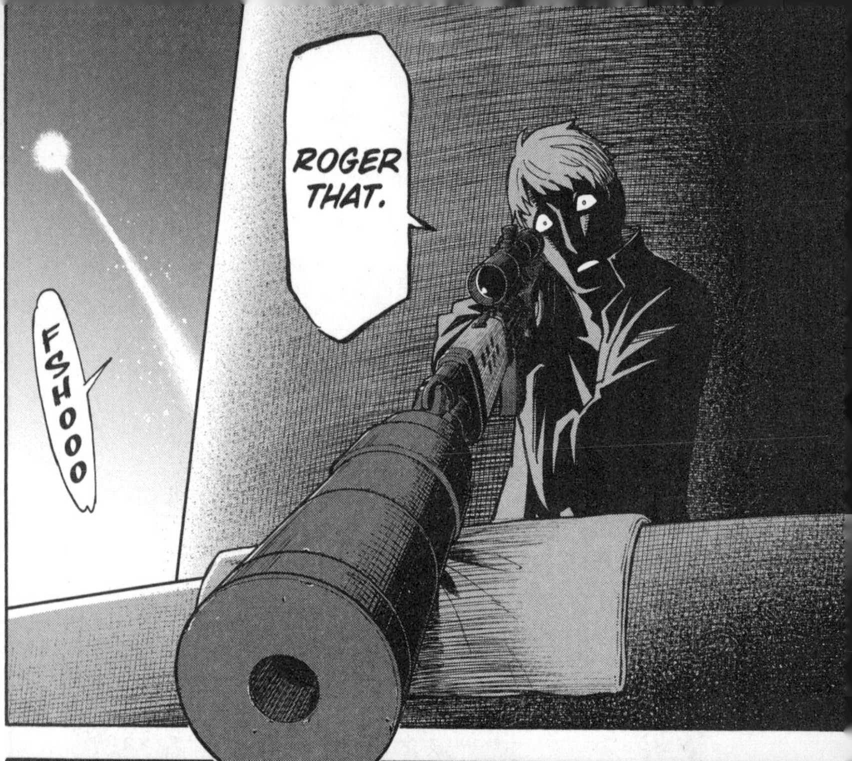
ROGER THAT.
FSHOOO

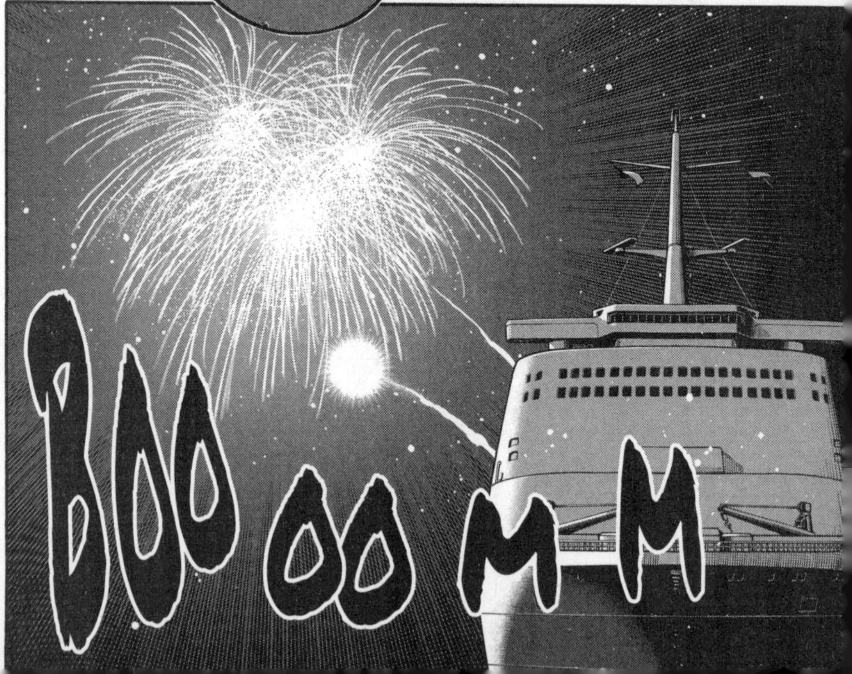
BOOOOMM

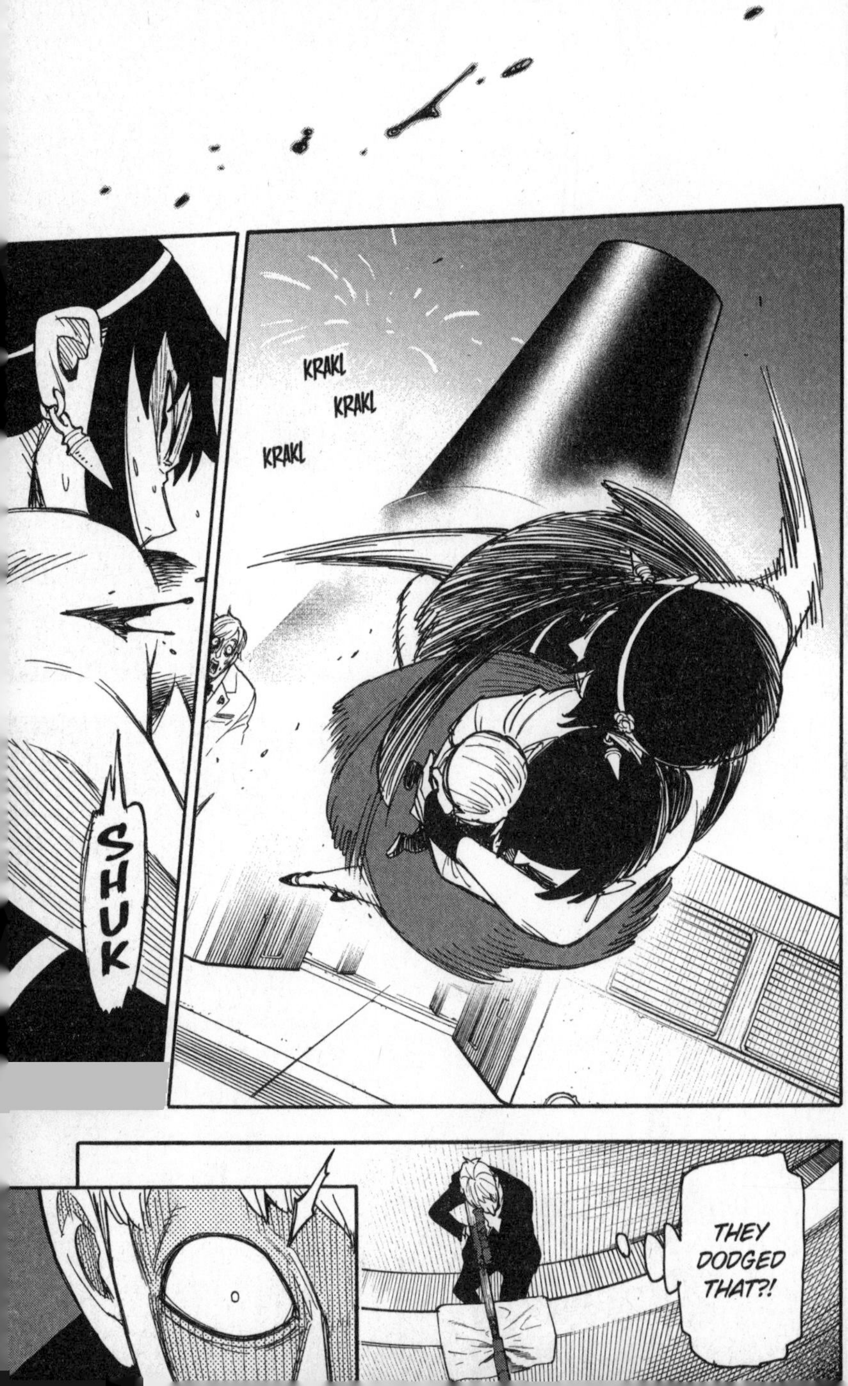
KRAKL
KRAKL
KRAKL
SHUK
THEY DODGED THAT?!

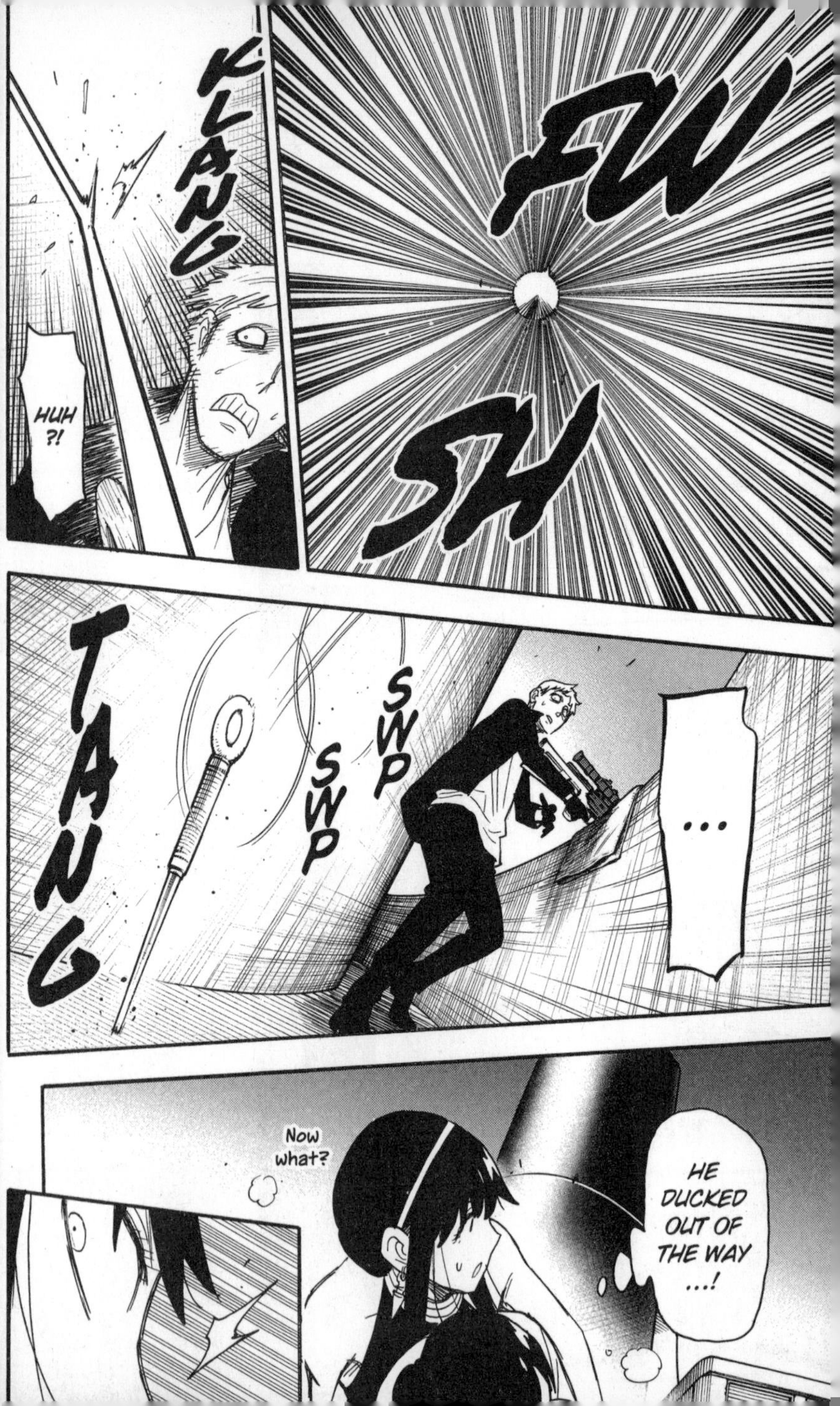
FWSH
KLANG
HUH?!
...
SWP SWP
TANG
HE DUCKED OUT OF THE WAY ...!
Now what?

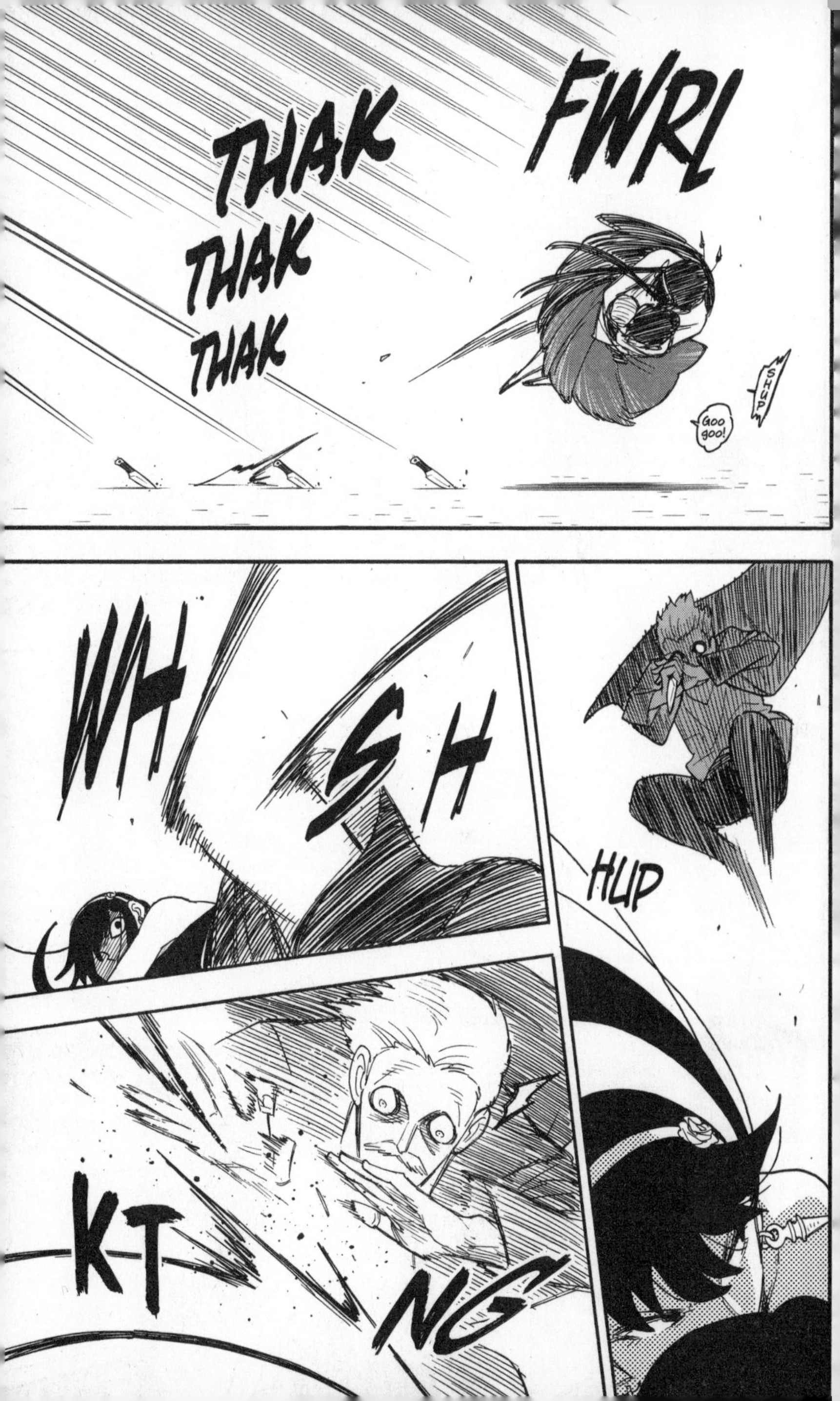
FWRL
THAK
THAK
THAK
SHUP
Goo goo!
HUP
WHSH
KTNG

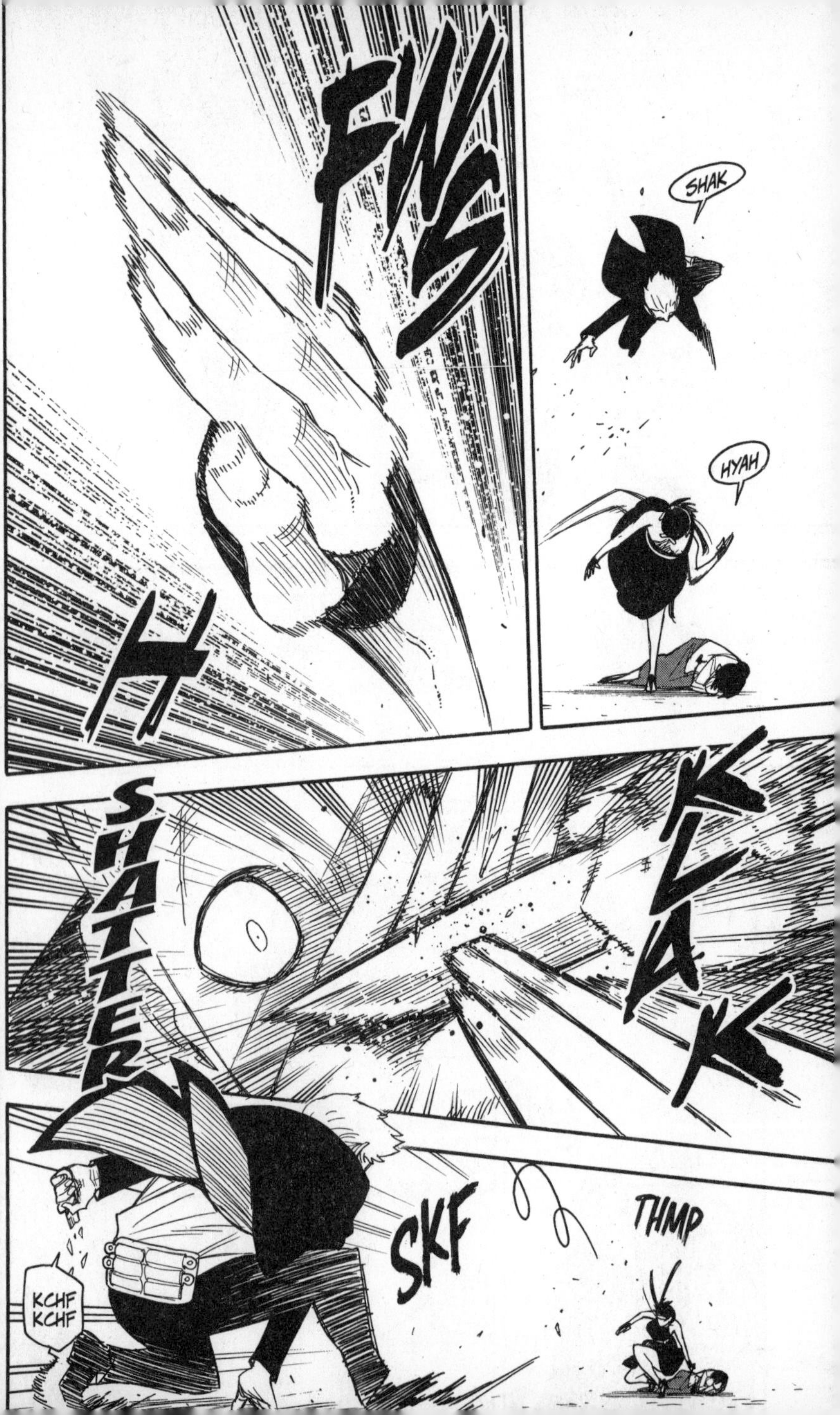

SHAK
HYAH
FWS
KLAK
SHATTER
THMP
SKF
KCHF KCHF

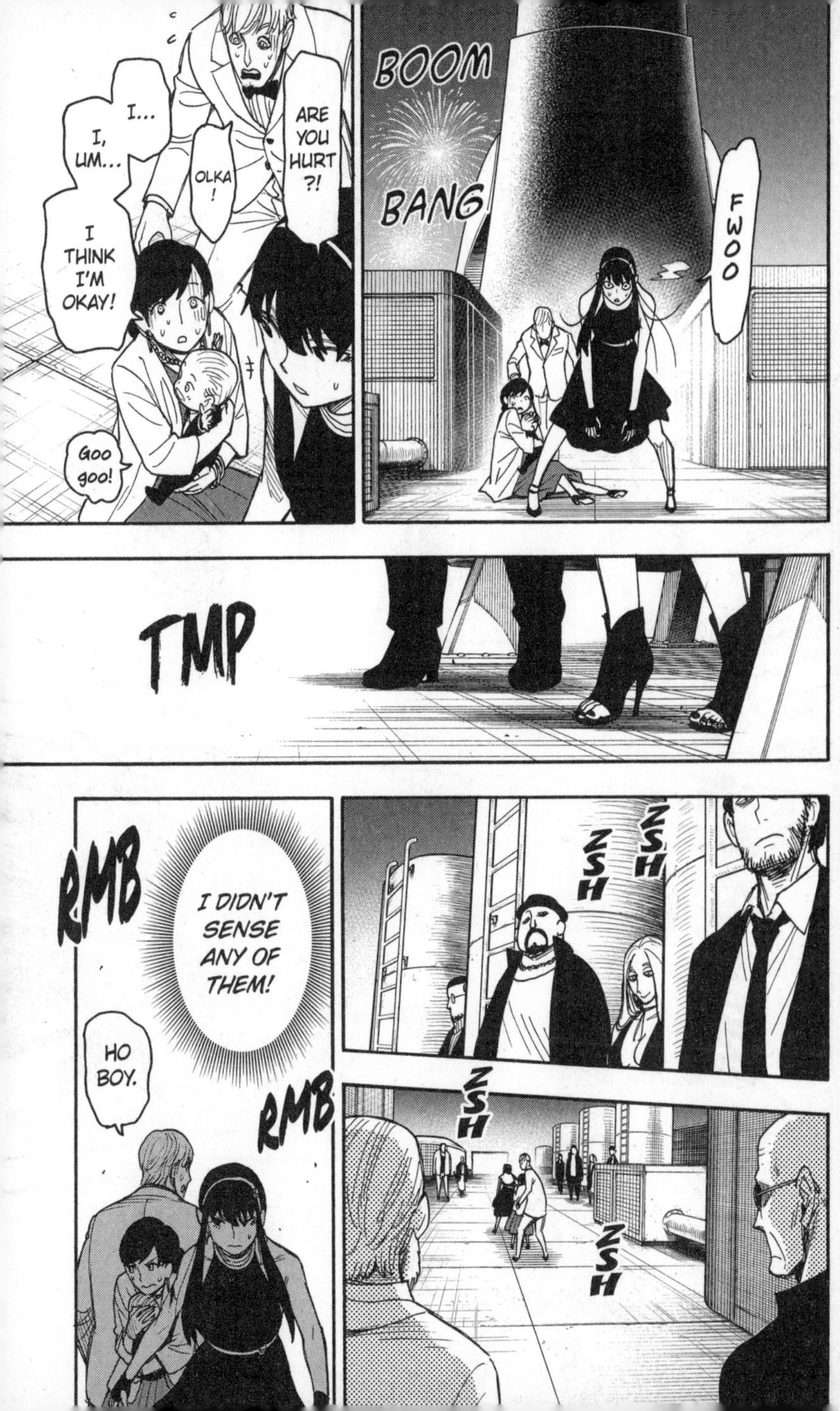
BOOM
BANG
FWOO
ARE YOU HURT?!
OLKA!
I...
I, UM...
I THINK I'M OKAY!
Goo goo!
TMP
ZSH
ZSH
ZSH
ZSH
RMB
I DIDN'T SENSE ANY OF THEM!
HO BOY.
RMB

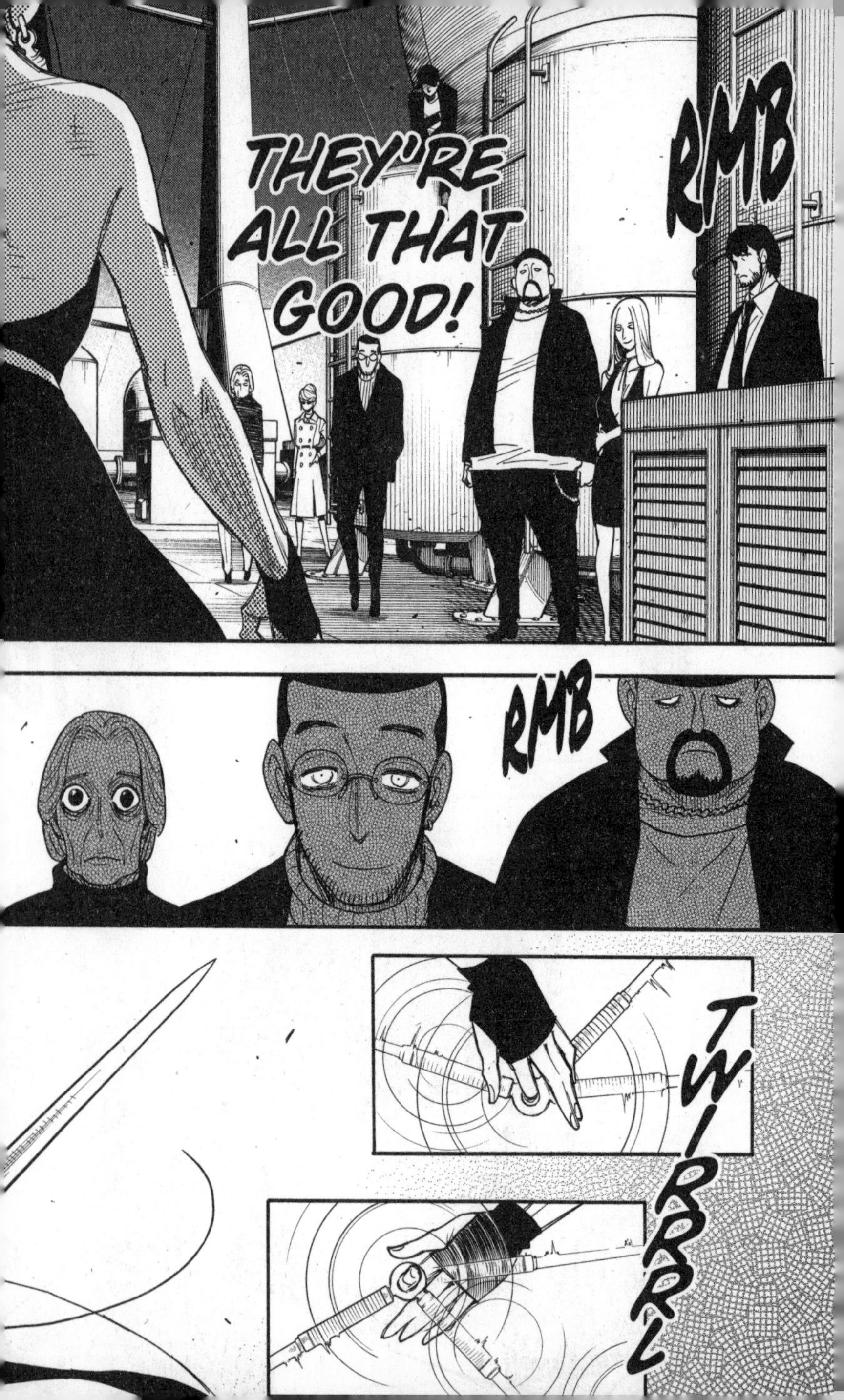
RMB
THEY'RE ALL THAT GOOD!
RMB
TWIRRRL

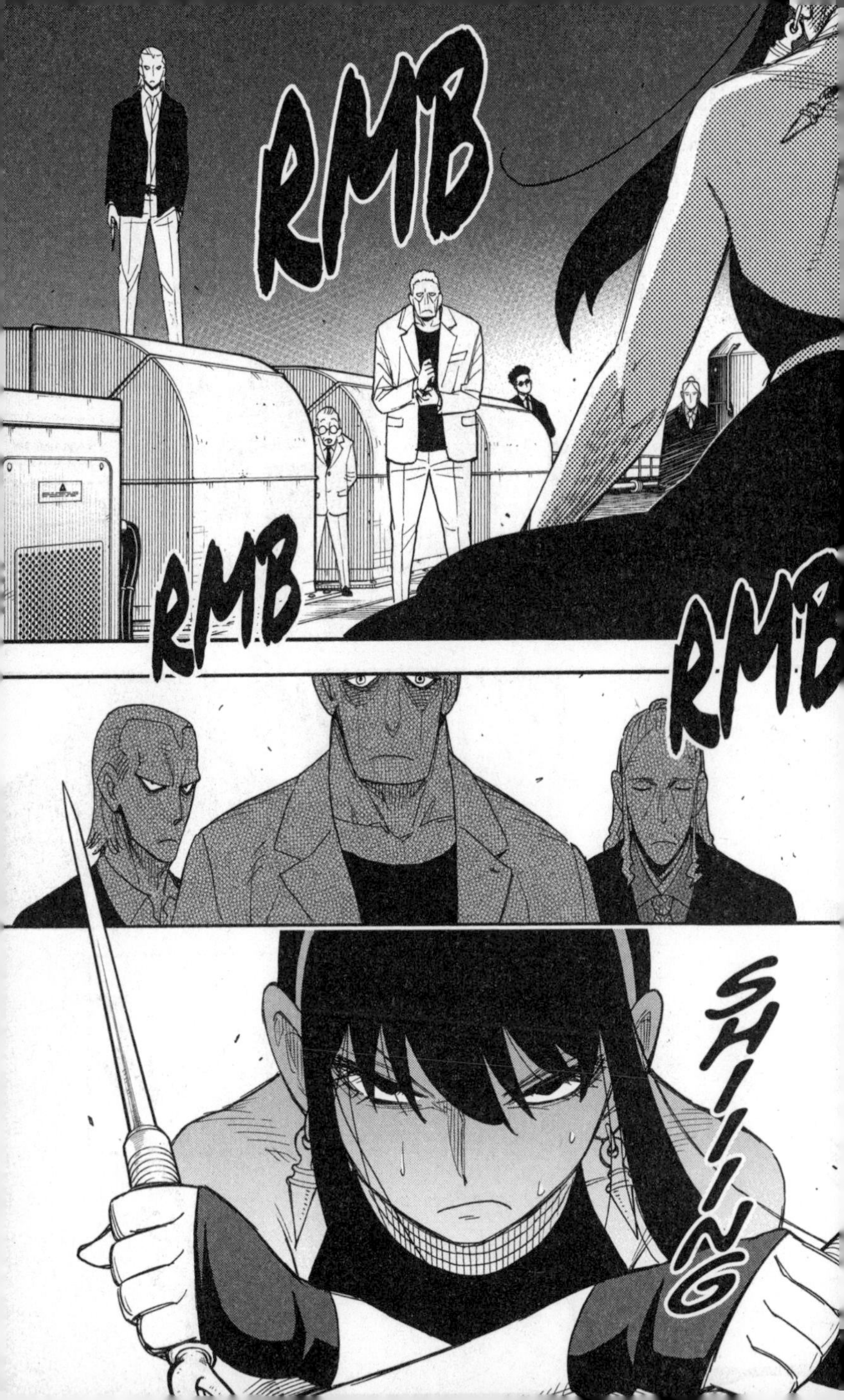
RMB
RMB
RMB
SHIIING

SPY×FAMILY

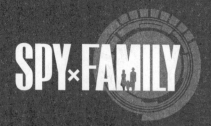

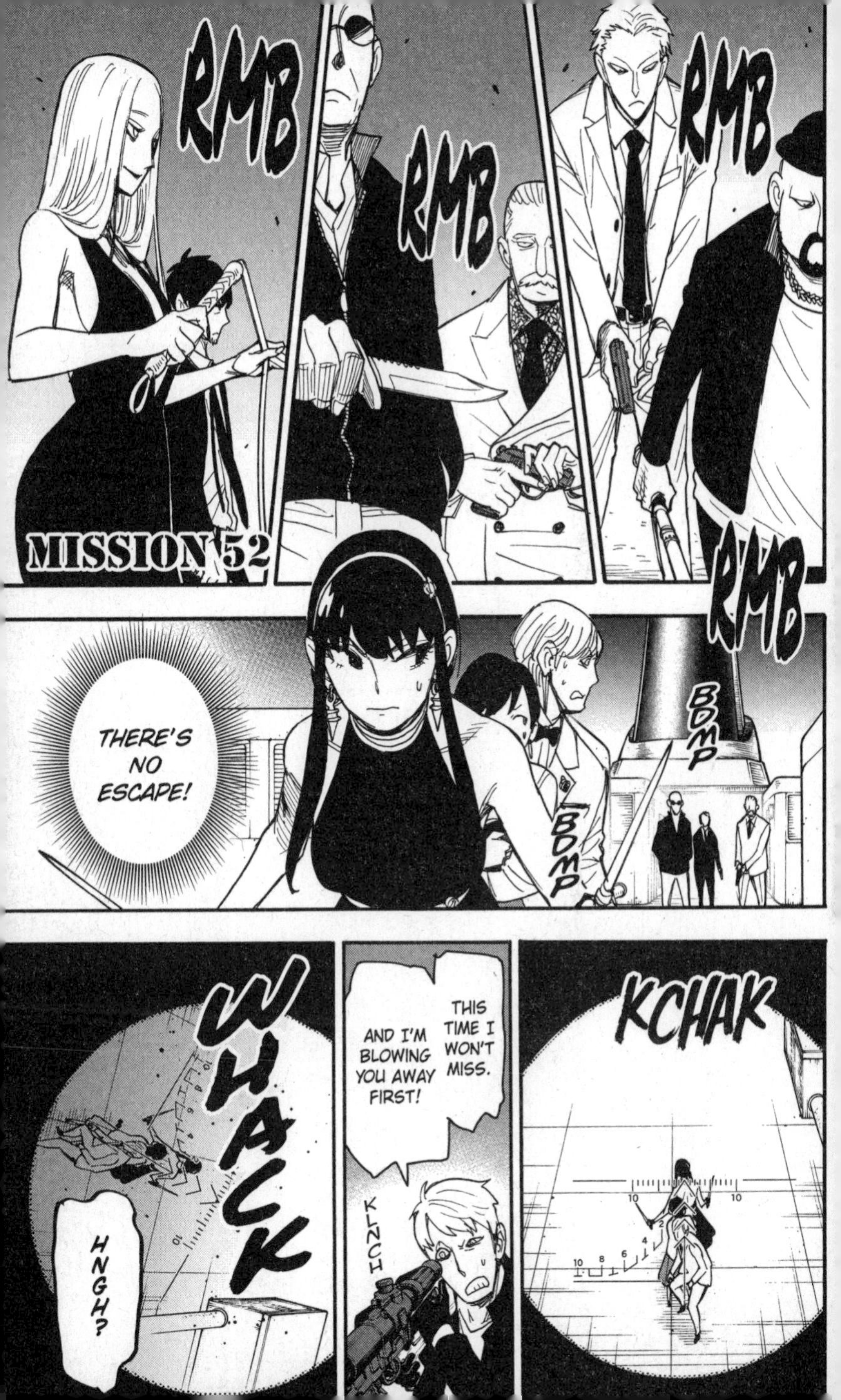
RMB
RMB
RMB
RMB
MISSION 52
RMB
BDMP
BDMP
THERE'S NO ESCAPE!
KCHAK
THIS TIME I WON'T MISS.
AND I'M BLOWING YOU AWAY FIRST!
KLNCH
WHACK
HNGH?

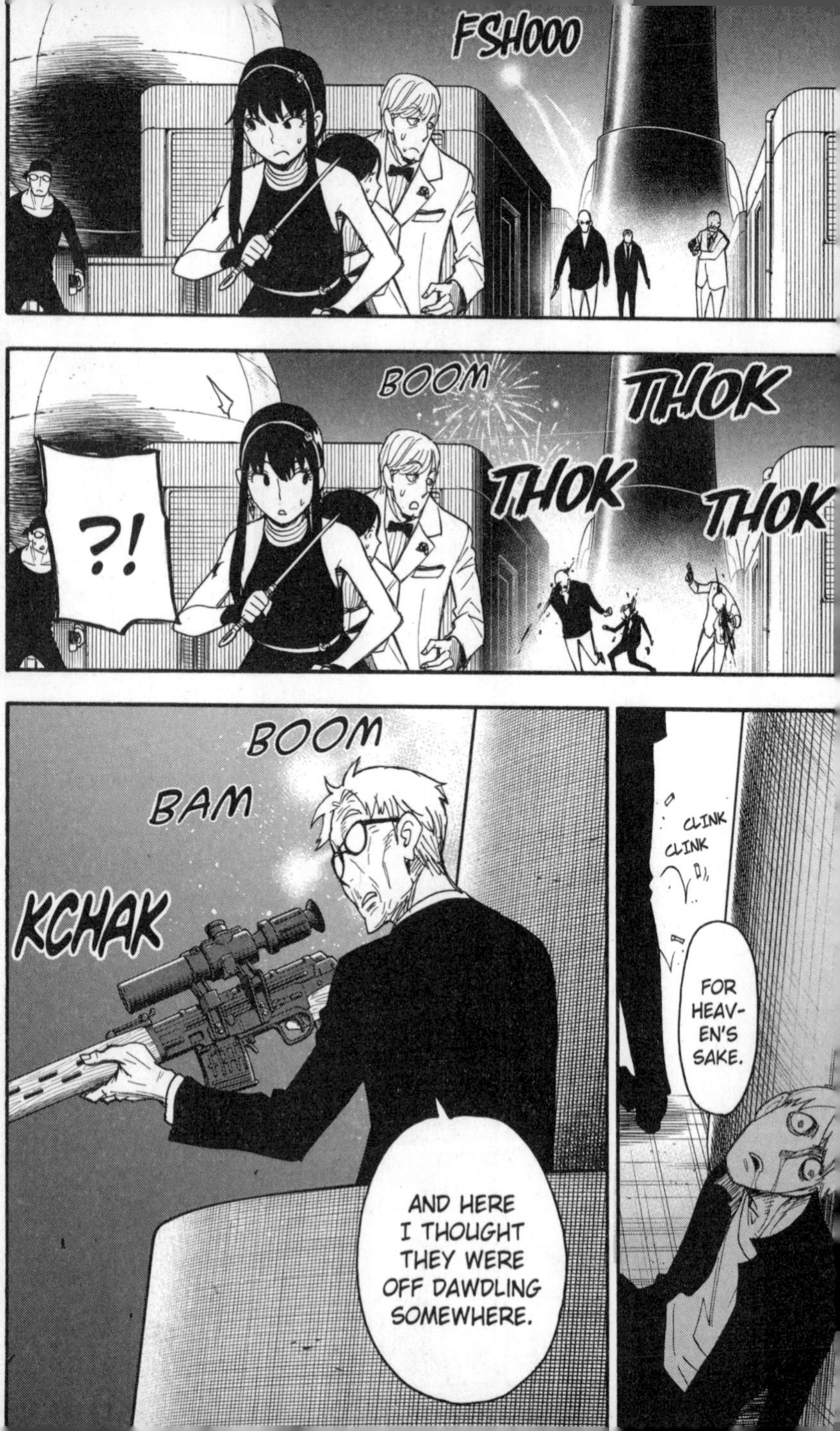
FSHOOO
BOOM
THOK
THOK
THOK
?!
CLINK
CLINK
FOR HEAVEN'S SAKE.
BOOM
BAM
KCHAK
AND HERE I THOUGHT THEY WERE OFF DAWDLING SOMEWHERE.

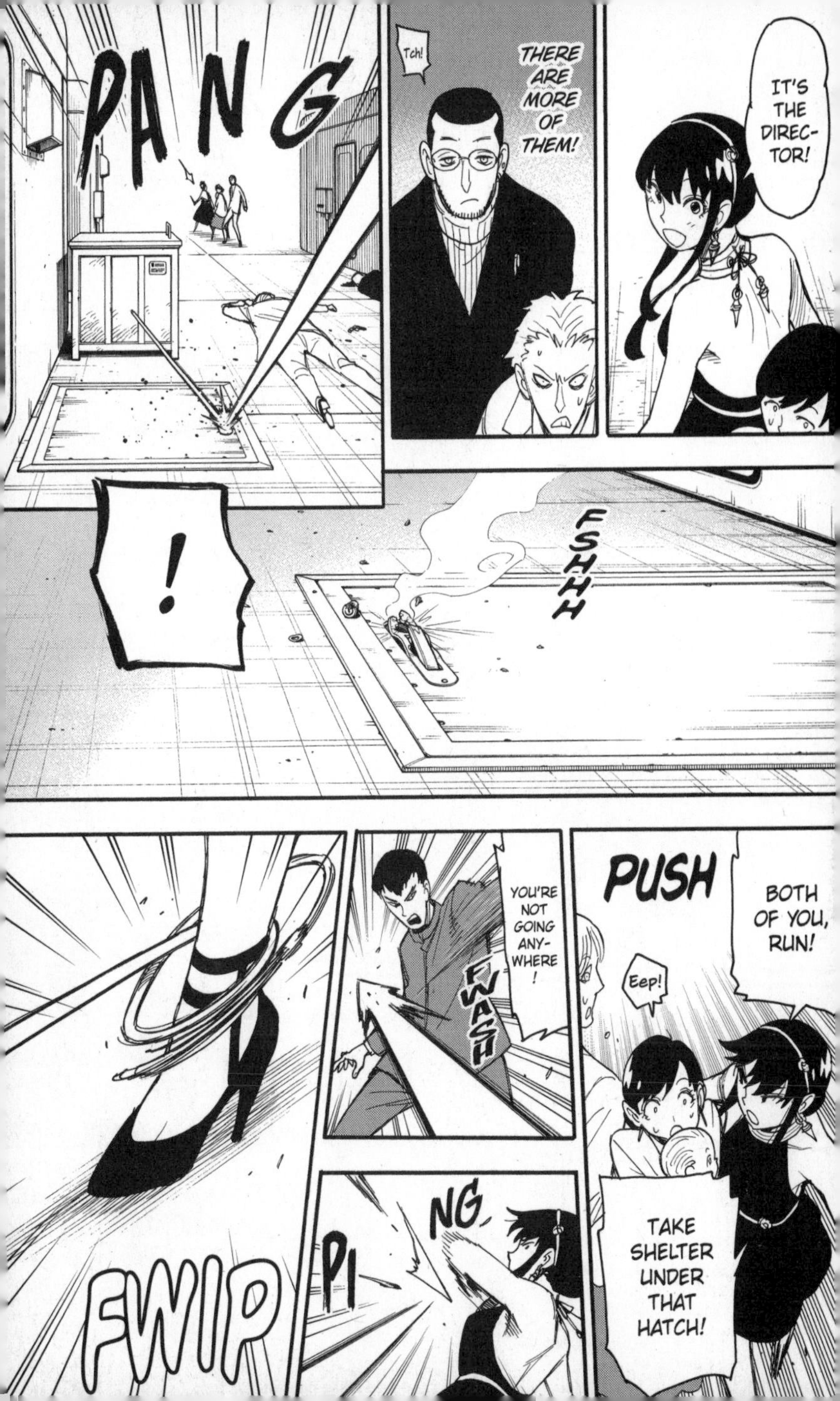
IT'S THE DIRECTOR!
Tch!
THERE ARE MORE OF THEM!
PANG
FSHHH
!
BOTH OF YOU, RUN!
PUSH
Eep!
TAKE SHELTER UNDER THAT HATCH!
YOU'RE NOT GOING ANYWHERE!
FWASH
PING
FWIP

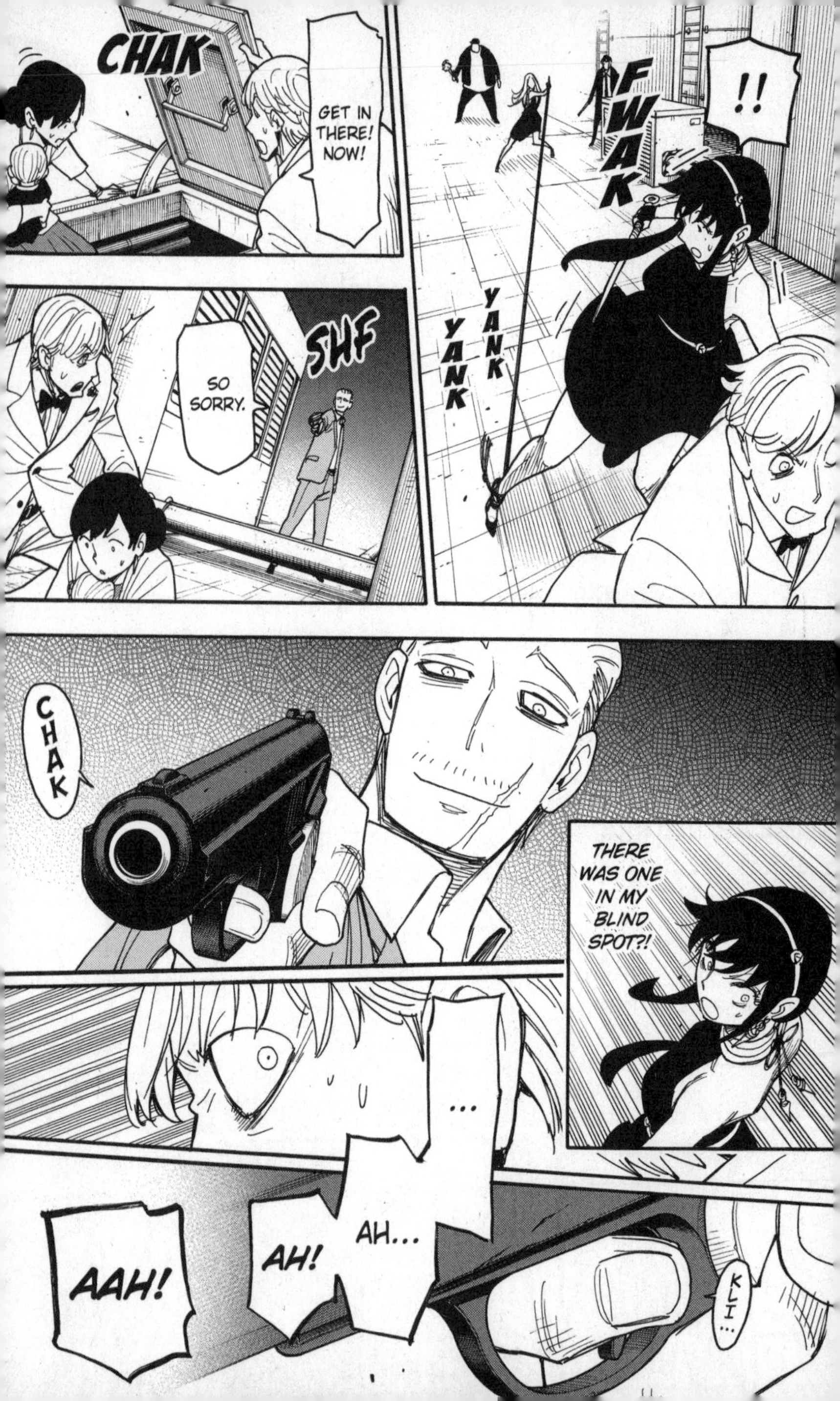
!!
FWAK
YANK
YANK
CHAK
GET IN THERE! NOW!
SO SORRY.
SHF
CHAK
THERE WAS ONE IN MY BLIND SPOT?!
...
KLI...
AH...
AH!
AAH!

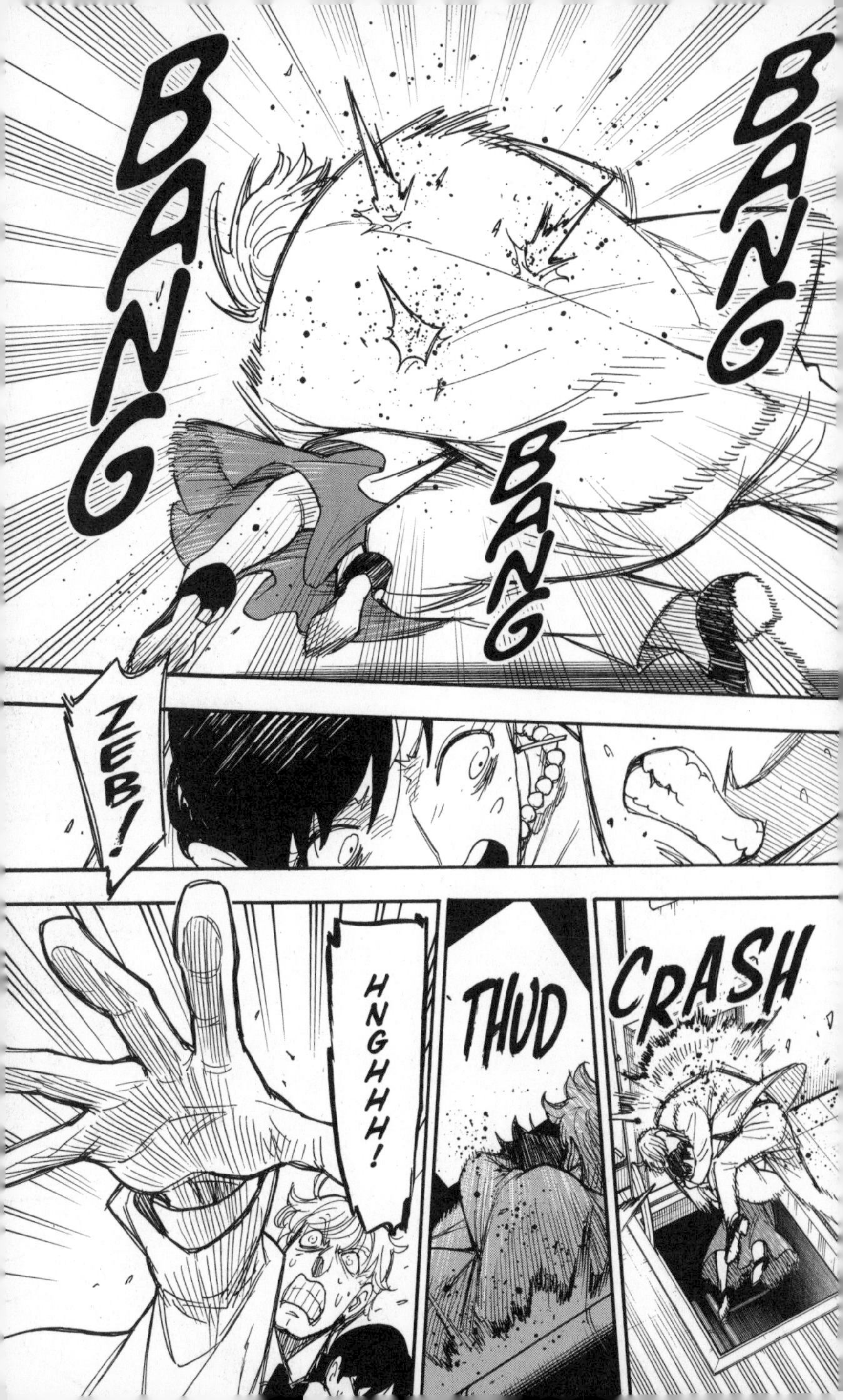
BANG
BANG
BANG
ZEB!
CRASH
THUD
HNGHHHH!

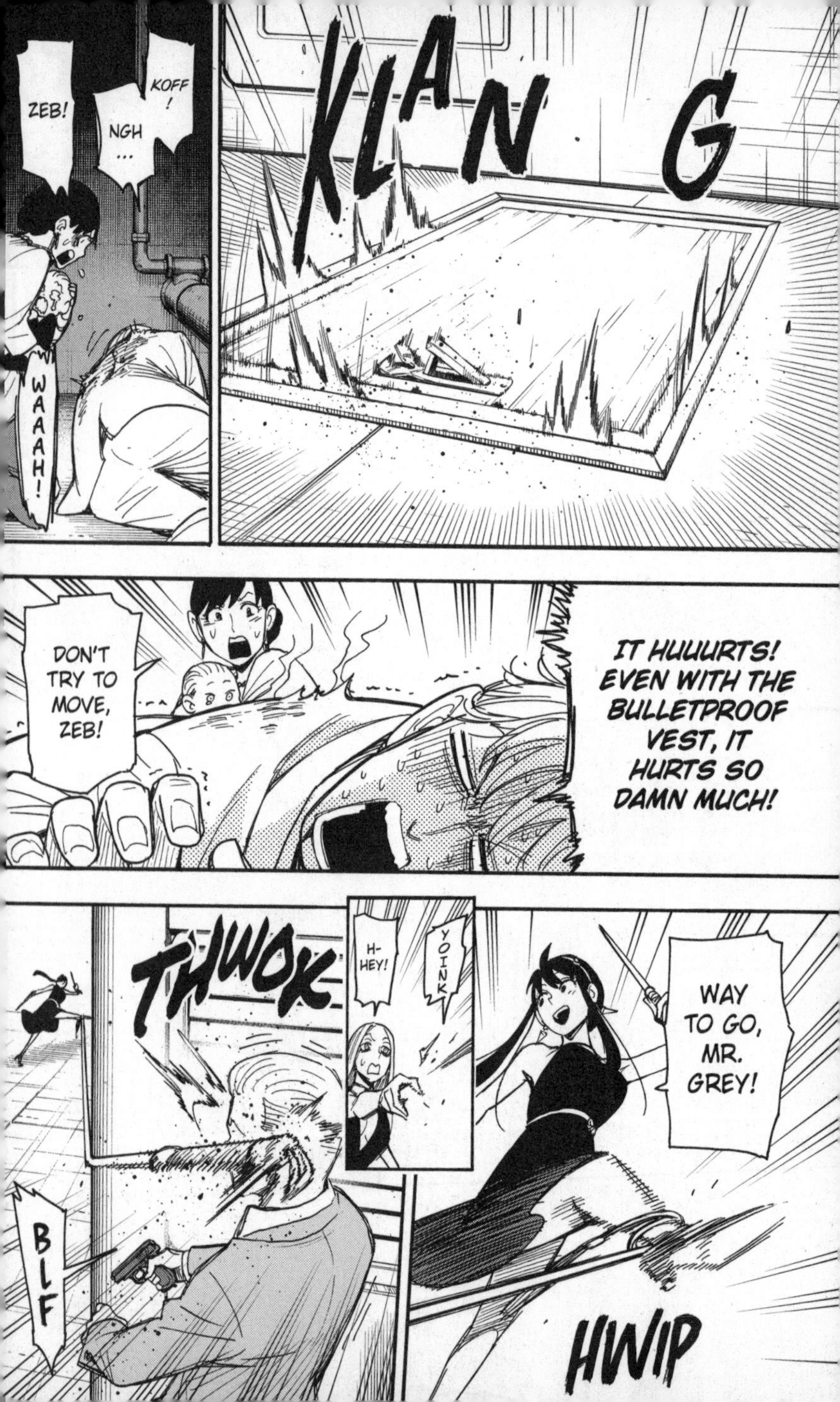
KLANG
KOFF! NGH...
ZEB!
WAAAAH!
IT HUUURTS! EVEN WITH THE BULLETPROOF VEST, IT HURTS SO DAMN MUCH!
DON'T TRY TO MOVE, ZEB!
WAY TO GO, MR. GREY!
HWIP
YOINK
H-HEY!
THWOK
BLF

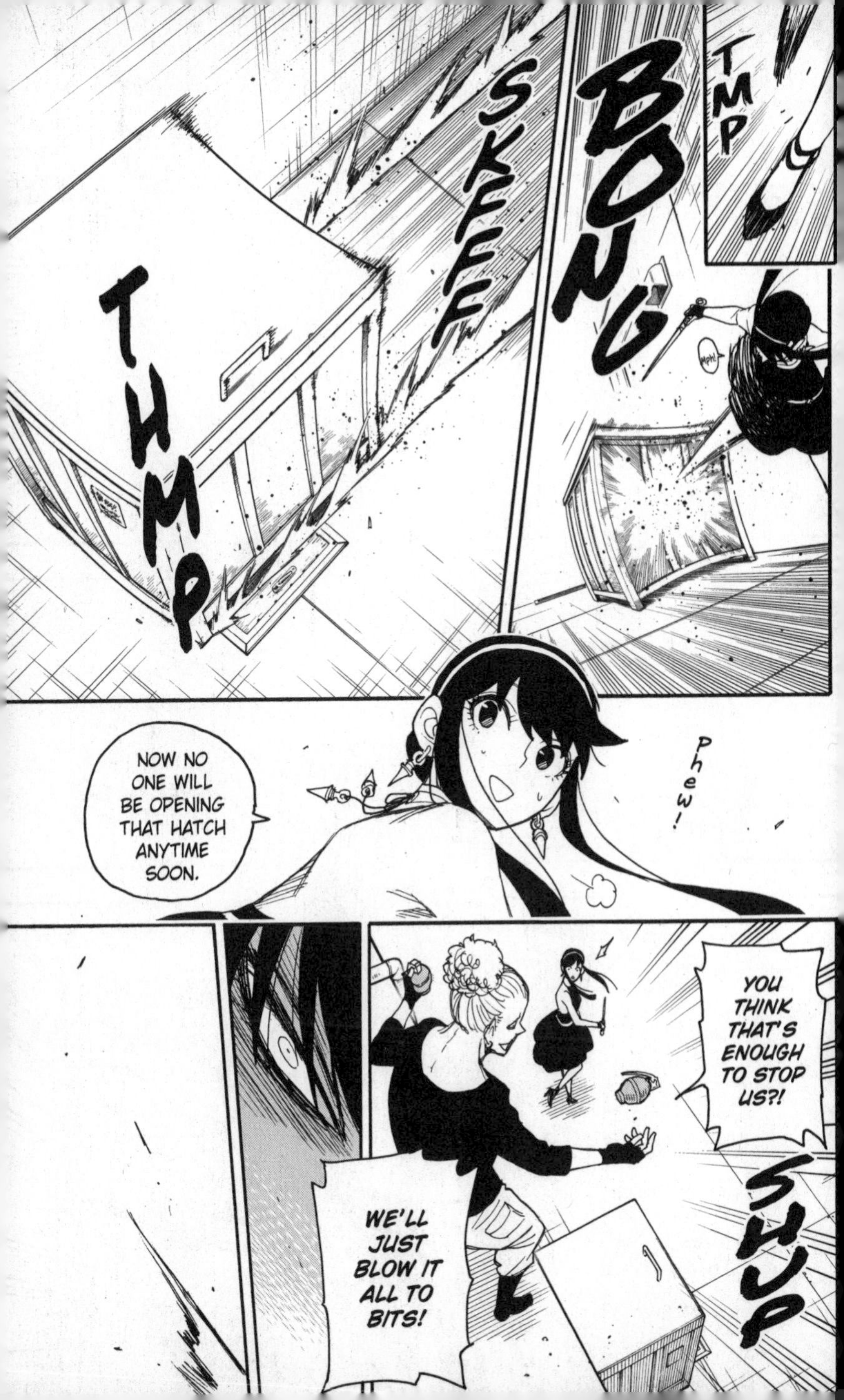
TMP
BONG
Mph!
SKFFF
THUMP
Phew!
NOW NO ONE WILL BE OPENING THAT HATCH ANYTIME SOON.
YOU THINK THAT'S ENOUGH TO STOP US?!
SHUP
WE'LL JUST BLOW IT ALL TO BITS!

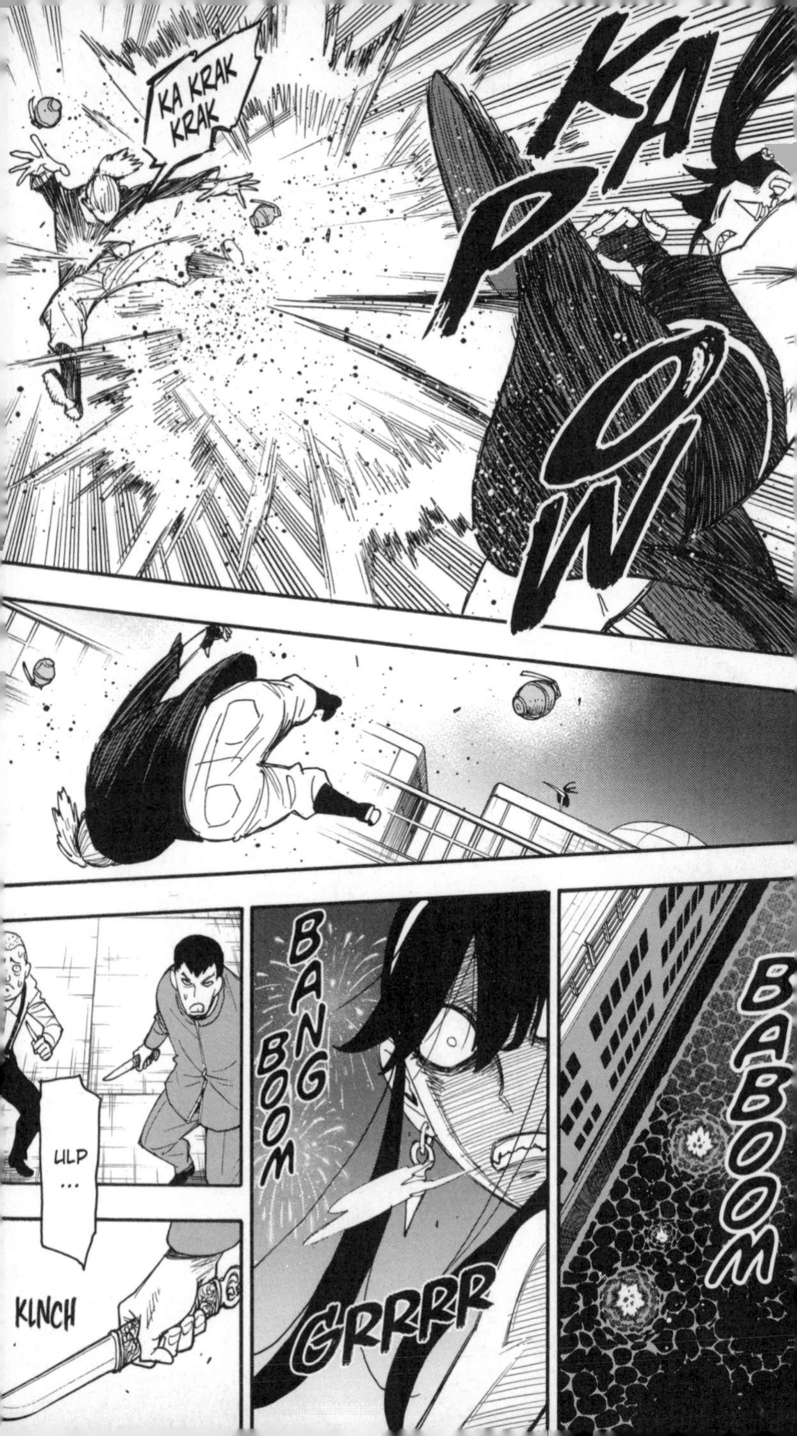
KAPOW
KA KRAK KRAK
BABOOM
BANG BOOM
GRRRR
ULP...
KLNCH

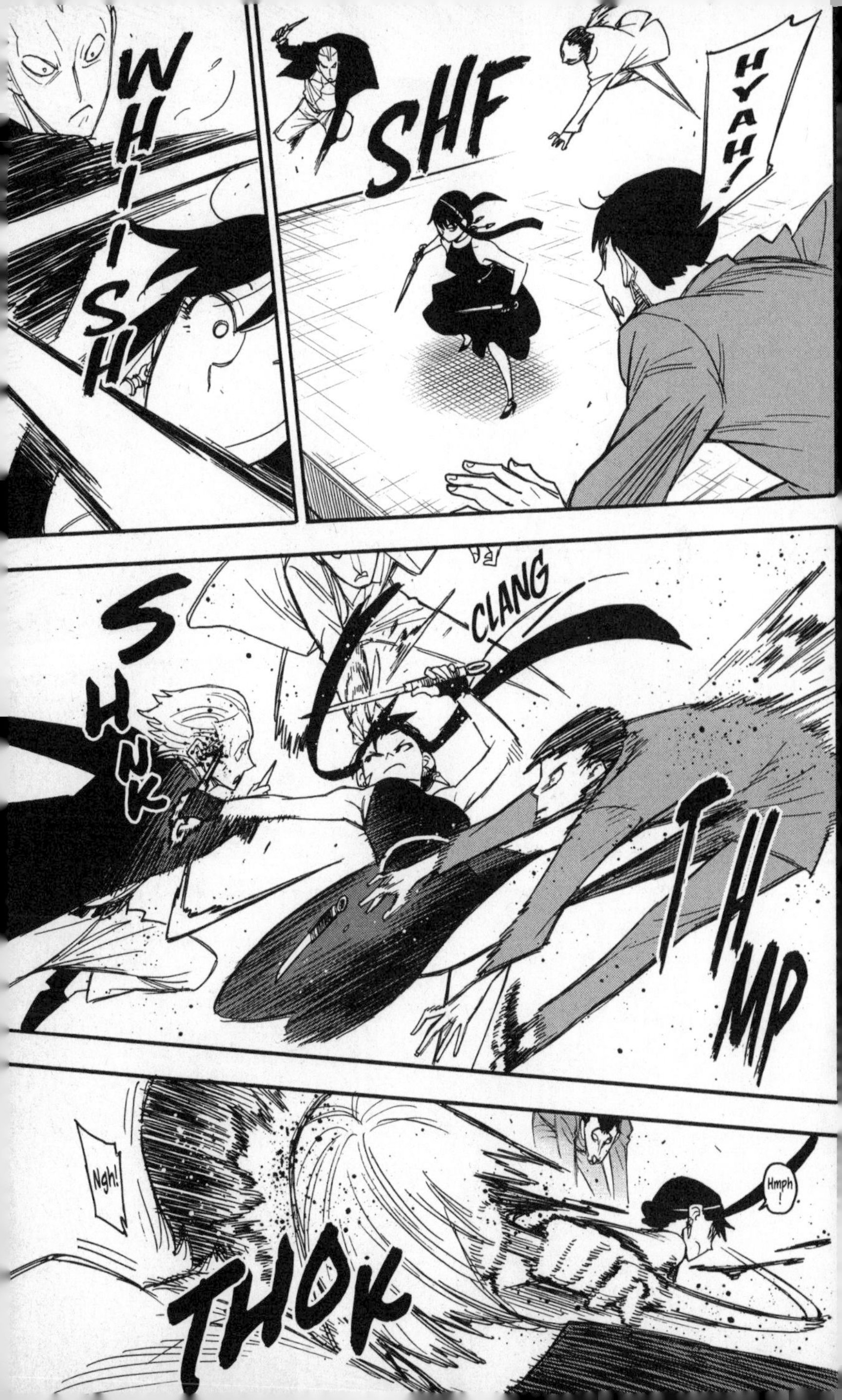
HYAH!
SHF
WHIISH
CLANG
THMP
SHUNK
Hmph!
Ngh!
THOK

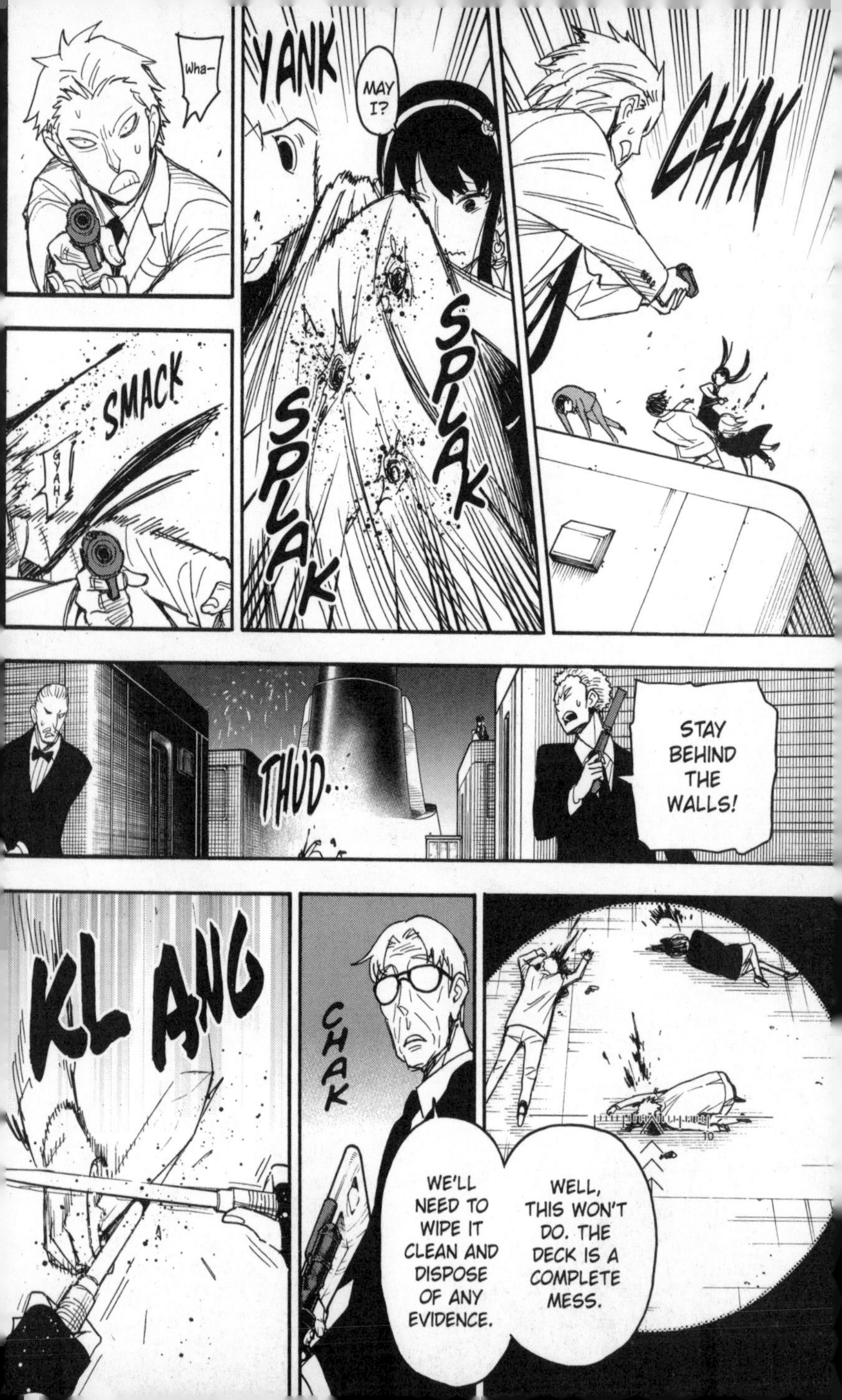
CHAK
YANK
MAY I?
SPLAK
SPLAK
Wha-
SMACK
GYAH!
STAY BEHIND THE WALLS!
THUD...
WELL, THIS WON'T DO. THE DECK IS A COMPLETE MESS.
WE'LL NEED TO WIPE IT CLEAN AND DISPOSE OF ANY EVIDENCE.
CHAK
KLANG

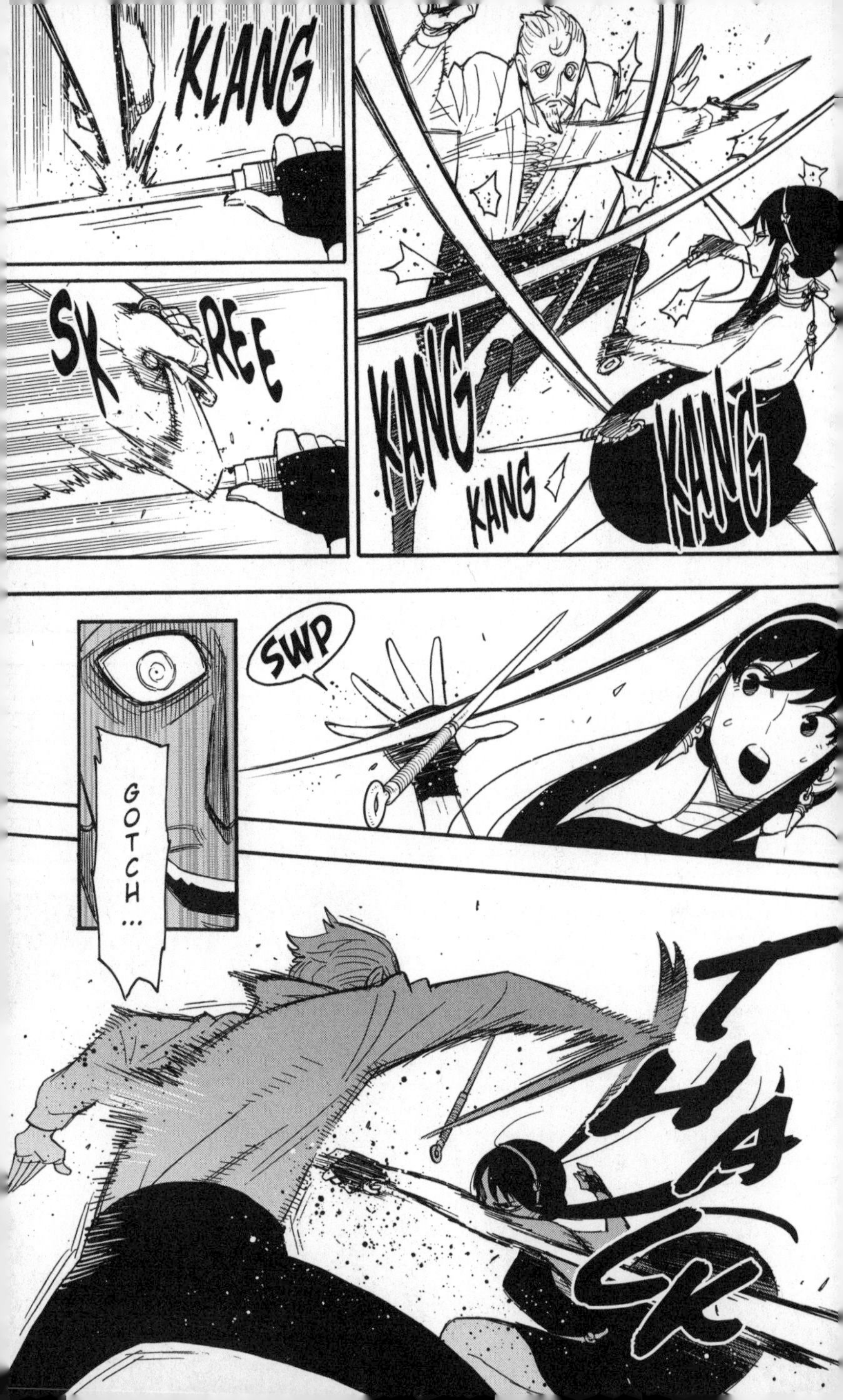
KANG
KANG
KANG
KLANG
SKREE
SWP
GOTCH...
THWACK

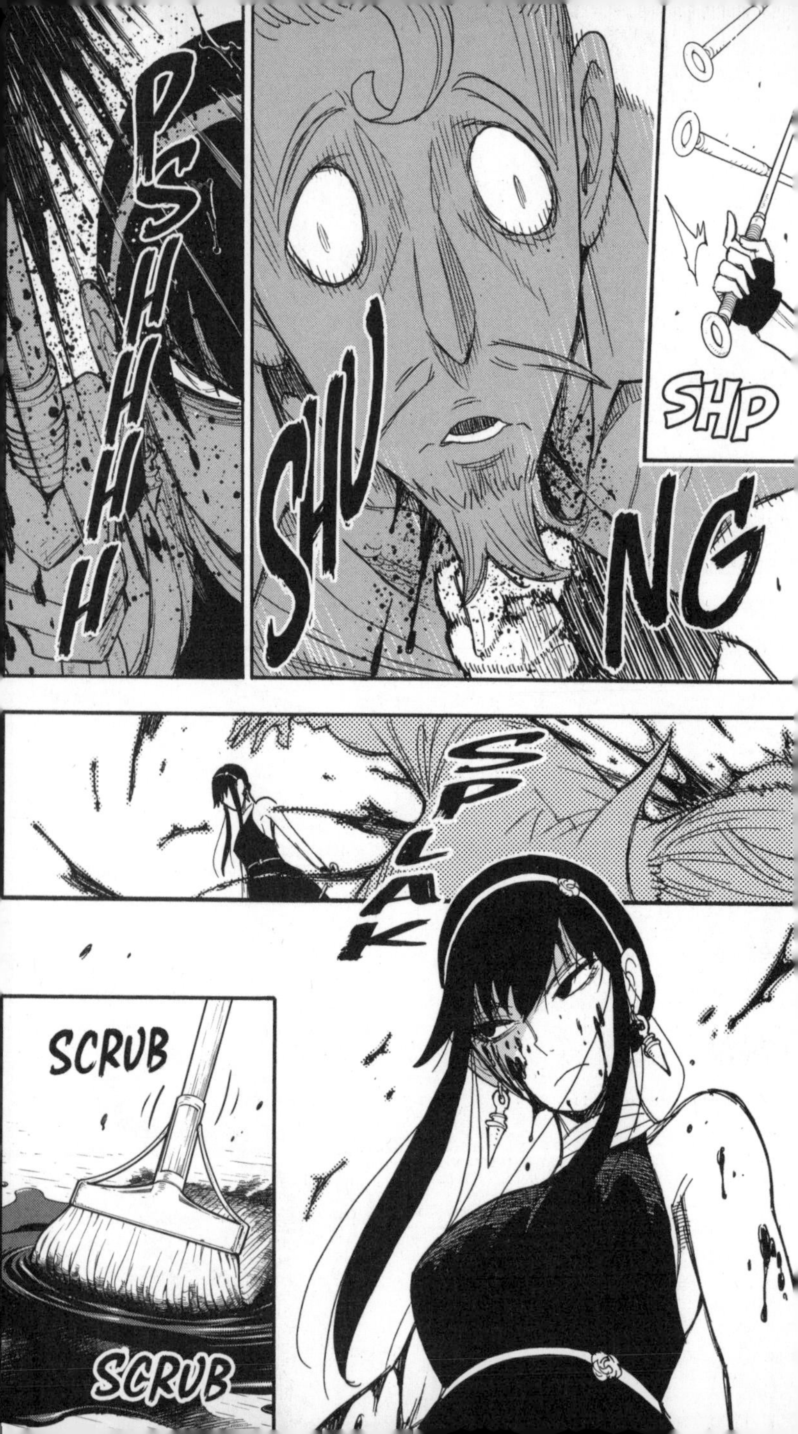
SHP
SHUNG
PSHHHHH
SPLAK
SCRUB
SCRUB

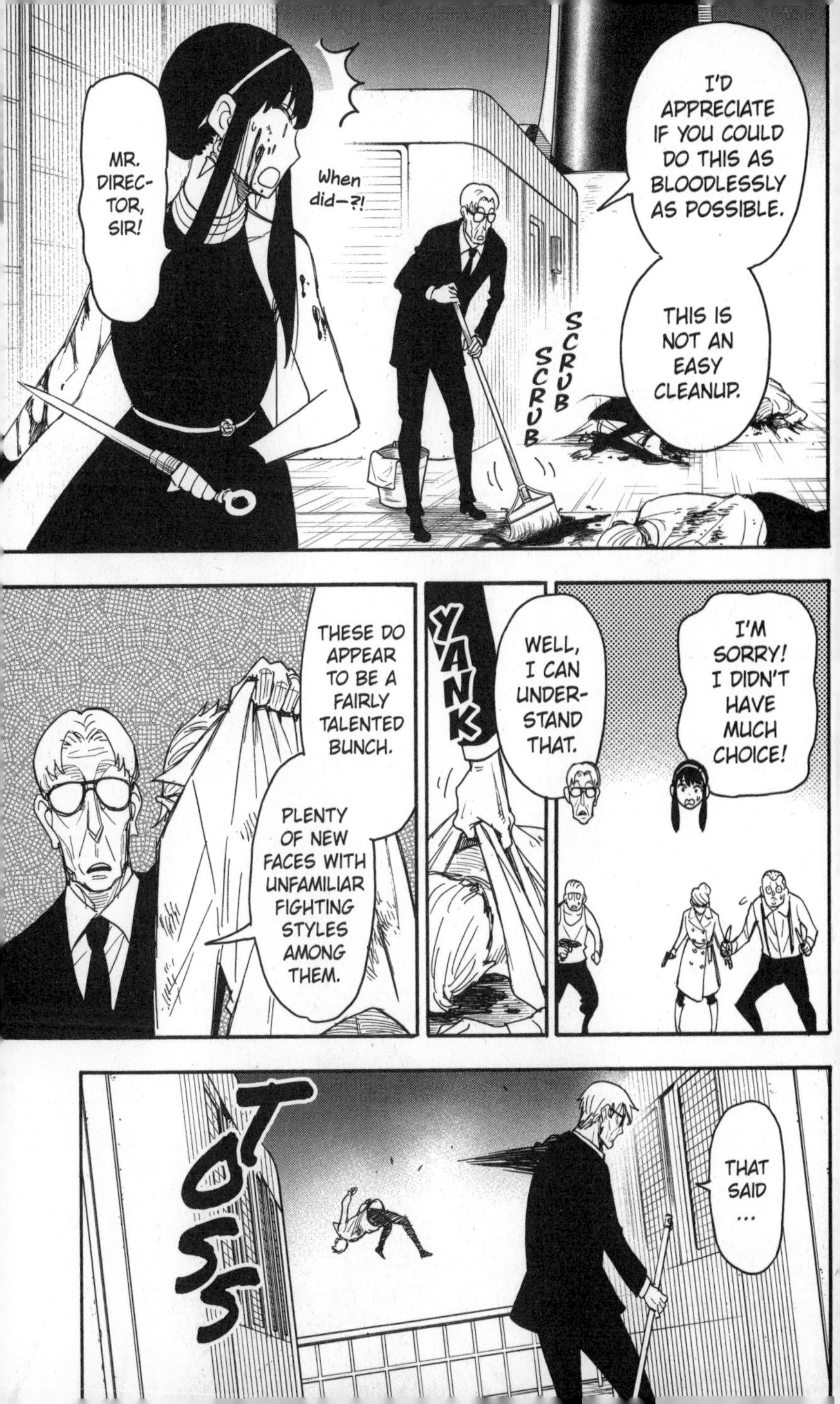
I'D APPRECIATE IF YOU COULD DO THIS AS BLOODLESSLY AS POSSIBLE.
THIS IS NOT AN EASY CLEANUP.
SCRUB SCRUB
When did—?!
MR. DIRECTOR, SIR!
I'M SORRY! I DIDN'T HAVE MUCH CHOICE!
WELL, I CAN UNDERSTAND THAT.
YANK
THESE DO APPEAR TO BE A FAIRLY TALENTED BUNCH.
PLENTY OF NEW FACES WITH UNFAMILIAR FIGHTING STYLES AMONG THEM.
THAT SAID ...
TOSS

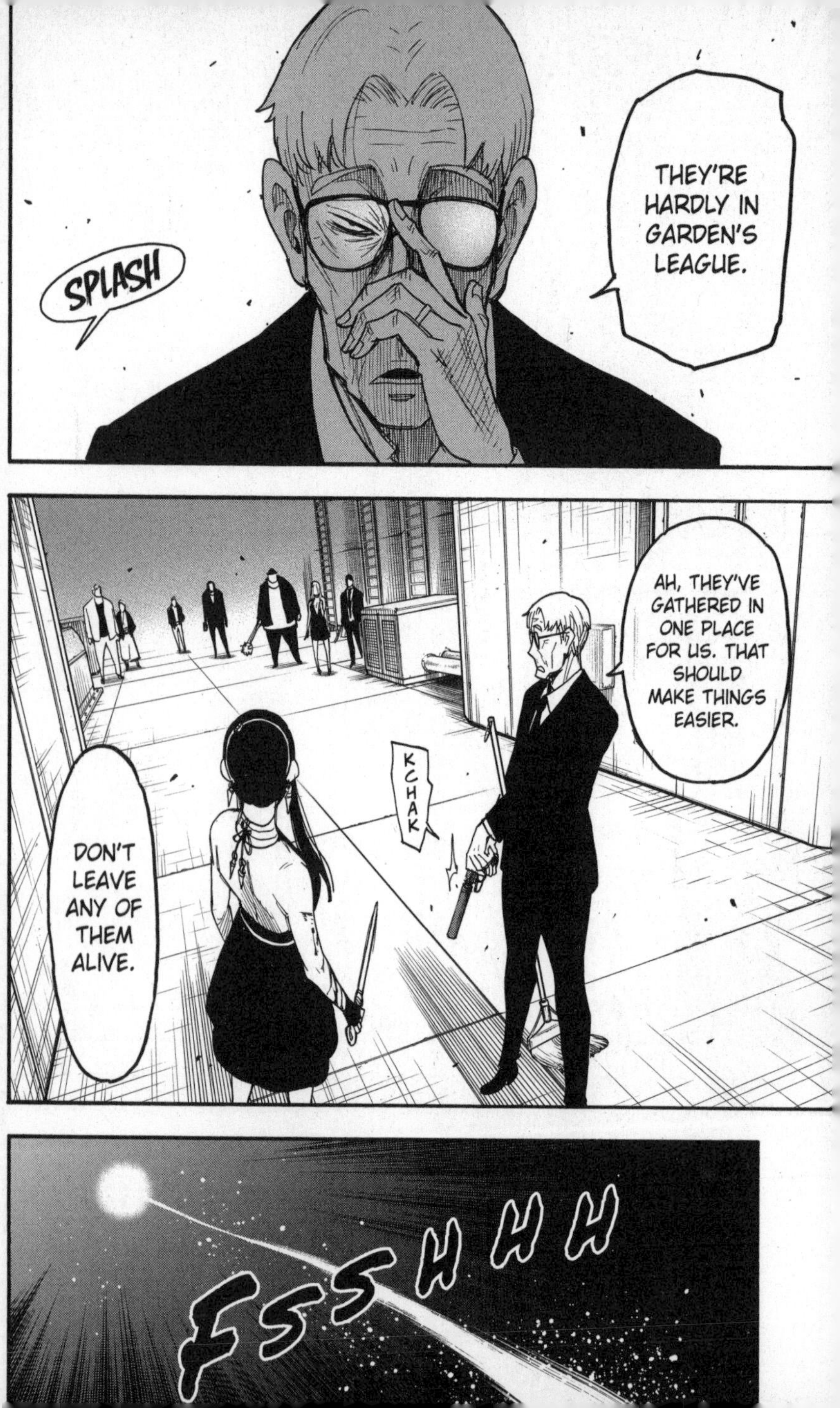
THEY'RE HARDLY IN GARDEN'S LEAGUE.
SPLASH
AH, THEY'VE GATHERED IN ONE PLACE FOR US. THAT SHOULD MAKE THINGS EASIER.
KCHAK
DON'T LEAVE ANY OF THEM ALIVE.
FSSHHHH

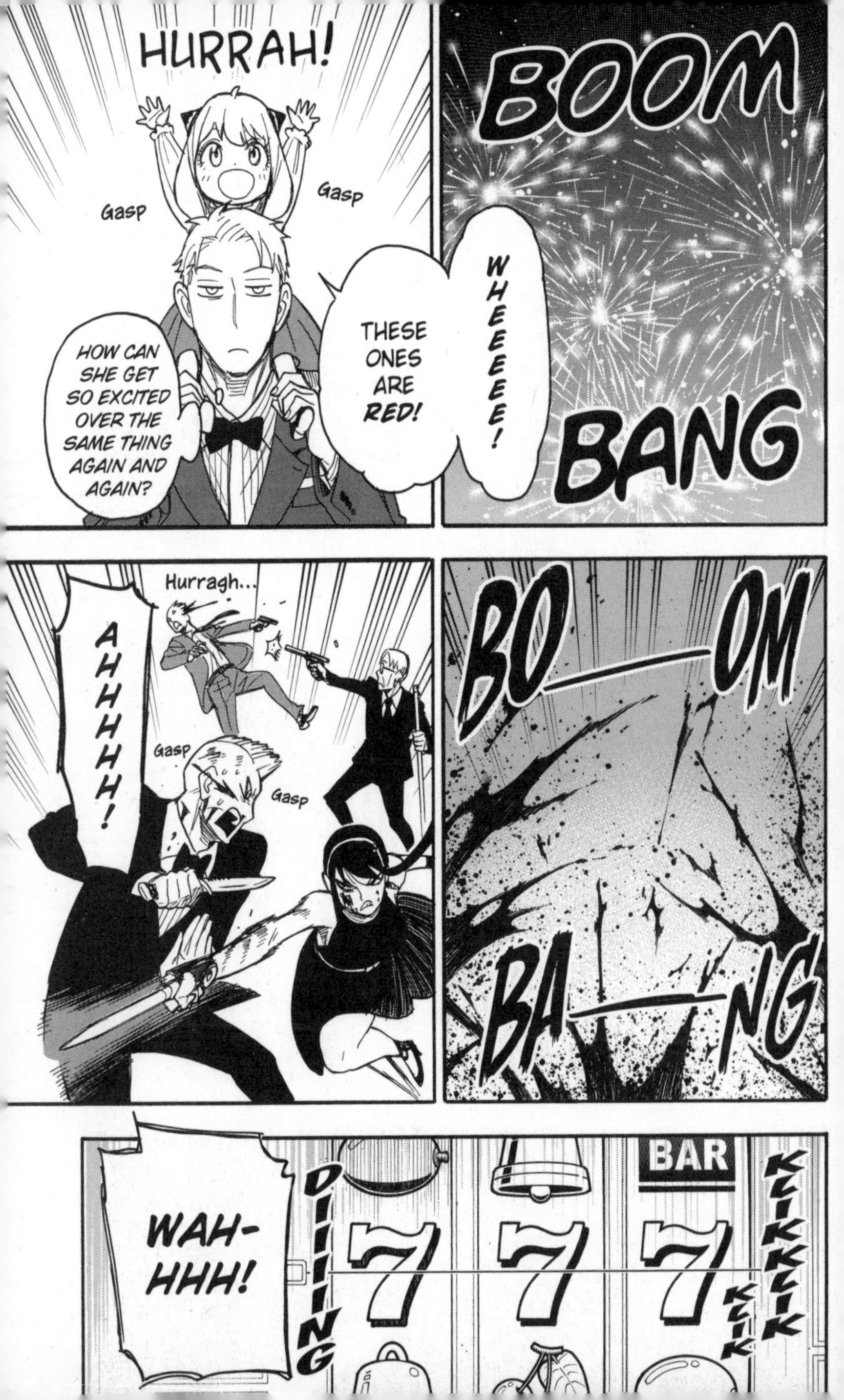
BOOM
WHEEEEEE!
BANG
HURRAH!
THESE ONES ARE RED!
Gasp
Gasp
HOW CAN SHE GET SO EXCITED OVER THE SAME THING AGAIN AND AGAIN?
BO—OM
BA—NG
Hurragh...
AHHHHHH!
Gasp
Gasp
KLIKKLIKKLIK
KLIK
BAR
DIIIING
WAH-HHH!

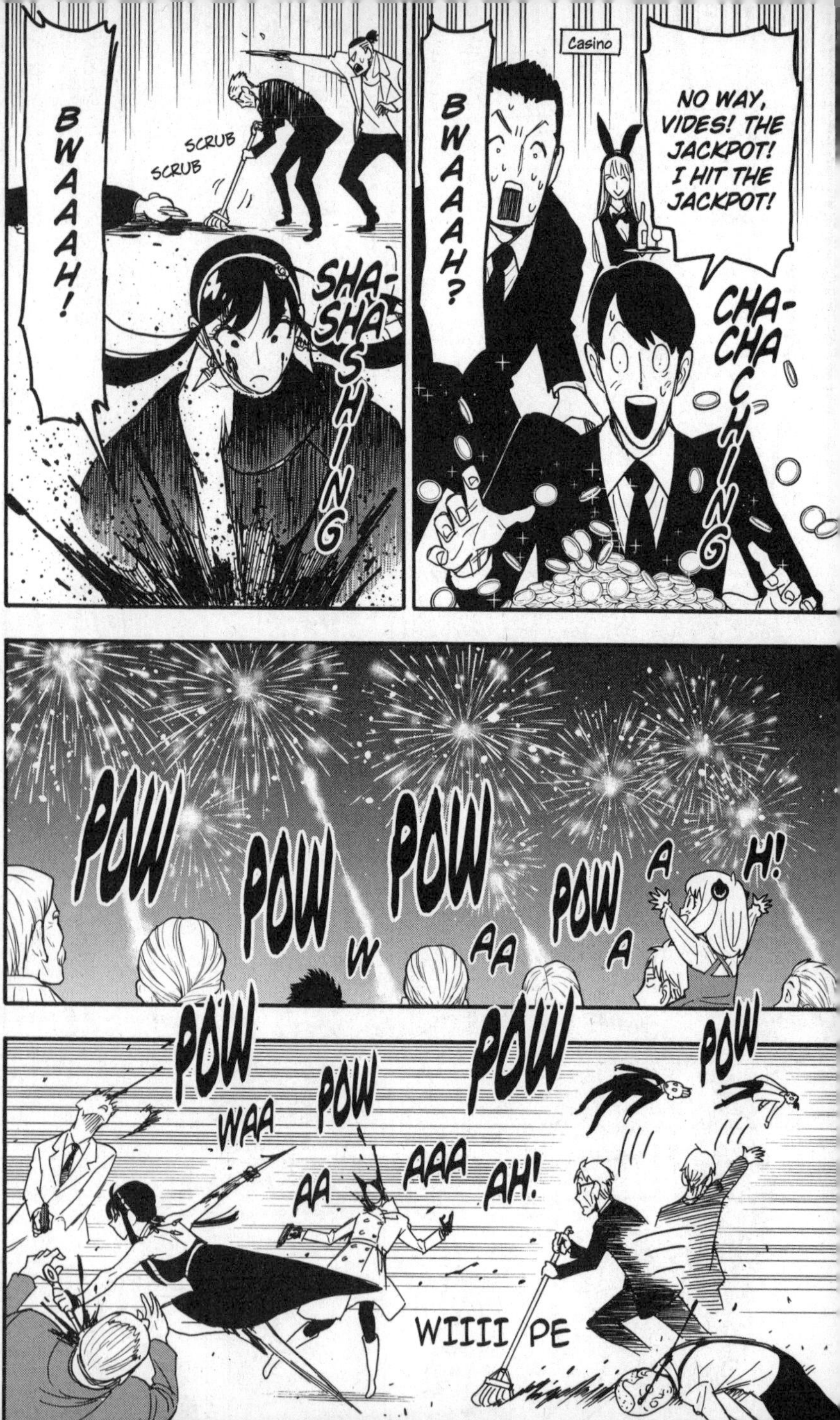
Casino
NO WAY, VIDES! THE JACKPOT! I HIT THE JACKPOT!
BWAAAAAH?
CHA-CHA-CHING
BWAAAAH!
SCRUB
SCRUB
SHA-SHA-SHING
POW
POW
POW
POW
A H!
AA
A
W
POW
POW
POW
POW
WAA
AA
AAA
AH!
WIIII PE

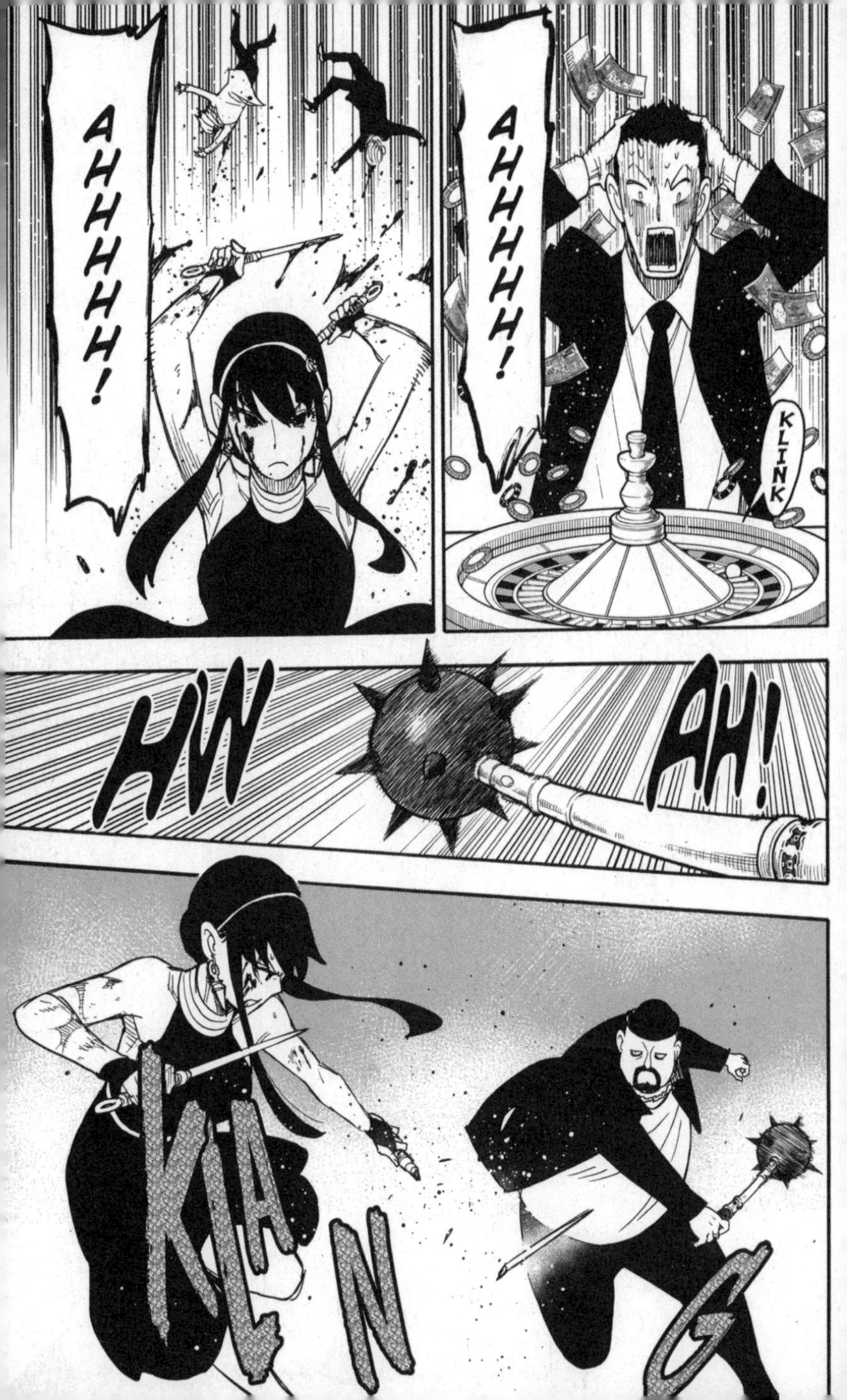
AHHHHH!
KLINK
AHHHHH!
HWAH!
KLANG

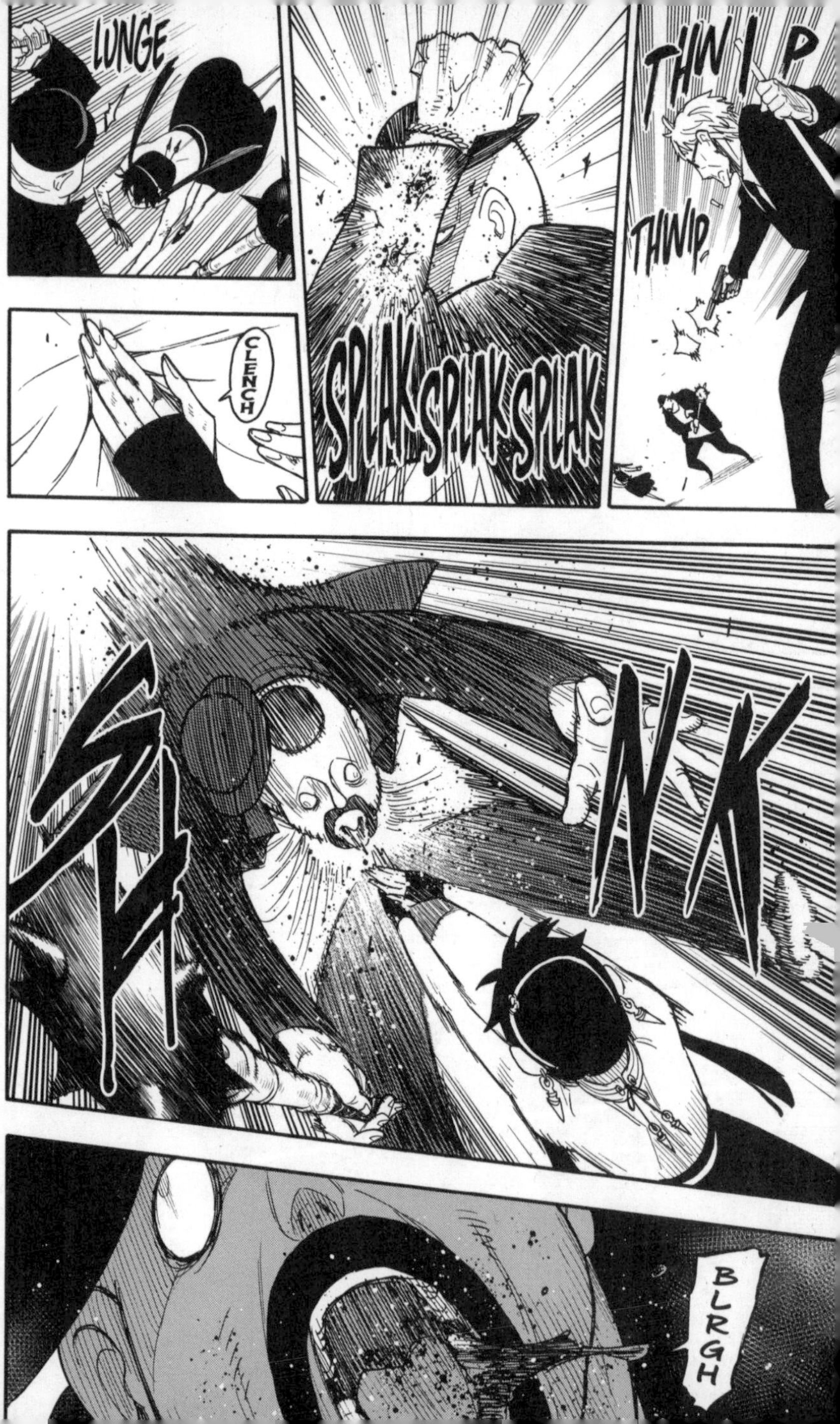
THWIP
THWIP
SPLAK SPLAK SPLAK
LUNGE
CLENCH
SHNK
BLRGH

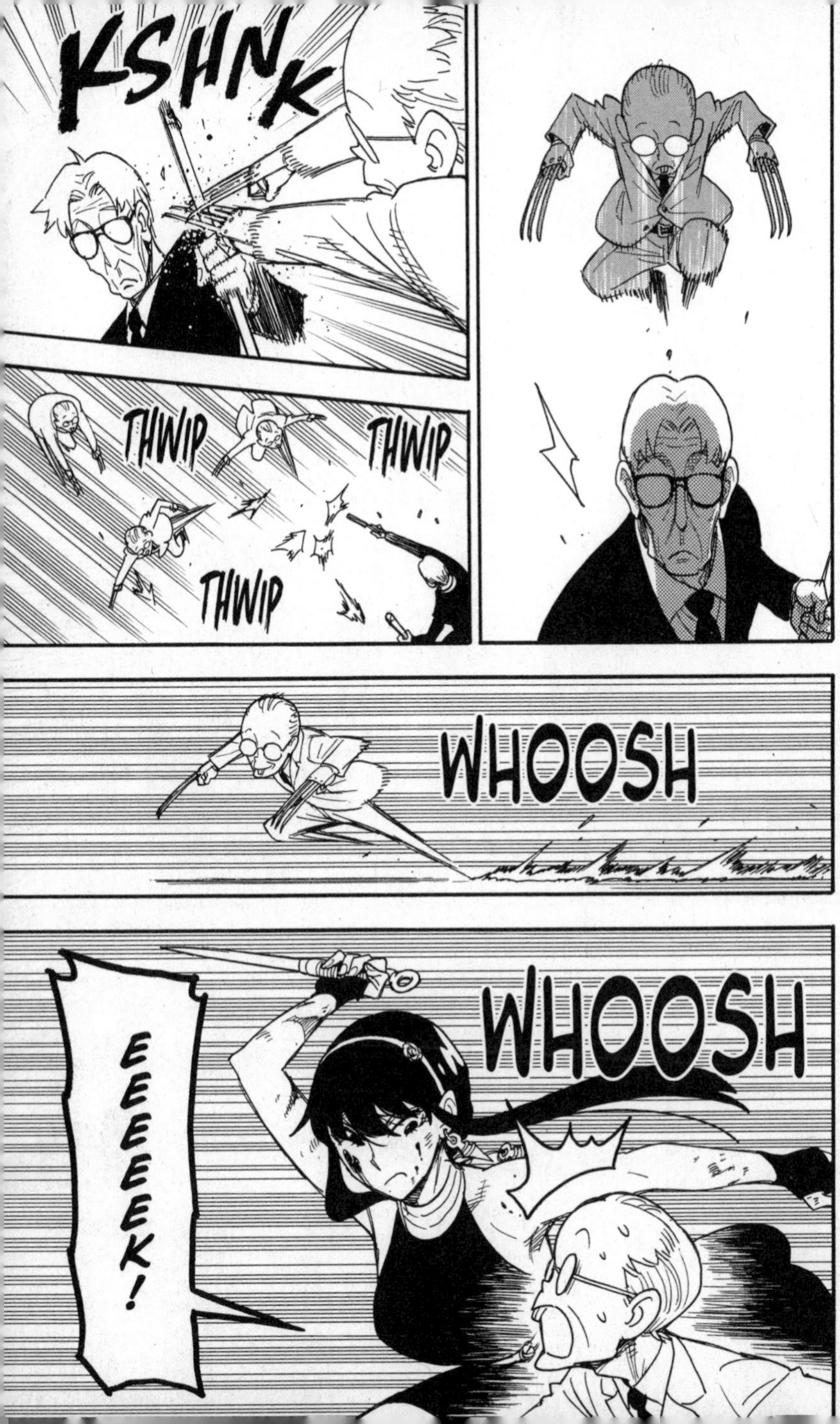
KSHNK
THWIP
THWIP
THWIP
WHOOSH
WHOOSH
EEEEEEK!

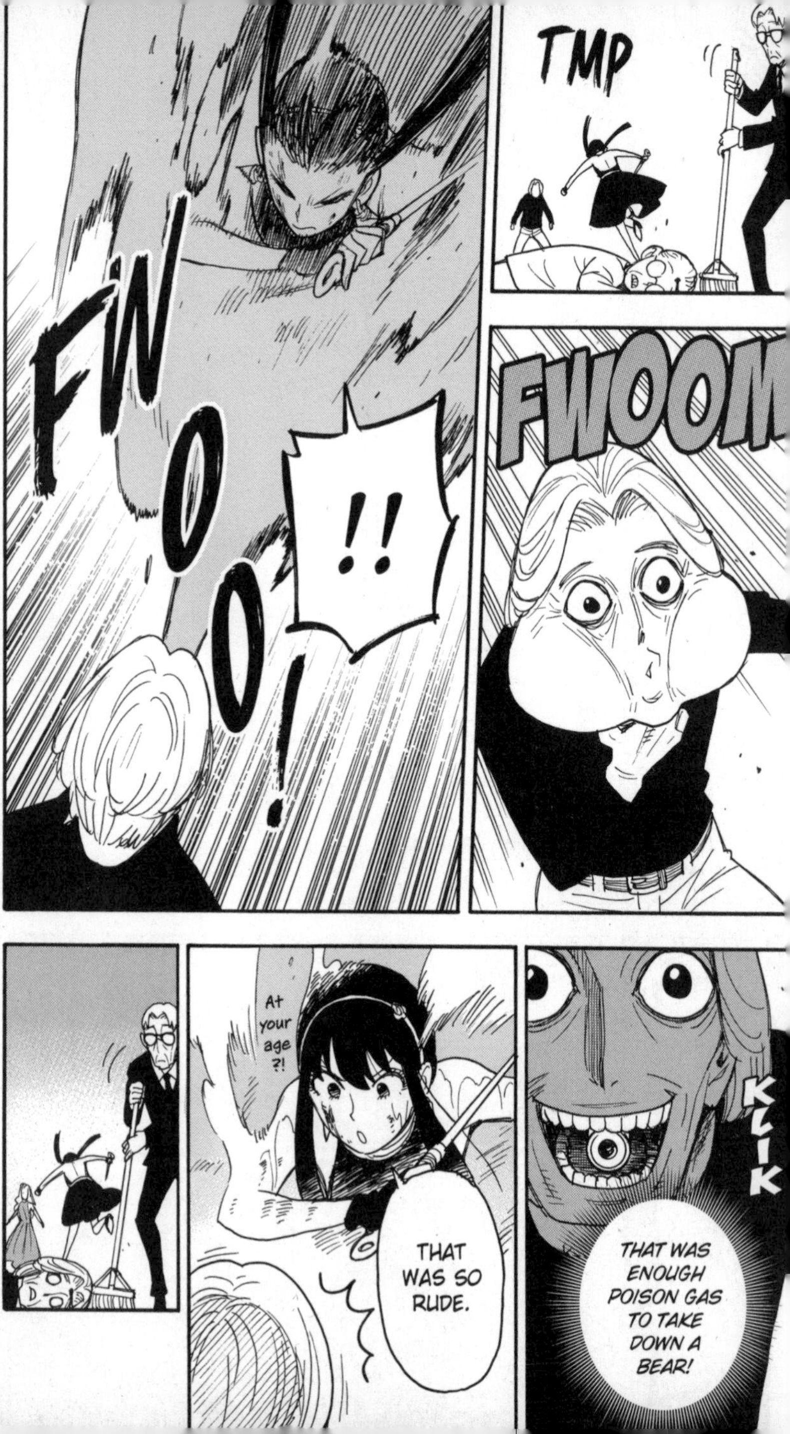
TMP
FWOOM
FWOOOO!
!!
KLIK
THAT WAS ENOUGH POISON GAS TO TAKE DOWN A BEAR!
THAT WAS SO RUDE.
At your age?!

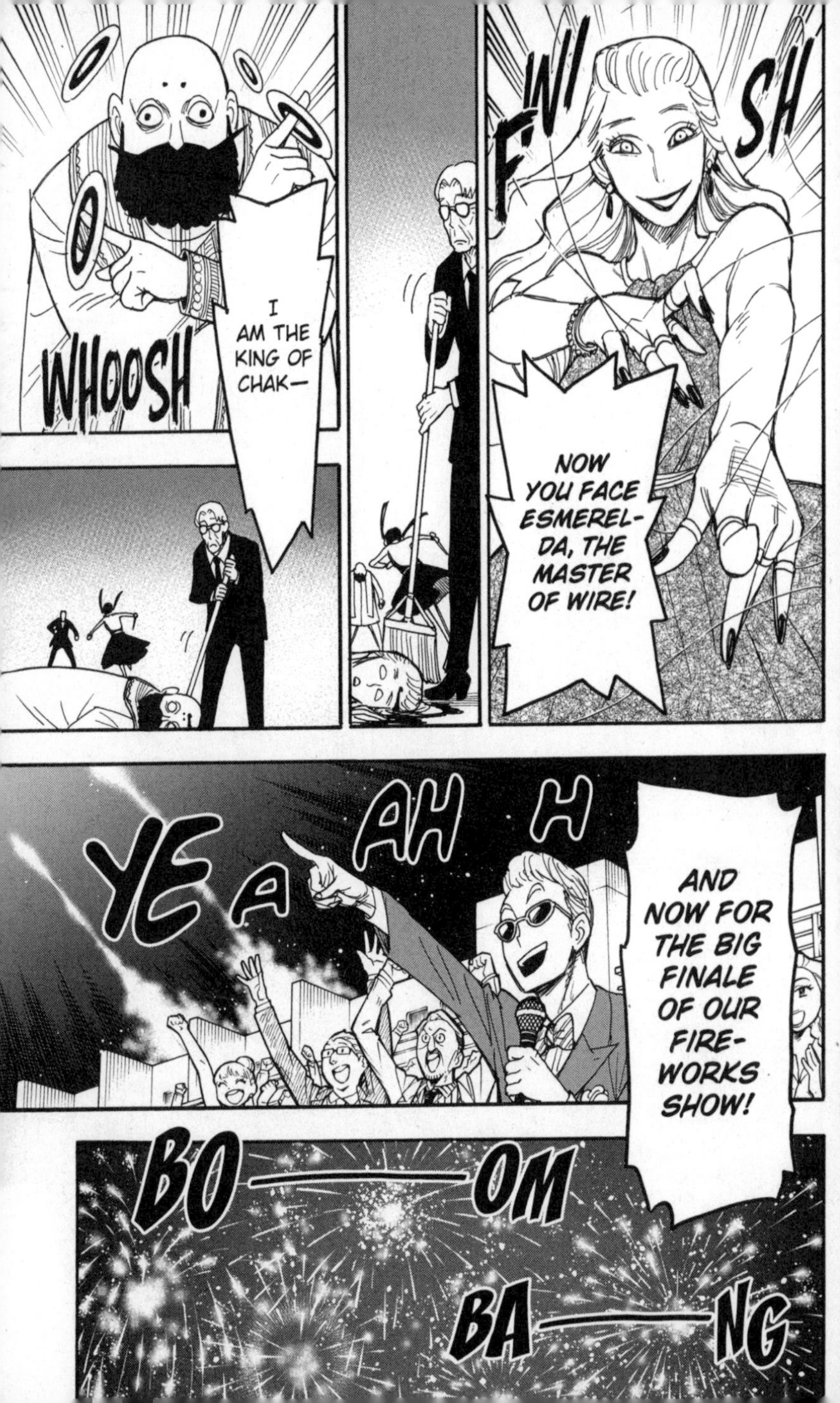

FWISH
NOW YOU FACE ESMEREL-DA, THE MASTER OF WIRE!
WHOOSH
I AM THE KING OF CHAK—
YEAAHH
AND NOW FOR THE BIG FINALE OF OUR FIRE-WORKS SHOW!
BO——OM
BA——NG

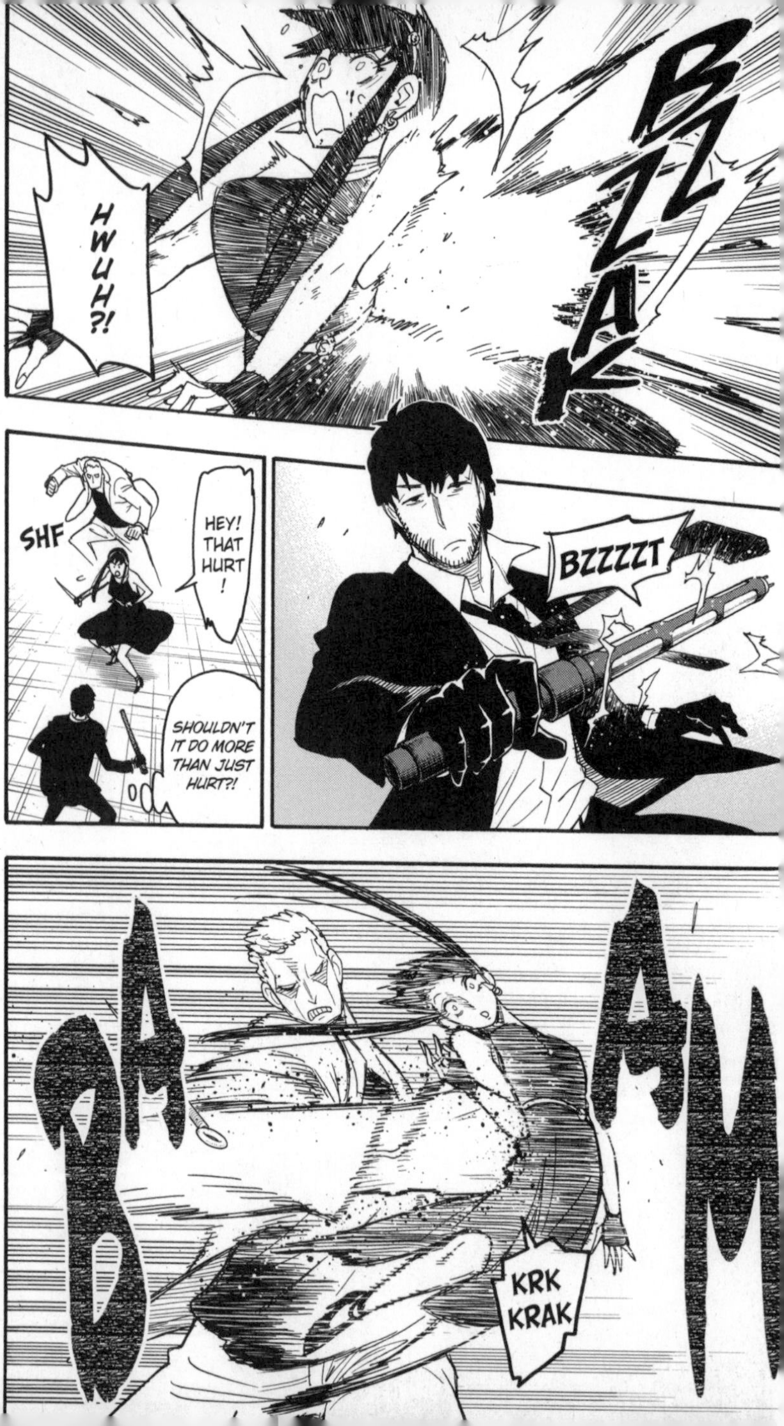
BZZAK
HWUH?!
BZZZZT
HEY! THAT HURT!
SHF
SHOULDN'T IT DO MORE THAN JUST HURT?!
BAM
KRK KRAK

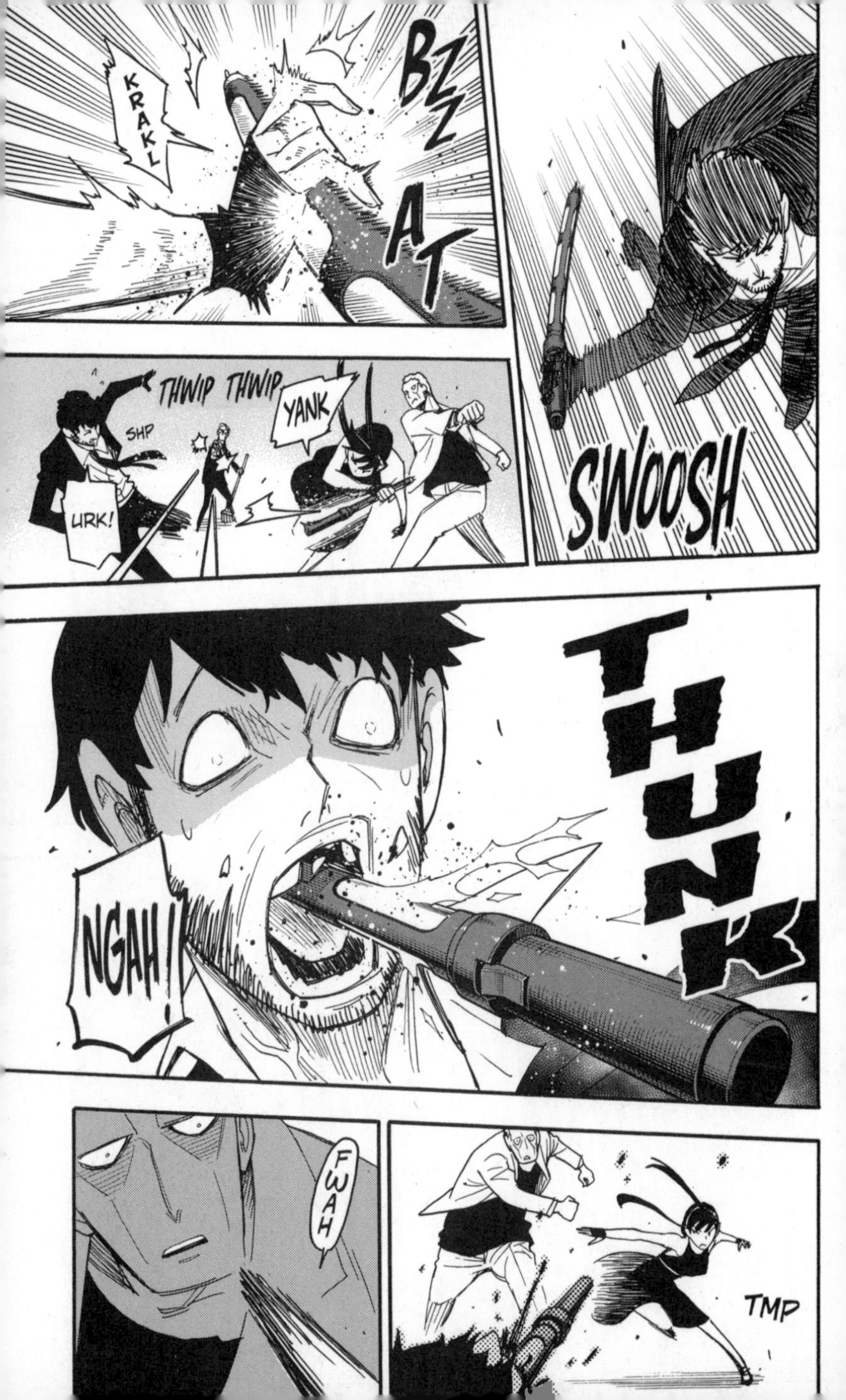

SWOOSH
BZZAT
KRAKL
YANK
THWIP THWIP
SHP
URK!
THUNK
NGAH!
TMP
FWAH

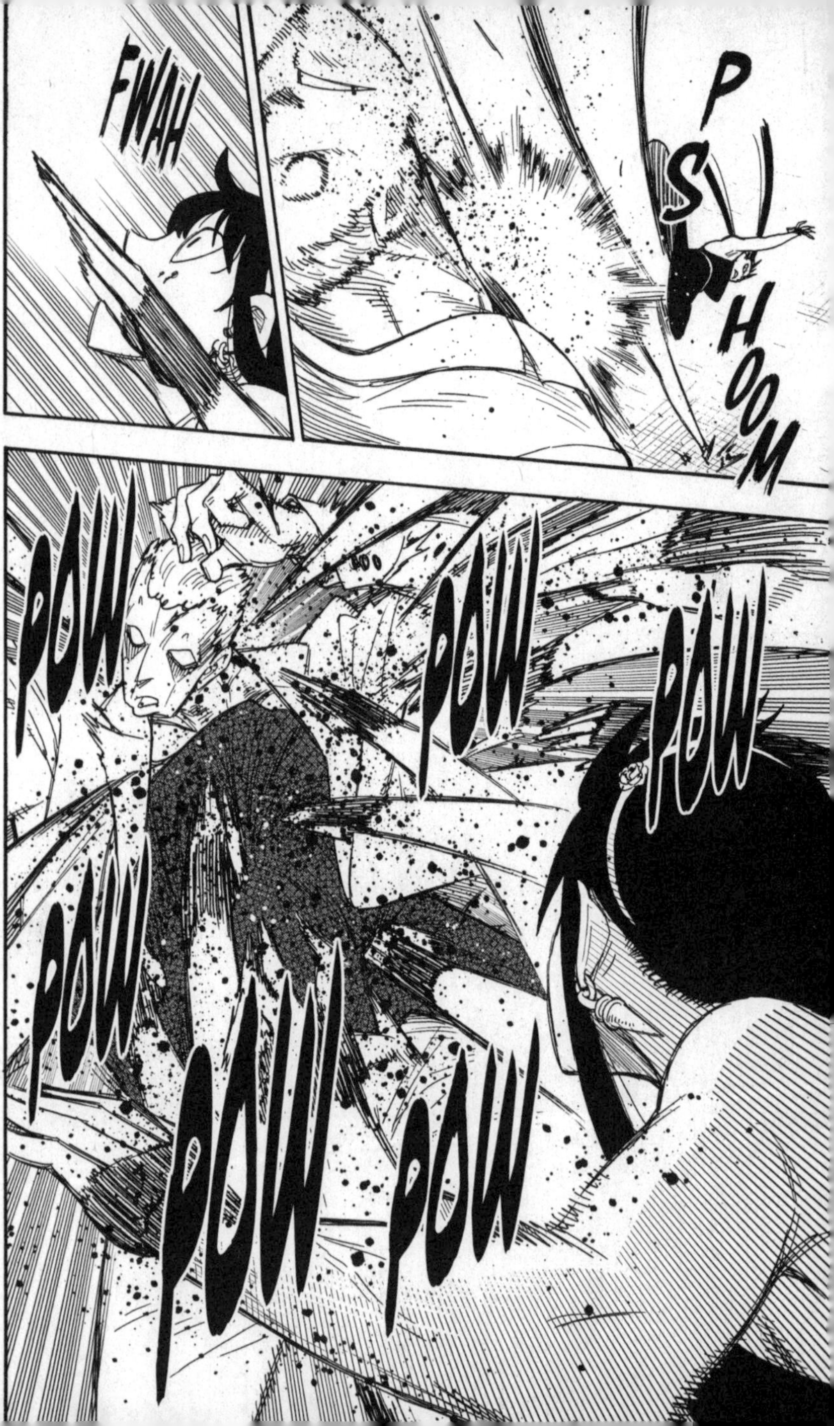
PSHOOM
FWAH
pow
pow
pow
pow
pow
pow
pow

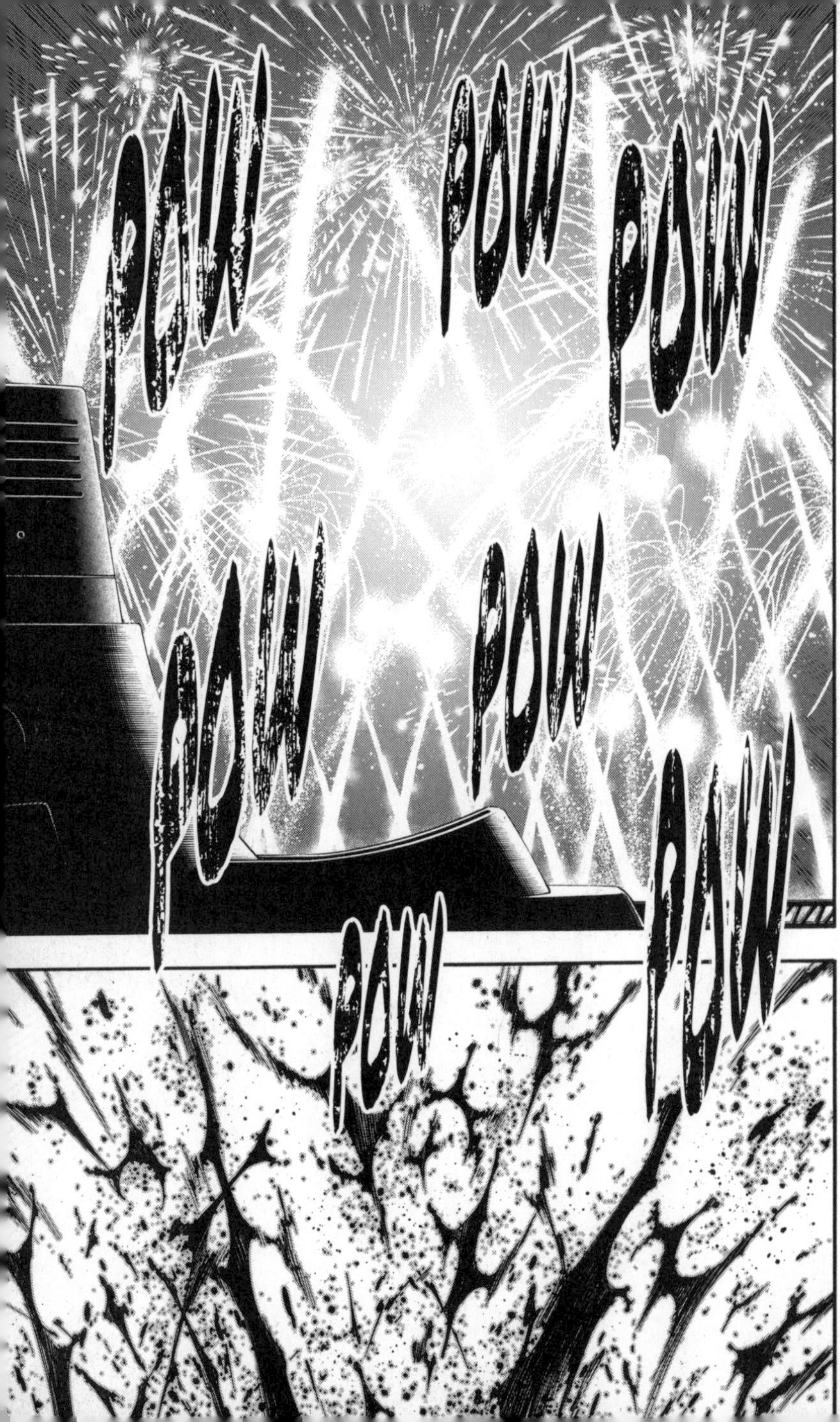
pow
pow
pow
pow
pow
pow

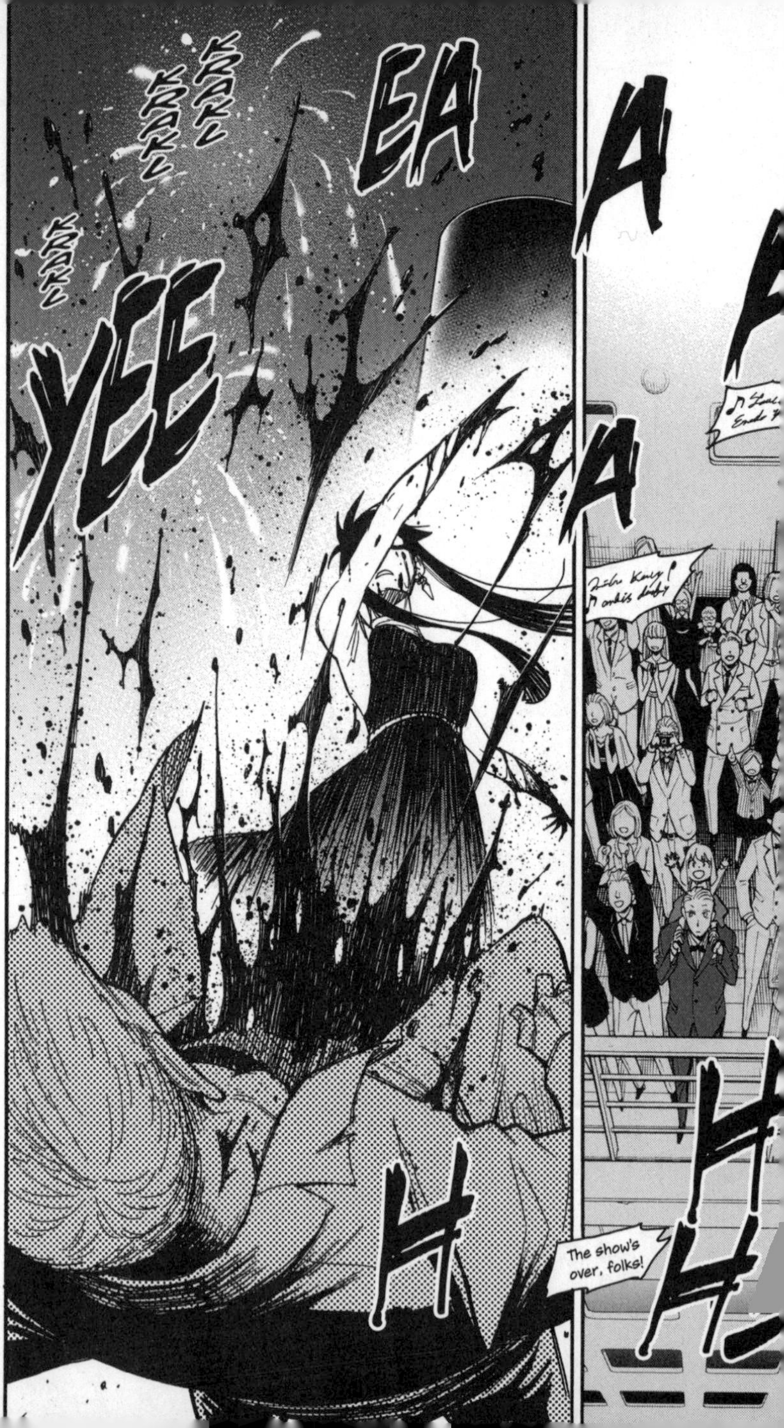
The show's over, folks!
YEE
EA
AAA
HHH

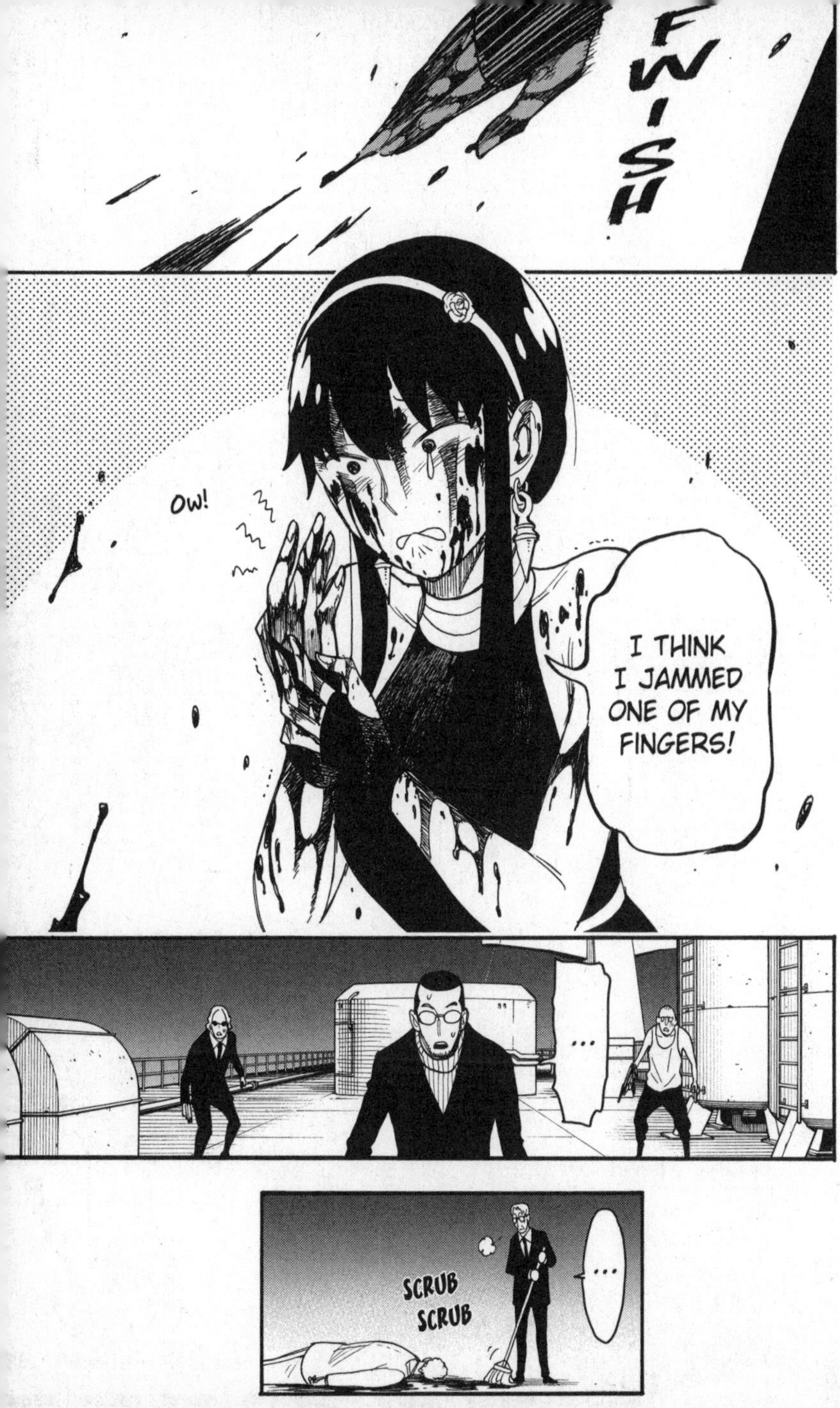
FWISH
I THINK I JAMMED ONE OF MY FINGERS!
OW!
...
...
SCRUB SCRUB

SPY×FAMILY

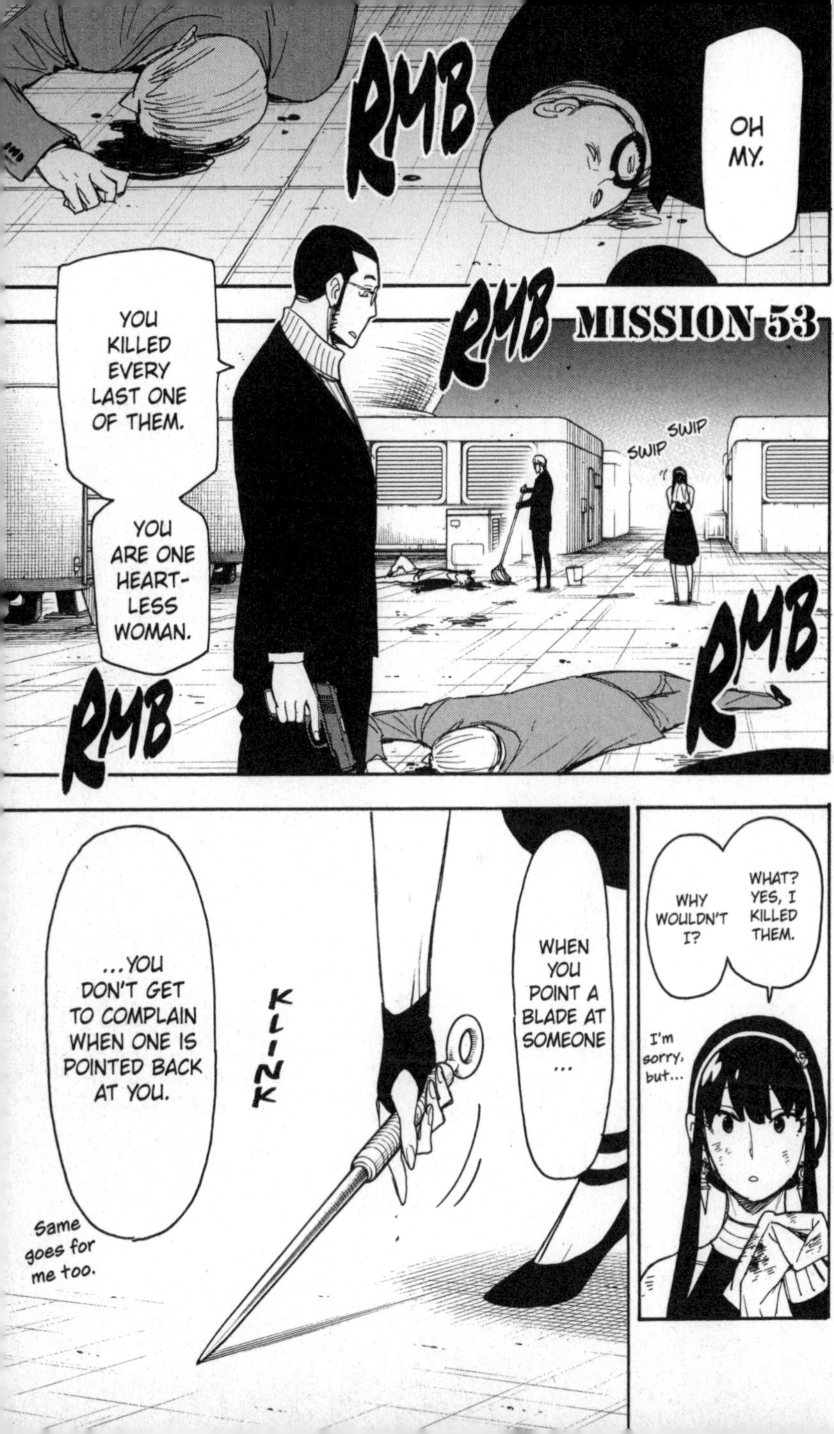
RMB
OH MY.
MISSION 53
RMB
SWIP SWIP
YOU KILLED EVERY LAST ONE OF THEM.
YOU ARE ONE HEART-LESS WOMAN.
RMB
RMB
WHAT? YES, I KILLED THEM.
WHY WOULDN'T I?
I'm sorry, but...
WHEN YOU POINT A BLADE AT SOMEONE ...
KLINK
...YOU DON'T GET TO COMPLAIN WHEN ONE IS POINTED BACK AT YOU.
Same goes for me too.

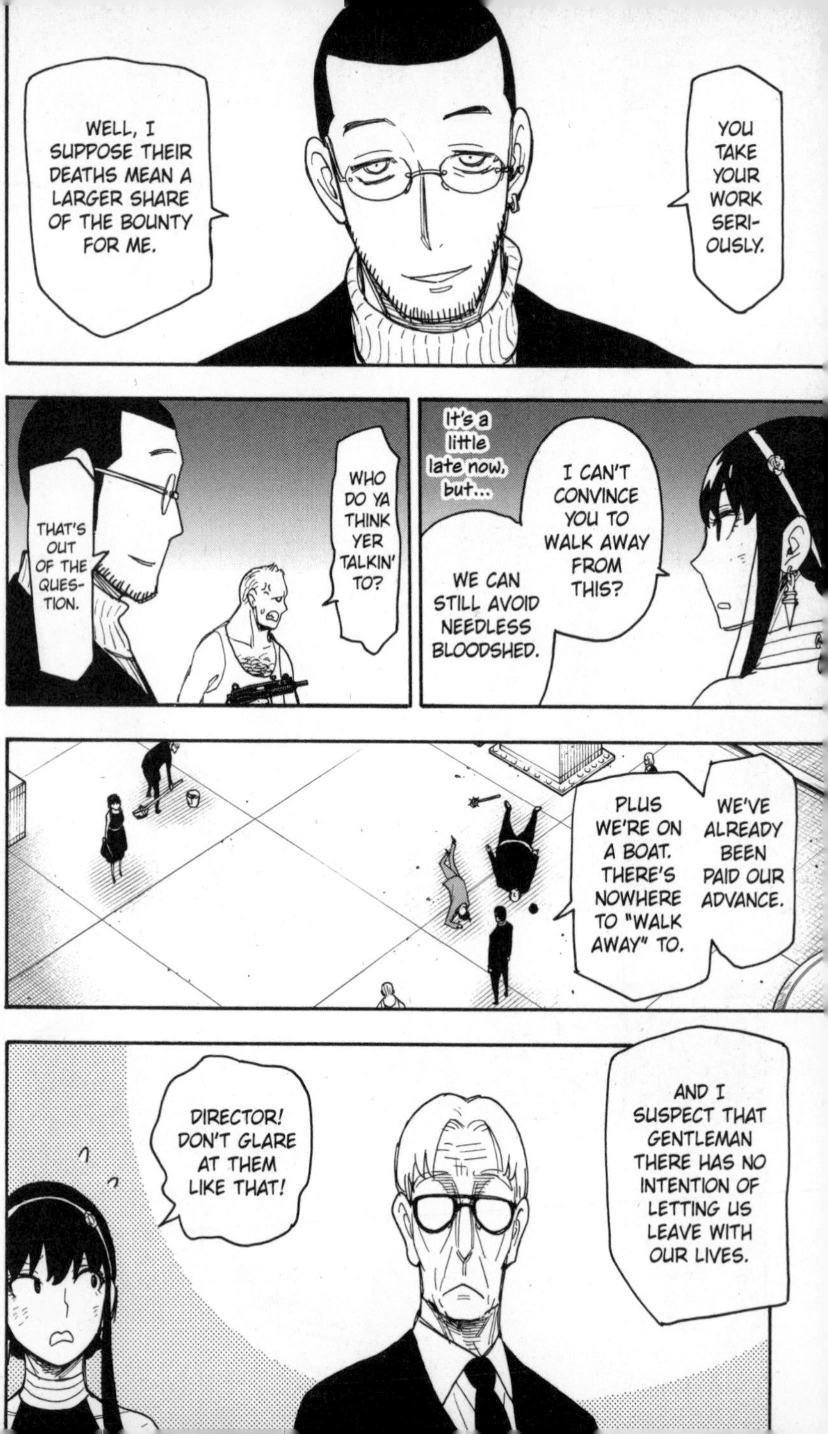
YOU TAKE YOUR WORK SERIOUSLY.
WELL, I SUPPOSE THEIR DEATHS MEAN A LARGER SHARE OF THE BOUNTY FOR ME.
It's a little late now, but...
I CAN'T CONVINCE YOU TO WALK AWAY FROM THIS?
WE CAN STILL AVOID NEEDLESS BLOODSHED.
WHO DO YA THINK YER TALKIN' TO?
THAT'S OUT OF THE QUESTION.
WE'VE ALREADY BEEN PAID OUR ADVANCE.
PLUS WE'RE ON A BOAT. THERE'S NOWHERE TO "WALK AWAY" TO.
AND I SUSPECT THAT GENTLEMAN THERE HAS NO INTENTION OF LETTING US LEAVE WITH OUR LIVES.
DIRECTOR! DON'T GLARE AT THEM LIKE THAT!

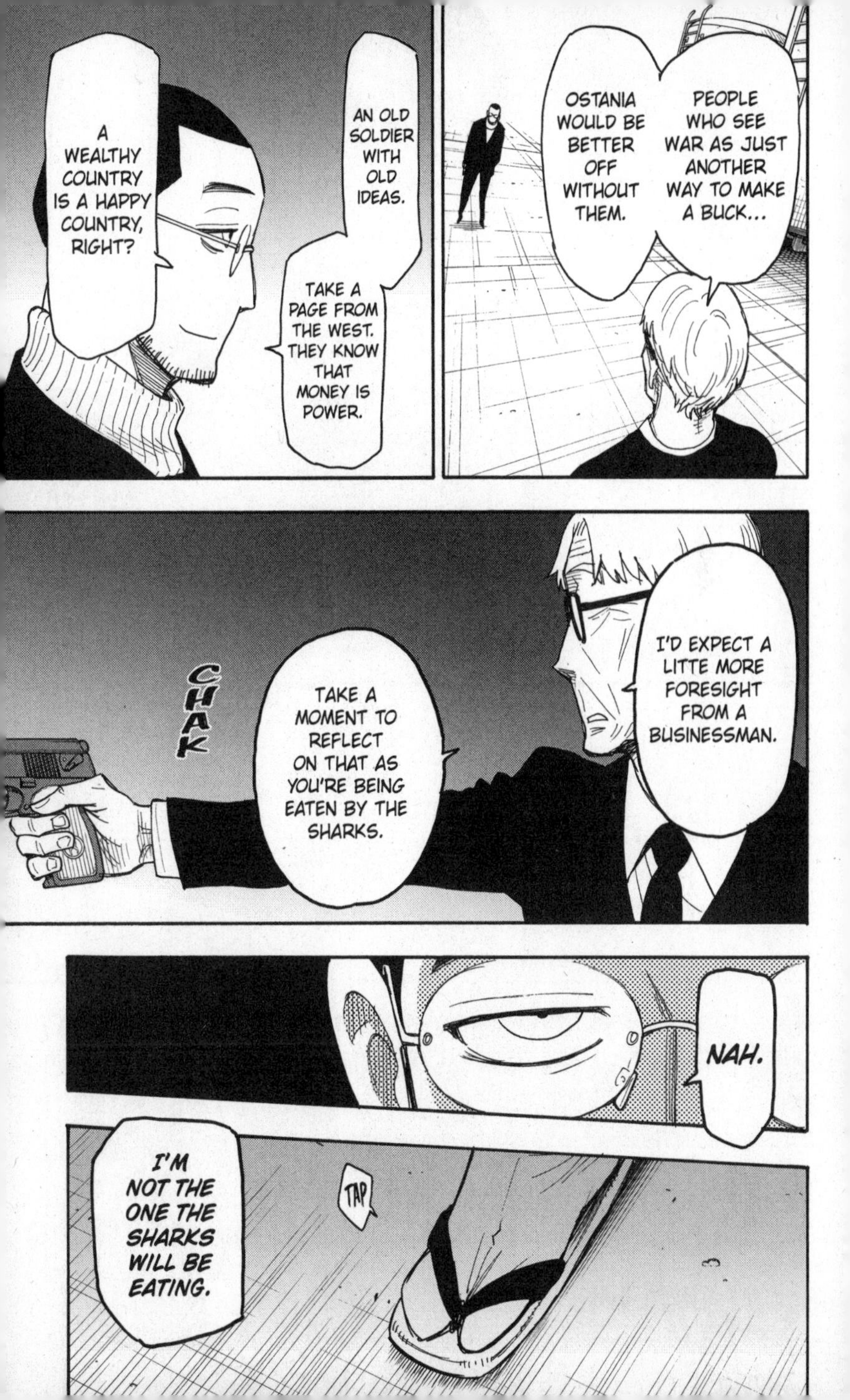
PEOPLE WHO SEE WAR AS JUST ANOTHER WAY TO MAKE A BUCK...
OSTANIA WOULD BE BETTER OFF WITHOUT THEM.
AN OLD SOLDIER WITH OLD IDEAS.
A WEALTHY COUNTRY IS A HAPPY COUNTRY, RIGHT?
TAKE A PAGE FROM THE WEST. THEY KNOW THAT MONEY IS POWER.
I'D EXPECT A LITTE MORE FORESIGHT FROM A BUSINESSMAN.
TAKE A MOMENT TO REFLECT ON THAT AS YOU'RE BEING EATEN BY THE SHARKS.
CHAK
NAH.
TAP
I'M NOT THE ONE THE SHARKS WILL BE EATING.

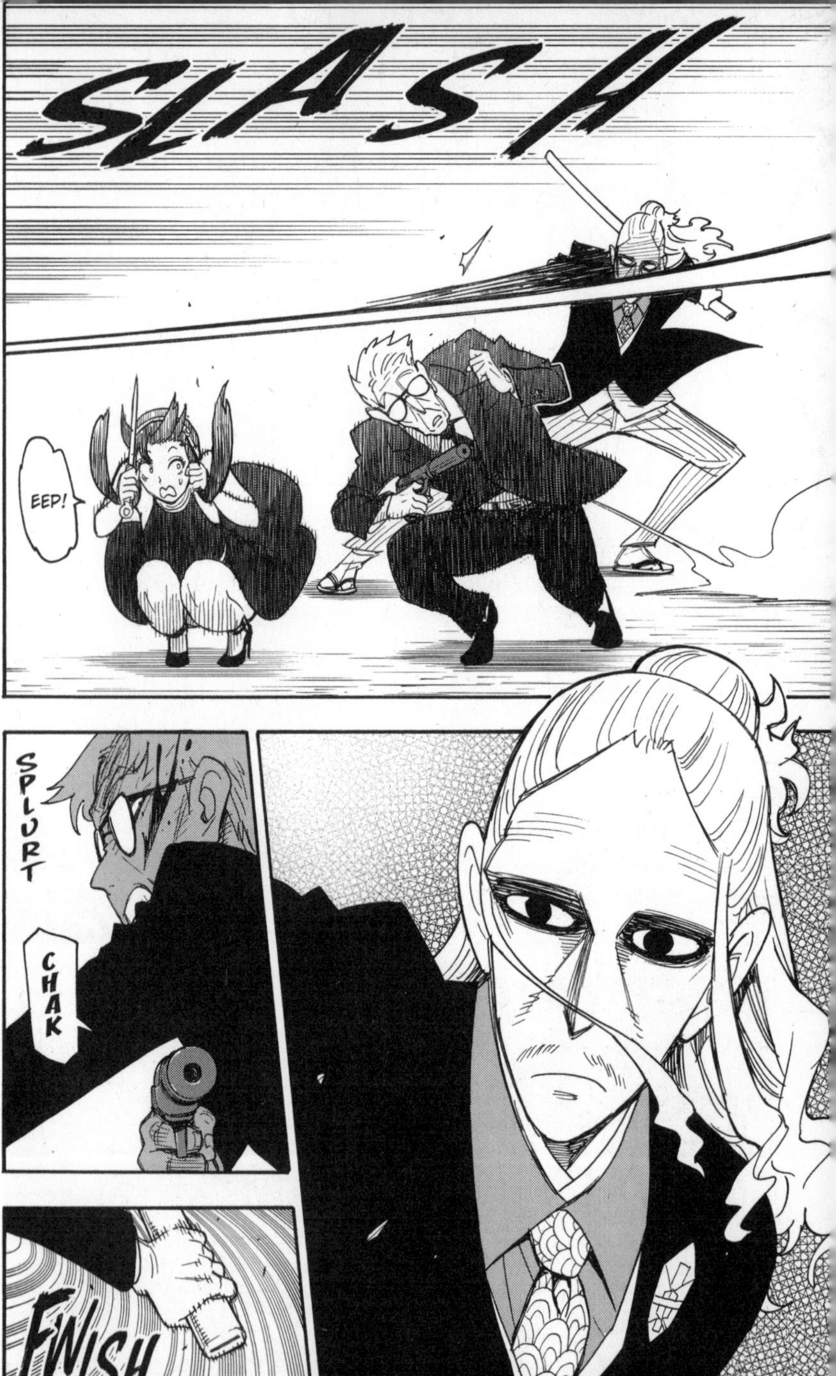
SLASH
EEP!
SPLURT
CHAK
FWISH

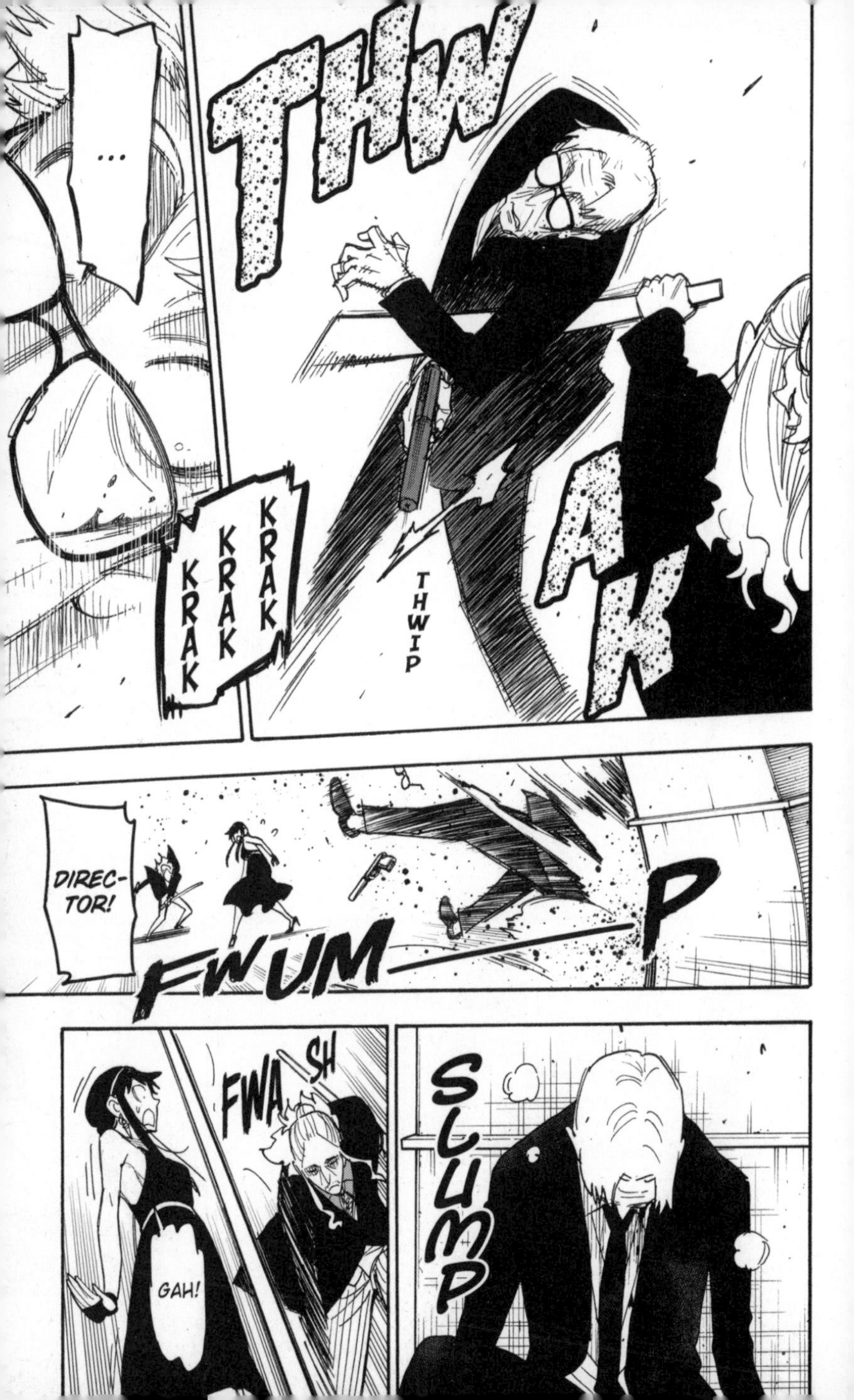
THWAK
THWIP
KRAK KRAK KRAK
...
FWUMP
DIRECTOR!
SLUMP
FWASH
GAH!

BAM

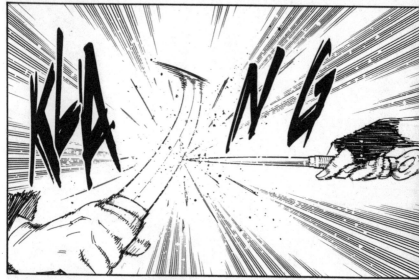

KLANG

HUFF
HUFF

AGH!
MY GRIP
STRENGTH
...

IT'S OVER.

SHING

SWIP
SWIP
SWIP

THWOK

FWAK

OW!

188

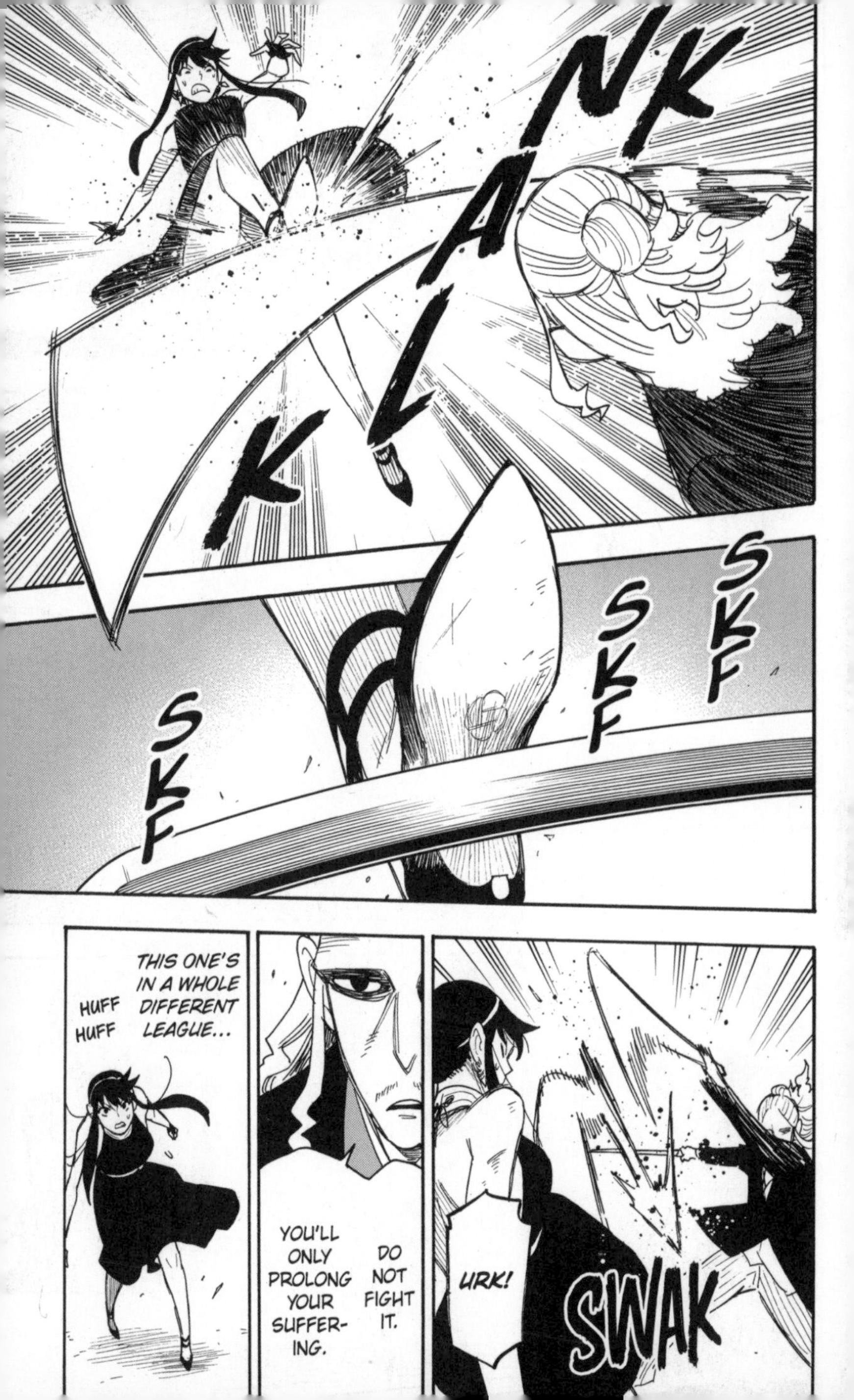
KLANK
SKF
SKF
SKF
SWAK
URK!
DO NOT FIGHT IT.
YOU'LL ONLY PROLONG YOUR SUFFER-ING.
THIS ONE'S IN A WHOLE DIFFERENT LEAGUE...
HUFF HUFF

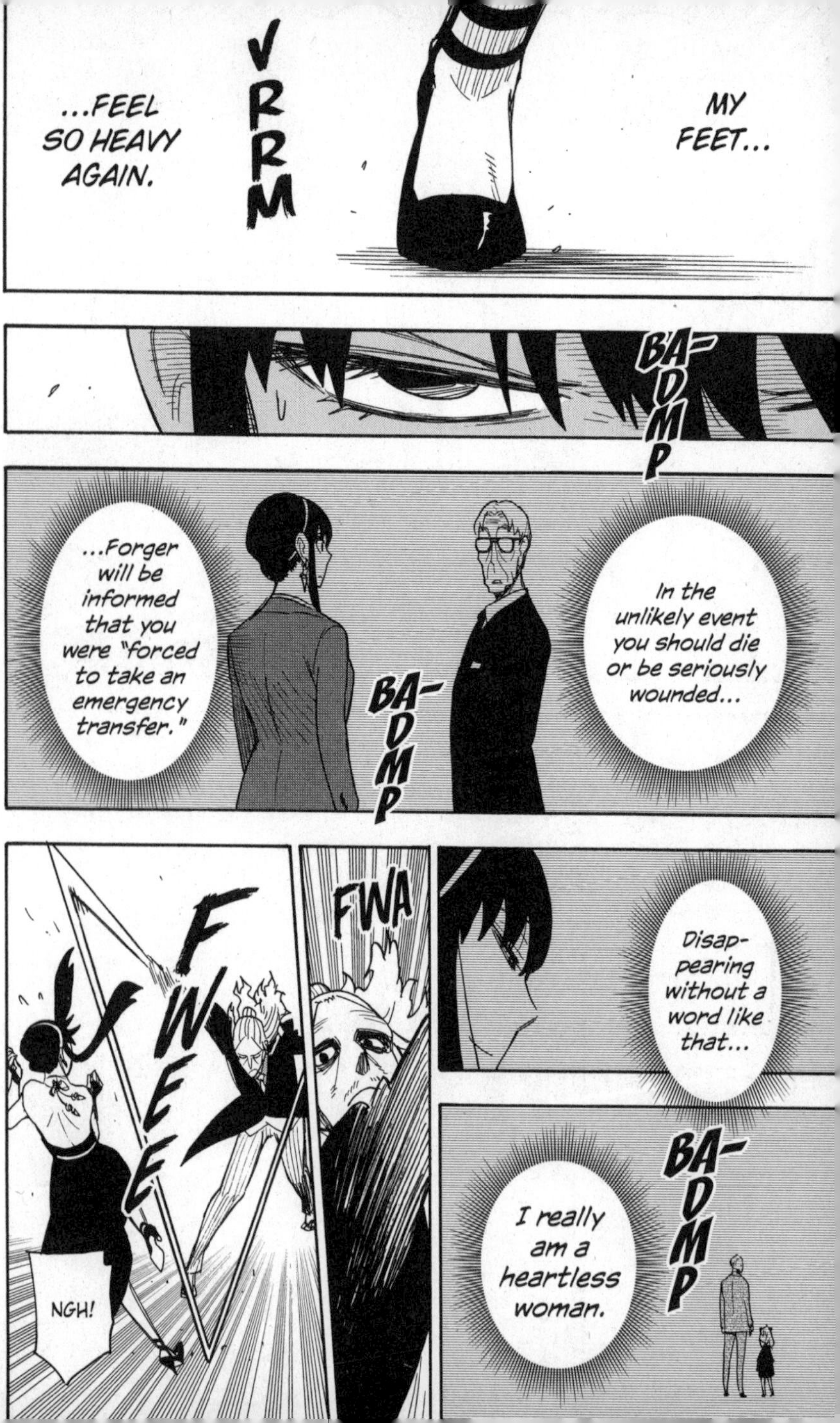
MY FEET...
VRRM
...FEEL SO HEAVY AGAIN.
BA-DMP
In the unlikely event you should die or be seriously wounded...
BA-DMP
...Forger will be informed that you were "forced to take an emergency transfer."
Disap-pearing without a word like that...
BA-DMP
I really am a heartless woman.
FWA
FWEEE
NGH!

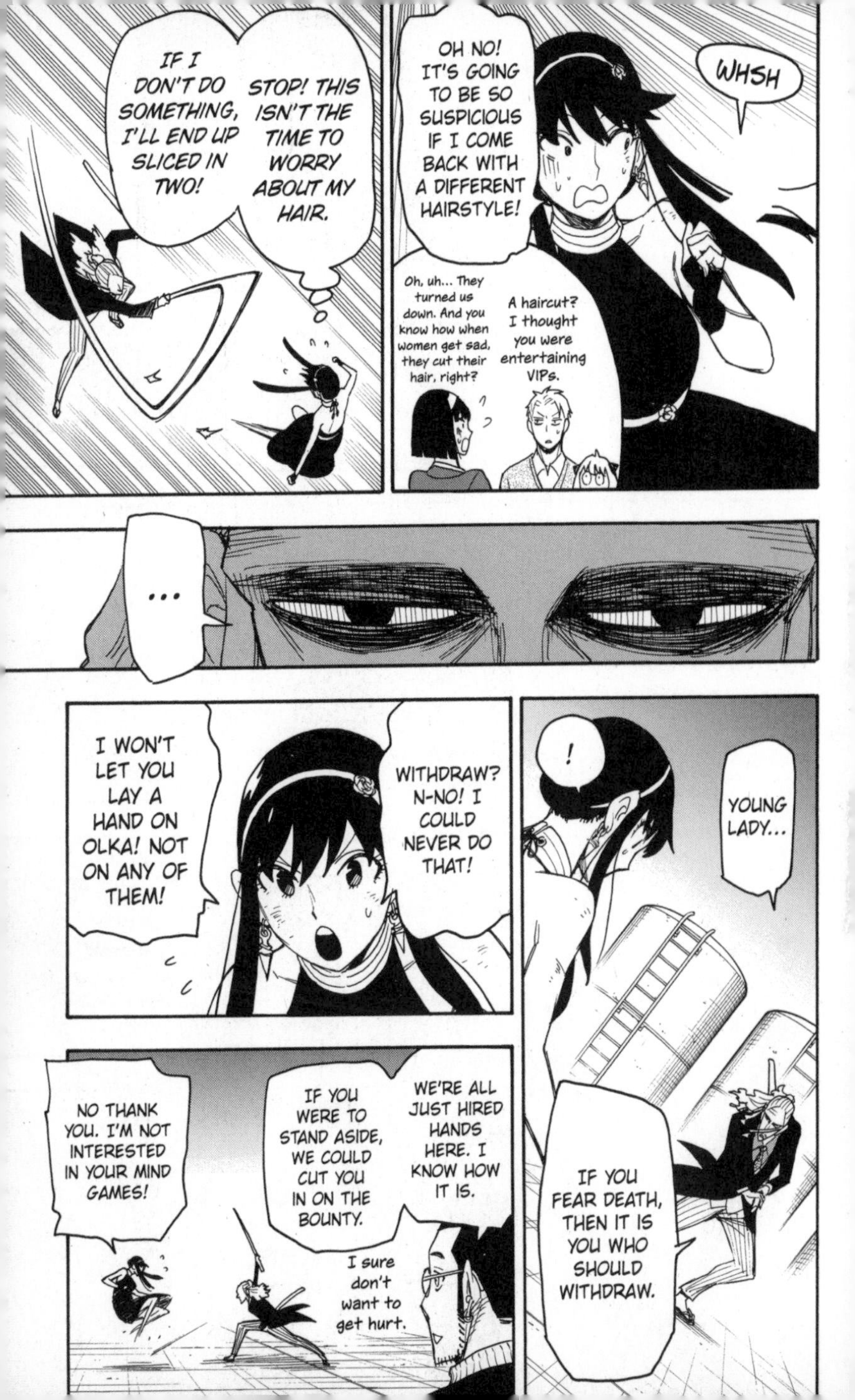
WHSH
OH NO! IT'S GOING TO BE SO SUSPICIOUS IF I COME BACK WITH A DIFFERENT HAIRSTYLE!
A haircut? I thought you were entertaining VIPs.
Oh, uh... They turned us down. And you know how when women get sad, they cut their hair, right?
STOP! THIS ISN'T THE TIME TO WORRY ABOUT MY HAIR.
IF I DON'T DO SOMETHING, I'LL END UP SLICED IN TWO!
...
!
YOUNG LADY...
IF YOU FEAR DEATH, THEN IT IS YOU WHO SHOULD WITHDRAW.
WITHDRAW? N-NO! I COULD NEVER DO THAT!
I WON'T LET YOU LAY A HAND ON OLKA! NOT ON ANY OF THEM!
WE'RE ALL JUST HIRED HANDS HERE. I KNOW HOW IT IS.
IF YOU WERE TO STAND ASIDE, WE COULD CUT YOU IN ON THE BOUNTY.
I sure don't want to get hurt.
NO THANK YOU. I'M NOT INTERESTED IN YOUR MIND GAMES!

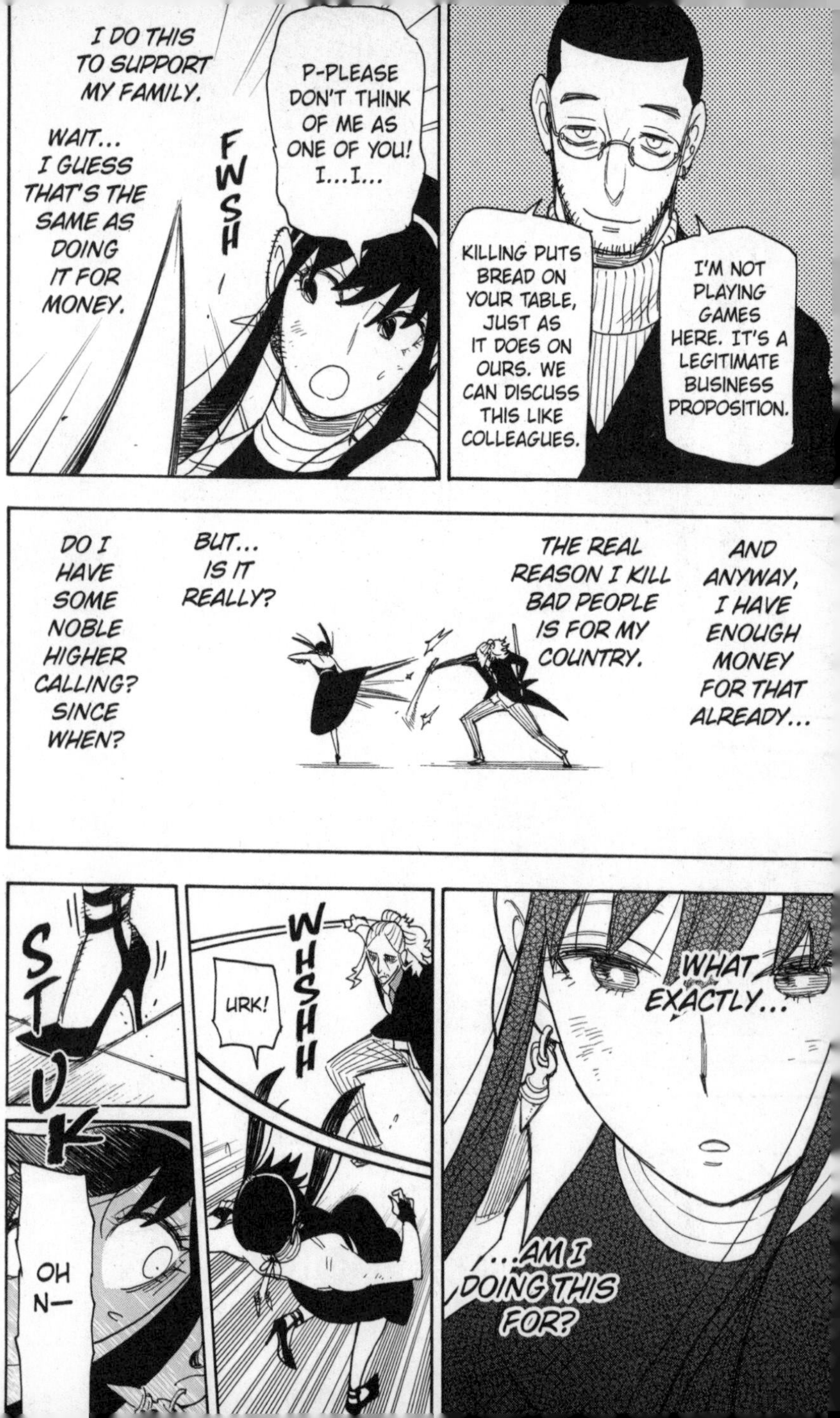
I'M NOT PLAYING GAMES HERE. IT'S A LEGITIMATE BUSINESS PROPOSITION.
KILLING PUTS BREAD ON YOUR TABLE, JUST AS IT DOES ON OURS. WE CAN DISCUSS THIS LIKE COLLEAGUES.
P-PLEASE DON'T THINK OF ME AS ONE OF YOU! I...I...
FWSH
I DO THIS TO SUPPORT MY FAMILY.
WAIT... I GUESS THAT'S THE SAME AS DOING IT FOR MONEY.
AND ANYWAY, I HAVE ENOUGH MONEY FOR THAT ALREADY...
THE REAL REASON I KILL BAD PEOPLE IS FOR MY COUNTRY.
BUT... IS IT REALLY?
DO I HAVE SOME NOBLE HIGHER CALLING? SINCE WHEN?
WHAT EXACTLY...
...AM I DOING THIS FOR?
WHSHH
URK!
STUK
OH N—

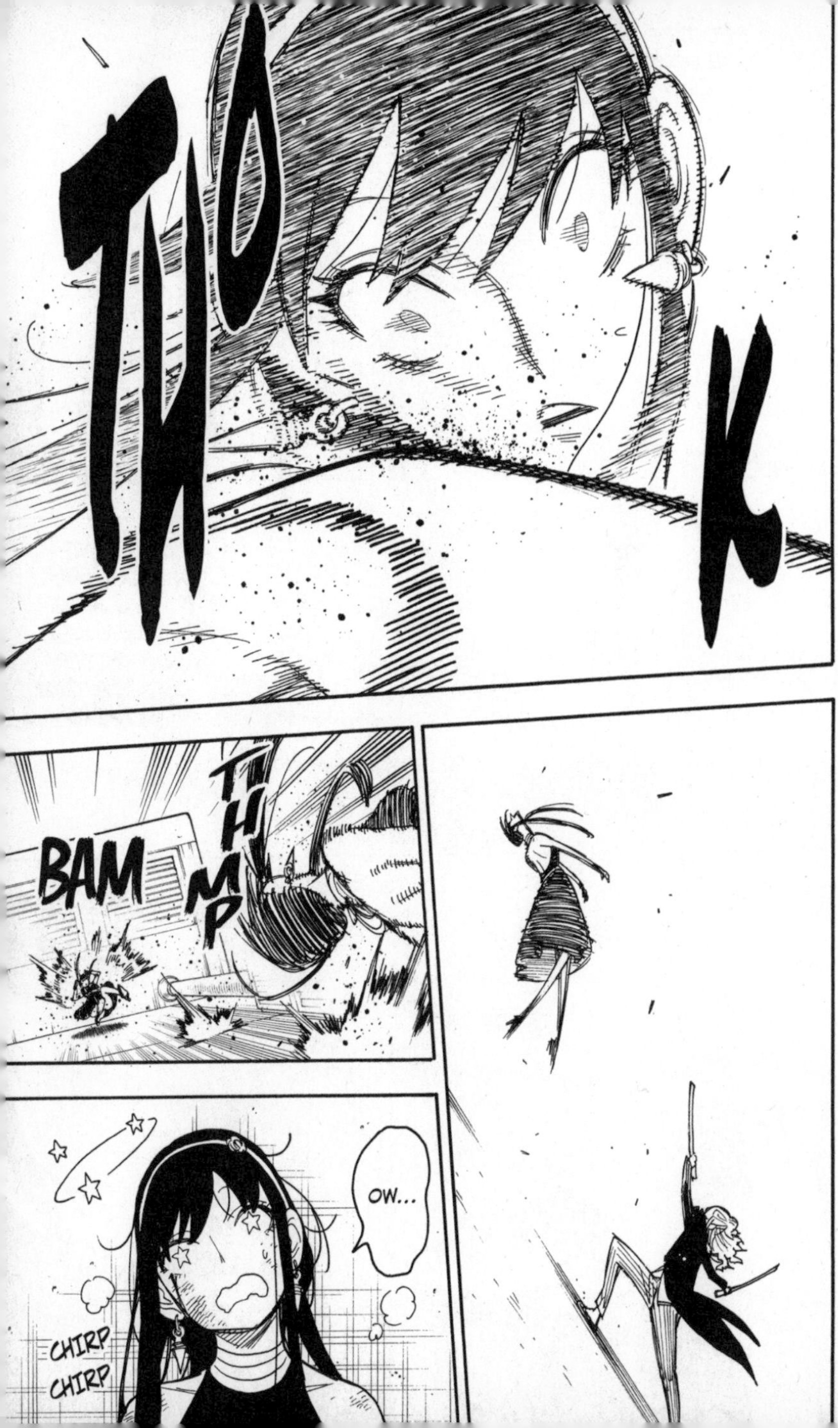
THOK
THMP
BAM
OW...
CHIRP
CHIRP

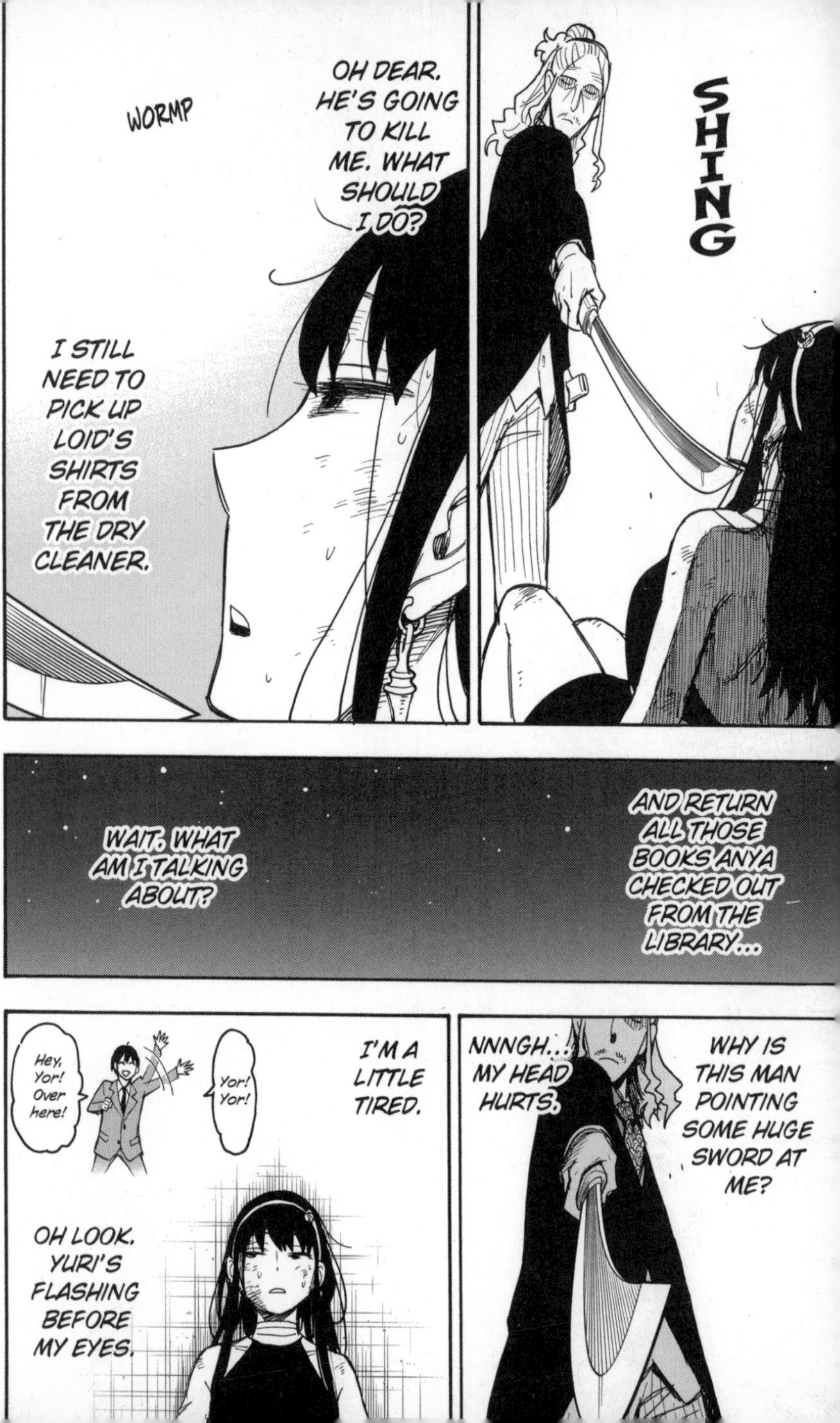
SHING
OH DEAR. HE'S GOING TO KILL ME. WHAT SHOULD I DO?
WORMP
I STILL NEED TO PICK UP LOID'S SHIRTS FROM THE DRY CLEANER.
AND RETURN ALL THOSE BOOKS ANYA CHECKED OUT FROM THE LIBRARY...
WAIT. WHAT AM I TALKING ABOUT?
WHY IS THIS MAN POINTING SOME HUGE SWORD AT ME?
NNNGH... MY HEAD HURTS.
I'M A LITTLE TIRED.
Yor! Yor!
Hey, Yor! Over here!
OH LOOK. YURI'S FLASHING BEFORE MY EYES.

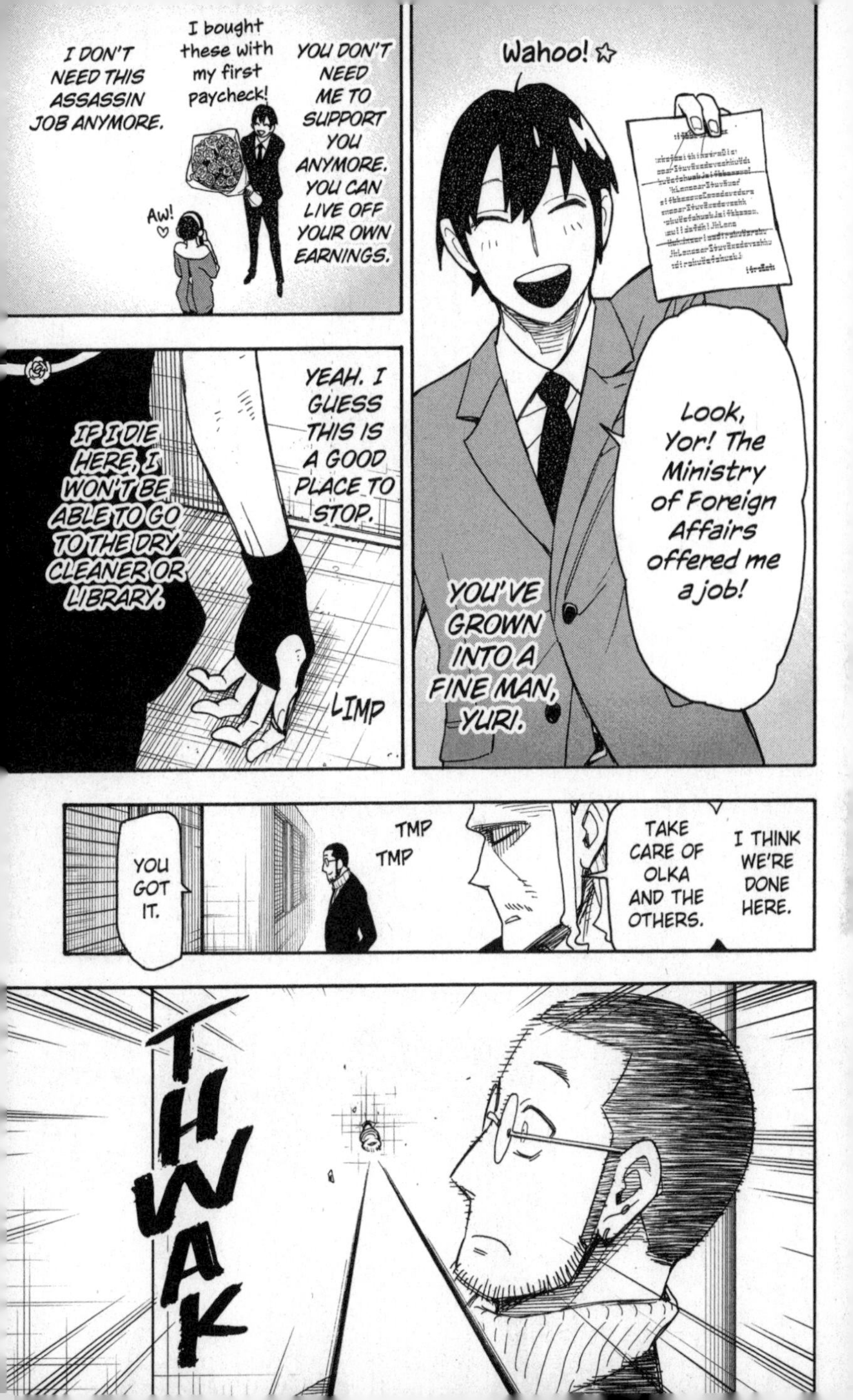
Wahoo! ☆
Look, Yor! The Ministry of Foreign Affairs offered me a job!
YOU'VE GROWN INTO A FINE MAN, YURI.
YOU DON'T NEED ME TO SUPPORT YOU ANYMORE. YOU CAN LIVE OFF YOUR OWN EARNINGS.
I bought these with my first paycheck!
I DON'T NEED THIS ASSASSIN JOB ANYMORE.
AW! ♡
YEAH. I GUESS THIS IS A GOOD PLACE TO STOP.
IF I DIE HERE, I WON'T BE ABLE TO GO TO THE DRY CLEANER OR LIBRARY.
LIMP
I THINK WE'RE DONE HERE.
TAKE CARE OF OLKA AND THE OTHERS.
TMP TMP
YOU GOT IT.
THWAK

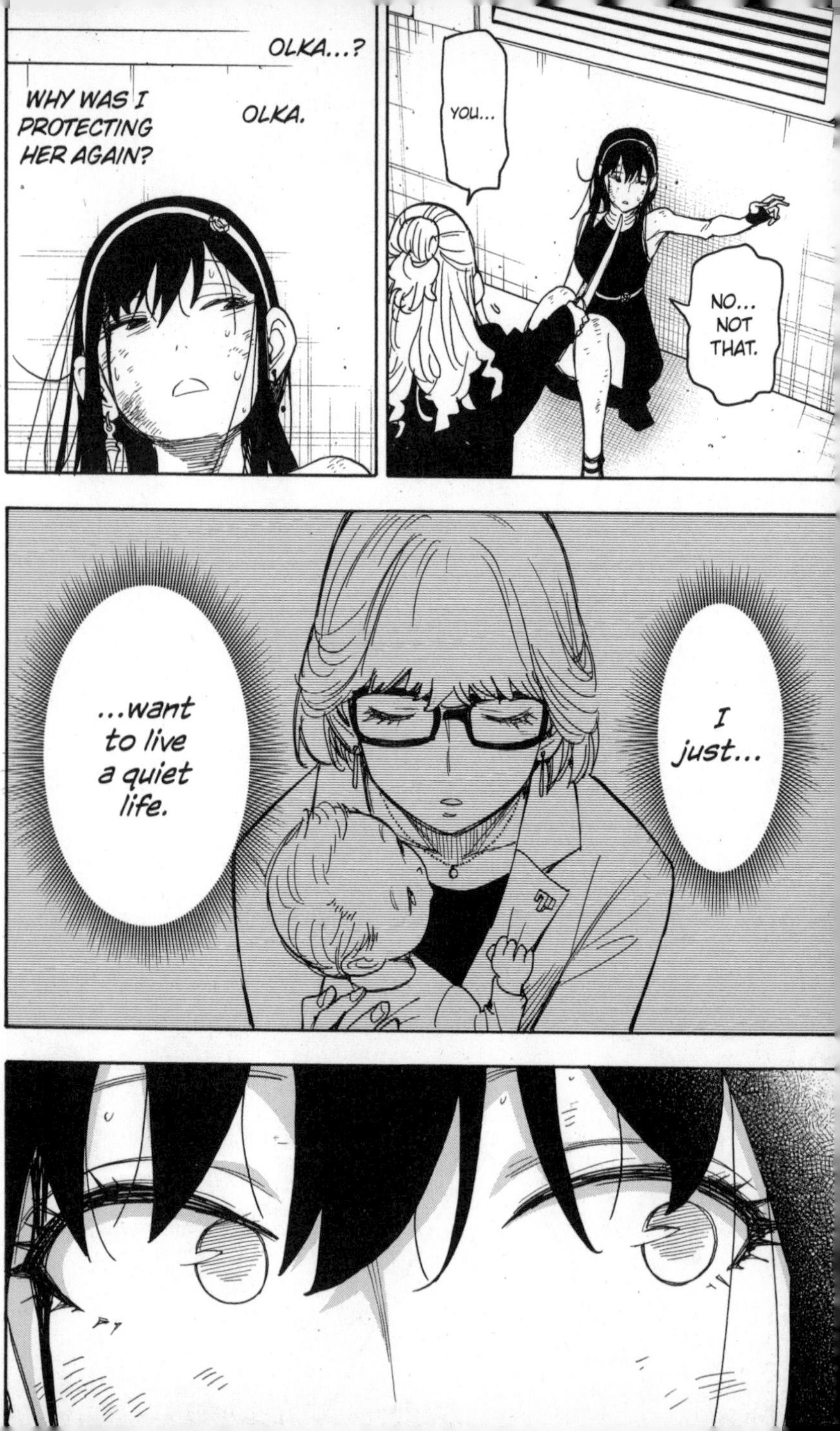
YOU...
NO... NOT THAT.
OLKA...?
OLKA.
WHY WAS I PROTECTING HER AGAIN?
I just...
...want to live a quiet life.

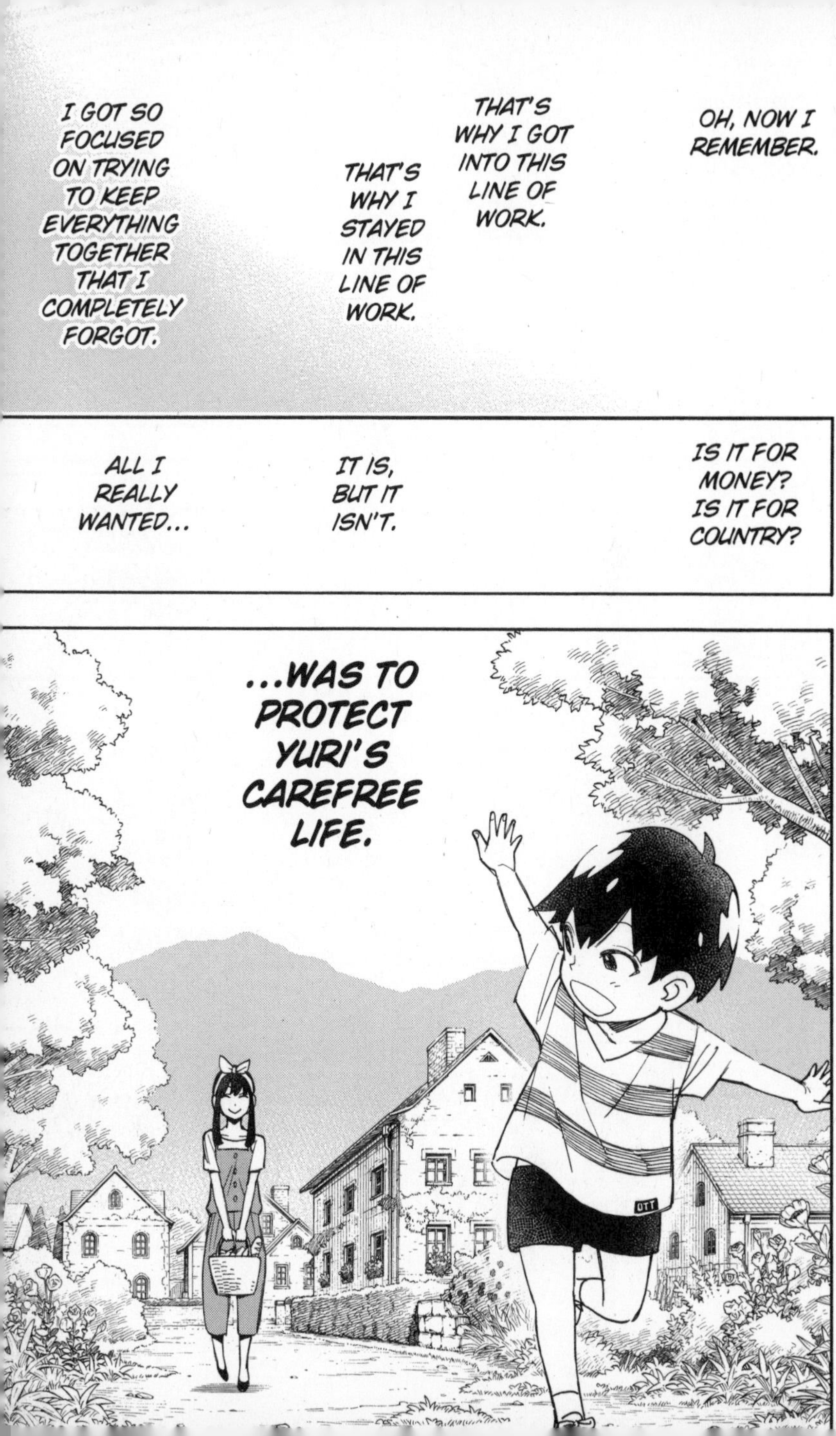
OH, NOW I REMEMBER.
THAT'S WHY I GOT INTO THIS LINE OF WORK.
THAT'S WHY I STAYED IN THIS LINE OF WORK.
I GOT SO FOCUSED ON TRYING TO KEEP EVERYTHING TOGETHER THAT I COMPLETELY FORGOT.
IS IT FOR MONEY? IS IT FOR COUNTRY?
IT IS, BUT IT ISN'T.
ALL I REALLY WANTED...
...WAS TO PROTECT YURI'S CAREFREE LIFE.

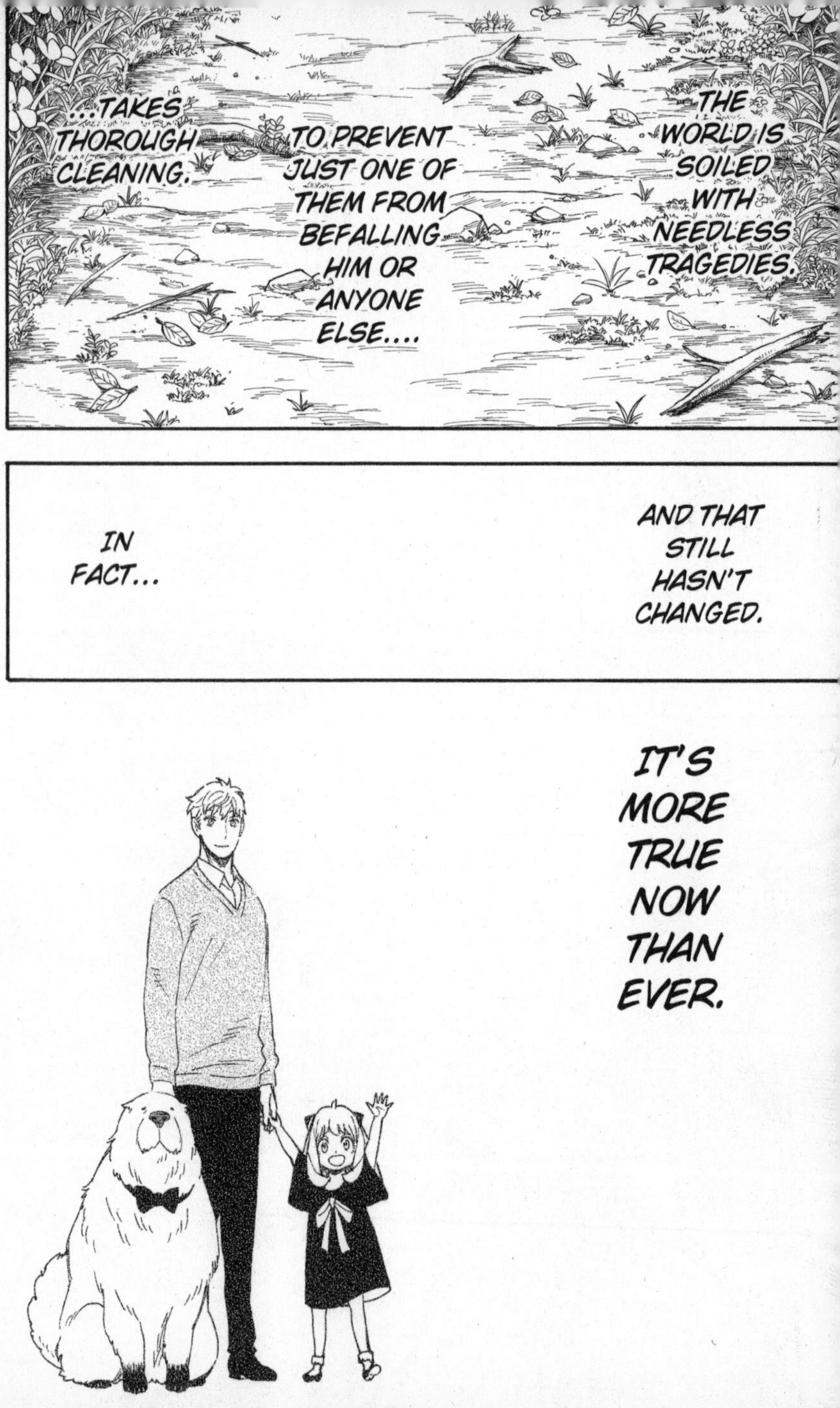
THE WORLD IS SOILED WITH NEEDLESS TRAGEDIES.
TO PREVENT JUST ONE OF THEM FROM BEFALLING HIM OR ANYONE ELSE....
...TAKES THOROUGH CLEANING.
AND THAT STILL HASN'T CHANGED.
IN FACT...
IT'S MORE TRUE NOW THAN EVER.

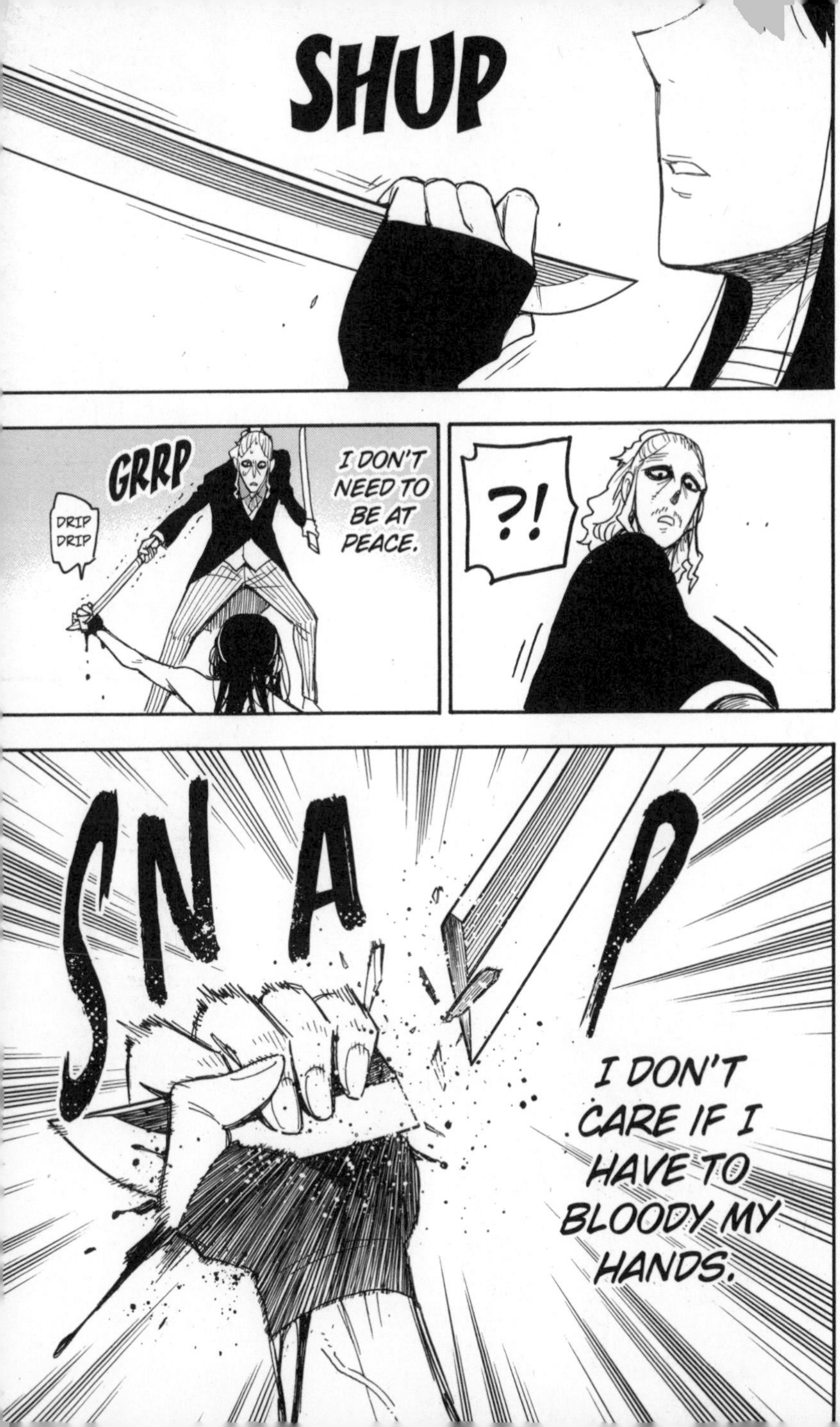
SHUP
?!
I DON'T NEED TO BE AT PEACE.
GRRP
DRIP DRIP
SNAP
I DON'T CARE IF I HAVE TO BLOODY MY HANDS.

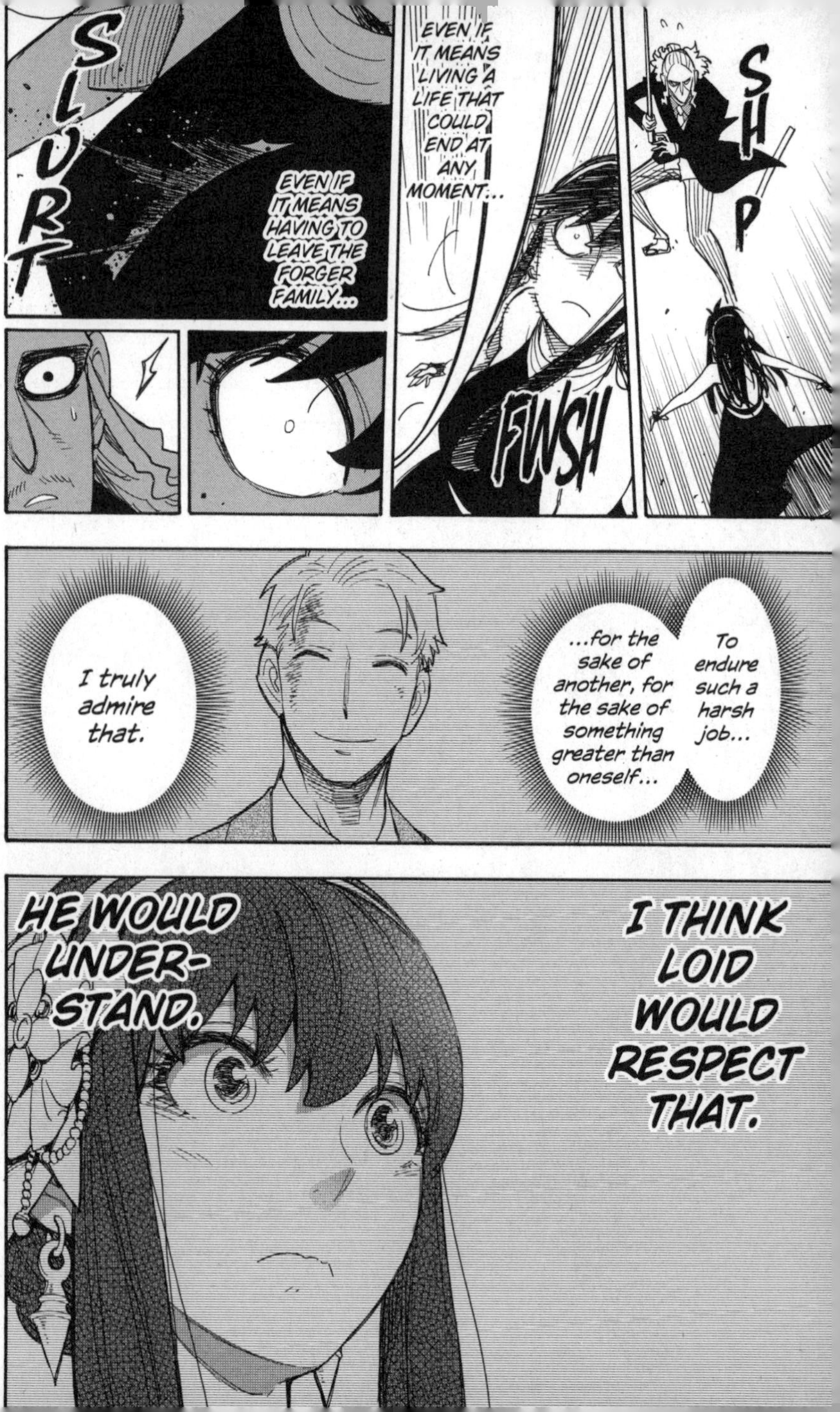
SHP
EVEN IF IT MEANS LIVING A LIFE THAT COULD END AT ANY MOMENT...
FWSH
SLURT
EVEN IF IT MEANS HAVING TO LEAVE THE FORGER FAMILY...
To endure such a harsh job...
...for the sake of another, for the sake of something greater than oneself...
I truly admire that.
I THINK LOID WOULD RESPECT THAT.
HE WOULD UNDER-STAND.

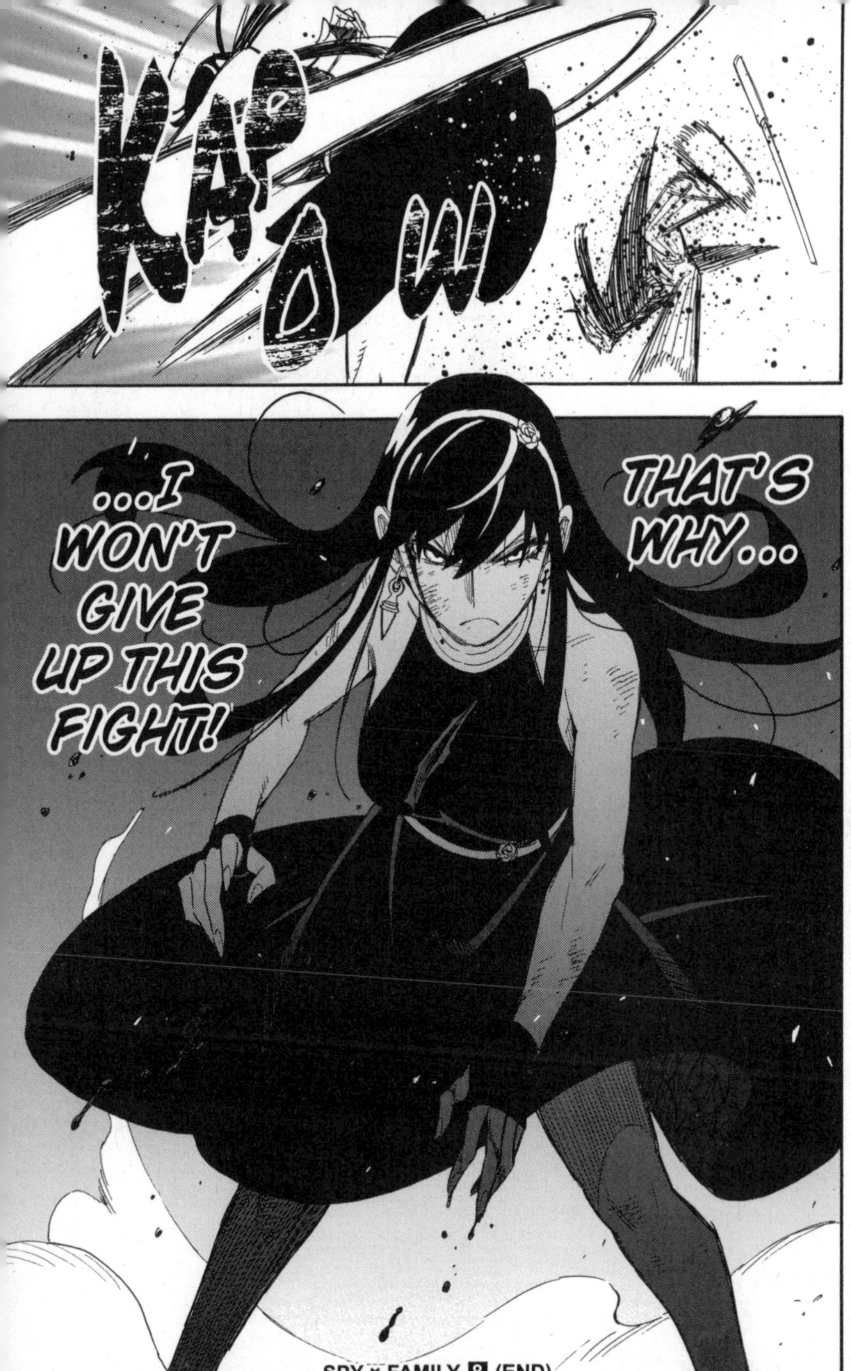
KAPOW
THAT'S WHY...
...I WON'T GIVE UP THIS FIGHT!

SPY × FAMILY 8 (END)

SPYxFAMILY VOL. 8

SPECIAL THANKS LIST

·CLASSIFIED·

ART ASSISTANCE	
SATOSHI KIMURA	HIKARI SUEHIRO
KAZUKI NONAKA	YUICHI OZAKI
MAFUYU KONISHI	MIO AYATSUKA
GRAPHIC NOVEL DESIGN	
HIDEAKI SHIMADA	ERI ARAKAWA
GRAPHIC NOVEL EDITOR	
KANAKO YANAGIDA	
MANAGING EDITOR	
SHIHEI LIN	

I ALREADY MENTIONED IT IN MY AUTHOR'S COMMENT, BUT THIS MANGA IS NOW GETTING AN ANIME! I AM TRULY GRATEFUL FOR ALL YOUR SUPPORT IN MAKING THIS HAPPEN. I HOPE YOU'LL ENJOY SEEING THE FORGERS IN MOTION AND HEARING THEM SPEAK.

I WILL CONTINUE WORKING HARD (AT MY OWN SLOW PACE) TO MAKE A MANGA WORTHY OF ADAPTATION, AND I'D BE DELIGHTED TO HAVE YOUR CONTINUED SUPPORT.

—TATSUYA ENDO

EYES ONLY READ & ~~DESTROY~~ EYES ONLY

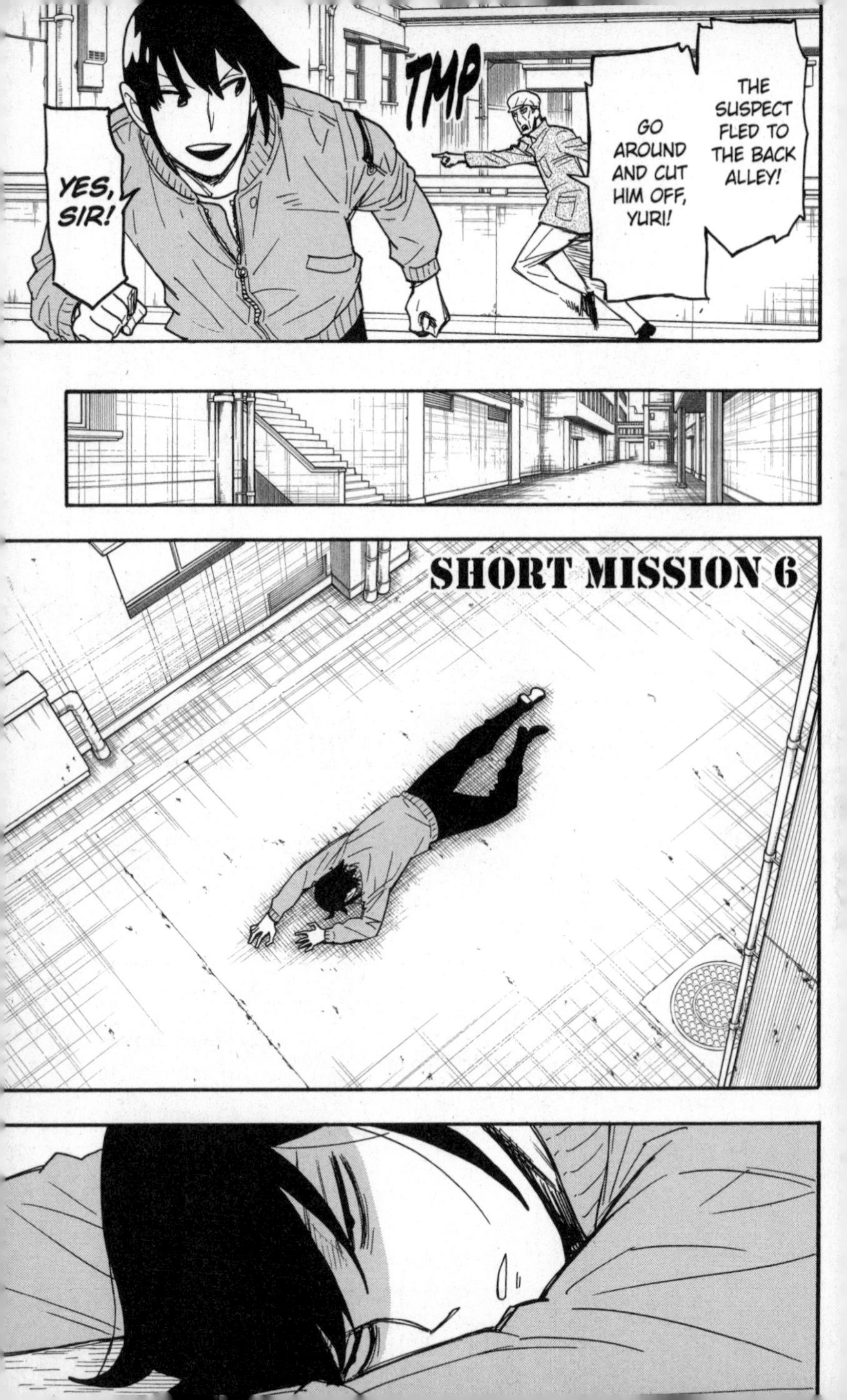
THE SUSPECT FLED TO THE BACK ALLEY!
GO AROUND AND CUT HIM OFF, YURI!
TMP
YES, SIR!
SHORT MISSION 6

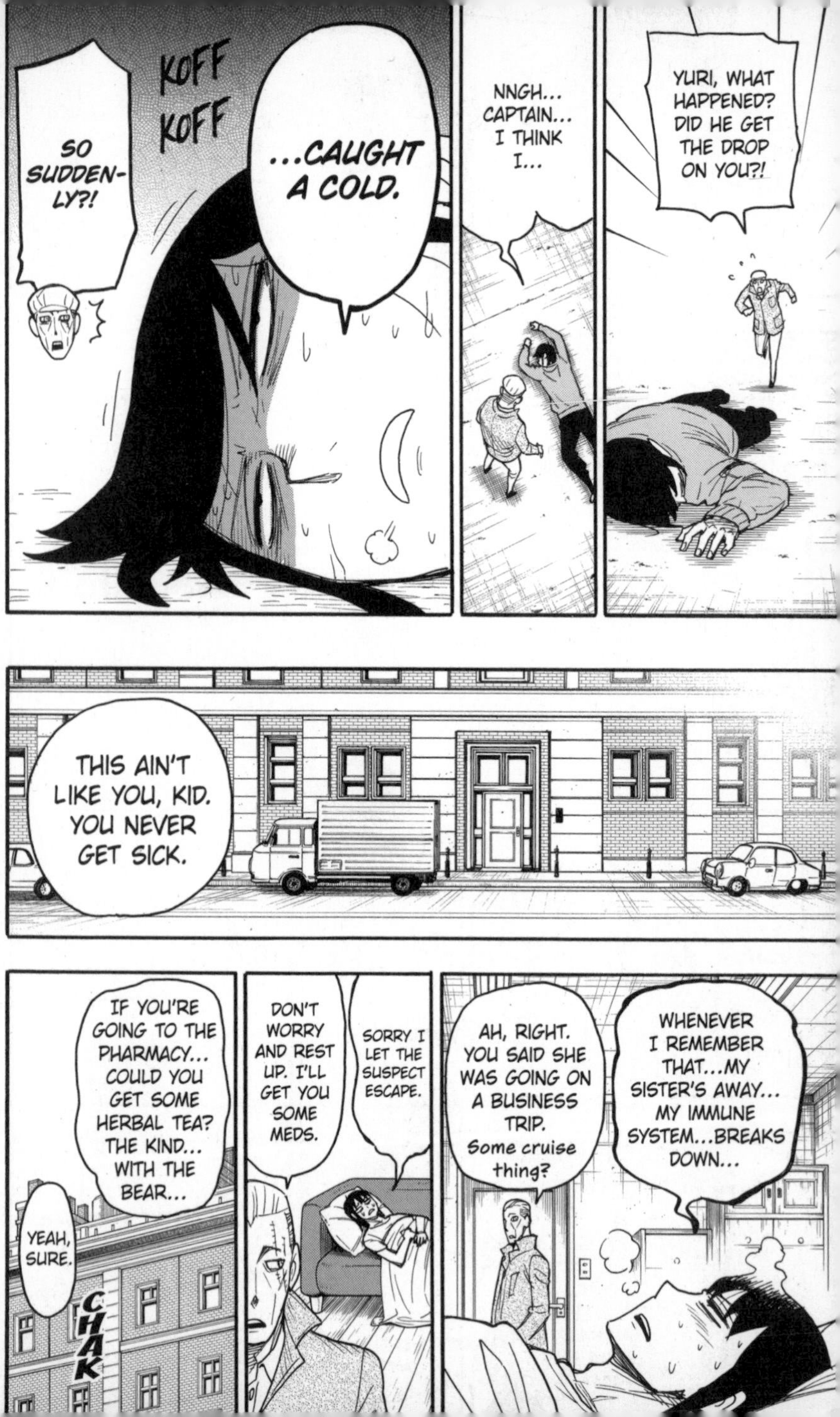
YURI, WHAT HAPPENED? DID HE GET THE DROP ON YOU?!
NNGH... CAPTAIN... I THINK I...
...CAUGHT A COLD.
KOFF KOFF
SO SUDDEN-LY?!
THIS AIN'T LIKE YOU, KID. YOU NEVER GET SICK.
WHENEVER I REMEMBER THAT...MY SISTER'S AWAY... MY IMMUNE SYSTEM...BREAKS DOWN...
AH, RIGHT. YOU SAID SHE WAS GOING ON A BUSINESS TRIP. Some cruise thing?
SORRY I LET THE SUSPECT ESCAPE.
DON'T WORRY AND REST UP. I'LL GET YOU SOME MEDS.
IF YOU'RE GOING TO THE PHARMACY... COULD YOU GET SOME HERBAL TEA? THE KIND... WITH THE BEAR...
YEAH, SURE.
CHAK

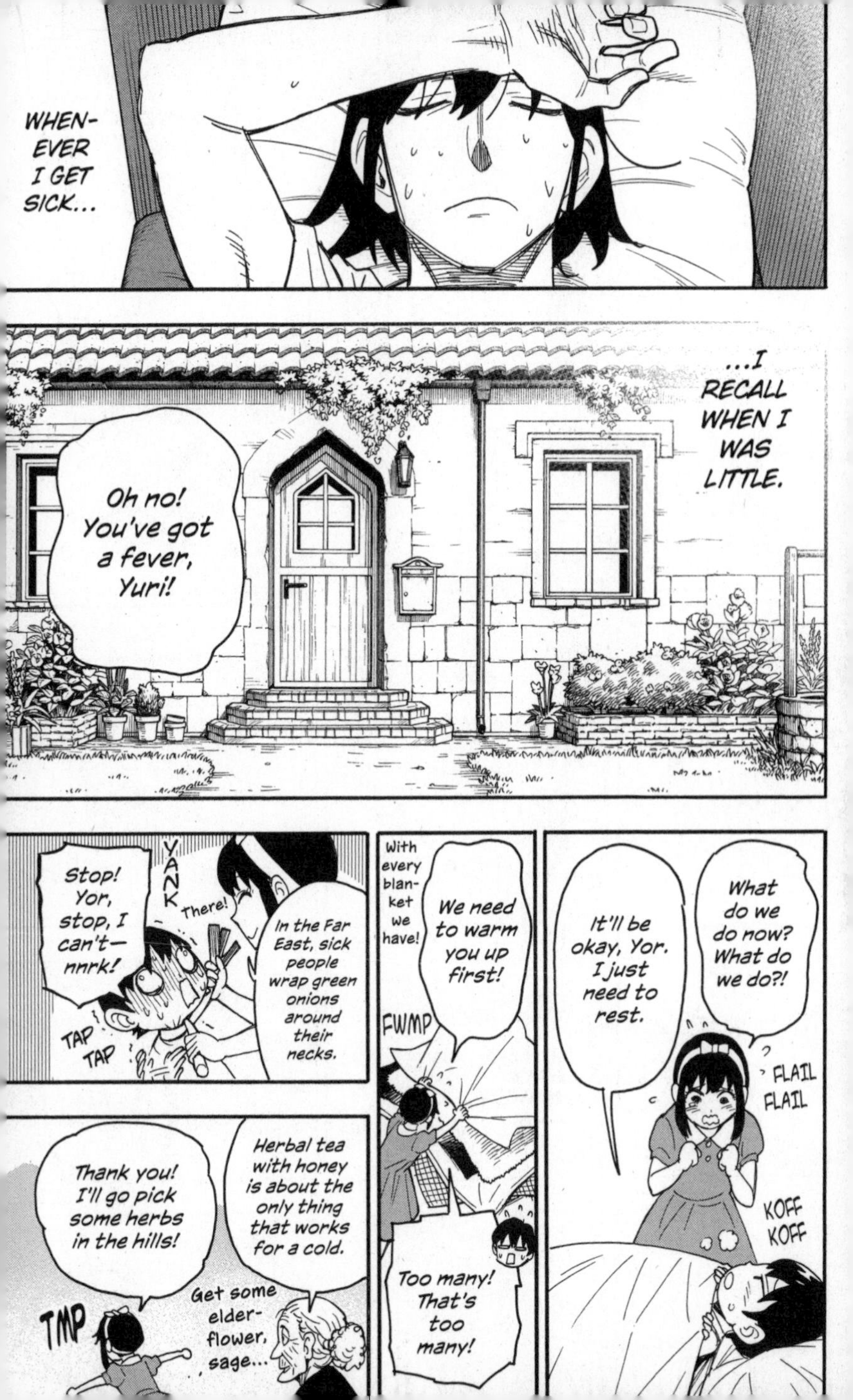
WHENEVER I GET SICK...
...I RECALL WHEN I WAS LITTLE.
Oh no! You've got a fever, Yuri!
What do we do now? What do we do?!
FLAIL FLAIL
It'll be okay, Yor. I just need to rest.
KOFF KOFF
We need to warm you up first!
With every blanket we have!
FWMP
Too many! That's too many!
In the Far East, sick people wrap green onions around their necks.
There!
YANK
Stop! Yor, stop, I can't— nnrk!
TAP TAP
Herbal tea with honey is about the only thing that works for a cold.
Get some elderflower, sage...
Thank you! I'll go pick some herbs in the hills!
TMP

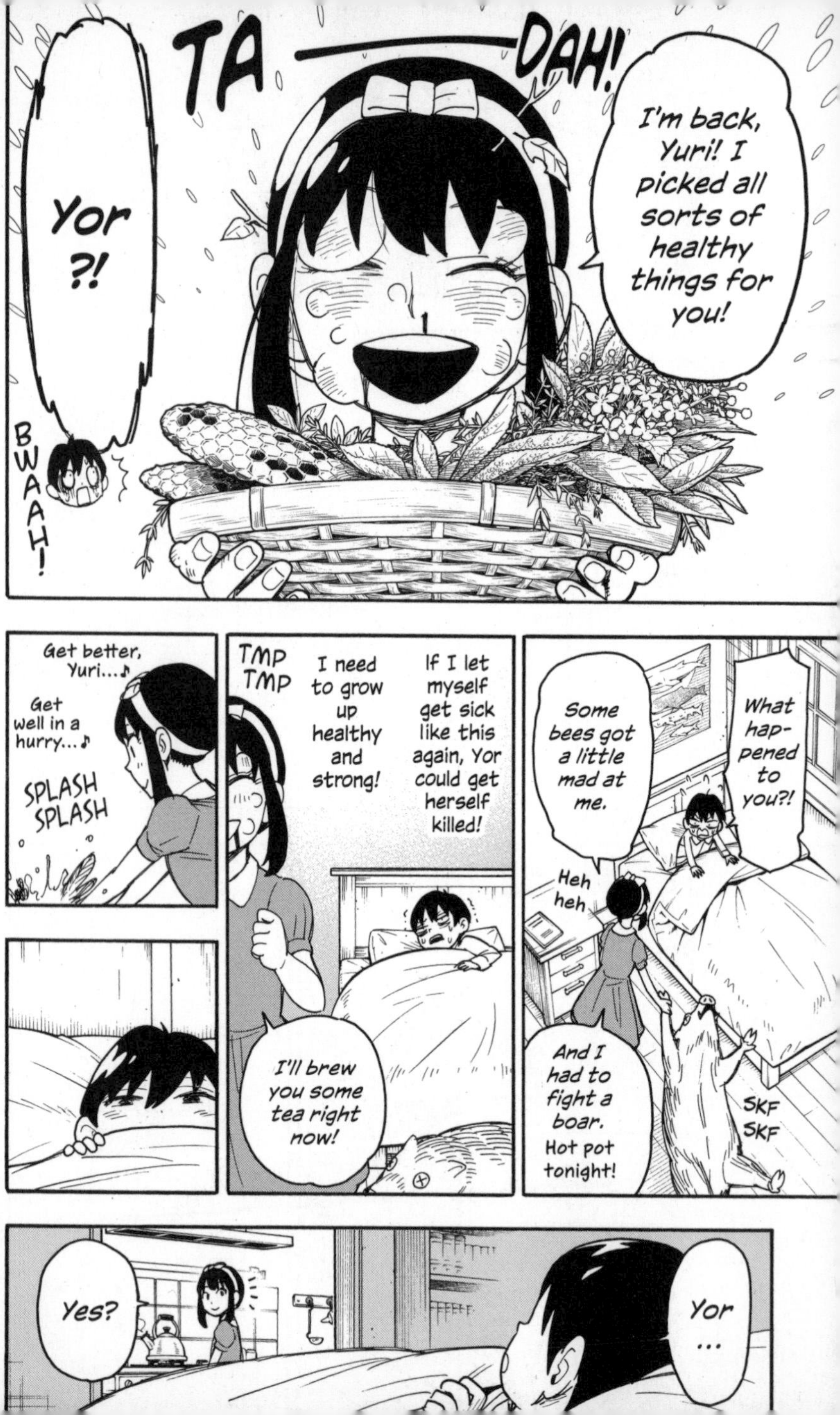
TA——DAH!
I'm back, Yuri! I picked all sorts of healthy things for you!
Yor ?!
BWAAAH!
What hap-pened to you?!
Some bees got a little mad at me.
Heh heh
And I had to fight a boar. Hot pot tonight!
SKF SKF
If I let myself get sick like this again, Yor could get herself killed!
I need to grow up healthy and strong!
TMP TMP
I'll brew you some tea right now!
Get better, Yuri...♪
Get well in a hurry...♪
SPLASH SPLASH
Yor ...
Yes?

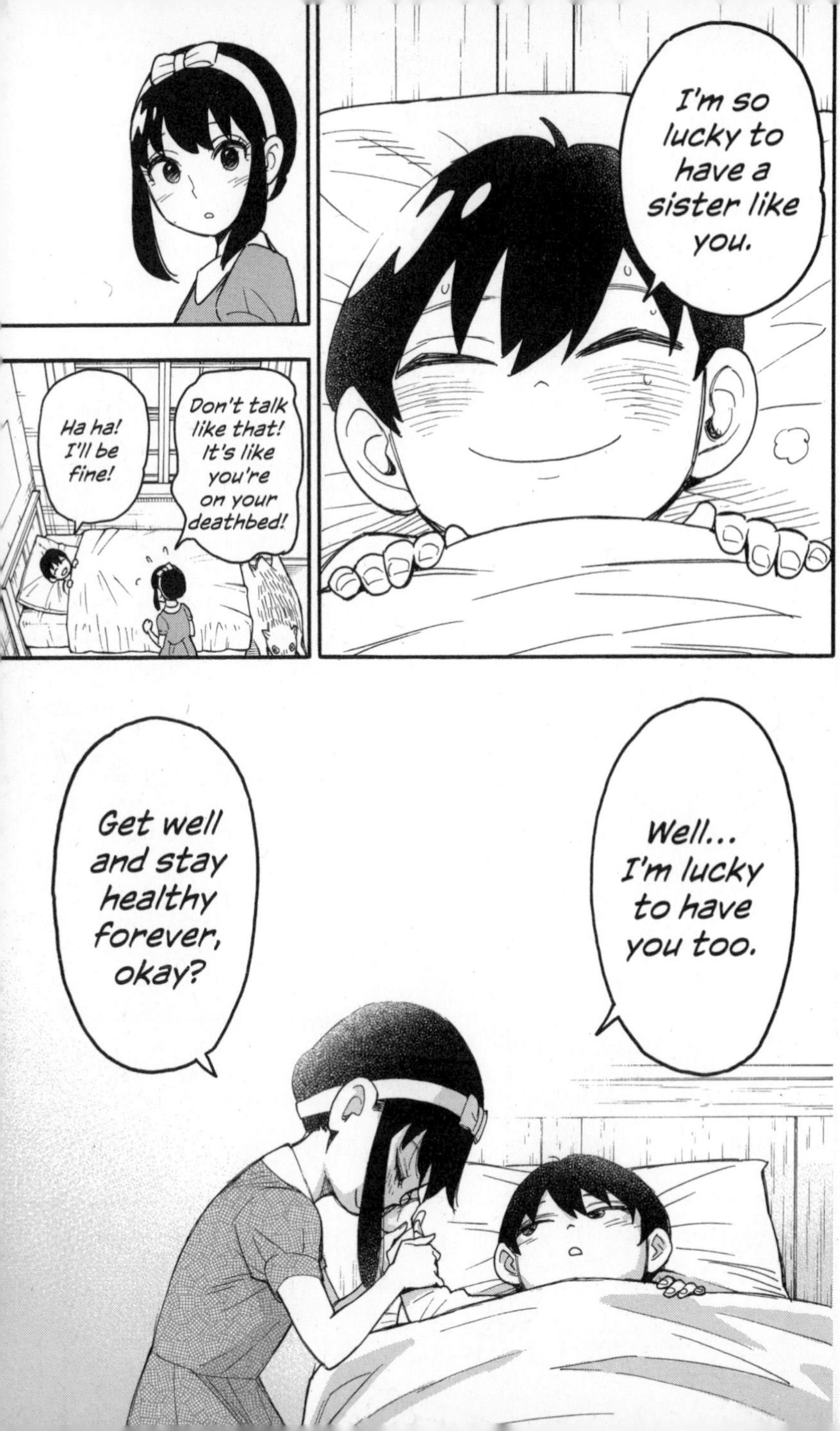
I'm so lucky to have a sister like you.
Don't talk like that! It's like you're on your deathbed!
Ha ha! I'll be fine!
Well... I'm lucky to have you too.
Get well and stay healthy forever, okay?

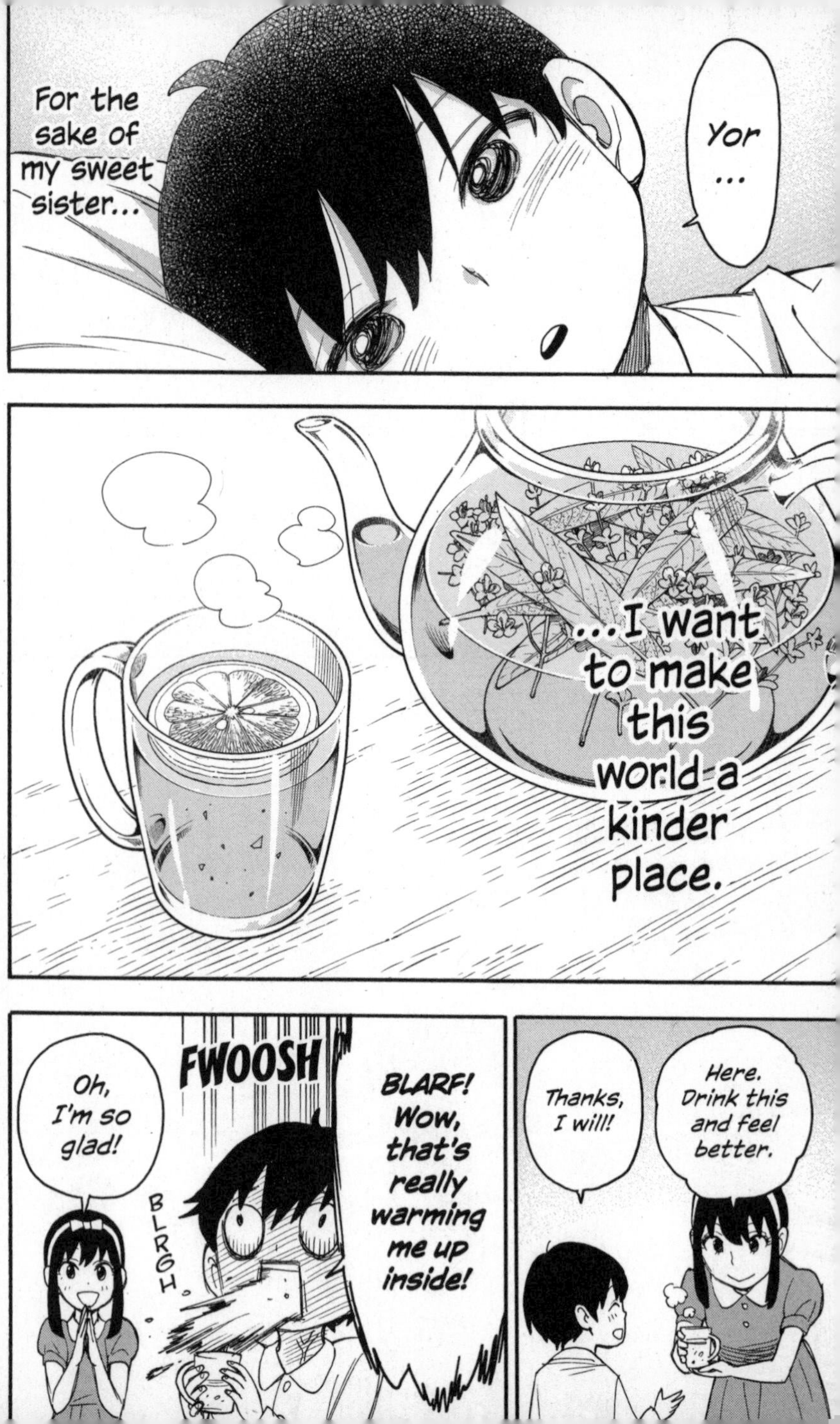
Yor ...
For the sake of my sweet sister...
...I want to make this world a kinder place.
Here. Drink this and feel better.
Thanks, I will!
BLARF! Wow, that's really warming me up inside!
FWOOSH
BLRGH
Oh, I'm so glad!

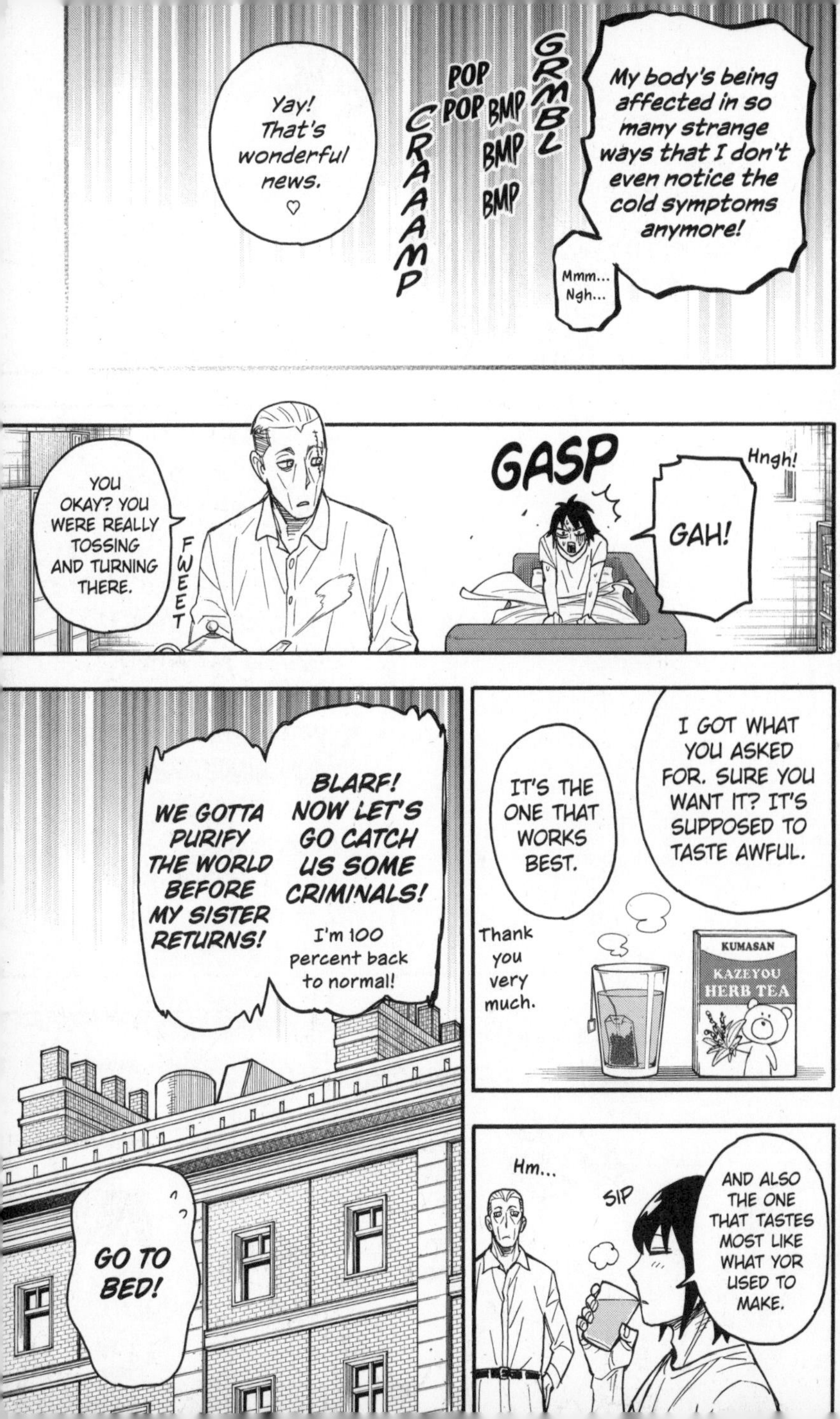
My body's being affected in so many strange ways that I don't even notice the cold symptoms anymore!
Mmm... Ngh...
GRMBL
POP POP
BMP BMP BMP
CRAAAAMP
Yay! That's wonderful news. ♡
Hngh!
GAH!
GASP
FWEET
YOU OKAY? YOU WERE REALLY TOSSING AND TURNING THERE.
I GOT WHAT YOU ASKED FOR. SURE YOU WANT IT? IT'S SUPPOSED TO TASTE AWFUL.
IT'S THE ONE THAT WORKS BEST.
Thank you very much.
KUMASAN
KAZEYOU HERB TEA
AND ALSO THE ONE THAT TASTES MOST LIKE WHAT YOR USED TO MAKE.
SIP
Hm...
BLARF! NOW LET'S GO CATCH US SOME CRIMINALS!
I'm 100 percent back to normal!
WE GOTTA PURIFY THE WORLD BEFORE MY SISTER RETURNS!
GO TO BED!

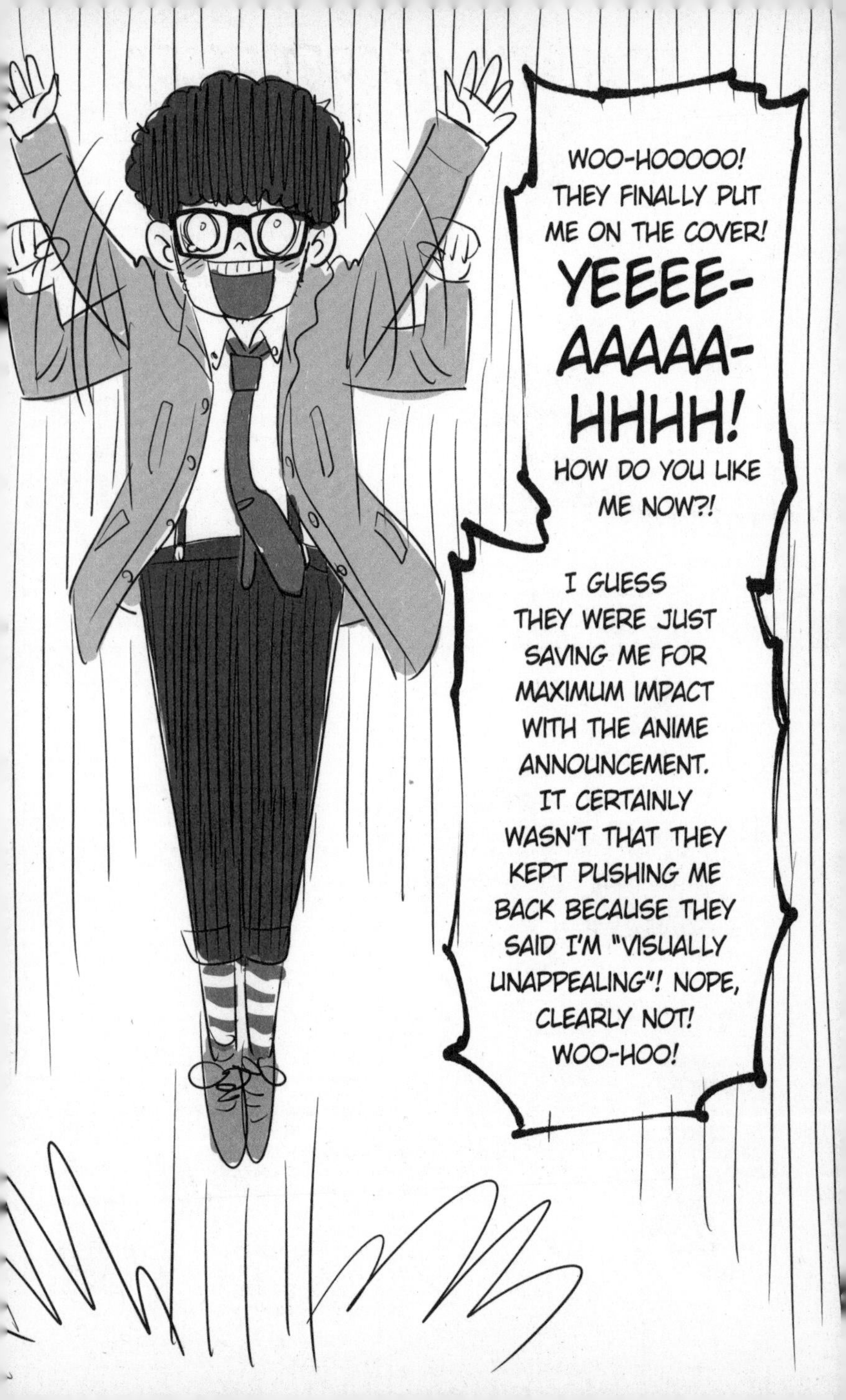
WOO-HOOOOO! THEY FINALLY PUT ME ON THE COVER! YEEEE-AAAAA-HHHH! HOW DO YOU LIKE ME NOW?!
I GUESS THEY WERE JUST SAVING ME FOR MAXIMUM IMPACT WITH THE ANIME ANNOUNCEMENT. IT CERTAINLY WASN'T THAT THEY KEPT PUSHING ME BACK BECAUSE THEY SAID I'M "VISUALLY UNAPPEALING"! NOPE, CLEARLY NOT! WOO-HOO!

FRANKY'S SECRET FILES

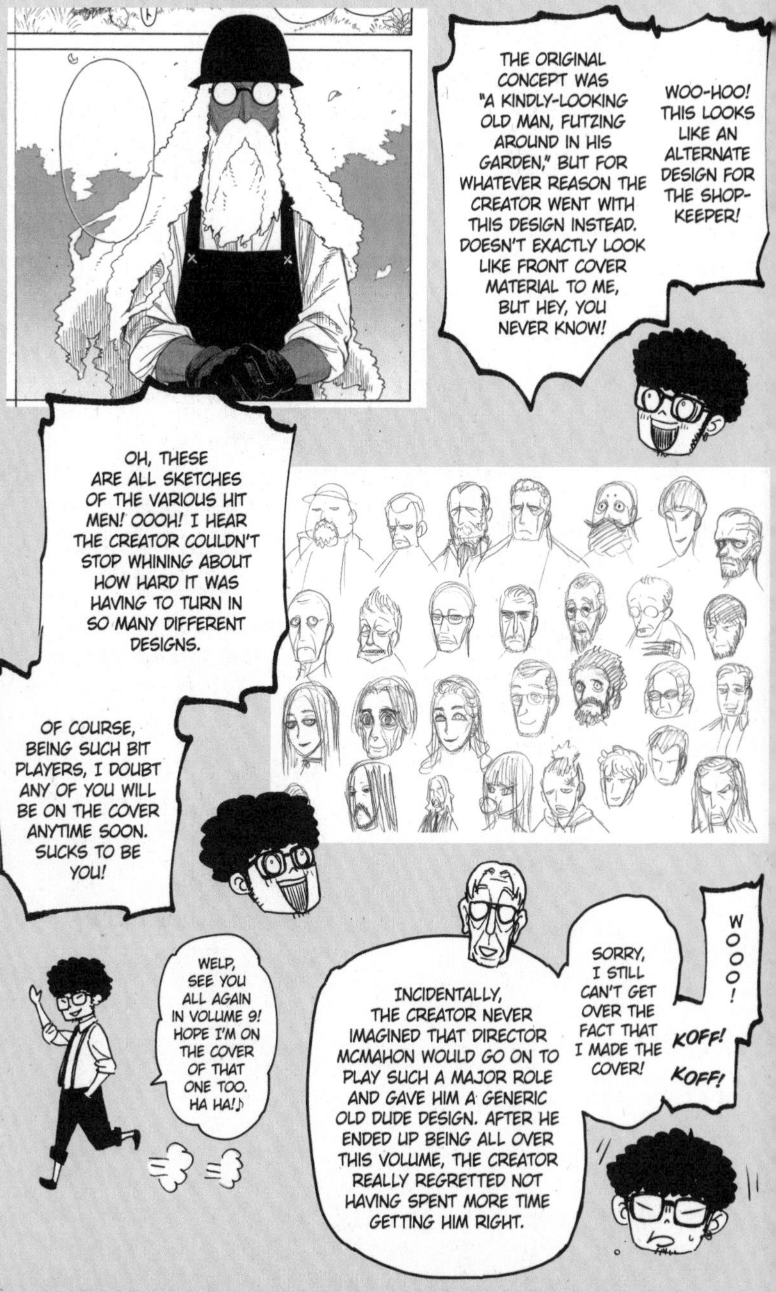
WOO-HOO! THIS LOOKS LIKE AN ALTERNATE DESIGN FOR THE SHOP-KEEPER!
THE ORIGINAL CONCEPT WAS "A KINDLY-LOOKING OLD MAN, FUTZING AROUND IN HIS GARDEN," BUT FOR WHATEVER REASON THE CREATOR WENT WITH THIS DESIGN INSTEAD. DOESN'T EXACTLY LOOK LIKE FRONT COVER MATERIAL TO ME, BUT HEY, YOU NEVER KNOW!
OH, THESE ARE ALL SKETCHES OF THE VARIOUS HIT MEN! OOOH! I HEAR THE CREATOR COULDN'T STOP WHINING ABOUT HOW HARD IT WAS HAVING TO TURN IN SO MANY DIFFERENT DESIGNS.
OF COURSE, BEING SUCH BIT PLAYERS, I DOUBT ANY OF YOU WILL BE ON THE COVER ANYTIME SOON. SUCKS TO BE YOU!
WOOO!
SORRY, I STILL CAN'T GET OVER THE FACT THAT I MADE THE COVER!
KOFF! KOFF!
INCIDENTALLY, THE CREATOR NEVER IMAGINED THAT DIRECTOR MCMAHON WOULD GO ON TO PLAY SUCH A MAJOR ROLE AND GAVE HIM A GENERIC OLD DUDE DESIGN. AFTER HE ENDED UP BEING ALL OVER THIS VOLUME, THE CREATOR REALLY REGRETTED NOT HAVING SPENT MORE TIME GETTING HIM RIGHT.
WELP, SEE YOU ALL AGAIN IN VOLUME 9! HOPE I'M ON THE COVER OF THAT ONE TOO. HA HA!♪

Great news! We're getting an anime adaptation!

—TATSUYA ENDO

Tatsuya Endo was born in Ibaraki Prefecture, Japan, on July 23, 1980. He debuted as a manga artist with the one-shot "Seibu Yugi" (Western Game), which ran in the Spring 2000 issue of *Akamaru Jump*. He is the author of *TISTA* and *Gekka Bijin* (Moon Flower Beauty). *Spy x Family* is his first work published in English.

SPY x FAMILY 8

SHONEN JUMP Edition

STORY AND ART BY **TATSUYA ENDO**

Translation **CASEY LOE**

Touch-Up Art & Lettering **RINA MAPA**

Design **JIMMY PRESLER**

Editor **JOHN BAE**

First published in Japan in 2019 by SHUEISHA Inc., Tokyo.
English translation rights arranged by SHUEISHA Inc.

Printed in Italy

Published by VIZ Media, LLC
P.O. Box 77010
San Francisco, CA 94107

10 9 8 7 6 5 4 3 2
First printing, September 2022
Second printing, September 2022

ratings.viz.com RATED T+ OLDER TEEN

PARENTAL ADVISORY
SPY x FAMILY is rated T+ for Older Teen and is recommended for ages 16 and up. This volume contains realistic violence.

VIZ MEDIA
viz.com

SHONEN JUMP

THE PROMISED NEVERLAND

STORY BY **KAIU SHIRAI**
ART BY **POSUKA DEMIZU**

Emma, Norman and Ray are the brightest kids at the Grace Field House orphanage. And under the care of the woman they refer to as "Mom," all the kids have enjoyed a comfortable life. Good food, clean clothes and the perfect environment to learn—what more could an orphan ask for? One day, though, Emma and Norman uncover the dark truth of the outside world they are forbidden from seeing.

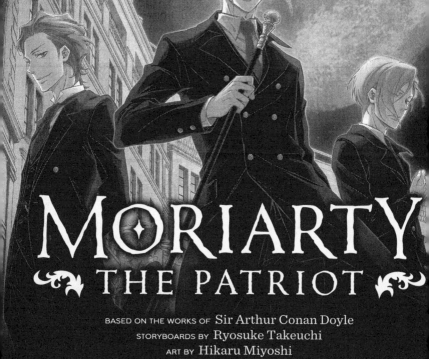

MORIARTY
❦ THE PATRIOT ❧

BASED ON THE WORKS OF Sir Arthur Conan Doyle
STORYBOARDS BY Ryosuke Takeuchi
ART BY Hikaru Miyoshi

THE UNTOLD STORY OF SHERLOCK HOLMES' GREATEST RIVAL, MORIARTY!

Before he was Sherlock's rival, Moriarty fought against the unfair class caste system in London by making sure corrupt nobility got their come-uppance. But even the most well-intentioned plans can spin out of control—will Moriarty's dream of a more just and equal world turn him into a hero...or a monster?

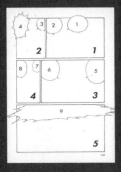

YOU'RE READING THE WRONG WAY!

SPY x FAMILY reads from right to left, starting in the upper-right corner. Japanese is read from right to left, meaning that action, sound effects, and word-balloon order are completely reversed from English order.